P9-COP-769

LANGUAGE AND LITERACY DEVELOPMENT

Solving Problems in the Teaching of Literacy
Cathy Collins Block, Series Editor

Recent Volumes

Language and Literacy Development
What Educators Need to Know

JAMES P. BYRNES *and* BARBARA A. WASIK

THE GUILFORD PRESS
New York   London

© 2009 The Guilford Press
A Division of Guilford Publications, Inc.
72 Spring Street, New York, NY 10012
www.guilford.com

All rights reserved

No part of this book may be reproduced, translated, stored in
a retrieval system, or transmitted, in any form or by any means,
electronic, mechanical, photocopying, microfilming, recording,
or otherwise, without written permission from the Publisher.

Printed in the United States of America

This book is printed on acid-free paper.

Last digit is print number: 9 8 7 6 5 4 3 2 1

Library of Congress Cataloging-in-Publication Data

Byrnes, James P.
  Language and literacy development : what educators need to know / James P.
Byrnes, Barbara A. Wasik.
    p. cm. — (Solving problems in the teaching of literacy)
  Includes bibliographical references and index.
  ISBN 978-1-59385-991-6 (hardcover : alk. paper) — ISBN 978-1-59385-990-9
(pbk. : alk. paper)
 1. Language arts (Elementary) 2. Literacy—Study and teaching.
3. Language experience approach in education. 4. Cognition in children.
I. Wasik, Barbara A. II. Title.
  LB1576.B98   2009
  372.6—dc22
                                                        2008032943

To Ruth and Thomas Wasik who,
from the very start, provided us with the love
and support we needed to accomplish our goals,
among them writing this book

About the Authors

James P. Byrnes, PhD, is Associate Dean for Academic Affairs in the College of Education at Temple University in Philadelphia. He is a Fellow of Division 15 (Educational Psychology) of the American Psychological Association and has served as Vice President of the Jean Piaget Society. An Associate Editor of the *Journal of Cognition and Development*, Dr. Byrnes has published over 70 books, chapters, or articles on several different areas of cognitive development, such as logical reasoning and mathematical learning. Dr. Byrnes has received grant funding from the National Science Foundation, the National Institutes of Health, and the U.S. Department of Education, and awards for his teaching and mentoring of undergraduate and graduate students. His most recent work has focused primarily on developing two comprehensive theoretical models, one on adolescent decision making and one on academic achievement. The model of academic achievement has been designed specifically to provide insight into ways to eliminate or substantially reduce gender, ethnic, and racial gaps in achievement.

Barbara A. Wasik, PhD, is Associate Professor and the PNC Endowed Chair in Early Childhood in the department of Curriculum, Instruction, and Technology in Education at Temple University in Philadelphia. Her research interests are emergent literacy and early intervention in beginning reading, with a specific focus on disadvantaged children. Dr. Wasik has extensive experience in program and curriculum development and is specifically interested in the role that teachers play in the development of children's language and literacy skills. She has written numerous articles on early literacy, one of which received the Dina Feitelson Research Award from the International Reading Association for outstanding research article. She is the coauthor of several books, including one with Carol Seefeldt, *Early Education: Three-, Four-, and Five-Year-Olds Go to School* (2nd edition). Also interested in educational policy issues, Dr. Wasik is the author of several papers that have affected teaching practices in classrooms.

Preface

The motivation for writing this book derives from several sources. The first was precipitated when an advisory committee commissioned by the State Department of Education (DOE) in Maryland in the late 1990s made a number of recommendations for improving the level of reading proficiency in Maryland students. One of these recommendations was to increase teachers' knowledge of theories and research regarding the development of language and literacy skills in children. In response, the state DOE mandated that all colleges of education statewide require a course on the development of language and literacy skills in their elementary education teacher preparation programs. One of us (JPB) was assigned the task of creating such a course since none was offered at the University of Maryland. He consulted with the coauthor (BAW) about the design of the course and accepted her suggestions for potential texts, given her expertise in the areas of language and literacy development. The consultations led, in turn, to the second motivation: Although there are several widely used and very good texts on the development of language, these texts have a strong developmental psychology as opposed to an educational orientation. Little attempt is made in these texts to explain the implications of research on language for classroom practice. The third motivation is that, although there are texts that either exclusively focus on language development or exclusively focus on literacy practices, no texts that we know of (1) focus on developmental trends and theories regarding language *and* literacy in young children (giving equal weight to each) and (2) discuss the instructional implications of this work in a manner that teachers could understand and find useful. As developmental psychologists who have spent our careers making psychological research accessible to educators, we wrote this book to fill this void.

The intended audiences are primarily students in preservice undergraduate programs who are training to become teachers and master's students who already have their teaching certificates but who want to learn more about the development of language and literacy skills so that they can be more effective in literacy instruction. However, the book should prove useful to a variety of educators in fields such as early childhood education, educational leadership, and educational policy, because the information is essential for making good decisions about curricula as well.

There is an unfortunate gap between the fields of developmental and cognitive psychology on the one hand and the field of education on the other. Scholars in the former disciplines know the theories and research but typically do not know how to apply this information to the classroom. In contrast, scholars and practitioners in the field of education know literacy practices but lack knowledge of the theories and research that could explain why practices are effective or ineffective. This book tries to bridge the gap. In so doing, we hope not only to help educators see the theoretical explanations behind sound instructional practices, but also to help developmental and cognitive psychologists understand how to apply their work on language and reading skills to actual classrooms. Thus, graduate students in developmental and cognitive psychology programs who have an interest in education should also find this book useful.

We have benefited from relationships formed over the years with colleagues who have expertise in areas such as language development, literacy, motivation, and early childhood education, among them Ellin Scholnick, Susan Gelman, Katherine Nelson, John Guthrie, Allan Wigfield, Kathy Wentzel, Min Wang, Darrell Morris, Nancy Karweit, Mary Alice Bond, Annemarie Hindman, Keith Stanovich, and Carol Seefeldt. In many ways, these individuals have helped to shape our perspective on the development of language and literacy skills. We would also like to thank Chris Jennison at The Guilford Press, who encouraged us to write this book and sought expert advice on how to improve it. Finally, we would like to thank our children, Julia and Tommy, for providing wonderful insight into the natural course of language and literacy skills in children by their own example, for coping with seemingly endless days in which we worked on this book, and for providing us the affection and support that helped to sustain us throughout the process.

JAMES P. BYRNES
BARBARA A. WASIK

Contents

Part III. The Development of Reading and Writing Skills

Part V. Instructional Techniques and Programs

LANGUAGE AND LITERACY DEVELOPMENT

PART  I

Introductory Issues

Introduction

Although not on par with topics such as politics and religion, questions regarding the education of children often evoke strong emotions and contentious debates. To illustrate, consider just a few of the educational battles that have been waged over the past 25 years. There have been arguments about whether school vouchers are a good idea, whether children should be taught phonics, whether math concepts should be emphasized instead of facts and procedures, and so on (Byrnes, 2001a). Politicians, teachers, parents, and researchers have all taken various sides in these debates, and many of these issues remain unresolved. It is fair to say, then, that there is a general climate of dissention and controversy in most matters pertaining to the education of children.

Given this climate, it may be surprising to learn that there seems to be very little dissention when it comes to opinions regarding the importance of early language development to the acquisition of literacy skills (e.g., Snow, Burns, & Griffin, 1998). Nearly everyone agrees that children can only become proficient readers by the end of third grade if they enter school with a specific set of spoken language competencies. The goal of this book is to explain the basis for this uncommon consensus by examining the parallel and interlocking age changes that occur in spoken language, reading, and writing.

In the next two sections of this chapter, we provide an overview of (1) the topics that will appear in subsequent chapters (i.e., what will be covered and why), (2) the kinds of questions we will ask in each chapter, and (3) our general approach. Careful reading of these sections is essential for getting the most out of Chapters 2 through 13.

OVERVIEW OF TOPICS

The chapters of this book are arranged into five main sections. In the first
section, which includes the present chapter and Chapter 2 (Brain Development, Language, and Literacy), we examine foundational issues, themes,
and approaches that frequently recur in subsequent chapters. The discussion
of neuroscience in Chapter 2 is designed to be accessible to those who have
little background in such matters, yet it also encourages and models critical
analysis of the research in the hope that the reader will not fall prey to the
overexuberance and overacceptance of brain research that often occurs in
the field of education today. At the very least, neuroscientific findings will
be shown to be useful for corroborating certain theories of language and
reading. For example, linguists propose that, among other things, competent speakers of a language have insight into both the syntax and semantics
of their language. In support of this claim, studies of brain-injured individuals show that people often have problems processing syntax when they experience damage to certain areas of their brain, but have problems with semantics when they experience damage to other areas of their brain (Byrnes,
2001b; Saffran, 2003). Relatedly, brain imaging studies show that different
parts of the brain are active when people focus on semantics versus syntax.
Imaging studies also show that reading and language tasks often activate
similar regions of the brain, thereby supporting the contention that there is
a fair amount of overlap in reading skills and language skills.

After examining such foundational issues, the next two sections of this
book (Parts II and III) provide insight into the nature of spoken language
competence and literacy, respectively. More specifically, the chapters in Part
II explain what it means to be a competent speaker of a language (Chapter
3) and review research on the development of three aspects of this competence: phonological (Chapter 4), semantic (Chapter 5), and grammatical
knowledge and processes (Chapter 6). In Part III, the focus shifts somewhat
to emergent literacy (Chapter 7), beginning reading skills (Chapter 7), reading comprehension (Chapter 8), and writing skills (Chapter 9). Parts II and
III are designed to provide educators with a clear sense of (1) what goes on
in most people's minds when they speak, read, or write, (2) the skills that
speaking, reading, and writing have in common, and (3) normative developmental findings in the areas of language and literacy (i.e., what most
children can do at different ages). After mastering the content in Parts II
and III, the reader will have a very clear sense of why spoken language
skills are important to the acquisition of early reading skills.

Whereas Parts II and III tend to emphasis general normative trends,
the chapters in Part IV provide insight into individual differences in the
level of reading skill manifested by fourth-grade children. By "individual
differences," we mean that some children become highly proficient readers

by the end of fourth grade, while others become average readers or worse. In Chapter 10, we show that one reason for such individual differences pertains to children's achievement motivation: Simply put, some children are more motivated to become proficient readers than others. We consider why such motivational differences exist. Other reasons for individual differences pertain to variables that are closely associated with a child's gender, ethnicity, family income, or language spoken at home (Chapter 11). Boys, Black and Hispanic children, children from impoverished families, and children whose primary language is not English show less reading skill at the end of fourth grade than girls, children who are European American, children who come from affluent families, and children who are proficient speakers of English. Once again, we examine why these differences exist and what can be done about them.

The final section of this book (Part V) includes two chapters that consider the instructional implications of the information presented in Chapters 2 through 11. An indispensable prerequisite for making good decisions regarding reading-related classroom practices and educational policies is to understand the nature and development of language and reading. Our goal is to help educators and policymakers understand *why* certain approaches or policies make sense (i.e., why they work) and why others are likely to fail. Whereas Chapter 12 (General Principles of Effective Instruction) uses contemporary theories and research to describe what all effective practices have in common, Chapter 13 (Language and Literacy Programs That Work) describes specific instructional practices and formal programs. The reader is asked to evaluate the latter programs using the information contained in Chapters 2 through 12.

GENERAL APPROACH OF THIS BOOK

There are two ways to appreciate the macrostructure on this book. The first is by examining the notions of instructional goals and developmental pathways. The second is by examining a set of five questions that appear in many of the chapters.

Instructional Goals and Developmental Pathways

Why should preservice and experienced teachers master the content of this book? Our selection of topics was guided by three main assumptions. The first assumption is that *teaching is a goal-directed activity*. In other words, teachers try to accomplish certain goals when they lecture or ask students to engage in various activities at school or at home. Some of these goals include (1) promoting students' understanding of particular content (e.g., main ideas in a novel), (2) improving students' scores on achievement tests, and (3) fostering students' interest in specific subject areas (e.g., science). For example, a teacher might say, "If I explain it this way, maybe students will understand it better" or "Instead of lecturing, I'll give students a group assignment that involves looking up the answers themselves; that way, they get to be social and feel like explorers."

From the assumption that teaching is goal-directed, it becomes rather straightforward to define *successful* or *effective instruction* as follows: Successful teachers know how to accomplish their goals and do so on a regular basis. Unsuccessful teachers, in contrast, try to make things happen in their classrooms but never seem to get the results they (or the people they answer to) want.

The second assumption that guided our selection of topics is that *teachers are more likely to attain their instructional goals on a regular basis if they have a detailed understanding of the inner workings of their students' minds than if they lack this understanding.* A good way to appreciate the logic of this assumption is to contrast the education of teachers with the education of other kinds of problem solvers such as, for example, car mechanics or physicians. Car mechanics and physicians are similar to teachers in that the former have goals they are trying to accomplish in their jobs (e.g., stop a rattling noise in an engine; lower cholesterol levels in a heart attack victim). Unlike teachers, car mechanics and physicians are taught about the inner workings of the entities they interact with when they received their education. That is, before actually working on cars, car mechanics learn about the parts of a car (e.g., battery, carburetor, brakes) and how these parts work individually and collectively. Similarly, before physicians are given the responsibility of improving the health of patients, they are taught about the parts of the human body (e.g., heart, lung, pancreas) and how these parts work individually and collectively. It is precisely this knowledge of "inner workings" that allows car mechanics and physicians to fix cars and improve the health of patients. They are not just told what to do in their courses; they are given information that helps them understand why their actions would be effective. In other words, car mechanics and physicians are given both *conceptual knowledge* (how things work) and *procedural knowledge* (how to fix things).

Teachers, in contrast, are typically given only procedural knowledge in their methods courses (e.g., step-by-step instructions on how to implement sustained silent reading in their classrooms). Chapters 2 through 11 describe the inner workings of children's minds. This information represents the conceptual knowledge that teachers need to know to promote the development of language and literacy skills. Chapters 12 and 13, in contrast, discuss methods or procedural issues (i.e., what to do; how to teach). In the absence of conceptual knowledge, children's minds are mysterious "black boxes," and teachers can only hope that their actions will be effective. This is analogous to drivers who have no idea what happens in a car engine when they turn a key; they hope the engine will start but have no idea what do when the engine does not start. In addition, teachers who lack conceptual knowledge are likely to fall prey to the many false promises that are made by curriculum developers and salespeople. Conceptual knowledge helps teachers be educated consumers of the various instructional packages on the market. They will know which packages are likely to help them meet their instructional goals and which will not. No drivers would take their cars to a mechanic who did not understand the inner workings of a car. Similarly, no patients would go to a doctor who did not understand the inner workings of the human body. Perhaps the biggest benefit of teachers having conceptual knowledge is that it enables them to create classroom activities and programs on their own, or to modify adequate programs to make them work better.

The third guiding assumption of this book is that *education is a developmental mechanism.* That is, education has the potential to transform or change an individual over time. To see what we mean by "transform," note that some children enter first grade with very underdeveloped reading skills (State 1), but eventually leave fourth grade with a reasonably high level of reading skill (State 2). Developmental scientists would explain this transformation (i.e., State 1 changing into State 2) by saying that these children were presented with education experiences that progressively instilled reading skills in them.

In addition to framing instruction in a new and useful way (e.g., as a transforming operation), such a developmental perspective has several other benefits. For example, if we view each child's education as a progression of states, or "snapshots" in time, we gain a unique and extremely informative understanding of the state that children may be in at any given time (Vygotsky, 1978). In particular, a child's current state (e.g., level of reading skill; level of motivation) can be viewed as an *outcome* that was produced by developmental mechanisms transforming earlier states. Paraphrasing Vygotsky (1978), an adult can only understand where a child currently "is" by understanding where that child has "been." By analogy, art enthusiasts would get a much deeper understanding of a particular painting or sculpture if they were to watch the artist progressively construct the painting or sculpture over time (and watch it take shape). If nothing else, enthusiasts would see that the first layers of paint determine the colors that emerge when subsequent layers are added (e.g., red painted over gray looks different than red painted over white). Similarly, once a sculptor commits to using a section of a block of stone to produce a shape (e.g., an arm), that decision determines what can be added next (e.g., a hand but not a foot or a nose—assuming the artist is a realist!). Whereas it is relatively easy to see how developmental mechanisms such as paint strokes or chisel blows can transform a piece of artwork over time, we do not always recognize how teacher actions (and educational experiences more generally) transform children over time.

Relatedly, it is often clear how prior states of an artwork constrain or determine how things will turn out later (e.g., once an arm is created, this action cannot be "undone" without starting over); however, it is not always obvious that prior states of children determine or constrain how they perform when developmental mechanisms (e.g., educational experiences) operate on them. But this point is crucial in understanding why one would not implement a particular instructional activity in the same way for all children of all ages or developmental levels. Instruction can only transform children into some desired end-state (e.g., proficient readers by age 9) if the children are in particular states when they experience this instruction. Children enter first grade in a variety of states, and only some children will benefit from various instructional packages and techniques as they are normally implemented or recommended by their curriculum developers. In other words, one size does not fit all.

One further benefit of a developmental perspective is the recognition that a child's current state is not only an outcome or product of prior states (as described above), it is also a step on the road to later developmental outcomes or states. Before drawing the implications of this insight, we should point out that we earlier only paraphrased half of a Vygotskian expression regarding the importance of a developmental perspective. The complete version is this: An adult can only understand where a child currently "is" by understanding where that child has "been" and where the child is "going." By considering where a child has been, teachers gain insight into the reasons why a particular instructional activity will or will not transform children in the way they want. But by considering where a child is going, teachers gain two additional insights. The first is that they recognize that each instructional decision has an effect on the developmental pathway a child will take. Each day in a classroom is like a fork in a road. Whereas certain activities cause a child to go in one direction toward a particular developmental outcome (e.g., a high level of skill and positive feelings about school), other activities could promote transformations in another, less desirable direction. As such, teachers can either facilitate or hinder children's development (Okagaki & Sternberg, 1991). The second insight is that teachers no longer ask themselves questions such as "How can I get this information into children's heads?" or "How can I cover this part of the required curriculum?" Rather, teachers consider the desired developmental outcome at the end of formal schooling and ask, "What I can do in my classroom to move children closer to that desired outcome?" and

"Will this activity move them closer to that outcome, will it sidetrack them, or will it promote regression in the opposite direction to earlier states?"

Recurrent Questions

In order to (1) promote a conceptual understanding of language and literacy, (2) facilitate comprehension of the material in Chapters 2 through 9, and (3) place the material in a developmental perspective, questions of the following form are asked and answered in Chapters 2 through 9:

- *The "nature of" question*: What is X (e.g., spoken language competence, phonological knowledge)? Here, the question focuses on the components of a skill in question. In other words, teachers ask, "What does it really mean to say that a person has X" (e.g., phonological knowledge)? This is the "inner working" knowledge teachers need.
- *The relevance question*: Why should teachers care about X? Here, we describe why it would be useful for teachers to know something about the phonological skills of children, their vocabulary, and so on. The literatures on language development and reading are vast. We only discuss work that has immediate or direct relevance to sound educational policy and practice.
- *The developmental trends question*: How does X normally develop? In light of the earlier discussion of the utility of a developmental perspective, answers to questions of this form address many of the states children pass through. In other words, the trends question focuses on developmental "snapshots" (what children know and are able to do at different ages).
- *The developmental mechanisms question*: Why does X develop in the manner described in answer to the developmental trends question? Here, we complete the developmental perspective by presenting theories that try to explain why children pass through developmental states as they do. For example, we consider why children start out with 1 word (State 1) in their vocabularies but end up with 5,000 to 10,000 words (State 2) by age 6 (see Chapter 5). As discussed earlier in this chapter, insight into mechanisms is crucial for figuring out how to promote the outcomes we want. For example, if we had a clear grasp of the mechanisms by which children learned vocabulary, we would be better able to create educational experiences that promote vocabulary growth in students.
- *The deficiencies question*: Who has deficiencies in X and how might these deficiencies affect a child's acquisition of reading skills? Chapters 2 through 9 describe the kinds of skills that children need to have to be competent speakers and proficient readers. One way to "bring such information home" is to examine developmental outcomes for children who lack or

who are deficient in these skills. For example, in Chapter 4 we explain why phonological processing skills are an important aspect of proficient reading. In support of this claim, we show that (1) children with reading disabilities have particular problems with phonological processing and (2) children with phonological deficits (e.g., children who are hearing impaired) are delayed in their acquisition of reading skills. We also examine strategies for helping children with these deficiencies learn how to read.

2

Brain Development, Language, and Literacy

MAIN IDEAS OF THE CHAPTER

1. Scientists have discovered that the brain of human adults contains several different kinds of cells that are arranged into a characteristic organization (its cytoarchitecture); this organization has been described in terms of an areal aspect (different areas perform different functions) and a laminar aspect (layers of the brain contain different kinds of cells).

2. There are seven main processes of brain development that eventually produce the characteristic cytoarchictecture of the adult brain: proliferation (creating the right total number of cells), migration (movement of the created cells to the right location), differentiation (transforming cells into the right types), growth (each cell increasing in length and width), synaptogenesis (cells creating connections with each other), regressive processes (eliminating connections and cell death), and myelination (coating cells with a fatty acid).

3. There are five factors that can affect the manner in which the aforementioned seven processes of brain development are carried out: (a) genetics, (b) environmental stimulation, (c) nutrition, (d) steroids, and (e) teratogens. These factors can either help or hinder the operation of the seven processes of brain development. When problems arise in brain organization, one or more of these factors could be responsible.

4. Although genes play an important role in shaping brain development, plasticity and environmental input show that children are not destined to have a particular brain; in other words, biology is not destiny.

As the second installment in the discussion of foundational issues, we turn next to the topic of brain development. We have included a chapter on this topic for several reasons. First, all aspects of human cognition (including language and literacy) are products of brain activity. When people are processing spoken language or expressing ideas themselves, their brains are active. Given that the brain is clearly involved in acts of communication, it seems reasonable to examine what we know about the neural basis of language and literacy to see if this information provides any clues to the functioning of these skills. Second, for over 100 years, researchers have documented the serious communication problems faced by individuals when particular regions of their brains are damaged or poorly developed. By examining brain development as it pertains to language and literacy skills, readers of this book may gain insight into the possible differences between individuals who acquire these skills in normative ways and individuals who lag behind their peers in one or more ways.

By way of a preview of the topics to follow, it is important to note that each of our brains has a specific *cytoarchitecture*. That is, it contains a certain number of neurons that are connected to each other in particular ways. Inasmuch as this cytoarchitecture is the computational foundation of our ability to think, use language, and read, scientists have often wondered whether talented individuals differ from less talented individuals in terms of the number of neurons in their brains, the types of neurons in their brains, and the interconnections among these neurons. Scientists have also tried to determine the extent to which a person's cytoarchitecture is determined by his or her genes. Although brain science has not advanced enough for us to know whether there is in fact a correlation between certain cytoarchitectures and talent, it has advanced enough for us to be able to say something about the role of genetics in the construction of individual brains. The goal of this chapter is to present information relevant to the latter issue and related issues.

In the first section of this chapter, the notion of cytoarchitecture is explored further as a means of laying the groundwork for subsequent sections. Then, consideration is given to the processes by which this cytoarchitecture is constructed during prenatal and postnatal development. Finally, the factors that facilitate or hinder optimal brain development are discussed.

FURTHER EXPLORATIONS OF CYTOARCHITECTURE: CELL TYPES AND BRAIN LAYERS

An interesting fact about the brain is that there is a certain degree of localization of cognitive functions in the cortex and elsewhere (Byrnes, 2001b; Kosslyn & Koenig, 1994). The evidence for the *areal organization* of the cortex comes from a variety of sources. With animal brains, for example, researchers can insert probes into an animal's cortex and show that a small cluster of cells are selectively active only when the animal is engaged in a particular kind of task (e.g., detecting vertical lines). With human brains, researchers have relied on other kinds of evidence such as *double dissociations*. A double dissociation exists when damage to one area of the brain causes a deficit in one aspect of a skill (e.g., semantic processing), while damage to another area causes a deficit in a different aspect (e.g., syntactic processing). Although it is important not to infer too much from such findings (because the localization is relative rather than absolute), researchers could reasonably argue that such evidence provides support for theoretical models that propose that a given skill (e.g., language) can be subdivided into specific component subskills (e.g., semantic and syntactic processing).

In addition to the areal organization of the brain into specific processing regions, the cortex also has a characteristic *laminar* organization (i.e., layers that extend deeper into the brain). A prerequisite to understanding the latter type of organization is to recognize that the brain contains a number of different types of cells that fall into two broad classes: *glial cells* and *neurons*. Glial cells are far more numerous than neurons, but they do not seem to play a role in the processing of information (as far as scientists know). Instead, they provide a number of other important functions including (1) providing firmness and structure to the brain, (2) forming the myelin sheath that surrounds the axons of long neurons and speeds up their firing, (3) providing a "scaffold" for neurons to latch onto during the process of cell migration (see below), and (4) taking up and removing some of the chemical transmitters that are released during synaptic transmission (Kandel, 1991).

Neurons, in contrast, do play a role in the processing of information and come in a variety of types that differ in terms of their shape, patterns of connectivity, and the neurotransmitters they release. The shape dimension underlies the distinction between *pyramidal cells* (see Figure 2.1) and other types of cells (e.g., star-shaped cells called *stellate cells*). The former comprise more than 80% of the neurons in the brain (Johnson, 1997; Moyer, 1980). The connectivity dimension underlies the distinction between excitatory and inhibitory neurons. The neurotransmitter dimension allows one to distinguish between neurons that excrete dopamine, neurons that excrete gamma-aminobutyric acid (GABA), and neurons that excrete serotonin.

Scientists discovered these various aspects of neurons in the midst of examining microscopic slides of brain tissue. This microscopic approach also revealed the fact that the cortex comprises six horizontal layers that differ in terms of the morphology, density, and functional properties of the neurons in them (Chenn, Braisted, McConnell, & O'Leary, 1997; Johnson, 1997). Layer 1 is the highest (most superior, closest to the scalp) layer and consists primarily of long, horizontal fibers that connect different regions of the cortex to each other. In the next layer down, layers 2 and 3 also contain horizontal fibers as well as small pyramidal cells that extend apical dendrites upward as well as collateral projections outward to neighbors. A *dendrite* is the branching portion of a neuron that receives neurotransmitters secreted by presynaptic neurons (see Figure 2.1). Layer 4 is the terminal point for many input fibers from subcortical regions (e.g., the

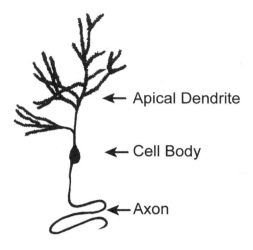

FIGURE 2.1. Basic structure of a pyramidal cell. From Byrnes (2001b). Copyright 2001 by The Guilford Press. Reprinted by permission.

thalamus). These inputs primarily make contact with the large number of stellate cells found in layer 4. Layers 5 and 6 are the most inferior (deepest) layers that have a high concentration of large pyramidal cells that project long-distance, output fibers to important subcortical sites as well as apical dendrites that extend upward to layers 4 and 1 (but not layers 2 and 3). Thus, all of the layers contain neurons that make either horizontal connections with neurons in other layers or vertical connections with neurons in the same layer (or both).

This laminar arrangement of cells is a defining characteristic of an adult brain. As such, it can be used to judge the relative maturity of children's brains at various ages. For example, a researcher may wish to consider whether 5-year-old children seem to have the same number of stellate cells in layer 4 as adults have (e.g., Huttenlocher, 1993). Similarly, researchers might consider whether the neurons in children's brains seem to make the same number of synaptic connections as the neurons in adults' brains. In the next section, these issues are considered further as the processes that create the laminar structure of the brain are explored.

SEVEN MAJOR PROCESSES OF BRAIN DEVELOPMENT

Prenatal development is often characterized in terms of structurally defined phases. That is, the boundaries of specific prenatal periods are set by the emergence of particular structural or anatomical features in an embryo or fetus (Purves & Lichtman, 1985). The period of the *zygote*, for example, begins when a sperm cell fertilizes an ovum and concludes when cell divisions within the zygote create a structure called a *blastula* (a hollow sphere of cells). Soon thereafter, the cells on the surface of the blastula invaginate along an indentation and create a groove called the *primitive streak*. The latter process is called *gastrulation* because it creates a structure called a *gastrula*. Somewhat later during a process called *neurulation*, two symmetrical, protruding folds of tissue emerge on the longitudinal surface of the gastrula, move closer together (like two ocean waves moving toward each other), and eventually fuse above the primitive streak to form the *neural tube*. One end of the neural tube eventually gives rise to the structures of the forebrain and midbrain. The other end eventually gives rise to the spinal cord (Johnson, 1997; Moyer, 1980). The end that gives rise to the forebrain and midbrain structures continues to develop and expand in such a way that a characteristic pattern of five convolutions and bulges appears by 5 weeks gestational age. (Imagine a partially inflated, shaped balloon attached to a straw.) Whereas the most anterior bulge is eventually transformed into the cortex, the second-most anterior bulge is eventually transformed into structures such as the thalamus and hypothalamus (Johnson, 1997).

Early on, scientists suspected that these bulges arose because the neural tube was manufacturing brain cells somewhere inside its walls. To confirm this suspicion, they used microscopic techniques to observe the formation of bulges *in vivo*. They found two regions within the neural tube (called *proliferative zones*) out of which brain cells emerged in rapid succession. Subsequent studies revealed that precursor cells within the zones produced approximately 100 generations of clones of themselves through *mitotic division* (Rakic, 1993). Mitotic division involves creating exact duplicates and splitting into two identical "daughter" cells with a full complement of DNA (as opposed to *meiosis* which creates gametes with half of the DNA of the parent cell). For some types of neuron, each precursor ends up producing 10,000 offspring cells. Given that the process of proliferation is largely over by the seventh prenatal month (in all areas except for the hippocampus) and that children's brains contain more than 10^{11} neurons, it follows that the two proliferative zones must produce progenitors at an explosive rate of 250,000 cells per minute (Johnson, 1997; Purves & Lichtman, 1985)!

Subsequent research revealed a second major process besides proliferation that is instrumental in determining the eventual configuration of cells in an adult brain: *migration*. To understand migration, it is helpful to imagine a (coronal) cross-section of the neural tube that has concentric circles corresponding to various layers (similar to a bull's-eye pattern). The proliferative zones lie near the innermost layer of the tube wall (close to the hollow of the tube or the target of the bull's eye). The neural tube expands in an outward, bulging manner because newly created cells migrate away from the proliferative zones to the outer layers of the tube wall. More specifically, as each generation of cells is produced through repeated cell division, they migrate farther and farther away from the inner wall (an inside-out, or radial progression). Hence, the cells that end up near the outer wall of the neural tube were some of the last ones produced during the process of proliferation. This outer layer is called the *cortical plate* because it ultimately becomes part of the cortex of a mature brain.

In vivo studies have revealed that neurons migrate to outer layers in one of two ways. In the first, newly created cells emerge from the proliferative zones and push older "siblings" away from the zones as they emerge (in the same way that an advancing crowd of protesters would push a line of police backward). In the second, newly created cells traverse along glial cells that are aligned in a perpendicular direction to the concentric layers of the tube (like spokes in a wheel). The glial cells secrete a substance to which the migrating cells adhere (Rakic, 1993), and the migrating cells themselves adhere to each other using recently discovered adhesion molecules (Edelman, 1992).

So far, we have described two processes that could produce a brain that has the right number of cells (proliferation) that are located in the right places (migration). Next, we have to consider how the brain manages to produce the various types of cells that are stereotypically distributed across the six layers of the cerebral cortex (as described above in the description of the laminar organization of the cortex). There are two ways that a developing brain could make sure that the right kind of cells (e.g., stellate cells) end up in the right layers (e.g., layer 4). One way would be to transform progenitor cells into the right type (via genetic transcription processes) immediately after they are produced within the proliferative zones. According to this approach, a cell would "know" what kind of neuron it will become even before it migrates. The second way would be to withhold transforming the progenitor cell until after it migrates to a particular layer. In the latter approach, chemicals secreted by neighboring cells "inform" the migrated cell what kind of cell it should become (Chenn et al., 1997). Recent experimental studies suggest that both of these processes seem to be involved in creating various types of neurons. In the absence of chemical signals from neighbors, postmitotic progenitors differentiate into one (and only one) type of cell. When these same cells are transplanted to atypical layers, however, they differentiate into cells typical for that layer.

The correlation between the birthdate of a cell and its final laminar position suggests that a neuron's phenotype might be determined early (Chenn et al., 1997). As noted above, there are two main classes of neurons in the cortex: pyramidal and nonpyramidal. Whereas the majority of pyramidal cells use excitatory amino acids as neurotransmitters, the majority of nonpyramidal neurons use inhibitory neurotransmitters (e.g., GABA). Moreover, whereas nonpyramidal cells are distributed uniformly across the six layers of the cortex, excitatory pyramidal neurons are only found in particular layers. Recent evidence suggests that local signals from neighbors have differing effects on neuronal specification, depending on when a cell was produced. For example, studies of regions that contain a large number of inhibitory neurons show that cells transplanted to that region during a certain phase of their development (the "S phase") fail to become inhibitory. Cells transplanted after this phase, however, express inhibitory neurotransmitters (Chenn et al., 1997).

With differentiation processes added to the mix, we now have a brain that has the right number and right type of cells located in the right layers. But to create a fully mature brain, several additional things have to happen. First, each brain cell has to grow in size and send projections to other cells. Second, these cells have to form synaptic connections with some of the cells to which they project. Third, an optimal numerical correspondence has to emerge between presynaptic and postsynaptic neurons. (Note: When two neurons are connected in a oneway chain by way of a synapse, the one earlier in the chain is called presynaptic; the next one to which it sends neurotransmitters is called postsynaptic). Finally, a myelin sheath has to form along the axons of many of the longer neurons. Let's examine each of these four processes a little further.

A fascinating aspect of neuronal growth processes is that neurons seem to seek out highly specific targets during their development. Even when the targets of these projections are transplanted to atypical locations in the brains of animals, the axons of the seeking neurons still find their targets (Chenn et al., 1997; Purves & Lichtman, 1985). Other evidence of neuronal specificity is the fact that there is a highly stereotyped pattern of lamina-specific axonal projections across individuals. For example, whereas layer 5 neurons make long-distance projections to targets such as the spinal cord and superior colliculus in most people, those in layer 6 make long-distance projections to the thalamus (Chenn et al., 1997). Unlike the synaptic connections that form in response to experience (see later in this chapter), the stereotyped, laminar patterning of connections among neurons seems to be largely determined by genes (Chenn et al., 1997; Goodman & Tessier-Lavigne, 1997).

Although the evidence is still coming in, it would appear that a combination of factors explain how it is that neurons can find their genetically determined targets. The first thing to note is that axons solve the daunting task of finding long-distance targets by proceeding in small steps (Goodman & Tessier-Lavigne, 1997). That is, they project a small distance and leave behind a new portion of axon. At each point, they make use of both local cues (e.g., chemoaffinity or attraction to certain "guidepost" cells along the way as well as repulsion toward other cells), and long-distance cues (e.g., a steady increase in the concentration of Neuronal Growth Factor [NGF] as the axon gets closer to the target). Then, gradations of molecular guideposts along the surface of targets help individual axons recognize their targets.

Once the projected axons of neurons are in close proximity to other neurons, a correlation of activity patterns in these neurons promotes the formation of synapses. In other words, if two neurons are always active at the same times, they are likely to form a synapse with each other. If they are active at different times, however, they are unlikely to form synapses with each other. In the developing fetus, these activity patterns seem to be intrinsic and spontaneous (i.e., they are not caused by afferent stimulation from the environment that travels from sensory organs along pathways and registers ultimately in the brain; they fire in an unprovoked manner). The first sign that a synapse is forming is that the membranes of the presynaptic and postsynaptic cells thicken at the site of the synapse in response to recurrent activity. The second sign is that the tip of the axon changes in appearance from looking like a *growth cone* (i.e., a starburst) to looking like a *synaptic bouton* (i.e., an oval with a flat bottom—imagine a cloth bag of marbles tied at the top). Then, three other changes take place: (1) circular vesicles containing neurotransmitters appear near the edge of the bouton (imagine a row of dots along the bottom of the bag), (2) the synaptic cleft between the bouton and the surface of the postsynaptic neuron's dendrite widens somewhat (i.e., forms a narrow oval shape), and (3) glial cells encase the boutons. The net result of all of these anatomical changes is that the information exchange between presynaptic and postsynaptic neurons can occur in a fast and efficient manner. From the standpoint of neuroscience, however, we need to know what a mature synapse looks like before we can say anything about changes in synapses that occur with age or experience. When a scientist counts the number of fully formed synapses in a region of a child's brain and an adult's brain, for example, he or she needs to be able to recognize a fully formed synapse.

In an adult brain, each of the approximately 10^{11} neurons makes a thousand or more synaptic contacts with other neurons (Goodman & Tessier-Lavigne, 1997). In addition, these neurons tend to form contacts in a stereotypical manner. For example, some neurons form synapses only on dendritic spines while others form synapses only on dendritic shafts. (Note: The spines are like circular leaves on a tree, and the shafts are like branches.) Early in development, however, this stereotyped patterning is not yet apparent and neurons make many more synaptic contacts than needed to create functional circuits for processing information. So, slides of brain tissue would reveal a lot of synapses all over the neuron in young children but a stereotyped reduced pattern in slides of adult brain tissue. One way that the overabundance of synapses is reduced with age (in many species) is through the death of neurons. A second way is through the process of axonal retraction. In the latter, a presynaptic neuron literally retracts its axon away from the postsynaptic neuron by shrinking in size. (Imagine a tree pulling back one of its branches away from a neighboring tree by making the branch smaller.)

What causes neurons to die and why do surviving neurons retract their axons? Many scientists believe that both of these processes reflect the fact that neurons have to compete for substances called *trophic factors* that are secreted by activated postsynaptic neurons (Purves & Lichtman, 1985; Reichardt & Farinas, 1997). To explain cell death, scientists note that only some of the axonal projections that make contact with target neurons will succeed in obtaining enough trophic factors to survive. Those that survive and become activated at the same time as postsynaptic neurons tend to form stable synapses with these postsynaptic neurons. To explain axonal retraction, scientists note that sometimes neurons fail to get enough trophic factor from one site but succeed in getting enough from other sites. Instead of dying, these neurons simply retract their axons away from the unsupportive areas.

The net result of the competition for trophic factors is an optimum balance between a population of innervating neurons and a population of innervated neurons (i.e., a functional circuit that has the right number of each class of cells). Presumably, the initial oversupply of neurons and synapses emerged phylogenetically as an evolutionary adaptation to guard against possible problems that might arise as brains are being constructed. To see the utility of this oversupply, consider the following thought experiment. Imagine a species that had a brain that contained 300 functional circuits (one circuit for each of 300 cognitive operations). Next, assume that each circuit must have 1,000 neurons configured in a particular way to work properly (total = 300,000 neurons). Finally, assume the proliferative zones in this species produce exactly 300,000 cells during development. A little reflection shows that a properly constructed brain would only be constructed in this species if all of the following happened during development: (1) all cells managed to migrate to the right locations, (2) chemical signals from neighboring cells were detected by the DNA transcription processes of all migrated cells, and (3) the axons of all cells found their targets. In effect, a properly functioning brain would only emerge if everything went right. But things often go wrong in nature, so the biological strategy of producing exactly the number of cells needed is obviously not the best way to go.

Shortly after the regressive processes of cell death and axonal retraction were discovered, scientists wondered whether all species relied on these two processes to the same extent. Some recent evidence suggests that lower-order species (e.g., rats) seem to rely more on cell death than higher-order species (e.g., humans). The opposite seems to be true for axonal retraction

(Huttenlocher, 1993). However, this conclusion is based on a few studies using postmortem techniques. Hence, more evidence needs to accumulate before strong statements can be made regarding interspecies differences in regressive processes.

The last two processes of brain development that should be discussed are *dendritic arborization* and *axonal myelination*. In addition to growing in size (length and width), neurons also sprout new dendrites (arborization) and acquire a myelin sheath along some of their axons. The addition of new dendrites is thought to be the primary neural basis of cognitive development (Quartz & Sejnowski, 1997). To get a vivid image of arborization, or neurons bathed in solutions that foster sprouting, imagine "Chia Pets" (those small ceramic animals that one covers with a seed paste and then waters)! Myelination, in contrast, is the process of adding a fatty-acid coating (myelin) to the axon of some neurons to speed up their firing. Myelin adds considerable mass to the brain beyond that produced by other types of growth. When the brain is finished maturing in late adolescence, it weighs four times as much as it did at birth (Johnson, 1997). Of course, a brain is never really finished changing in an absolute sense because there is a constant shifting of synaptic contacts with experience (see later in this chapter). In addition, the brain often shrinks in size for inactive, undernourished individuals who live beyond the age of 80.

In a way, the foregoing discussion of brain development could be transformed into a checklist for determining the state of development in a child's brain. As noted earlier, autopsies have been used to determine the kinds of cells that normally appear in specific layers and the number of synapses that form between cells in various regions of the brain. This "final state" can serve as the reference point for developmental comparisons. For example, one could ask, "How many cells are present in Layer 4 at ages 1, 4, 7, 10, and 13?" "How many synapses per neuron are there, on average, in an adult brain and a child's brain?" Moreover, once we know how things should "look" in an average adult brain that developed in an average environment, we can consider the effects of various substances or experiences on brain development. For example, we can compare the brains of individuals who smoked cigarettes for many years to those of individuals who did not smoke to see if there are differences in the number of neurons in particular regions, the number of synapses formed by these neurons, and so on. In the next section, we explore the latter theme more fully.

FACTORS AFFECTING BRAIN DEVELOPMENT

In the previous two sections, the focus was on describing the general characteristics of mature brains (e.g., the laminar organization of the cortex), as well as the processes that produce these general characteristics (e.g., migration). This reveals how all of our brains are similar at a basic level. In the present section, the primary goal is to elucidate the factors that produce *individual differences* in brain structure. Five such factors will be described in turn: (1) genetics, (2) environmental stimulation, (3) nutrition, (4) steroids, and (5) teratogens.

Genetics

Long before scientists discovered genes, they knew that some intrinsic (i.e., nonenvironmental) factor was responsible for producing the large-scale physical differences that can be observed among species (Edelman, 1992). Today, we know that this intuition was clearly correct. The human brain looks very different than other mammalian brains (including our closest ape cousins) chiefly because of a difference in genetic instructions. But what about the more subtle differences in brain structure that arise between individuals of the same species (Goldman-Rakic, 1994; Talairach & Tournoux, 1988)? Everyone's brains look a little different. Relatedly, the precise location of particular areas of the brain (e.g., Broca's area) differs slightly among individuals. Are these within-species differences also caused by genetic differences? In order to answer this question, we need to expand upon our earlier descriptions of proliferation, migration, and differentiation. Then, we can consider the implications of this expanded analysis for two related lines of genetic research.

The most important variable that explains between-species differences in brain size is the length of the proliferation phase. As Finlay and Darlington (1995) note, an additional 17 doublings of precursor cells can yield 131,000 times the final number of neurons (roughly the difference in the number of neurons found between the brains of humans and shrews). How does a developing brain know when to stop proliferating cells? One possibility is that the proper number of mitotic divisions is encoded somewhere in the DNA of precursor cells. Another possibility is that precursor cells continue to double until they receive signals that enough cells have migrated to various locations in the brain (Chenn et al., 1997). Regardless of which of these possibilities turns out to be the case, it is clear that proliferation is largely under the control of genetic instructions.

The same could be said for migration and differentiation. Earlier in this chapter, we saw how proliferated cells seem to be genetically destined to become particular types of cells and migrate to particular levels as soon as they leave the proliferative zones. However, we also saw that this predestination is not set in stone. Once again, signals from neighboring cells seem to play a role determining the ultimate fate of particular cells. Thus, one could summarize the role of genetics so far by saying that genes largely constrain how things turn out, but there is a certain degree of protective flexibility built into the system.

One other point worth noting pertains to the probabilistic nature of migration. As cells migrate, they overlap, pass by, make contact with, and adhere to one another in a complex way (Edelman, 1992; Rakic, 1993). As a result, there is no way to know for sure where a given cell will end up when it migrates (Chenn et al., 1997). The stochastic, "bump-and-grind" quality of the migration process means that genetic instructions are not really analogous to blueprints. Whereas two houses built from the same blueprint would turn out to be identical (in terms of their size, location of rooms, etc.), two brains built from the same set of genetic instructions could be rather different.

The latter point provides a nice segue to a second line of work that provides further insight into the role of genetics in brain development. Researchers who have conducted neuroscientific studies of twins have revealed two important findings. First, people who have exactly the same genetic instructions (i.e., monozygotic, or MZ, twins) sometimes develop brains that are structurally different (Edelman, 1992; Segal, 1989; Steinmetz, Herzog, Schlaug, Huang, & Lanke, 1995). In fact, MZ twins have been found to develop brains that are mirror images of each other (e.g., one has a dominant left hemisphere, while the other has a dominant right hemisphere).

However, researchers have also found that there can be a relatively high concordance rate between MZ twins for disorders that are alleged to have a neurological basis. By "concordance rate," it is meant that both of the twins have the same phenotype (i.e., both have the disorder, or both lack the disorder). In a study of the genetic basis of reading disability, for example, DeFries, Gillis, and Wadsworth (1993) found that 53.5% of MZ twins were concordant for reading problems, compared to just 31.5% of dizygotic (DZ) twins. Note, however, that both of these concordance rates are considerably lower than 100%, which suggests that there is not a deterministic, one-to-one correspondence between genes and brain structure. Also, when DeFries et al. estimated the heritability of reading disability from their data, they found that genetics accounted for 44% of the variance in reading profiles (which means that 56% is explained by nongenetic factors). Later studies produced somewhat higher concordance rates and heretibility estimates (e.g., Knopik, Alarcon, & DeFries, 1997), but the overall findings are essentially the same. Since MZ twins are highly similar in terms of their height and weight ($r = .97$), it would appear that reading disability is probably not a product of proliferation problems. Rather, it would seem that reading problems arise from other aspects of brain development (e.g., formation of synapses; pruning of axons).

A final way to assess the relative importance of genes for brain development is to examine disorders such as Down syndrome (DS) in which there is a known linkage between specific genes and neurological pathology. DS, or trisomy 21, is the leading cause of mental retardation in the United States. It results from the nondisjunction of a portion of the 21st chromosome during meiotic division of gametes (usually the ovum), so that three copies of that portion are present in the cells of the affected individual instead of the usual two (Coyle, Oster-Granite, Reeves, & Gearhart, 1988; Hassold, Sherman, & Hunt, 1995). The presence of this extra genetic material produces a number of anatomical and health-related differences between individuals with DS and unimpaired individuals (Coyle et al., 1988; Kemper, 1988). Of particular interest here are the differences related to brain structure. Individuals with DS tend to have brains that are smaller and less developed than those of unimpaired children and adults. In addition, individuals with DS tend to have 33% fewer cortical neurons, less complex patterns of connectivity, reduced levels of myelin, and apical dendrites that are abnormal in appearance (e.g., fewer spines and elongated necks). Taken together, these findings suggest that the extra genetic material probably interferes with the processes of proliferation, synaptogenesis, and myelination.

Although much more can be said about the role of genes in brain development, the preceding discussion of developmental processes (e.g., proliferation), twin research, and genetic disorders is sufficient for drawing several broad conclusions. First, it seems clear that certain changes in genetic instructions can lead to large-scale changes in brain volume and patterns of connectivity. For example, a 2% change in the amount of genetic material (e.g., shifting from 46 to 47 chromosomes) can produce a 33% difference in brain structure (e.g., the number of cortical neurons in the brains of DS vs. unimpaired individuals). But even when people have the same genes, there is still a chance that they could have brains that differ somewhat in terms of their size, shape, and areal organization. The lack of one-to-one correspondence between genes and brain structure means that researchers should not assume that two individuals definitely have different genes simply because their brains are different in size or in organizational structure. Perhaps more to the point, researchers should not argue with certainty that two people have different brains because they have different genes (consider the case of identical twins), nor argue with certainty that two people must have the same genes because their brains seem to be anatomically identical (two unrelated people who share few genes could have identical brains).

Environmental Stimulation

In essence, then, we see that genes only partly explain why we have the brains that we do. The second factor that is instrumental in sculpting the brain is environmental stimulation. In order for animals to respond adaptively to their environment, they have to be able to form mental representations that match their experiences (Greenough, Black, & Wallace, 1987; Johnson, 1997). For example, they need to be able to recognize conspecifics (e.g., their mothers and their siblings), as well as store new, adaptation-relevant experiences in memory (e.g., the fact that fire can burn). Many animals come into the world ready to learn such things, using a prewired circuitry that is closely aligned with their external sense organs.

The prewired circuitry consists of (1) cortical neurons that receive, process, and store input signals from the environment and (2) afferent neurons that bring these input signals to the brain from the various sensory organs. Postmortem studies reveal that the afferent neurons from particular sensory organs terminate in the same general regions for all people (e.g., area V1 in the occipital lobes in the case of afferents coming from the eyes). By necessity, then, it would be expected that all people would process and store input signals from particular organs in roughly the same regions of the cortex (Johnson, 1997). But it is important to note that this areal organization is jointly a function of the preset location of afferent projections and environmental stimulation. Take away the afferents and we would not develop particular types of representations (e.g., visual representations of people we know) in particular regions of the cortex (e.g., area V1). Similarly, we would obviously not develop representations of events in the world without experiencing these events. Each of these counterfactual claims has been tested empirically.

For example, surgical studies with animals have shown that atypical cortical maps can be created by redirecting the input fibers that extend from the thalamus to new areas. Normally, a neural tract that carries visual information from the eyes projects upward and backward from the thalamus (located in the middle of the brain) to area V1 of the occipital lobe in the cortex (in the back of the head). Scientists have redirected this tract such that it projects to, for instance the frontal lobe in the front of the head. They have found that cells in the frontal lobe then process visual information the same way cells in the occipital lobe normally do! In addition, studies have shown that animals will create new projections and new representations in a cortical area even after some of the thalamic projections that normally project to that area have been severed (e.g., Recanzone, Schreiner, & Merzenich, 1993). A similar type of plasticity has been observed in human infants who have suffered brain injury or had portions of their brains removed to relieve epilepsy (Johnson, 1997). Normally, the neural regions responsible for language skills are in the left hemisphere for most right-handed people. Infants who have had their left hemispheres removed to relieve constant seizures develop language areas in their remaining right hemispheres. Thus, whereas the laminar organization of the cortex seems to be largely intrinsically determined (i.e., preprogrammed by genes and unrelated to afferent stimulation that comes into the cortex), the areal organization seems to be jointly determined by pre-existing projections and environmental input (Chenn et al., 1997; Johnson, 1997). To understand the latter point by analogy, imagine that the neural assemblies in the cortex that process sounds or letters are like employees of a credit card company who operate in their own cubicles. Imagine further that outside phone calls from their customers are analogous to afferent stimulation from the environment. The company could not do its business if someone (e.g., the boss) had not placed the workers there and hooked them up to phone lines and each other via a computer network. But their computer databases would all be empty if their customers never called in. Thus, a functioning company requires both preset architectures ready to receive input and the input itself.

However, studies show that environmental stimulation can have different effects on brain structure depending on when it occurs in development (Greenough et al., 1987). For example, animals can be permanently blinded if they are reared in total darkness for 2 weeks right after birth. However, if the deprivation occurs somewhat later in the postnatal period, their visual skills develop normally. To explain such time-dependent results, Greenough et al. (1987) proposed that mammalian brain development involves two types of neural plasticity: experience-expectant and experience-dependent.

Experience-expectant plasticity exploits regularities in the environment to shape developing neural systems. Appropriate circuits develop if the animal experiences these regularities (e.g., contrast borders, movement). The mechanism of change in experience-expectant plasticity appears to be an early overproduction of synapses followed by a pruning of exuberant projections in response to experience. As noted earlier, the overproduction of synapses is said to take place in order to compensate for possible problems that arise during proliferation and migration (to make sure that there are enough neurons to form a functional circuitry). The pruning takes place because the neurons must compete for a limited supply of trophic factors (as described earlier).

The second type of plasticity, *experience-dependent*, is thought to have evolved to allow the animal to form representations of unique features of its environment (e.g., characteristics of its own mother, sources of food and haven, native language properties). The mechanism of change here is not the elimination of excessive synapses as much as the creation of new synapses (Greenough et al., 1987; Quartz & Sejnowski, 1997). Or, more accurately, new learning is probably best conceived of as the reorganization of synapses (elimination of some combined with the addition of others).

In sum, then, we can attribute the fact that most of us can see (or hear) correctly to the fact that we had appropriate visual (or auditory) experiences when we were young. In contrast, we can attribute the fact that we represent a particular sensory experience in a particular region of the cortex to the fact that (1) afferents project to that region and (2) we had the experience. It is in this way that experience can sculpt our brains and create a dynamic type of circuitry.

Nutrition

Numerous experimental studies with animals have shown that malnutrition can have different effects on brain development depending on when it occurs (Winick, 1984). Scientists explain such time-dependent outcomes by arguing that early (i.e., prenatal) malnutrition slows the rate at which cells are proliferated, thereby reducing the total number of neurons and glial cells in an animal's brain. Later malnutrition, in contrast, slows the rate at which the already proliferated cells grow in size or acquire a myelin sheath. Whereas the latter problems can be ameliorated by providing enriched diets to malnourished animals, the former problem of too-few cells cannot be corrected in this way. Such findings suggest, then, that prenatal malnutrition would cause more permanent harm to developing human brains than postnatal malnutrition (because proliferation largely occurs during the prenatal months in humans).

In support of this claim are various correlational studies of malnourished and normally fed children around the world (e.g., Streissguth, Barr, Sampson, Darby, & Martin, 1989; Winick, 1984), as well as a recent quasi-experimental study conducted by Pollitt, Gorman, Engle, Martorell, and Rivera (1993). These researchers gave either a high-protein, high-calorie supplement ("Atole") to poor Guatemalan pregnant women and their children, or a low-protein, lower-calorie supplement ("Fresco"). Some children received the supplement postnatally, while others received it both prenatally and postnatally. Children were followed longitudinally and given various assessments when they were preschoolers and adolescents. At the preschool assessment, Pollitt et al. found that children given the Atole supplement performed significantly better than children given the Fresco supplement, even after controlling for gender, age, and socioeconomic status. However, the findings were largely limited to motor skills. At the adolescent assessment, the Atole supplement was associated with higher cognitive skills, but it explained only 1% to 5% of the variance in these abilities. Factors such as gender, socioeconomic status, and schooling explained much more of the variance. In line with the findings with animals, however, Pollitt et al. found that children who started supplemental feeding after 24 months showed less benefit than children who received the supplement before and after birth.

Taken together, such studies suggest that nutrition has the potential to affect two important aspects of brain development: proliferation and myelination. Studies have also shown that brain development can be enhanced in most children by making sure that they have adequate levels of protein and fatty acids in their diets (Winick, 1984). For children who have the condition known as *phenylketonuria (PKU)*, however, a high-protein diet could prove disastrous if it is left unchecked. Children with PKU are unable to convert the amino acid phenylalanine into the amino acid tyrosine (Diamond, Prevor, Callender, & Druin, 1997). As a result, they experience two main problems. First, high levels of phenylalanine in the bloodstream cause progressive brain damage and mental retardation. Second, tyrosine is a precursor to dopamine. Circuits comprised of dopaminergic neurons cannot work properly when the level of dopamine is too low.

Whereas the first problem can be alleviated by having children with PKU avoid foods that contain high levels of phenylalanine (a strategy that has been in place for many years), researchers have not yet figured out how to solve the second problem (Diamond et al., 1997). As a result, many children with PKU still experience subtle cognitive deficits.

Steroids

Scientists believe that steroids affect brain development for four reasons. First, the brain is one of several organs in the body that contain receptors for estrogens and related substances (e.g., cortisol and other stress hormones). As such, there is reason to think that it would be transformed during prenatal development in the same way that other so-called steroid target tissues (e.g., genitalia) are transformed (Kelley, 1993). Also, excessive amounts of stress hormones could promote the death of neurons in certain key areas of the brain. The second reason relates to the consistent patterns of gender differences that have been found in areas such as cognitive skills, psychological disorders, and violent behavior. Many scientists believe that the consistency of these differences argues in favor of inborn structural differences in the brains of men and women (Halpern, 1992).

The third reason derives from various experimental studies of animals. In one line of research, scientists uncovered gender differences in brain structure that are visible to the naked eye (Breedlove, 1994). Other studies have shown that sex hormones can alter the brains and behaviors of animals. For example, female rats exposed to androgens have been found to engage in sexual behaviors that are characteristic of males (e.g., mounting).

The fourth reason derives from several recent studies that have compared the brains of three groups: homosexual men (group 1), heterosexual men (group 2), and heterosexual women (group 3). The logic of this comparison is as follows: If sexual attraction to men is brain-based, then the brains of people in group 1 should look more like the brains of people in group 3 than the brains of people in group 2 (Breedlove, 1994). Researchers recently demonstrated this expected pattern for a region of the hypothalamus that has been implicated in sexual functioning. The region was significantly larger in group 2 than in either group 1 or 3 (which did not differ).

While the results of all of these studies are certainly intriguing, it cannot be said that they convincingly demonstrate that the human brain is sexually dimorphic. The first problem relates to a high level of inconsistency in the evidence reported by researchers who have used either magnetic resonance imaging (MRI) or postmortem methodologies within human brains. Some have found structural differences that are consistent with the behavioral evidence (e.g., larger spatial areas in men); others report differences that are opposite to what would be predicted (e.g., larger spatial areas in women); and a third group has found no structural differences at all (Beaton, 1997; Breedlove, 1994; Driesen & Raz, 1995; Giedd et al., 1996). The second problem is that human behavior is far more flexible and context-sensitive than animal behavior (Breedlove, 1994; Byrnes & Fox, 1998). As such, there is little reason to think that humans and animals would respond in the same way to some experimental intervention (e.g., an injection of androgens). Third, the brain regions targeted by experimental interventions have not been consistently related to sexual behaviors in either animals or humans. Finally, it is not at all clear why the size of a particular brain region would necessarily relate to behaviors in a meaningful way (Beaton, 1997; Breedlove, 1994).

Thus, even though there is reason to think that steroids could alter the brains of men and women, scientists have found little hard evidence of this transformation. This lack of evidence either means that sexual dimorphisms do not exist or that scientists have not been looking in the right places (using the right metrics). With respect to the latter possibility, note that few researchers have investigated whether steroids alter (1) the distribution of particular types of cells in given regions or (2) patterns of connectivity. Such differences could not be detected with MRI technology, but they could be detected in postmortem studies.

Teratogens

Any foreign substance that causes abnormalities in a developing embryo or fetus is called a *teratogen*. Researchers identify teratogens through retrospective analyses, prospective longitudinal studies, and prospective experimental investigations. Using the retrospective technique, mothers of children who are born with birth defects are interviewed to determine whether they may have ingested something (e.g., alcohol) or been exposed to something (e.g., a virus) that could have altered the course of their child's development *in utero*. Using the prospective longitudinal technique, pregnant women are interviewed regarding their behaviors during their pregnancy and followed for years after they give birth. Of interest is the association between their exposure to teratogens and developmental outcomes in their children. Using the prospective experimental technique, pregnant animals are exposed to various dosages of suspected teratogens. Their offspring are then analyzed for the presence of physical or behavioral anomalies.

Scientists consider a substance to be a teratogen only if both of the following are true: (1) A sufficient level of evidence has accumulated from retrospective or prospective studies to show a consistent linkage between the substances and birth defects, and (2) the dosages utilized in prospective experimental studies are not unrealistically high. Many common substances (e.g., caffeine and nicotine) have been found to produce birth defects when given at extremely high and unrealistic dosages, but not when given at more realistic levels. Such substances are generally not considered teratogens by scientists, but they may nevertheless appear on lists of to-be-avoided substances issued by the federal government, or on the warning labels of packages. The government takes a more cautious approach since it often takes time to determine whether a substance really is dangerous. Hence, government officials think it is better to be safe than sorry.

Generally speaking, two types of teratogens have been the subject of numerous investigations: viruses and drugs. Viruses reproduce themselves by invading a host cell (e.g., a neuron), releasing their nucleic acids into the surrounding tissue, and co-opting the host cell's metabolic machinery. In mature organisms, this invasion usually results in transient symptoms such as lethargy and fever. In developing organisms, however, a viral infection can have more permanent effects if it occurs when the organism's cells are in the midst of proliferating, migrating, or differentiating. Viruses such as rubella have been linked to a range of birth defects including microencephaly (i.e., a small head and brain). It is not yet clear whether other viruses are also linked to abnormal brain development in the same way, but the key seems to be whether the virus targets particular kinds of tissues. Cold viruses and flu viruses target tissues in the nose and lungs, respectively, and do not target developing embryonic tissue (such as developing neurons).

As for drugs, numerous prospective and retrospective studies have been conducted to determine whether substances such as lead, alcohol, marijuana (cannabis), cocaine, caffeine, nicotine, aspirin, acetaminophen, and antihistamine are teratogens. Maternal exposure to high levels of lead has been found to be associated with higher rates of fetal loss (i.e., spontaneous abortion), but, despite popular reports in the media, lower levels do not appear to produce large-scale cognitive deficits or physical abnormalities in children (Bellinger & Needleman, 1994). Maternal consumption of alcohol, however, has been consistently linked to a range of cognitive and motor deficits (Barr, Streissguth, Darby, & Sampson, 1990; Streissguth et al., 1989; Streissguth, Sampson, Barr, Bookstein, & Olson, 1994). In heavy drinkers and alcoholics, prenatal exposure to alcohol occasionally leads to a disorder called Fetal Alcohol syndrome, which has an incidence rate of about 3 per 1,000 births. As for marijuana, cocaine, caffeine, nicotine, aspirin, acetaminophen, and antihistamine, the collective evidence from prospective and retrospective studies with humans suggests that these substances do not appear to be consistently related to long-term cognitive or motoric deficits (Barr & Streissguth, 1991; Hinds, West, Knight, & Harland, 1996; Streissguth et al., 1994). Experimental studies with animals, however, have found teratogenic effects for all of these substances. In each case, there is evidence that the substance has the potential to interfere with the processes of proliferation, migration, and differentiation. In the final section of this chapter, we explore possible reasons why these drugs seem to affect the offspring of animals more than the offspring of humans.

Summary

The preceding discussion focused on five factors that have been found to produce individual differences in brain structure: genes, environmental stimulation, nutrition, steroids, and teratogens. This analysis revealed that two people could develop different brains because they (1) had different genes, (2) had differing levels or types of environmental stimulation, (3) ingested differing levels or types of food, (4) were exposed to differing levels or types of steroids, or (5) were exposed to differing levels or types of teratogens. The evidence as a whole, however, suggests that most of the structural differences that might arise between people would tend to be rather small and subtle. Large-scale differences in brains might only arise when several of these factors work in concert, or when extreme values of the individual factors are involved (e.g., shifting from 46 to 47 chromosomes; reducing diets by 60%; rearing animals in the dark; drinking large quantities of alcohol daily).

CONCLUSIONS AND CAVEATS

In a certain sense, this chapter represents a "how to" manual for building a human brain. The standard model of this brain is clearly the default option that is likely to emerge in all but the most adverse environments. The underlying principles behind this high degree of adaptive success appear to be two notions:

1. *Overproduction*: Build more brain cells and synaptic connections than most people will need; if proliferation, migration, differentiation, and synaptogenesis are somehow slowed or altered, there may still be enough cells around to create functional circuits.
2. *Flexibility and plasticity*: Augment genetic instructions with cellular feedback loops; make use of both experience-expectant and experience-dependent learning processes; make use of alternative brain regions if the typical brain region lacks functional circuits (the latter mostly applies to young children).

These two principles combined with physical aspects of the intrauterine environment (e.g., crowding, passive migration) also mean that individual differences in brain structure will be the norm rather than the exception (even in identical twins). However, in most cases, the differences that emerge in brain structure will tend to be rather subtle. Whether any of these smaller differences are responsible for either individual differences in behavior or phenotypic similarity in twins is currently a matter of controversy.

Moreover, it is important to point out that much of what we know (or, rather, believe) about brain development is still tentative and fairly controversial. To a large extent, the lack of certainty is due to the fact that researchers have had to resort to experimental studies with animals to determine the possible role of certain factors in development (e.g., environmental stimulation, hormones). Interspecies differences clearly cloud the conclusions that can be drawn from such studies. Moreover, studies with humans are, by necessity, correlational rather than experimental. Any linkages between background variables (e.g., nutrition) and outcomes (e.g., brain size) could be spurious.

What, then, are the implications of the research on brain development for psychological theory, educational practice, and public policy? We have seen that the adult form of a person's brain is jointly a function of (1) genetic instructions that specify the length of the proliferative phase and the kinds and locations of neurons that are produced; (2) mechanical processes involved in the movement of cells and progressive lengthening of axons; (3) chemical signals between neurons (neurotransmitters that are sent across synapses as well as other signals that help guide axonal projections and inform the differentiation process); (4) environmental stimulation that causes clusters of neurons to fire together, form synapses with each other, and create functional areas of the cortex (e.g., for vision or math); and (5) other factors that interfere with the normal processes of sculpting (e.g., teratogens and diseases). We have also seen that there is not a one-to-one relationship between genes and the final cytoarchitecture of someone's brain and that the human brain is highly plastic in the sense that it can reorganize itself and overcome obstacles imposed by the environment. However, the ability of the brain to overcome problems varies over time. For example, whereas the effects of prenatal malnutrition on the brain seem to be relatively permanent, the effects of postnatal malnutrition seem to be reversible.

When confronted with these tentative conclusions, a variety of reactions seem possible. Some have used the findings in this chapter and related findings to argue in favor of the *constructivist orientation* to cognitive development (e.g., Quartz & Sejnowski, 1997). The constructivist orientation lies midway between a *nativist orientation* (that espouses the idea that mental representations of such things as faces, math skills, and grammatical categories exist at birth prior to environmental input) and an *empiricist orientation* (that espouses the idea that the mind is blank slate that is entirely shaped by environmental input). Among developmental psychologists, there is an ongoing, vigorous debate between nativist and constructivist camps, so presumably the findings can be used to bolster the position of the constructivists. Relatedly, most mathematics and science educators espouse the constructivist philosophy these days (Byrnes, 2001a), so these educators may use the findings to their advantage as well. However, there is a large gap between finding support for the metatheoretical belief system of constructivism and finding support for a particular theory or instructional technique that is consistent with this paradigm (e.g., Piaget's theory or the instructional approach advocated by the National Council of Teachers of Mathematics). There are many ways to conceptually and behaviorally implement constructivism (in the same way there are many ideas, behaviors, and rituals consistent with the religious beliefs of a particular type of religion such as Christianity).

Relatedly, some have used the time-dependent relation between environmental input and brain sculpting to argue in favor of starting foreign language and music instruction in the preschool period, for example (before a presumed critical period is over) rather than later in development. Others, in contrast, have argued that nothing at all can be concluded from the time-dependent effects of the environment because they only apply to cases of extreme deprivation (Bruer, 1998). We tend to agree more with the latter than the former reaction, but we add that the findings are nevertheless important for the attitudes we take toward children. There is an unfortunate tendency for scientists, educators, and ultimately parents to take a deterministic, pessimistic view of abilities and disabilities. The findings regarding plasticity and environmental input show that children are not destined to particular outcomes due to their genes. In other words, there is much we can do to improve skills in children. The sooner we start, the sooner the sculpting and plasticity can begin. In the same way, the findings show that gender and ethnic differences in abilities may be relatively easy to eliminate and that parental guilt over "giving" their children a malady with a presumed genetic basis (e.g., reading disability, autism) may be misguided. The stochastic, mechanical quality of brain maturation may be the culprit in many cases (i.e., things just did not go as planned by the genes).

The Development of Spoken Language Competence

3

An Overview of Spoken Language Competence

Vignette: Ms. Filano's preschool class is getting ready to take a field trip to the local grocery store. As the children line up to get their coats, Ms. Filano notices that Miguel is squeezing glue onto his line partner's hand. Since Miguel is typically a very compliant child, Ms. Filano asks quizzically, "What are you doing with the glue, Miguel?" Miguel replies, "You said that we needed to stick together, so I was making sure that Sam and I do." Children younger than 5 often interpret the literal meaning of our words.

MAIN IDEAS OF THE CHAPTER

1. Competent speakers know many different ways to express the same communicative goals (e.g., they can ask for something politely or rudely); the most skilled and successful language users choose ways of communicating that accomplish their goals while also helping them to maintain positive social relationships with others.
2. Teachers should care about children acquiring spoken language competence because children who enter school with high levels of phonological, semantic, and grammatical knowledge learn to read better than children who enter school with lower levels of these forms of knowledge.
3. In terms of developmental trends, few children younger than the age of 5 show high levels of insight into ideas such as utterances having multiple or implicit meanings. Moreover, young children tend to be literal, concrete, and largely truthful. After age 5, use of more varied communicative devices (e.g., sarcasm, indirect requests, white lies) increases steadily and seems to level off by late childhood (but sometimes later). The key aspect of children's mastery of these communicative devices is their ability to comprehend and control utterances that are figurative or intentionally false. Depending on the communicative goal of a speaker, false statements may be expressed to (a) convey a negative attitude in a muted way (as in sarcasm), (b) make someone laugh (as in humor), (c) spare someone's feelings (as in white

lies), or (c) avoid punishment (as In other kinds of lies). As children grow in their ability to recognize the multiple goals of other speakers (and "get inside their heads" more generally), children also become more apt to respond correctly to nonobvious indirect requests and to possibly express themselves in more polite ways, as well.

4. The developmental mechanisms responsible for the developmental trends in communicative skills include (a) multiple opportunities to converse with others and fulfill their communicative goals, (b) increases in vocabulary, and (c) increased exposure to examples of sarcasm, indirect requests, and so on with age.

5. Three groups have particular trouble with the skills identified in this chapter: children and adults who have autism, adults who have sustained damage to their right hemispheres through strokes, and adults who have sustained damage to their frontal lobes through traumatic brain injury.

This chapter and the next three chapters provide a detailed description of spoken language competence. The goal is to give you considerable insight into the "inner workings" of children's minds so that you can understand how to foster, or take advantage of, children's spoken language skills in the classroom (see Chapter 1). As a means of promoting this insight efficiently and consistently, the following questions will be asked and answered in each chapter:

- The *"nature of"* question inquires into the components of the focal skill in question for a given chapter (in this case, spoken language competence).
- Answers to the *relevance question* provide an explanation as to why preservice and experienced teachers should care about whether children ever master this skill.
- The *developmental trends question* focuses on snapshots of skills over time (what children can do at different ages).
- The *developmental mechanisms question* pertains to theories that try to explain why skills change in the manner described in the answer to the preceding developmental trends question.
- The *deficiencies question* asks whether there are populations of children who lack some or all of the key skills involved in the focal competence and whether these children experience problems when they learn to read.

Organizing chapter topics in this way will help you see commonalities of issues across chapters and also places the focal competence in developmental perspective (see Chapter 1 for the importance and utility of the developmental perspective). In what follows, we answer these five questions as they pertain to the case of spoken language competence. The answers provide a broad but useful overview of the nature and development of communicative abilities. Chapters 4, 5, and 6 provide more detail on three core aspects of communicative competence that we only touch on in this broad characterization (i.e., phonological, semantic, and grammatical processing).

THE "NATURE OF" QUESTION: What Does It Mean to Say That a Child Has Spoken Language Competence?

One way to answer this question is to consider what people mean when they say that a friend is fluent in a foreign language such as French. Informally, people usually mean that the friend (1) knows the meaning of a number of French words, (2) pronounces these words correctly, and (3) puts the right endings on these words and arranges them into proper sequences. Linguists call these three aspects of competence *semantic knowledge, phonological knowledge,* and *grammatical knowledge,* respectively (Berko Gleason, 2005; Hoff, 2001). This triadic definition of spoken language competence is certainly reasonable because it would hardly make sense to say that someone knew French if that person only knew a handful of French words, or pronounced these words awkwardly, or always put the wrong endings on words (e.g., the male ending on adjectives assigned to female nouns, second-person verb endings when speaking in the first person). In Chapters 4, 5, and 6, the development of phonological, semantic, and grammatical knowledge in English speakers is explored in detail. For the purposes of this overview chapter, we can simply note that competent speakers of a language have at least these three forms of knowledge.

In addition, however, spoken language competence involves other abilities, as well. For example, think of friends to whom you would assign the label "good conversationalist." What is it about these individuals that causes you to believe that they are skilled in the area of conversations? Do they initiate conversations themselves or are they provoked reluctantly into making polite banter? Do they dominate conversations and "talk through" partners or do they engage in a more egalitarian give-and-take? Do they take the needs of the listener into account or do they drone on about topics that are unfamiliar, too complicated, or of little interest to their conversational partners? Answers to these questions show that communicative competence involves more than phonology, semantics, and grammar. It also involves (1) a desire to communicate with others (i.e., convey ideas to them and receive ideas back), (2) respect for others, (3) a desire to get along with others, (4) reciprocity and turn taking, and (5) lack of egocentrism (Ninio & Snow, 1999). Egocentric individuals have a difficult time putting themselves in someone else's shoes and think everyone knows what they know. In light of these five additional aspects of spoken language competence, one might expect shy and socially isolated individuals to have deficiencies in conversational skills (Ninio & Snow, 1999), or expect that these individuals would not come to mind when one thinks of good conversationalists. One might have similar expectations for overly assertive, rude, and self-centered individuals.

A third way to understand spoken language competence is similar to the second in that it connects language abilities to social competence in general. However, it adds important new insights, as well. The central idea involves the recognition that *language use is a form of goal-directed or intentional behavior* (Bloom, 1998; Ninio & Snow, 1999; Searle, 1983). In other words, the claim is that we *use language in order to have certain effects on listeners.* For example, sometimes we communicate because we want to provide information to others (e.g., "Hey, Bill, did you know that World Cup tickets are on sale?"). Here, the primary intended outcome is a change in the listener's knowledge base (though these knowledge changes sometimes provoke changes in the person's behavior, as well). Other times, we communicate to change people's opinions or persuade them to a particular point of view (as in argumentative essays or congressional debates). Still other times, we say things to alter people's behavior or make them do things. For example, Hart and Risley (1995) found that a large percentage of the utterances directed toward children by parents have to do with either getting children to do something (e.g., wash their hands) or getting them to stop doing something (e.g., stop yelling). Conversely, children often say things to parents to have their own needs met (e.g., as when a child says, "Mommy, I'm hungry" as a means of getting something to eat). To get a sense of a speaker's intentions or communicative goals, one merely needs to ask, "Why did he say that?" or "What was she trying to accomplish by saying that?"

But, as many parents of teenagers and spouses fully understand, there are many ways to express the same intention and have an effect on listeners. Although a direct, brutally honest way of expressing an idea gets the point across (e.g., "Dad, you won't be wearing *that* shirt when you chaperone at the school dance tonight, will you? You look like a nerd!"), it is usually the case that a less direct, gentler utterance can have the same effect without hurting a person's feelings (e.g., "Hey, Dad, how about wearing that new blue shirt I got you for your birthday? You look great in it and it would mean a lot to me"). It can be argued that an important part of spoken language competence is "building up a tool kit" of possible ways to express the same communicative intention (Ninio & Snow, 1999). In other words, *competent speakers know a lot of different ways to express themselves, and they choose their utterance options wisely in particular situations.*

What does it mean to "choose options wisely?" Theories of decision making specify that one key aspect of good decision making is the ability to satisfy multiple goals with one's options (Byrnes, 1998). For example, imagine the case in which a person has two goals (e.g., goal 1 = drive a reliable car; goal 2 = save money). Imagine next that this person has two options. One option allows him or her to satisfy both goals (e.g., a car that is both reliable and reasonably inexpensive). The other option, in contrast, only satisfies one goal (e.g., a car that is very reliable but very expensive). The wise decision in this case is to choose the option that satisfies both goals. The same can be said for choosing utterances wisely. In general, the idea is to *figure out how to accomplish primary communicative goals (e.g., get the listener to do something) while maintaining positive social relationships with others.*

The converse ability is also useful. That is, individuals with high levels of spoken language competence are adept at correctly inferring the communicative intentions of others when they serve as listeners or recipients of utterances directed toward them. For example, a wife might say the following to her husband 1 week before her birthday: "I just finished a book by Anita Shreve. It was great. I'd like to read more of her stuff." The husband, if he is skilled at picking up indirect requests or hints, might realize that in saying this statement, the wife was hoping that he would buy her another Anita Shreve book for her birthday. Or, sometimes people in dating situations say things like "I think we should spend a little time apart" or "Can we be friends instead of lovers?" as ways of expressing the idea that the relationship is close to over. So, if we connect our previous discussion with the present one, it appears that one way to demonstrate a lack of social skills is to be routinely dominating and rude as a speaker (as described earlier in this chapter). A second way is to be a listener who regularly fails to "get the hint."

Linguists and philosophers who study the "meaning behind the meaning" and the use of expressions as instrumental, goal-directed acts fall in the field of *pragmatics* (Ninio & Snow, 1999) These scholars sometimes attempt to delineate various "rules" of conversation such as the four principles of cooperation proposed by Grice (1975): (1) the *quantity principle*: Be informative, but use the right amount of information in doing so (i.e., say no more or no less than what is required); (2) the *quality principle*: Be truthful, and avoid making assertions for which you have insufficient evidence; (3) the *relation principle*: Be relevant (i.e., don't introduce random thoughts that have little to do with the current topic of conversation); and (4) the *manner principle*: Avoid ambiguity by being brief and orderly. In regard to the quantity principle, saying too little can be a problem, as in the case in which a letter of recommendation for a professor has the single line: "Mr. Jones has excellent penmanship." The reader is left to infer that the applicant has no other notable abilities, including those that would be useful for being a successful college professor (e.g., research skills, writing skills, teaching skills). Conversely, saying too much can be a problem, as well. For example, a listener would not want a lengthy dissertation on the history of watches in response to the question, "Do you happen to know the time?"

Some have argued that various communicative devices such as *irony*, *sarcasm*, *metaphor*, *lying*, and *humor* become effective, in part, through an intentional violation of Grice's cooperative principles. As noted earlier, one need not be direct or brutally honest to accomplish one's communicative goals. Sometimes one can be equally or more effective using sarcasm and humor, which often have the effect of muting or softening the message (Creusere, 1999). The interesting aspect of irony, sarcasm, metaphor, and humor is that the speaker and listener know that the speaker does not really mean what is being said. For example, when a father says to his children in an annoyed tone, "Well, isn't this fun!" after being stuck with them in a traffic jam for one hour, the father does not really mean that being in a traffic jam is fun. Hence, speakers who use devices such as irony or sarcasm intentionally violate Grice's quality principle to have an effect on their listeners. Similarly, metaphors and other forms of figurative language (e.g., idioms) are not intended to be taken literally. For example, a speaker who uses the idiom *let off steam* within the sentence, "He went outside to let off some steam" does not mean the person actually let off steam (as a tea kettle would). Rather, the speaker means that the person was angry and left the situation to calm down. As for jokes, they often bend, distort, or exaggerate the truth for comic effect (e.g., as when Woody Allen said that he was expelled from New York University for looking into the soul of the boy next to him during a philosophy exam). Other times, jokes require holding in mind two meanings of the same expression (e.g., "Why did Snoopy quit his job as a cartoon character?" Because he was tired of working for *Peanuts*). Because the speaker and listener know that the speaker is not telling the truth or being literal as a means of getting some other idea across or to make the listener laugh, no harm is usually done. In contrast, lies are intentionally false utterances that only the speaker knows, at first, are not true. Moreover, the goal of a lie is not to get the listener to focus on the opposite meaning (as in irony or sarcasm), or to enhance understanding through a mapping to a familiar analogous idea (as in metaphor), or to make the listener laugh (as in a joke). Rather, the goal of a lie is to deceive the listener for some other purpose (e.g., the speaker wants to avoid getting in trouble or wants to avoid hurting someone's feelings). In any event, these aspects of spoken language competence illustrate once again that speakers have many options at their disposal to accomplish their communicative goals. These options include being direct, polite, indirect, ironic, sarcastic, metaphorical, idiomatic, humorous, and deceitful.

Whereas some scholars who study pragmatics focus on such communicative options, others delineate the various kinds of *speech acts* that people use (e.g., Searle, 1969). For example, any given utterance can serve to (1) express the speaker's beliefs about some state of affairs (e.g., "It's raining outside"), (2) request information from others (e.g., "Do you know what time it is?"), (3) cause a formal or legal definition to take effect (e.g., "I christen you *Queen Elizabeth II*" or "I now pronounce you man and wife"), or (4) demand that others perform some behavior (e.g., "Stop that at once"). Competent speakers of a language know the usual grammatical form and intonation patterns of such declaratives, interrogatives, imperatives, and so on. For example, interrogatives in English have a rising intonation and either a fronted auxiliary (e.g., *can* or *do*), a fronted verb (e.g., *is* or *are*), or a question word (e.g., *what* or *where*). Thus, the choice of words, intonations, and structures clearly matters when one wants to have a desired effect on a listener. For example, you may not get an answer if you do not execute a question correctly (the listener may not know it was a question). Competent speakers acquire the knowledge they need to accomplish their communicative goals and execute a variety of speech acts.

In stressing the goal-directed aspect of language in this book and discussing this perspective before discussing the traditional topics of phonology, semantics, and grammar, we are aligning ourselves with a variety of scholars in the *functionalist* perspective on language acquisition (Ninio & Snow, 1999; Tomasello & Brooks, 1999). Functionalists represent a controversial minority in the fields of linguistics and philosophy. The latter fields are currently dominated by scholars who take a strong *formalist* orientation (e.g., Chomsky). Formalists stress the autonomy of language (from the rest of cognition and specific situations) and consider it important to develop rule-governed models that could generate well-formed utterances "on their own." In addition, these scholars tend to believe in the innate origins of language skills, and they also tend to consider goals, context effects, and implicit meanings as epiphenomena or tangential to the core or "real" issues in linguistics (such as phonology, semantics, and grammar). In contrast, functionalists argue that children learn new pronunciations, words, and grammatical structures precisely *because* they are interested in specific topics, want to communicate more effectively, and want to get along more effectively with others (Bloom, 1998; Ninio & Snow, 1999). As we shall see, formalist and functionalist orientations have very different implications for instruction. As such, it clearly matters who is "right" in this regard. Instruction based on one of these perspectives is more likely to be effective than instruction based on the other perspective.

THE RELEVANCE QUESTION: Why Should Teachers Care about Whether Children Acquire Spoken Language Competence?

There are several reasons why spoken language skills are important to success in school. Perhaps the most convincing argument pertains to the empirical evidence that children who enter school with high levels of phonological, semantic, and grammatical knowledge learn to read better than children who enter school with lower levels of these forms of knowledge (see Chapters 4, 5, and 6). A second reason pertains to a child's ability to form positive social relationships in school and adapt to the demands of the classroom. Whereas socially rejected children do poorly in school and are at risk for a variety of problems later in life (Rubin, Bukowski, & Parker, 1998), socially skilled children do better in school and engage more readily in school tasks. As suggested earlier, there is a nontrivial correlation between social competence and (1) conversational skills, (2) the ability to produce and comprehend implicit meanings, and (3) use of humor (Masten, 1986; Ninio & Snow, 1999; Spector, 1996). As such, teachers would be far better off to have a classroom full of socially competent children than a classroom full of socially incompetent children. If nothing else, the former kind of classroom will be more harmonious and have higher levels of positive affect than the latter kind of classroom. In addition, students with high levels of social skills are more likely to be engaged in classroom tasks and to comply with verbal commands of teachers.

A third reason for focusing on spoken language competence pertains to the fact that most narrative texts (e.g., novels) and plays contain dialogues between characters. Very often, comprehending the fictionalized communicative exchanges in these works requires the ability understand such things as indirect requests, irony, sarcasm, and humor. Further, narratives may also require comprehension of metaphors, as well as the ability to detect deception and intentionally false statements uttered by characters. In addition, metaphors and analogies are also used rather frequently in science texts to help students understand difficult content (e.g., the myelin sheath on neurons is often said to be analogous to the insulation that covers electrical wires). Studies also suggest that teachers and classroom materials use idioms around 10% of the time. Thus, it would be nearly impossible for students to comprehend many narrative or expository texts if they were deficient in the abilities to comprehend indirect requests, sarcasm, deception, humor, or figurative language.

THE DEVELOPMENTAL TRENDS QUESTION:
How Does Spoken Language Competence Change over Time?

As noted in Chapter 1, the developmental trends question is all about "snapshots" of abilities over time. Generally speaking, analyses of developmental trends for any given ability show that children nearly always demonstrate higher levels of ability at each successive age. That is, 2-year-olds nearly always show more competence than 1-year-olds, 3-year-olds nearly always show more competence than 2-year-olds, and so on. Another common finding is that components of the skill are often added, elaborated, or integrated with other components as children get older. What happens in the case of spoken language competence? Let's examine the developmental trends for the four aspects of spoken language competence that were discussed earlier in this chapter in response to the "nature of" question.

Component 1: Phonological, Semantic, and Grammatical Knowledge

Children incrementally add to and refine their phonological knowledge and grammatical knowledge between birth and age 5 or 6 (see Chapters 4 through 6). After that time, little changes in their capacities to (1) recognize or produce the sound patterns of their native language, (2) add appropriate endings to words (e.g., -s to the end of verbs in the third person, -ed to past tense verbs), and (3) arrange words in proper grammatical order (Hoff, 2001; Menn & Stoel-Gammon, 2005; Tager-Flusberg, 2005). In contrast, developmental increases occur both before and after age 5 in the case of vocabulary (i.e., semantics).

Component 2: Conversational Skills

Even children between ages 1 and 3 show the ability to sustain alternating turns in communicative exchanges (Ninio & Snow, 1999). However, young children interrupt and talk out of turn more often than older children and adults. In addition, the former use fairly primitive devices to hold the floor (e.g., "And then. . . . ") and often utter statements that are not contingent on, or relevant to, what was just said (Hoff, 2001; Ninio & Snow, 1999). Preschoolers are also more likely to incorrectly assume knowledge on the part of their listeners than older children. For example, it sometimes appears that preschoolers think that listeners (even relative strangers) know all of their friends and all of the events that they experience. For instance, in response to a statement such as "Hey, Grandma! Billy and I went on the Blaster today!" a grandmother might say, "Who is Billy? A friend of yours? What is the Blaster?" Relatedly, an early study by Piaget (1926) suggested that preschoolers often (though not always) engage in collective monologues in which they seem to talk past each other and respond in noncontingent ways in their conversations (e.g., Child 1: "My dad is a fireman!" Child 2: "We had pizza for dinner last night!"). Further, younger children also sometimes violate Grice's quantity cooperative principle (see above) by talking endlessly about the travails of their favorite television characters to adults who tend to be far more interested in other topics.

This is not to say, of course, that young children are completely egocentric or that they are incapable of taking the needs of their listeners into account. Studies clearly suggest that even 2- and 3-year-olds know how to initiate conversations, choose appropriate conversation partners, adjust their speech to the age of the listener, and so on (Shatz & Gelman, 1973). However, preschoolers are novices when it comes to having conversations and benefit greatly from having patient and supportive adults as listeners (Hoff, 2001; Ninio & Snow, 1999). Older children, in contrast, are simply more adept and need less scaffolding from adults. For example, one study of peer conversations (i.e., Dorval & Eckerman, 1984) showed that 2nd graders responded in a contingent and relevant way to their conversational partners 60% of the time. Whereas 60% is a respectable figure, the percentage of relevant turns was found to be 90% of the time in 9th graders, 95% in 12th graders, and 100% of the time in adults. Thus, children continue to improve in their conversational skills after the preschool period and after the first few years of elementary school.

Component 3: Communicative Goals

Even preverbal children seem to have a wide array of intentions that they try to express through gestures and actions (Bates, 1976; Carpenter, Mastergeorge, & Coggins, 1983; Hoff, 2001; Ninio & Snow, 1999). For example, they make nonword sounds and gestures (e.g., points) as a means of (1) directing another person's attention (as in declaratives) and (2) prompting others to do something for them (as in imperatives). In addition, researchers have observed children trying to accomplish communicative goals such as requesting, greeting, acknowledging, and so on through a variety of pragmatic behaviors.

With the onset of language in the one-word stage, many of these same intentions are expressed now with words. For example, a child may say "cookie" with a particular intonation to show a listener a cookie (as in, "Did you know that this thing is called a cookie?"), and this child may also say "cook-eeee!" with an insistent and whiny tone as a means of having a cookie given to him or her (as in "Mom, I want a cookie!"). As these examples indicate, the earliest attempts at expressing communicative goals fall short of the full requirements of the communicative devices used by older children and adults. By age 5, however, children often have enough control over conventional syntactic constructions that they can express a wide range of declaratives, imperatives, interrogatives, and so on. In their play, moreover, they can imitate some of the forms used by others in various cultural rituals (e.g., "Say aahh!"—a doctor's office; "I now pronounce you man and wife"—a wedding ceremony). Finally, they eventually shift from using a single kind of construction to express a particular communicative goal, to understanding how to use a variety of constructions to express the same intention (Ninio & Snow, 1999). Complete mastery of this many-to-one system is not evident until well beyond the preschool years, however.

Component 4: Comprehension and Use of Communicative Devices

When do children demonstrate the ability to comprehend and use indirect requests, polite expressions, irony, sarcasm, verbal humor, metaphor, and lies to accomplish their communicative goals? In the case of indirect requests, most studies suggest that children below the age of 5 have an easier time understanding direct requests than indirect requests, though even 2-year-olds perform pretty well when given indirect requests in conventional formats (Elrod, 1986; Garvey, 1975; Ledbetter & Dent, 1988) and perform even better when these utterances are accompanied by eye gazes and gestures (Kelley, 2001). However, it is not clear what to make of children's ability to respond appropriately to conventional indirect requests such as "Can you hand me that?" because they could effectively ignore the first few words (i.e., "Can you . . . ") and merely respond to the last few words as a simple imperative (i.e., . . . "hand me that"). Eye gazes and points can further clarify a speaker's intent in such cases. Some studies have shown that 3-year-olds correctly respond to indirect requests that do not explicitly state what is wanted (e.g., "I wonder what this thing is called") as little as 30% of the time; 5-year-olds do better but have been found in some studies to correctly respond only 50% of the time (Elrod, 1986; Ledbetter & Dent, 1988). In a study of older children, Ackerman (1978) found that first graders correctly predicted the behavior of story characters 62% of the time when these characters were given indirect requests (e.g., a mother says, "It's 10 o'clock" to a child who is still awake doing homework as a means of getting the child to stop and go to bed). In contrast, third graders and adults responded correctly 88% and 96% of the time, respectively. Thus, children seem to show improvement after age 6 in their understanding of indirect requests that fail to explicitly state desired behaviors.

With respect to polite expressions, surprisingly few studies have documented changes in the frequency with which children use polite structures to accomplish their goals (Ninio & Snow, 1999). Most studies have focused, instead, on the considerable amount of effort expended by middle-class mothers to get their children to use more polite constructions (e.g., "What's the magic word?"). These efforts presumably do increase the overall frequency of polite forms, but this speculation awaits empirical confirmation in large-scale, normative studies. One small-scale study found no age increases between 8 and 12 in the ratings children gave to the politeness of various direct and indirect requests (Garton & Pratt, 1990), but it is one thing to know how to say things politely and quite another to actually use polite forms on a regular basis. Garton and Pratt (1990) did not measure how often children actually were polite, so their findings cannot be used to draw inferences about age changes in the frequency of polite forms.

Turning next to irony and sarcasm, researchers have generally found that 5- and 6-year-olds show less understanding of ironic and sarcastic comments than older children and adults (Creusere, 1999). Without contextual support (e.g., certain intonations and prior story events that clearly scaffold the sarcastic intention), younger children sometimes equate irony and sarcasm with deception or mistakes. In other words, they do not recognize the speaker's goal as being one of expressing an attitude (e.g., irritation) toward a situation, using the muting device of sarcasm. Instead, they assume the speaker is trying to deceive when he or she states something that clearly is not true.

Comprehension of verbal humor (e.g., puns or jokes such as the Snoopy example earlier) also seems to be a later-emerging skill in children. In other words, children older than 8 seem to get the point of verbal jokes and witty statements more readily than children below the age of 8 (McGhee, 1971; Spector, 1996). Younger children, in contrast, are more apt to laugh at other kinds of nonverbal humor (e.g., visual humor or slapstick). This shift from visual comprehension to more conceptual understanding has also been found for children's comprehension of metaphors and idioms (Gentner, 1988; Qualls & Harris, 1999). For example, younger children appreciate visual metaphors such as "a snake is like a hose" more readily than they appreciate "a tire is like a shoe" or "a cloud is like a sponge." Understanding of the latter continues to develop between the ages of 8 years and adulthood. As for familiar idioms (e.g., *let off steam, put one's foot down, read between the lines*), children show good mastery by the fifth grade (Qualls & Harris, 1999).

Earlier in this section, we discussed how children younger than 6 tend to interpret expressions literally and tend to confuse sarcasm with lying. The latter confusion, of course, implies that young children know what lying entails. In line with this implication, studies using a variety of methodologies (e.g., parent report, observation of naturalistic situations, experiments) have demonstrated that preschoolers understand how to deceive and often do make false statements to cover up their transgressions (Lewis, Stanger, & Sullivan, 1989; Polak & Harris, 1999; Talwar, Lee, Bala, & Lindsay, 2002; Wilson, Smith, & Ross, 2003). For example, in an often-used methodology, 3-year-olds are asked not to touch an attractive toy while an experimenter leaves the room briefly. Most do, of course, and 80% of the latter deny that they did to the experimenter when he or she returns.

Older children may be even more inclined to tell falsehoods. In a large-scale, 3-year study of children when they were first, second, and third graders, parents and teachers were asked to report on the frequency with which children told lies (Gervais, Tremblay, Desmarais-Gervais, & Vitaro, 2000). Whereas parents reported that their children lied occasionally (58%) or frequently (6%), teachers reported that 21% and 2% of their students lied occasionally or frequently, respectively. This discrepancy between parents and teachers either reflects the different amount of time teachers and parents spend with children, or the fact that children have fewer chances to lie or be caught in the classroom than at home. Either way, the rate of reported lying was found to be very stable across the 3 years of the study, so it would appear that the frequency of lying plateaus somewhat in the early elementary grades.

Depending on one's moral stance, the pervasiveness and stability of occasional lying to cover up minor transgressions in childhood can be perceived either as a normative, natural behavior or as a matter of concern. Frequent and persistent lying, in contrast, is best viewed as a problematic behavior regardless of one's moral stance because it is linked to social rejection by peers and disruptive behavior in the classroom (Gervais et al., 2000). The link between lying and social problems provides further support for the claim made earlier in this chapter that spoken language skills are an important aspect of social relationships with peers and teachers.

One further way to illustrate the linkage between communicative skills and social relations pertains to studies that analyze the different kinds of lies told by children. Whereas there may not be age changes in the overall frequencies of occasional or frequent lying after age 5, children do appear to tell more "white lies" with age (Broomfield, Robinson, & Robinson, 2002; Talwar & Lee, 2002). White lies are false statements that are uttered in order to spare someone's feelings (as when one compliments a friend's cooking even when the dish is not very tasty). Again, one could either view increases in white lies either as a troubling trend or as a positive sign of increased politeness and concern for others.

In sum, then, a similar pattern emerges for all communicative devices that require insight into Gricean cooperative principles, multiple meanings, and implicit meanings: Few children younger than the age of 5 show high levels of insight into these matters. Moreover, young children tend to be literal, concrete, and largely truthful. After age 5, use of more varied communicative devices increases steadily and seems to level off by late childhood (but sometimes later). The key aspect of children's mastery of these communicative devices is their ability to comprehend and control utterances that are figurative or intentionally false. Depending on the communicative goal of a speaker, false statements may be expressed to (1) convey a negative attitude in a muted way (as in sarcasm), (2) make someone laugh (as in humor), (3) spare someone's feelings (as in white lies), or (4) avoid punishment (as in other kinds of lies). As children grow in their ability to recognize the multiple goals of other speakers (and "get inside their heads" more generally), children also become more apt to respond correctly to nonobvious indirect requests and to possibly express themselves in more polite ways, as well.

THE DEVELOPMENTAL MECHANISMS QUESTION:
What Factors Promote Changes in Spoken Language Competence?

In the previous section on developmental trends, we examined the ways in which four components of spoken language competence change with age. Two general trends emerged in this examination: (1) The components initially emerge between ages 1 and 6, and (2) nearly all components continue to improve considerably after age 6. In what follows, we examine possible explanations of these age trends for each component in turn. As noted in Chapter 1, understanding developmental mechanisms is crucial for knowing how to enhance spoken language skills in children in early childhood and beyond.

Component 1: Phonological, Semantic, and Grammatical Knowledge

Developmental mechanisms for these core aspects of language are examined more fully in the next three chapters. For the present purposes, it is sufficient to note that children need to have multiple opportunities to speak, and be spoken to, in order for there to be growth in their phonological, semantic, and grammatical knowledge. Every time children learn a new word, they refine both their phonological representations and their semantic knowledge (Metsala & Walley, 1998). Whereas large-scale refinements in phonological representations and pronunciations largely cease after age 7, increases in vocabulary after this point are evident in individuals who read broadly, watch informative television programs (e.g., on PBS), and have conversations with others who use words that are unfamiliar to them (Bloom, 2000). As for grammatical knowledge, it appears that children need to know at least 400 words before they begin to demonstrate early grammatical insights. Hence, we see that vocabulary growth affects syntax in the early preschool years, as well. After the point at which children begin to put two words together (around 18 to 24 months), they slowly build up the complexity of their syntactic constructions, bit by bit, until around age 5 (Tomasello & Brooks, 1999). These improvements seem to occur primarily because of children's intrinsic desire to communicate in a competent, more complete, and more accurate manner. The average child may engage in 400,000 or more communicative exchanges with others per year (Hart & Risley, 1995), so these elaborations and refinements may also reflect extensive practice. Imagine how well a child could play one of Mozart's sonatas if he or she practiced portions of that piece 400,000 times per year!

Discussion Topic: James and Carlos are both 6-year-olds who are just entering first grade. Whereas James has extensive phonological, semantic, and grammatical knowledge, Carlos has limited levels of these forms of knowledge. Why might this be the case? Take some time to develop an explanation. Once done, assume that your explanation of this outcome is correct. What could someone do to make sure that Carlos's little sister (who just turned 1) looks more like James than her brother (in terms of phonological, semantic, and grammatical knowledge) when she enters first grade?

Component 2: Conversational Skills

The factors responsible for changes in children's abilities to initiate and maintain conversations in an effective manner are not entirely clear at this point. Earlier, we noted that parents and other adults are skilled at supporting conversations through their patience and questions that provide scaffolds for children. Peers are likely to be less patient, less willing or able to provide scaffolds, and less competent themselves when it comes to communicating effectively. When their friends interrupt, drone on, or respond with random or unrelated responses, children may see, firsthand, examples of poor conversational skills. Hence, they could learn vicariously from the mistakes of their peers and attempt to not make these same mistakes themselves. Moreover, they are also likely to experience the consequences of their own ineffective communication (e.g., irritation or confusion expressed by listeners, peers avoiding them, and comments such as "Whoa! That was random!"). These consequences could lead them to change their style and refine their skills. Either way, one of the key factors is having opportunities to engage in conversations with adults and other children. However, children also have to be willing and able to take advantage of these opportunities.

Discussion Topic: Describe a home environment that provides many opportunities for conversations; contrast this with a home environment that provides few opportunities. Do the same for classroom environments. Finally, how would shy children respond to conversational opportunities presented to them at home or school? How competent would shy children be if they made little of the conversational opportunities presented to them? Also, who would have more opportunities to have conversations? A shy child or a gregarious child? Why?

Component 3: Communicative Goals

We saw in the developmental trends section of this chapter that even preverbal children engage in behaviors to accomplish a wide variety of communicative goals. We also learned that four aspects of their performance change with age: (1) children start to use spoken language to fulfill their goals instead of using nonverbal behaviors; (2) they eventually learn all of the syntactic constructions and intonation patterns associated with various speech acts (e.g., how to ask questions in a complete, grammatically correct way with rising intonation); (3) they shift from a one-to-one mapping of goals and constructions to a many-to-one system; and (4) they try to accomplish several goals at once with the same construction (e.g., have a request fulfilled and maintain positive social relations by being polite). Again, little is known about why these changes take place. One may speculate that children discover that they are often misunderstood or fail to get what they want when they use imperfect or ambiguous constructions. Thus, reactions from others provide feedback. Moreover, we saw that some parents vigorously work on getting their children to be more polite. In most other areas of their lives, children modify their goal-directed behaviors in response to failure or feedback. Perhaps this is true in the case of language, as well.

In addition to feedback, other factors are implicated by the work of Carpenter, Nagell, and Tomasello (1998). These researchers observed infants and their mothers interacting during seven monthly visits when the infants were 9 to 15 months of age. They found the following developmental sequence in infants: First, infants and mothers shared attention to the same objects. Next, the infants started to follow the attentional gaze of their mothers (e.g., their mothers looked interested at something, and the infants directed their attention to the same object or event). Finally, infants began to direct the attention of their mothers. This trend shows that infants progressively recognized that their mothers have intentions, attentional foci, and so on just like themselves. A second study showed that two variables predicted early-language skills in infants: (1) the amount of time infants spent in joint attention with their mothers and (2) the degree to which mothers used language that followed their infants focus on attention. Collectively, these studies show that infants may need a certain kind of scaffolding and responsivity from their mothers to recognize that other people have minds similar to their own. This insight, in turn, may give them a sense of how to say or do things in order to have an effect on other people's minds and behavior.

Discussion Topic: Imagine that you conducted a study that compared the five most socially competent children in the third grade of a particular school to the five least socially competent children (using peer or teacher nominations). Here, you observed them interacting during recess and while they worked on classroom tasks together. What would you expect to find when you counted how often particular children in the two groups: (1) initiated conversations and got favorable responses back to these initiations (as opposed to being ignored or rejected), (2) said something but the listener asked for clarification, or (3) asked others to do something (e.g., supply information, play a particular game) and the listener complied? In other words, would you expect children in one group to have their communicative goals fulfilled more often than children in the other? Why?

Component 4: Comprehension and Use of Communicative Devices

Why are children older than 5 more likely than children younger than 5 to understand indirect requests, irony, sarcasm, verbal humor, metaphor, and idioms? Why are they more likely to tell white lies after age 5, as well? One possibility is that children may start out with the default assumption that there is only one way to express a communicative goal and that people are nearly always truthful, literal, and referential (e.g., speakers describe what they see or describe memories of real situations in a straightforward way). To see why this may be a reasonable assumption on the part of young children, think back to when you were first learning how to use a particular word processing package (e.g., *Microsoft Word*). You may have assumed that there was only one way to perform an operation such as delete a word (e.g., highlight it with a mouse using a sweeping motion and pressing the delete key). But as you progressed, you learned that there are a number of other ways to delete words (e.g., double-clicking the word and hitting control-X on the keyboard).

A second possibility is that children younger than 6 are rarely confronted with examples of nonliteral utterances. If young children never hear sarcastic remarks, for example, how would they know how to interpret them? Observational studies of parents and children show, in fact, that parents do not use indirect requests and figurative language with their children very often (Sell, Kreuz, & Coppermath, 1997). The low rate of expressing such devices could be due to the fact that parents correctly infer that their children will not understand these expressions, or to the fact that children tend not to respond to these expressions as parents desire. In support of the latter proposition, parents have been found to sometimes follow up indirect requests with direct requests when children do not immediately comply with their wishes (e.g., "I want you to go to bed now" said after "It's 10 o'clock" fails to get the child to stop doing homework). A similar finding occurs with preschool teachers. Teachers are much more likely to use direct requests than indirect requests, perhaps because preschoolers were more likely to comply with the former than with the latter (MacKensie-Keating, McDonald, Tanchak, & Erickson, 1996). It is likely that other avenues for insight into language such as children's books and television shows also tend to be heavy on the direct and literal when they target preschoolers. Books and television shows designed for older children tend to have more frequent use of communicative devices such as sarcasm, metaphor, and idiom. In keeping with the idea of exposure, it has also been found that children from different countries, differential regions of the United States, and different ethnic groups are not familiar with the same idioms. In other words, children from Australia know different idioms than children from the United States, children from the Northwest United States know different idioms than those in the Southeast, and children who are African American know different idioms than children who are European American (Qualls & Harris, 1999).

A third possible explanation derives from literatures on other kinds of goal-directed behaviors and skills. Skills are normally acquired in three phases (Anderson, 1990). In the first phase, the person makes a lot of mistakes and needs to pay close attention to what he or she is doing (think back to when you first learned to drive, first learned a new dance step, and so on). In the second phase, the person shows considerable mastery of the technique but is still somewhat deeply immersed in the behavior itself. Hence, he or she cannot reflect upon his or her own performance. In the third phase, the person not only shows a high level of mastery, he or she is also able to step back and think about his or her performance at a metacognitive level. It has been repeatedly shown that people take about 10 years to attain a high level of skill in areas such as music, sports, chess, and so on, but only if they practice a skill about 4 hr a day (Ericsson, 1996). Children engage in language use far more than 4 hr a day, so it might be expected that they would attain high levels of mastery after 6 or 7 years of practice. It is probably not coincidental that the ability to produce and understand figurative language emerges after age 5 and after children show high levels of accurate phonological, semantic, and grammatical knowledge. To get jokes and so on, two meanings of sentences need to be compared at a conscious level.

The age trends for white lies may simply reflect the efforts of parents to get children to be more polite in their dealings with others. With increased memory capacity to consider multiple aspects of a situation (Byrnes, 2001a), children may be able to coordinate several goals at once (e.g., the main goal of the utterance and the goal to maintain positive social relations).

Discussion Topic: If it is true that young children show little facility with sarcasm, verbal humor, and so on because they are not exposed to these devices very often, one might conclude that we could improve children's understanding of these devices by increasing their level of exposure. However, if it is also true that children often fail to understand or respond to indirect requests, sarcasm, and so on, increased exposure to these devices might have little effect. Is there anyway around this apparent "Catch-22"? Do we need to wait until children show full mastery of basic phonology, vocabulary, and grammar (e.g., age 5 or so)? What makes you think so?

THE DEFICIENCIES QUESTION: Are There Populations of Children or Adults Who Lack Some or All of the Key Skills of Spoken Language Competence? Do These Individuals Experience Problems When They Learn to Read or after They Have Learned to Read?

In principle, there are two populations of individuals who could shed light on the importance of spoken language competencies. The first includes individuals who are simply delayed in the expression of spoken language skills because they failed to have adequate input or practice. Given continued practice and exposure, such individuals would be expected to ultimately attain adequate levels of competence (but a few years later than their peers, perhaps). One would expect, for example, that children who move from Tennessee to Oregon, or from Australia to the United States would eventually learn local idioms simply through exposure. If it is also true that children gain insight into various communicative devices after they practice using literal language correctly for some time (see above), then it would be expected that children who rarely engage in conversations or rarely read would eventually demonstrate skill in understanding sarcasm, idioms, and metaphor a few years later than their more talkative and bibliophilic peers.

Individuals in the second category, in contrast, have neurological problems that limit or undermine the efficacy of short-term interventions, simple exposure, or routine practice. To illustrate, it has recently been observed that individuals who have been diagnosed with three, seemingly disparate, disorders all have highly similar deficits in their communicative skills: (1) children and adults who have autism, (2) adults who have sustained damage to their right hemispheres through strokes (RHD), and (3) adults who have sustained damage to their frontal lobes through traumatic brain injury (TBI) (e.g., automobile crashes). Each of these groups show the following problems: overly literal language comprehension, difficulty comprehending narrative humor, injection of socially inappropriate, disinhibited, or tangential comments during conversations, overtalkativeness, poor verbal fluency, impairment in prosody, and difficulty reading emotion in facial expressions (Martin & McDonald, 2003). In some cases, moreover, problems in understanding pragmatic language are observed even when the individual demonstrates adequate levels of phonological, semantic, and grammatical knowledge. The fact that all three disorders lead to similar problems despite differences in the locale of brain dysfunction (i.e., individuals with autism have been found to have underdeveloped cerebellums) implies that *higher-order language skills require the coordinated functioning of multiple brain regions working in concert.* Should any of the component areas of this system become compromised through developmental processes or injury, an individual loses the ability to do more than comprehend and produce well-formed but literal expressions. Although it is too early to know for sure, recent efforts at intervention suggest that brain regions in homologous portions of the opposite hemisphere (e.g., the left in the case of those with right-hemisphere damage) become more active after a period of training (Carpenter et al., 2001). At some point we will know the extent to which the communicative problems of individuals with autism, RHD, and TBI can be remediated through training.

4

The Development
of Phonological Skills

Vignette: "Let's play our clapping game," says Ms. McGuire, a kindergarten teacher. "Is everyone ready?" "Yes," reply the group of students in unison as they sit around teacher aide Ms. Brabson on the circle-time carpet. "OK, listen carefully so that you can clap to the number of syllables that you hear in each word that I say. *Dog.* The children clap once. "Very good. Now let's try *kit-ten.*" Ms. Brabson repeats, *kit-ten,* and the children clap twice. Now, let's try that new word that we learned in our book. "Let's try *spa-ghet-ti.*" Ms. Brabson repeats the word very slowly so the children can hear all of the sounds. All 16 children stare at her without one hand moving. Johnny soon interjects, "Ms. Brabson, it's bisketti. Why you say it so funny?"

MAIN IDEAS OF THE CHAPTER

1. There are two kinds of phonological processing skills that children have to master to be able to communicate effectively and perform well in school: receptive and productive. Children who have *receptive phonological skills* have the ability to recognize the typical sound patterns of their native language when they serve as listeners in communicative exchanges. These recognition abilities occur at four levels: phoneme, syllable, word, and prosody. Children have high levels of *productive phonological competence* if they can (a) produce all of the phonemes of their native language, (b) combine these phonemes into higher units such as syllables, onsets, rimes, and words, and (c) create multiword expressions that have the characteristic prosodic features (i.e., global characteristic sound) of their native language.
2. Researchers have devised three models of receptive skills (i.e., the cohort model, neighborhood activation model [NAM], and connectionist models) and have also

provided a detail theoretical analysis of productive skills. At present, connectionist models are the most promising because they are able to solve a number of key theoretical problems (such as the parsing problem).

3. Teachers should care about phonological processing skills in children because (a) children who show the most phonological processing skill at age 3 or 4 become the best readers in first grade; (b) the link between phonological processing and reading is corroborated by the finding that the core deficit in children who are reading disabled is the ability to analyze sounds in spoken words; and (c) if children do not form stored representations of the sound patters of words, they will not build up a spoken vocabulary and will not, therefore, acquire spoken language competence. Children who fail to acquire adequate levels of spoken language competence, in turn, will be unable to benefit from traditional reading instruction.

4. The developmental progression for receptive skills is as follows: (a) At birth, infants can recognize the prosodic features of their native languages; (b) by 4 months, they can discriminate several consonantal and vowel contrasts; (c) by 8 months, they can do three new things: discriminate more subtle or hard-to-detect contrasts, use syllables and rhythmic patterns to parse an utterance stream, and hear individual words in passages; and (d) by 12 months, they can use phonetic, phonotactic, and syllable stress patterns to parse utterances into individual words. In addition to these developmental increases, however, children also seem to become less sensitive to some (but not all) non-native vowel contrasts by 6 months and some (but not all) non-native consonant contrasts by 12 months. Between the ages of 1 and 7, children seem to progress from the ability to recognize whole words to the ability to recognize progressively smaller portions of words (e.g., whole words → then syllables, onsets, and rimes, → then, eventually, phonemes).

5. The developmental progression for productive skills is as follows: (a) marginal babbling and pronunciation of certain vowels by 7 months, (b) frequent use of 11 consonant and 3 vowel sounds by 12 months (also production of their first word by 12 months), (c) correct pronunciation of nearly all consonants and vowels at least some of the time by age 3, and (d) correct pronunciation of various blends and difficult combinations by age 7.

6. These age trends in productive and receptive skills have been explained by appealing to brain maturation, exposure to language in the environment, and children's motivation to communicate.

7. Children who lack phonological processing skills (e.g., children who are reading disabled, children with language learning or hearing impairments) have particular problems when they learn to read.

In Chapter 3, we discussed spoken language competence as consisting of a variety of skills. Whereas some of these skills were described in detail, others were discussed only briefly to avoid duplicating more comprehensive accounts that appear elsewhere in this book. In this chapter, we provide a more complete account of one of the latter kinds of skills: the ability to recognize, and correctly pronounce, a number of words in one's language. These phonological skills are described using the five recurrent questions discussed in Chapter 1 as an organization framework.

THE "NATURE OF" QUESTION: What Does It Mean to Say That a Child Has Phonological Processing Competence?

There are two kinds of phonological processing skills that children have to master to be able to communicate effectively and perform well in school: receptive and productive. Children who have *receptive phonological skills* have the ability to recognize the typical sound patterns of their native language when they serve as listeners in communicative exchanges. In traditional accounts, these recognition abilities are said to occur at four levels: phoneme, syllable, word, and prosody (Nygaard & Pisoni, 1995). When listeners analyze sounds at the phoneme level, they can tell the difference between individual phonemes such as *buh* and *puh*. *Phonemes* are the smallest units of sound in a language that, when changed, cause a change in meaning (e.g., *pat* means something different than *bat*). English contains 45 different phonemes that a child eventually has to recognize and discriminate. Children growing up in countries where English is not the native language usually need to learn phonemes that differ from those in English. Moreover, some languages have fewer than 45 phonemes while others have more than 45.

At the syllable level, a listener can "hear" the number of syllables in a word (e.g., they know that *bod-i-ly* has more syllables than *bo-dy*). *Syllables* are composed of phonemes and are, therefore, one level higher up. Words, in turn, are composed of syllables (and, by implication, composed of phonemes, as well). At the word level, listeners can recognize words that are already in their vocabularies (e.g., *trouble*) and also know when a word is not familiar. For example, are the words *festiculate*, *blerpo*, and *evanescent* real English words? If you said "No" or "I'm not sure," that means that you do not recognize the words because sound-based copies are not stored in your memory (or at least not retrieved from memory). To recognize anything (e.g., a face, a song, a word, a scent), you need a copy or representation of it stored in your memory that is matched to what you see, hear, or smell.

At a still higher level of abstraction is the prosody level. *Prosody* includes such aspects as speaking rate, rhythmic patterns, pitch, and intonation changes. For example, you can probably tell when someone is speaking Japanese versus German even if you do not know any Japanese or German words. This characteristic, global "sound" of a language is what linguists mean by prosody. Having prosodic listening skills is a little like being able to recognize various styles of music (e.g., rock, jazz, folk, rap) even when songs are sung in different languages (e.g., a rock song sung by a German-speaking group sounds a lot like a rock song sung by an English-speaking group).

In addition to the traditional sound categories of phoneme, syllable, word, and prosody, it is also important to acknowledge units of sound called onsets and rimes. The *onset* of a word is the initial sound that can be used to create alliterations. For example, in the alliteration "The crocodile cracked crystals," the last three words all have the same onset (i.e., *cr-*). The *rime* of a word, in contrast, is the portion of a word that remains when one removes the onset (and vice versa). As the name implies, one creates words that rhyme by selecting words that all have the same rime or ending (e.g., *cat*, *hat*, and *fat* all have the -*at* rime). We would say, then, that children who have high levels of receptive phonological skills have the ability to recognize sounds at the phoneme, syllable, onset, rime, word, and prosody levels.

In addition to these receptive abilities, however, phonological processing competence also includes the ability to produce these sound patterns oneself when one serves as a speaker in communicative exchanges. Children would be said to have high levels of *productive phonological competence* if they can (1) produce all of the phonemes of their native language, (2) combine these phonemes into higher units such as syllables, onsets, rimes, and words, and (3) create multiword expressions that have the characteristic prosodic features of their native language. Note that it is often possible to have some of these abilities without having the others. For example, children may be able to recognize all of the phonemes in their language and be able to produce individual phonemes but still not be able to combine sounds into syllables or words or identify the onset or rime of words. Similarly, comedians such as Billy Crystal or Robin Williams can sound as if they are speaking French, Japanese, or German without using real French, Japanese, or German words. They can do this because of their deft imitation of the prosodic features of these languages (e.g., speaking rates, intonations, pauses, and sounds common in these languages).

But one key issue in ascribing phonological competence to an individual pertains to the degree of match between (1) that individual's representations and productions and (2) the representations and productions of other speakers with whom the individual comes into contact. In order for communication to occur, a person has to have stored representations of sounds, words, and prosody that match the sounds, words, and prosodic features that the person hears in his or her immediate environment. The match does not have to be perfect, but it has to be close enough that intended meanings could be extracted. For example, one of us (JB) used to have a job as a salesperson in a department store. When asked by a customer with an unfamiliar Southern accent one day, "Can you tell me where to find the *dohs*?" it took 5 minutes of clarifying questions to find out that the customer was trying to buy a door. (Both parties had a good laugh when the confusion was resolved.) Similarly, when college instructors who are from a country other than the United States are still trying to master English and teach in the United States, English-speaking students often complain that they have no idea what the instructor is saying in class (that the person is "hard to follow"). Similarly, U.S. tourists often experience problems when they try to negotiate traveling in other countries due to their atypical pronunciations and cadence (even when traveling in Great Britain). Hence, nonstandard pronunciations coupled with nonstandard prosody can cause a lot of problems for listeners. These examples of comprehension failures can be contrasted with cases in which the pronunciation is off-base but still is interpretable. For example, listeners who grew up in Chicago usually have little trouble understanding the utterances of a Bostonian (e.g., "Oh no! It's raining, and I just washed my *cah*!") or the utterances of the cartoon characters Elmer Fudd (e.g., "Where is that wascally wabbit?") and Sylvester the Cat (e.g., "Thufferin' thuccotash!").

But in addition to issues of communication, a second key issue in ascribing phonological competence is the nature and quality of a child's phonological representations. In particular, a child may be able to match whole words to stored representations in a global manner but may not be able to match portions of words to each other (e.g., phonemes, onsets, or rimes). As will be explained more fully in Chapter 7, children have to be able to decompose words into smaller portions if they want to be able to read. In addition, however, it is not enough that their brains can register matches of portions of words at an unconscious level. They have to be able to consciously reflect upon sound segments and matches, as well.

Theoretical Models of Phonological Knowledge and Skill

As will be discussed shortly, it is important to go beyond the overview provided in the previous section by providing more detail about receptive and productive competencies. In what follows, we examine theoretical perspectives on each of these component skills in turn. These perspectives provide the detail missing from the preceding discussion.

Models of Receptive Skill

As noted earlier in this chapter, the receptive component of phonological processing involves the matching of incoming sounds to stored representations (Jusczyk, 1997; Metsala & Walley, 1998; Swingley & Aslin, 2002). For example, if person X says to person Y during dinner, "Can you hand me the salt?" person Y needs to match each of the words *can*, *you*, *hand*, and so on to stored representations of each of these words in his or her memory in order to begin the process of deciphering the request.

However, it is one thing to say that listeners have stored representations of sound patterns (as stated above) and quite another to have a detailed, accurate model of what these representations are like. To be useful, theories need to provide such models. To see this, consider how car mechanics and people who know little about cars both know that automobiles have engines under their hoods. What makes car mechanics different is that they also have a clear sense of engine parts, how these parts are connected, and how they function. As noted in Chapter 1, it is this "inner workings" knowledge that allows car mechanics to solve engine problems and make sure that cars operate smoothly. In the same way, we provide an analogous level of detail about phonological skills so that you can acquire the knowledge you need to enhance phonological skills and solve phonology-related problems in children.

Over the years, researchers have proposed different theoretical models of stored representations of sound patterns and the matching process. What makes the theorizing particularly difficult is the fact that people are able to recognize instances of a particular word even when this word is spoken by different individuals (Jusczyk, 1997). How is it that we all hear the same word *salt* when it is spoken by the following three individuals? (1) a slow-talking man with a deep voice and a certain local accent, (2) a fast-talking woman with a slightly higher voice (and possibly different accent), and (3) a soft-spoken child with an even higher voice (and possibly imperfect pronunciation). The sound waves emitted from these three speakers are all different in frequency and other physical characteristics, yet listeners would know that all three said *salt*. The ability to determine that the word *salt* was uttered in each case is all the more amazing given the fact that differences due to speaker characteristics can be magnified by the words surrounding *salt*. If the man, woman, and child all used *salt* in different sentences, the problem of detecting invariance is made even more difficult. It is vital that researchers eventually solve this invariance puzzle because the solution will necessarily have something important to say about the precise nature of our stored representations of sound patterns and the matching process.

Another phenomenon that must be addressed by any viable theory of speech perception is called *categorical perception* (Jusczyk, 1997). Researchers have found that people tend to hear discrete categories rather than continua when researchers morph one sound (e.g., /p/ pronounced *puh*) into another (e.g., /b/ pronounced *buh*) using a synthesizer. In other words, even though the physical characteristics of the sound are changing little by little throughout the morphing process, there is a range of sounds that all sound like *buh* and another range that all sound like *puh*. Moreover, sounds within each range sound pretty much the same. Once the morphing process reaches a certain threshold, however, all of a sudden the listener hears *puh* instead of *buh*. This tendency to hear discrete categories rather than continua is very similar to the tendency to see categories of color rather than continua. Physicists can slowly change the frequency of light that is emitted from a laser (e.g., from 350 hz to 500 hz). Given frequencies below the range (e.g., 300 hz), the light will be seen as a particular color (e.g., green). Within the range, a different color is observed (e.g., yellow). Above the range (e.g., 550 hz), a third color will be seen (e.g., red).

The third problem facing a theorist is called the *parsing problem* (Jusczyk, 1997; Pinker, 1997). The parsing problem arises for anyone who does not yet speak a particular language (e.g., a 1-year-old learning English or a monolingual foreign-exchange student who just moved to a country where a language different from his or her own is spoken). The basic question is this: How does someone subdivide an utterance into its separate words when one does not know where one word ends and another begins? To get a sense of the parsing problem yourself, try to find television or radio stations in which people are conversing in a language you do not know (e.g., Spanish or French). Record a segment of the program and see if you can tell how many words each person used in a particular conversational turn. To illustrate the process somewhat imperfectly for now, imagine that an exchange student from another country says the following to you (i.e., makes the following sounds in sequence): "*ek-skyoo-say-mwah, oo-seh-troov-lay-twa-let-faam?*" If we assume that each sound between the hyphens is a syllable, the utterance has 11 syllables total. How many words did this person speak? Where does one word end and another begin? Take a pencil and lightly draw a line that cuts (i.e., parses) the string of sounds above into individual words (where you think each word begins and ends).

It turns out that the sequence of 11 phonemes corresponds to eight French words: *Excusez-moi, où se trouve les toilettes femmes?* (In English, this translates to, *Excuse me, can you tell me where the ladies' bathroom is?*) Conceivably, the utterance could have had only two words (one with four syllables and another with seven) or as many as 11 one-syllable words. Superficially, there is nothing in the input that clearly indicates that there are 8 words and not other possibilities. The fact that it is very hard to parse utterances into words is a major problem for the language learner. Given that words are the building blocks of languages (i.e., we string words together into sentences), children would not be able to distill these building blocks out of the utterances they hear. As result, they could not create their own sentences. By analogy, imagine that Lego blocks came in a package in which the blocks were connected to each other in a rod. Imagine next that a child could not see the individual blocks (he or she could not see seams between each block). How could a child ever build anything using the blocks if he or she could not break the rod up into individual Lego pieces?

Unfortunately, researchers have yet to devise a theory that successfully resolves the invariance problem, the categorical perception problem, and the parsing problem. Researchers have, however, devised models that can account for specific kinds of experimental phenomena (Nygaard & Pisoni, 1995). For example, the cohort model of Marslen-Wilson (1989) was designed to account for the fact that people can identify words based on only partial input (much the way they can "name that tune" using just the first few notes). The model assumes that within the first 100 to 150 ms of exposure to a word, all stored representations compatible with that word are activated from memory (e.g., *calamity*, *cash*, *cat*, *caterpillar*, and *catch* are all activated for the initial segment of a word). As more of the input comes in over the new few milliseconds (e.g., *cat . . .*), the candidates that are incompatible with the additional segment (e.g., *calamity* and *cash*) are eliminated from further consideration.

The neighborhood activation model (NAM) of Goldinger, Pisoni, and Luce (1995) can also account for the ability to identify words quickly even when one is presented with only partial input. However, it can also explain why response times are faster for certain words than for others. Unlike the cohort model that assumes that a large number of candidate words are indiscriminately activated with partial input, NAM assumes that only those representations that reside in the same "lexical neighborhood" as the target word are activated at first. A lexical neighborhood consists of a set of representations for words in which each "neighbor" differs from the others by one phoneme. For example, *bat*, *cat*, and *fat* are all neighbors, as are *mute*, *mate*, and *mite*. Words that have many neighbors (e.g., *bat*) are said to reside in dense neighborhoods. Words that have few neighbors (e.g., *orange*) are said to reside in sparse neighborhoods. The assumption of neighborhoods allows NAM to predict that a made-up word like *vaby* will activate a word such as *baby* (Swingley & Aslin, 2002) because its phonemes and rime portion is shared by words such as *baby*. The cohort model cannot make such a prediction or others that rely on the idea of density.

Other models have been proposed to account for other sorts of findings and, unfortunately, bear little similarity to either the cohort model or NAM. For example, the motor theory of speech perception begins with the parsimonious assumption that people may use many of the same representations to recognize words as they use to produce words themselves (Nygaard & Pisoni, 1995). To produce a word, a person retrieves a mental program from memory (much like retrieving a mental program when trying to remember how to add fractions). Then, when a person hears the same word spoken by others, he or she matches this input to the program used to produce the same sound. This analysis implies that young infants will not be able to recognize sounds until they can produce these sounds through babbling or articulation of complete words (Jusczyk, 1997).

Although the results of many studies can be said to be consistent with the predictions of the motor theory, these findings could be explained by other models as well (Nygaard & Pisoni, 1995). A further problem is that preverbal infants show the ability to recognize input well before they produce speech themselves (see below under the "developmental trends" question).

In addition, however, none of the models described so far provide sufficient levels of detail regarding the nature of the stored representations. For example, it is one thing to say that there are cohorts or neighborhoods and quite another to describe what each element in a cohort or neighborhood is like. Similarly, it is one thing to say that we have stored motor programs and quite another to describe these programs in detail. Imagine if instructors in automobile repair schools only told car mechanics that there are engine parts under the hood that exist in cohorts or neighborhoods (and did not describe these parts in detail). Without having a clear sense of the parts and their precise nature, mechanics would be at a loss when it came time to fix cars.

Fortunately, there are other models that do provide more detail on the nature of representations for sound patterns. Most of these models derive from the connectionist paradigm (e.g., Elman, 1989). To illustrate the general connectionist approach, consider the model presented in Figure 4.1. Connectionists argue that it is always possible to decompose a representation for something (e.g., the sound form of a word) into a set of atomic elements called *units* (represented by ovals in Figure 4.1). In some models for speech perception, there are units for phonemes, units for syllables, and

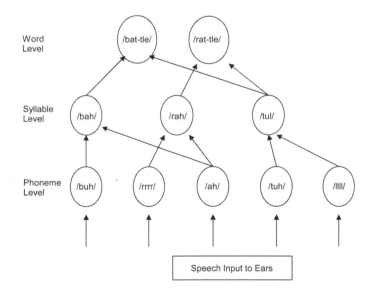

FIGURE 4.1. Example of a connectionist model for sound forms for words.

units for entire words. Other models may have units for onsets and rimes in addition to, or instead of, units for phonemes and syllables. Each unit has a particular job to perform such as detecting the presence of a particular phoneme (e.g., /b/ or *buh*). When the eliciting or input stimulus has the target sound (e.g., the word *baby* has the phoneme *buh*), the unit is said to "fire" or become activated. When it becomes activated, the unit sends along its activation to other units that it is connected to (connections are denoted by arrows in Figure 4.1). For example, if the input were the word *battle*, the unit for the phoneme *buh* in Figure 4.1 would sends its activation to the unit for *ba*. Similarly, the unit for *tuh* would send its activation to the unit for *tul*. This phenomenon of sending activation along a network is called *spreading activation*.

However, the amount of activation that each unit sends depends on the degree of *associative strength* that it has with the other units. Associative strength tends to be high between two units if they are often active at the same time, and lower if they are not usually active at the same time. Thus, the input and natural co-occurrence of sounds in a person's ambient environment determines the associative strength between units. For example, the phonemes *buh* and *-at* co-occur often in English spoken words (e.g., *bat*, *battle*, *battlefield*, *batch*). As such, their units might be highly associated and send a fair amount of activation to each other when one is stimulated. In contrast, the phonemes *buh* and *puh* do not usually occur in sequence very often (e.g., "words" such as *bpat* and *bpattle* do not exist). As such, one unit would not tend to send activation to the other when only one has been stimulated.

Connectionists also assume that each unit will only become activated if the input sent to it reaches a certain threshold. For example, let's assume that a unit for the rime *-at* requires a certain amount of input activation to fire (e.g., 70 on some scale constructed by the theoretical modeler). If a unit for the onset *b-* only sends activation corresponding to half that amount (e.g., 35), the unit for *-at* will not become fully active through spreading activation. However, if other units send similar amounts of activation to the unit for *-at* at the same time, the collective amount of activation will cause the unit for *-at* to become active.

Because of the various assumptions discussed so far, connectionist models do a pretty good job of explaining the performance of participants in many studies of speech perception. For example, connectionist models can account for the ability to identify words from partial input as well as effects deriving from lexical neighborhoods. In addition, connectionists can use the idea of summated, spreading activation to account for the phenomenon of categorical perception, and to account for the finding that made-up words like *vaby* tend to activate units for real words like *baby*.

Perhaps most important, connectionist models can be used to help resolve the parsing problem. The source of this resolution actually derives from a topic in phonology called *phonotactics* (Jusczyk, 1997; Menn & Stoel-Gammon, 2001). This topic pertains to the restrictions that are placed on the location of sounds in words in each language (i.e., the beginning, middle, or ends of words). Languages differ with respect to which sounds can go where, but all have restrictions of one sort or another. For example, the sound corresponding to the *n* in *ran* does not sound the same as the sound corresponding to the *n* in *rang*. Whereas the /n/ sound in *ran* can occur at the beginning of English words (e.g., *nasty*), the /n/ sound in *rang* cannot occur there. In contrast, the latter often does occur in the beginning of words in certain African languages. Similarly, English words can end in the combination *luh + puh* (e.g., *help*, *kelp*), but this combination cannot occur at the start of English words (there are no words such as *lpittle*). Another general restriction in English is that words cannot begin with two consecutive stop consonants but can begin with combinations of stops and liquids (e.g., *pl*) or fricatives and stops (e.g., *st*).

The various restrictions on the locations of sounds can go a long way to help listeners figure out where words begin and end (Juszcyk, 1997). When sound combinations co-occur frequently in sequence, the associations among sounds cause sounds to "bundle" together in our minds. It is for this reason that the utterance, "Call Peter for dinner" would parse naturally into the constituent words *Call*, *Peter*, *for*, and *dinner*. Notice how the phonemes corresponding to the *c*, *a*, and *l* in *Call* are permissible combinations and frequently co-occur in sequence in speech. These sounds would bundle together. Note also that the phonemes corresponding to the *l* at the end of *Call* and the *p* at the start of *Peter* cannot occur at the beginning of words (as noted above). All of the phonemes in *Peter* can occur together in sequence, so these can bundle together. This bundling combined with the impossibility of *Luh + puh* at the start of words causes a parse between *Call* and *Peter*. Finally, no English words start with the combination of phonemes corresponding to *rf* (at the end of *Peter* and start of *for*), so *Peter* and *for* would distill into distinct words, and so on. Thus, the input of language helps associations and permissible combinations form. It is relatively straightforward to model the bundling process in computer simulations using the actual correlations among sounds in words. Hence, connectionist models may well provide the solution to a major issue in the field of language development (i.e., the parsing problem) that many have alleged to be resolvable only by assuming a strong form of nativism.

However, connectionist models do have their problems. Perhaps the biggest shortcoming is a failure to address the invariance problem described earlier in this chapter. Models such as those in Figure 4.1 lack enough detail to be capable of explaining why a word such as *salt* can be recognized even when it is said by very different speakers.

Theoretical Analysis of Productive Skills

When we say that someone knows how to pronounce words correctly, what exactly does this involve? Most adults have spent very little time analyzing their own speech patterns and behaviors. As a result, they could not immediately tell someone how to move component parts of their vocal tracts or indicate which sounds are made using similar vocal behaviors. In contrast, scholars who hold appointments in departments such as linguistics or speech and hearing tend to spend a great deal of time categorizing sounds and the actions needed to produce these sounds. For the present purposes, it is not necessary to summarize all of the scholarly work on phonology in these two fields. Rather, it suffices to give a sense of the kind of knowledge that is implicit in adult production. This description, in turn, will provide a useful backdrop for understanding some of the developmental trends that are discussed later in this chapter.

Analysis of adult productive capabilities shows that competent speakers of a language know how to make two kinds of sounds: *vowels* and *consonants* (Menn & Stoel-Gammon, 2001). Vowels and consonants are primarily distinguished in terms of how much air is obstructed by the vocal tract when these sounds are produced. Speakers make a vowel sound (i.e., *aaaa, eeee, iiii, oooo, yuuu*) by vibrating the vocal chords and altering the shape of their mouths. The differences in obstructed air among the different vowels are minimal (e.g., *yuuu* may obstruct a bit air more than *eeee*). As an experiment, try to say all of the vowels to get a sense of changes in the shape of your mouth, and of the amount of air that is obstructed when each vowel is produced. Now, place your hand on your Adam's apple and repeat the process to feel the vibrations of vocal chords. Any sound that requires sustained vocal chord vibration is called a *voiced* sound (Menn & Stoel-Gammon, 2001). All vowels are voiced.

In contrast, not all consonants are voiced. For example, whereas *buh*, *mmmm*, *nnnn*, *vuh*, *zzz*, *juh*, and *guh* all involve voicing, consonants sounds such as *shh*, *hhh*, *fuh*, *ess*, *puh*, *tuh*, and *kuh* involve very little, if any, voicing. In addition to voicing, other distinctions among consonants have to do with the how much air is obstructed by the lips and tongue. For example, *stop consonants* are produced by completely stopping airflow (e.g., *buh*, *puh*, *tuh*, *duh*, *kuh*, and *guh*). *Fricatives*, in contrast, let out a little more air than stops (e.g., *fuh*, *ess*, *shhh*). *Affricatives* begin like a stop and end like a fricative (e.g., *juh*). Then, there are sounds that are in-between vowels and consonants that let more air pass than fricatives but not so much air as vowels (e.g., *glides* such as *yuh* and *wuh*; *liquids* such as *rrr* and *luh*). Finally, speech scientists distinguish among sounds according to the place of articulation. Some sounds, such as *buh, puh,* and *mmmm*, are made by pressing the lips together; others, such as *vuh* and *fuh*, are made using the bottom front teeth and top lip. If you know Latin, you will not be surprised to learn that the former sounds are called *bilabial*, while the latter are called *labiodental*. In addition, sounds can be made by touching the tip of the tongue to the little bump behind the top front teeth (*tuh*, *duh*, *luh*). These consonant sounds are given the descriptor *alveolar* because that is the name of the ridge behind the front teeth (i.e., the alveolar ridge). If you would like to impress your friends, point out to them that *buh* is a bilabial, unvoiced stop consonant.

What is important to notice for the present purposes is that competent speakers know how to use their lips, tongue, jaw muscles, teeth, vocal chords and other tissues in the back of the mouth (e.g., the flap of velar tissue in the back of the mouth used for sounds such as *guh*) to make sounds that other people in their immediate surroundings will readily recognize. Some of these sounds are harder to make than others at first (as we shall see later in this chapter). Also, seemingly small differences in vocal tract movements can make a big difference in what sound is produced. To test this, practice making the sounds *tuh*, *duh*, and *luh*. All use the alveolar ridge in pretty much the same way. Similarly, consider how *puh* and *buh* use the lips in very similar ways. The only difference is the timing of when the voicing begins relative to point at which one releases the closure of lips. When the release from lip closure precedes vocal chord vibration by intervals greater than 25 ms, English-speaking adults hear *puh* (Jusczyk, 1997). The temporal gap between lip closure release and vocal chord vibration is called *voice onset time* (VOT). In contrast, when the VOT is less than 25 ms, listeners hear *buh*. Try saying the sounds *wuh* and *ruh* several times and you may gain insight into Elmer Fudd's problem. If all of these subtleties in movements and place of articulation were not enough, consider blends and other combinations of multiple consonants (e.g., the initial sounds in words such as *sprite*). Perhaps it is no wonder that children take up to 6 years to fully master all of the sounds in English or that recent immigrants sometimes have trouble when they move to countries that have phonemes that differ considerably from those they already know how to produce.

THE RELEVANCE QUESTION: Why Should Teachers Care about Whether Children Acquire Phonological Processing Competence?

There are three primary reasons why teachers should care about the receptive and productive phonological skills of children:

1. As will be discussed more fully in Chapter 7, the ability to analyze the sounds in spoken language (e.g., identify rimes; identify the number of syllables or phonemes in a word) is one of the best predictors of who learns

to read in grades 1 to 3. Children who show the most phonological processing skill at age 3 or 4 become the best readers in grade 1.

2. The link between phonological processing and reading is corroborated by the finding that the core deficit in children with reading disabilities is the ability to analyze sounds in spoken words (Stanovich & Siegel, 1994). Children with reading disabilities cannot "hear" onsets, rimes, and phonemes in the same way that children without reading disabilities can. Children have to be able to analyze the sounds in words in order to map these sounds onto graphemes such as letters (e.g., *buh* onto the letter *B*). Studies have also shown a predictive relationship between early spoken language problems and later problems in learning to read.

3. More generally, if children do not form stored representations of the sound patterns of words, they will not build up a spoken vocabulary and will not, therefore, acquire spoken language competence. As noted above, words are the building blocks of language. Children who do not acquire adequate levels of spoken language competence will be unable to benefit from traditional reading instruction.

In essence, then, teachers and school officials need to be very concerned about the phonological processing skills that students bring to first grade. When large numbers of children in a school system enter first grade with limited phonological skills, officials in these systems need to address this problem through early intervention programs and policies.

THE DEVELOPMENTAL TRENDS QUESTION: How Does Phonological Processing Competence Change over Time?

Given the answers that were provided to the "nature of" question earlier in this chapter, the "developmental trends" question can be rephrased into the following, more specific variants: What kinds of receptive phonological skills do children have at birth, age 1, age 2, and so on? What kinds of productive skills do they have at the same ages? When do they provide evidence that they can recognize sounds at the phoneme, syllable, onset, rime, word, or prosody levels? When can they combine sounds into syllables and words? When does their speech take on the characteristic prosodic features of their surrounding environment? In what follows, answers to such questions are provided. In keeping with the organizational scheme used for the "nature of" question, age trends pertaining to children's receptive and productive skills are discussed in turn. Before examining these skills, however, it is important to briefly examine the methods used by researchers to reveal receptive and productive skills.

Methods Used to Reveal Phonological Skills

The need for an introductory discussion on methods becomes apparent when one considers the challenges posed by trying to assess the phonological skills of young infants. Whereas researchers can simply ask adults whether they heard a *puh* or *buh* sound emanating from an apparatus, this approach cannot be used with preverbal infants. Instead, researchers have to resort to other methods that try to exploit some of the skills and tendencies that are evident in even newborns. The most widely utilized skills and tendencies of infants include the fact that (1) very young infants can turn their heads or vary the rate at which they suck on pacifiers in response to particular stimuli, (2) infants have preferences for certain kinds of stimuli, (3) infants get bored when the same stimulus is repeated over and over, and (4) infants show increased interest and attention when a new stimulus is presented after another one had been presented for many trials in a row.

In one experimental approach that makes use of some of these known attributes of infants, researchers repeatedly play one sound for 20 to 30 trials (e.g., *puh*) and then introduce a different sound (e.g., *buh*) for the next 20 to 30 trials. If an infant had been sucking on a pacifier at a certain rate when the first sound was presented during the first block of trials, the infant might show less and less sucking over time (indicating boredom). Similarly, if an infant had been turning his or her head to hear a particular sound coming from a speaker on the right, the infant may turn less and less often each time the sound is repeated during the first block of trials. This phenomenon of diminished response to the same stimulus over time is called *habituation*. However, if a new stimulus is introduced after the old stimulus had been presented for 20 to 30 trials, the infant may rapidly speed up his or her sucking or turn his or her head to hear the new sound. This phenomenon is called *dishabituation* (also an *orienting response*). When it occurs, we know that the infant can tell the two sounds apart. When the infant shows continued habituation, however, that suggests the infant does not hear a difference in the two sounds. The technique that examines changes in the rate of sucking is called *high-amplitude sucking* (Jusczyk, 1997).

Alternatively, a researcher may use a procedure in which the infant discovers that two different outcomes are linked to two different behaviors. For example, if an infant sucks on a pacifier at a rate of 60 sucks per minute, an experimental apparatus may play a recording of the voice of the infant's mother. In contrast, if the infant sucks at a rate of 30 sucks per minute, the device plays a tape of an unfamiliar female. Alternatively, if the infant turns his or her head to the right, he or she may get to hear someone speaking in English. If the infant turns his or her head to the left, he or she may get to hear someone speaking in Polish. Either way, when infants show differential responding to the two stimuli (e.g., maintaining a sucking rate of 60 sucks per minute to hear the mother), this behavior suggests that the infant can tell the two stimuli apart. The technique that utilizes head turns is called the *conditioned head-turn* procedure (Jusczyk, 1997).

As for productive skills, the typical approach is more observational than experimental. For example, one may merely record the spontaneous babbling of an infant once a month for a year. With older children, one can tape-record a conversation between the child and the experimenter or between two children. Planned discussion topics may be used to elicit certain, hard-to-produce words for children of a focal age group (e.g., *spagetti* for 3-year-olds). These tapes can be coded for the phonemes, syllables, and words correctly produced.

Other methods used with older children require them to be more analytical than reactive or spontaneous. The object of such analytical methods is to see whether children can determine the phonemes, onsets, rimes, or syllables in sets of words (Stahl & Murray, 1998). For example, researchers may present a word like *pink* and ask children what it would sound like if the final sound (*kuh*) were eliminated (correct answer: *pin*). Or, on some trials, children may be asked to substitute one phoneme for another rather than delete phonemes (e.g., replace the *puh* in *pink* with *luh*). To assess children's appreciation of rimes, children may be presented with a triad of words (e.g., *hat, bat, bus*) and asked which one does not sound like the others (correct answer: *bus*). To assess appreciation of individual phonemes, children may be given a word such as *hat* and asked to tap once for each of the sounds (phonemes) it contains (correct answer: three taps for *huh, ah,* and *tuh*). Alternatively, they may be given multisyllabic words and asked to clap once for each syllable. Finally, to get a sense of the degree to which the stored representations of words reside in "neighborhoods" and are segmented into syllables, onsets, rimes, or phonemes, a researcher may use a *gating task* (Metsala & Walley, 1998). Here, one plays larger and larger segments of a word until a child can recognize it (analogous to "name that tune"). All of the aforementioned analytical tasks have been used to determine the level of *phonological awareness* in children aged 3 to 8 (Stahl & Murray, 1998). The subset of tasks that specifically require attention to individual phonemes are thought to assess a highly refined form of phonological awareness called *phonemic awareness*. Performance on phonological and phonemic awareness tasks has been found to be highly correlated with performance on reading achievement tasks.

Age Trends in Receptive and Analytical Skills

Quite a number of studies of the receptive skills of infants have been conducted since the early 1970s using procedures such as high-amplitude sucking and conditioned head turns. For expository purposes, it is helpful to group the findings according to the ages of the children tested. In particular, the findings relating to four specific age ranges are discussed in turn: (1) birth to age 4 months, (2) age 5 to 8 months, (3) age 9 to 12 months, and (4) age 13 months and older.

Birth to Age 4 Months

Newborns have been found to prefer listening to (1) tape recordings of people speaking in the language of their caregivers rather than in another language, and (2) tape recordings of their own mother reading a children's book rather than a female stranger reading the same book (e.g., DeCasper & Fifer, 1980). Such preferences are not likely to reflect hard-wired predispositions encoded in a child's genes. What if a child born to Russian-speaking parents were adopted by English-speaking parents soon after birth? What good would it do the child to prefer to listen to Russian in such a situation? Rather, these findings reflect the fact that infants can hear muffled versions of their mother's voices in utero. Over time, this prenatal exposure creates stored representations of the native language in children's minds, but these representations only encode aspects of speech that get through the low-pass filter created by the amniotic fluid and surrounding tissues of the mother's uterus and abdomen (Jusczyk, 1997). It has been shown that this low-pass filtering eliminates essentially all features of speech except for prosodic features. To get a sense of what this may sound like to an infant, think of what it sounds like to hear a conversation in an adjacent hotel room or office. Even if the actual words or sounds made by the people in the next room cannot be made out, it still may be possible to know whether the language spoken is English (based on the prosodic features you can hear).

So, the evidence suggests that even newborns have the ability to hear prosodic differences between one language and another (as long as they have been exposed to one of these languages). What else can infants in the age range of birth to 4 months do? With respect to consonants, studies suggest that very young infants can tell the difference between synthesized versions of the stop consonants *pa* and *ba* (Eimas, Siqueland, Jusczyk, & Vigorito, 1971). As soon as the voice onset time exceeds 25 ms (as explained above), infants seem to consider the sound to be *pa* (just like adults). If the voice onset time is less than 25 ms, however, the infants seem to consider the sound to be *ba* (just like adults). The same study demonstrated that infants are like adults in one other way as well: These sounds were perceived categorically.

Other studies of consonantal contrasts showed that 2-month-olds can hear differences relating to place of articulation (e.g., *ba* vs. *ga*; Morse,

1972), nasality (e.g., *ba* vs. *ma*; Eimas & Miller, 1980), the liquid versus glide distinction (e.g., *ra* vs. *la*; Eimas, 1975), and differences among allomorphs (Jusczyk, 1997). *Allomorphs* are the variants of a phoneme that derive, in part, from the location of the sound in a word. Note how the /t/ sounds in *tap*, *stop*, and *pat* are all slightly different. Finally, infants have also been found to discriminate vowel and consonantal contrasts that do not appear in their native language (Jusczyk, 1997). For example, the English contrast between *pa* and *ga* does not appear in the Kenyan language Kikuyu, but Kenyan infants in the age range of 1 to 4 months could discriminate these sounds.

Other studies of infants in this age range have shown that they can discriminate between vowel sounds of their native language, as well (Swoboda, Moore, & Leavitt, 1976; Trehub, 1973), even when the pitch of the speaker and other features vary irrelevantly (Eimas & Miller, 1980; Jusczyk, Pisoni, & Mullinex, 1992; Kuhl & Miller, 1982). In other words, infants tended to treat certain vowel sounds the same regardless of whether they were produced by a woman or a man, and regardless of whether the speaker spoke slowly or quickly.

Ages 5 to 8 Months

The primary achievement evident in this second age range is that infants can now handle more subtle or hard-to-detect differences in sounds (Jusczyk, 1997). For example, they discriminate contrasts between (1) stops and glides (e.g., *ba* vs. *wa*), (2) two fricatives (e.g., *fuh* and *thuh*), and (3) two very similar vowel sounds (e.g., the /a/ sound in *cat* vs. *caught*). In addition, whereas infants continue to respond as if they can discriminate non-native consonant contrasts during this age period (the way they did during the prior age period), they provide no evidence that they continue to discriminate between certain non-native vowel contrasts. When such findings first appeared, it was interpreted as showing two things: (1) Children seem to lose their sensitivity to non-native vowel contrasts over time; and (2) this loss in sensitivity occurs earlier for vowels than it does for consonants.

In studies examining the ways in which infants can use cues to solve the parsing problem, 6-month-olds showed that they seem to use the stress of syllables and rhythmic patterns to parse. For example, whereas English often places stress on the first syllables of words (e.g., *happy*, *father*), Norwegian uses the opposite stress pattern. When presented with sound patterns that have the "strong first–weak second" structure, 6- and 7-month-old infants responded as if they parsed the stream between each strong-weak syllable pairing (Jusczyk, 1997). So, if they heard *mother father*, they would parse the stream at the junction between the two words (between the weakly stressed second syllable of *mother* and strongly stressed first sylla-ble of *father*).

By the time infants are 7½ months old, they also seem to be able to de-tect individual words in extended utterance streams. To demonstrate this ability, researchers first exposed infants to a list of individual words for sev-eral trials. Then, the infants were exposed to short passages that may or may not contain the words that they had heard on the list. When given a choice of passages that either did or did not contain the words, infants showed a preference for the former (Juszcyk, 1997).

Ages 9 to 12 Months

By 9 months of age, infants show a preference for made-up words that have the phonetic and phonotactic properties of their language (Jusczyk, 1997). In other words, they prefer to listen to words that have (1) the same pho-nemes as those found in their own language and (2) phonemes arranged in orders that are permissible in their language. In addition, other studies have shown that the infants ages 9 to 12 months seem to not only have a prefer-ence for words that have permissible combinations of phonemes, but also contain highly frequent combinations of phonemes and the syllable-stress patterns of their language (Jusczyk, 1997; Jusczyk, Luce, & Charles-Luce, 1994). This apparent emphasis on phonetic, phonotactic, and syllable-stress patterns in 9-month-olds has not been found in 6-month-olds. This age difference suggests that 9-month-olds would be able to use phonotactic, rhythmic, and stress patterns to parse an utterance stream into separate words. By 10½ months, infants have been found to no longer need all three of these cues to parse utterances appropriately. For example, they have been found to ignore atypical syllable-stress information (e.g., a weak–strong pattern) in favor of phonotactic and rhythmic information to parse an utterance the way an adult might (Jusczyk, 1997).

In addition to acquiring information that can help infants parse their own language effectively, there is also evidence that older infants show even less sensitivity to non-native contrasts than was the case for younger in-fants. In particular, whereas infants provide little evidence that they dis-criminate certain non-native vowel contrasts by the time they are 6 months old, they provide little evidence that they discriminate certain non-native consonant contrasts by the time they are 12 months old (Jusczyk, 1997).

When the first studies of non-native contrasts first appeared, the find-ings were taken as evidence that there is a critical period of language acqui-sition (and that foreign language instruction should begin as early as possi-ble before infants lose important abilities). However, subsequent studies have shown that the apparent "loss" of discrimination occurs for some contrasts but not for others. For example, 12-month-olds reared in English-speaking homes have been found to respond as if they discriminate between clicking (consonantal) sounds that are important in certain African languages but not in English. In addition, the primary evidence for infants making discriminations is their showing a preference for one contrast over another. If infants do not show a preference for particular contrasts at 12 months, does that mean that they cannot tell the difference between sounds, or that they have no preference?

Regardless of the true meaning of the non-native contrast studies, it is clear that by 12 months of age, infants show many (but not all) of the receptive phonological skills that adults have. Perhaps, most important, they can use their knowledge to parse the speech stream into words and thereby provide themselves with the building blocks they will need to create their own sentences.

Ages 13 Months and Older

As children progress through the preschool and elementary school years, they continue to show improvements in their phonological processing skills. To understand the nature of these improvements, it is first necessary to reintroduce the concept of analytical (or metacognitive) thinking that was discussed earlier in this chapter. The basic idea is that there are two ways to process the sounds in words. One way involves responding to these sounds in an automatic and implicit manner. Another way is to consciously reflect on the sounds in words such that patterns can be noted, thought about, and described. In the former approach, your brain merely registers similarities and differences in sounds (much the way a connectionist model might respond to input). In the latter, words are objects of thought themselves and are, therefore, examined in a conscious, reflective way. Research suggests that children can unconsciously register properties of a speech stream well before they can analyze and comment on these properties.

Another way to increase the difficulty of a speech task (besides asking children to analyze sounds consciously) is to ask children to consider increasingly more specific units of analysis (Goswami, 1998; Stahl & Murray, 1998). As discussed several times in this chapter, the continuous speech stream can be subdivided into individual words. Words, in turn, can be subdivided into syllables (if a word is polysyllabic) or onsets and rimes (if a word is monosyllabic). Syllables, in turn, can be subdivided into onsets and rimes (e.g., the *bat-* of *battle* can be subdivided into *b-* and *-at*). Finally, onsets and rimes can be subdivided into individual phonemes. There is good evidence that, in all areas of perception, children show a developmental progression from being able to process objects and sounds in a global, holistic manner, to being able to process specific, "internal" features of objects and sounds (Aslin & Smith, 1988). With objects, for example, children may initially lump dogs and horses into the same category when they are young because of a global judgment that these animals have the same general shape. Later on, however, analysis of specific features (e.g., different facial characteristics, different tails) leads children to create two distinct categories.

These two kinds of shifts in children's thinking (i.e., implicit-to-conscious and global-to-specific) lead one to expect that children may first process words at a holistic, global level before they start to recognize similarities and differences among words at more specific levels. For example, the global-to-specific shift might lead a researcher to predict that toddlers would not be able to hear the similarities among words that have the same onsets (as in alliteration) or the same rimes (as in words that rhyme), but somewhat older children (e.g., 3- and 4-year-olds) might be able to acknowledge similarities based on onsets and rimes. Additionally, one would predict that children would not be able to indicate the number of syllables in a word until several years after they demonstrate the ability to register syllable information implicitly. Thus, if 9-month-olds demonstrate implicit registering of syllables (as was shown to be the case earlier in this chapter), the ability to consciously indicate the number of syllables in a word might not be evident until age 3 or 4. Further, one would not expect children to identify or manipulate the individual phonemes in a word (e.g., drop the final *kuh* sound in *pink*) until sometime after they show analytical mastery of larger segments of words such as syllables, onsets, or rimes. Thus, if children show mastery of syllables, onsets, and rimes at age 3 or 4, they might not be expected to demonstrate the ability to identify or manipulate individual phonemes until they are 5 or 6.

It turns out that all of these predictions have been confirmed in a number of studies conducted over the past 30 years (Stahl & Murray, 1998). Thus, phonological awareness of syllables, onsets, and rimes precedes phonemic awareness. Note that the apparent late emergence of phonemic awareness around age 5 or 6 does not contradict the findings reported earlier in this chapter that young infants can discriminate between *pa* and *ba* (or other contrasts). Recognizing individual phonemes or consonants (e.g., *ba*) within a cluster of phonemes that comprise a word (*bat*) is not the same as being able to distinguish two different phonemes that are presented in isolation. In the same way, hearing the difference between the single C note played on a piano and an F played on the piano is not the same as hearing these notes and identifying them in the song "Happy Birthday" when this song is played in the key of C.

To further illustrate the development of phonological age trends in children older than 13 months, consider a study conducted by Carroll and Snowling (2001). After training children to identify words that rhyme or have the same onset, these researchers found that the percentages of children who were above chance on the rhyming task were 29%, 58%, and 76% at ages 44 months (3 years, 8 months), 48 months (4 years, 9 months), and 56 months (4 years, 8 months), respectively. For alliteration, the percentages were 5%, 29%, and 55%, respectively. Note that these percentages are higher than one would expect in the general population given the fact that children are not normally trained in rhyming and alliteration in the way children in this study were (rhyming would happen informally in the contexts of nursery rhymes and book reading). Training was focused and involved corrections for right and wrong answers. Moreover, it occurred three times over the course of a year and lasted for nearly a week each time.

There are two alternative interpretations of the age trends that occur after 13 months that have been discussed so far. The first is that children's stored representations become increasingly segmented with development (Metsala & Walley, 1998). As these representations change from being unsegmented wholes (e.g., *bat*) to having two or more segments (e.g., an onset and a rime as in *b-+ -at*), children become equipped to solve tasks that require the ability to identify or manipulate more specific sound segments. This segmentation is thought to occur progressively over time and may not be completed for familiar words until children are 5 or 6. In contrast to the lack-of-segmentation hypothesis, the second interpretation is that children's representations of words are segmented even when they are only 1 or 2, but children do not have conscious or easy access to these representations (or their segments) until after age 3 or so. For the present purposes, the latter hypothesis can be dubbed the lack-of-conscious-access hypothesis.

Evidence for the first (lack of segmentation) hypothesis is somewhat scant because most of the studies that tested this proposal either have been conducted using children older than 5 (see Metsala & Walley, 1998 for a review) or relied on relatively indirect evidence (Carroll & Snowling, 2001). Using the gating task, for example, studies show that (1) 5- to 7-year-olds need to hear more of a word to identify it than adults and (2) younger children with reading disabilities need to hear more of a word than their same-age peers who do not have reading disabilities. Advocates of the lack-of-segmentation hypothesis argue that holistic representations force younger children to hear essentially all of a word before it can be identified.

However, the lack of segmentation hypothesis is not the only possible explanation for such developmental and individual differences on the gating task. There are findings from studies that used other kinds of tasks that are also consistent with the lack of segmentation hypothesis (e.g., detecting mispronunciations, listening to contrastive pairs such as *rake–lake*), but these findings can be interpreted in other ways, as well. Moreover, the age differences on all of the aforementioned tasks are relative rather than absolute (adults do perform better, but all age groups perform fairly well).

To further illustrate the equivocal nature of some of the findings that are used to support the lack-of-segmentation hypothesis, Carroll and Snowling (2001) recognized that it is possible to solve rhyming tasks using a global matching strategy rather than through the use of representations that are segmented into onsets and rimes. Words such as *beach* and *dish* sound similar even though they do not share phonemes, onsets, or rimes. The similarity probably derives from the fact that (1) both words begin with stop consonants, (2) the vowels in each are both close front, and (3) the final consonants involve frication just beyond the alveolar ridge. Using word triads that contained rhymes and globally similar distractors (e.g., *top, mop, tap*), children who were nearly 5 were only 60% successful even though they had received three bouts of week-long training in rhymes (as discussed earlier). When no distractors were used, they were correct 80% of the time. Thus, when they are successful, are children using global matching strategies, or are they matching rime segments?

Additional problems for the lack-of-segmentation hypothesis come from studies conducted by Griffiths and Snowling (2001) and Swingley and Aslin (2002). Griffiths and Snowling (2001) found that older children with dyslexia (aged 10–15) did not differ from age-matched controls in their performance on the gating task. What was found to be impaired in the children with dyslexia was the ability to retrieve phonological representations from memory. In other words, the segmented representations seemed to be stored in memory, but they could not be readily accessed in a form that supported the mapping of letters to sounds in words.

Swingley and Aslin (2002) found evidence that the representations of 14- and 15-month-olds seem to be encoded in finer detail (i.e., segmented) than previously believed. Their task was based on the following logic: If early representations lack phonetic detail, infants should be indifferent to small variations in pronunciations (e.g., they would ignore the differences between *vaby* and *baby* in the same way that children initially ignore visual appearance differences between horses and dogs). Infants watched a monitor in which two pictures were displayed (e.g., an apple and a truck). They were then asked questions that referred to one of the objects using correct pronunciations (e.g., *apple*) and close mispronunciations (e.g., *opple*). For example, they might hear, "Where is the apple?" Infants looked significantly longer at objects when their labels were correctly pronounced, suggesting that they did notice small changes in phonetic detail. If infants do segment representations in more detail than the lack-of-segmentation hypothesis would predict, it would seem that the primary developmental change concerns the ability to access and reflect upon these representations.

Further evidence for the distinction between having segmented representations and reflecting upon them come from recent brain imaging studies. Burton, Small, and Blumstein (2000) asked adults to make "same–different" judgments on the first sounds of word pairs. Some pairs did not require segmentation because the different pairs only varied in the voicing of the initial consonant (e.g., *dip–tip*). Other pairs required segmentation because the stimuli differed not only in the voicing of the initial consonant but also in their vowels and final consonants (e.g., *dip–ten*). The performance of adults on such auditory word pairs was compared to their performance when they were asked to make same–different judgments about the pitch of tones. Results showed that the superior temporal lobes of participants (see Chapter 2) were more active during both speech conditions than when participants listened to tone pairs. However, regions of the frontal lobe (near the Broca's area) were also active only when the pairs required segmentation. The authors speculated that " . . . frontal activation is a product of segmentation in speech processes, or alternatively, working memory demands required for such processing (p. 679)." The findings that (1) phonological processing occurs in both the temporal and frontal lobes and (2) segmentation involves frontal areas are consistent with other studies, as well (Devlin, Matthews, & Rushworth, 2003; Zatorre, 2003). Given the claim that the frontal lobes mature more slowly than other brain areas and are thought to be associated with metacognitive skills and working memory (see Chapter 2 or Byrnes, 2001b), such findings seem to corroborate the lack-of-access hypothesis.

However, all of the findings discussed above that seem to favor the lack-of-access hypothesis can be also interpreted in multiple ways. Inasmuch as neither hypothesis is supported by unequivocal or airtight evidence, firm conclusions about whether representations become increasingly segmented over time must await further studies in this area.

Age Trends in Productive Skills

Accounts of age changes in productive skills often discuss developmental trends using the global categories of early achievements (birth to 12 months) and later achievements (13 months to 7 years). The following discussion utilizes this traditional organizational scheme.

Early Achievements (Birth to 12 Months)

A useful perspective for describing developmental trends in children's early ability to produce speech in phonetically acceptable ways is the five-stage framework proposed by Stark (1986). In the first stage of Stark's framework (*reflexive crying and vegetative sounds*), newborns cry, sneeze, burp, and make other kinds of sounds that are associated with hunger, digestion, and so on. These sounds sometimes require closure of the vocal tract, vocal chord vibration, and stoppage of airflow. In this way, children are practicing some of the vocal movements needed for speech sounds.

In the second stage (*cooing and laughter*), infants who are 6 to 8 weeks old start making pleasant sounds that evoke positive responses from others. Cooing is the earliest form of such sounds. Coos sometimes have the *aa-aah* sound (stress on the first syllable, rising intonation followed by falling). When infants are 16 weeks old, they start to exhibit laughing in addition to cooing and crying. Infants who can cry, coo, and laugh exercise different aspects of the vocal tract and could, again, be thought of as preparing for using similar vocal behaviors to produce speech.

The third stage (*vocal play*) begins when many infants are between 17 and 30 weeks old. It is during this phase that infants start making their first vowel sounds and other sounds that eventually morph into speech sounds (e.g., friction sounds). When children are 2 to 3 months of age, they make their first consonant sounds (usually the velars *guh* and *kuh*). A few months later, when infants are 6 months old, they make consonants that are articulated at the front of the mouth, such as *muh*, *nuh*, *puh*, *buh*, and *duh*. (It is perhaps no accident that baby names for mothers, fathers, and grandparents are *Ma-Ma*, *Da-Da*, *Pop-Pop*, and *Nana*!) Sometimes all of the aforementioned sounds are strung together in extended series. Such productions have been given the label *marginal babbling*.

Canonical babbling, however, does not typically emerge until infants are 7, 8, or 9 months old (when they are in the fourth stage called the *reduplicative babbling* stage). Canonical babbling is distinguished from marginal and other forms of babbling using two criteria: (1) the presence of true syllables and (2) the syllables are produced in reduplicated series of particular consonant–vowel (CV) combinations (e.g., *ma-ma-ma-ma-* . . .). Canonical babbling is also significant in that it does not emerge in children who are deaf (Oller & Eilers, 1988).

When children are around 10 months old, they enter the final stage of Stark's (1986) framework (*nonreduplicative babbling*). Here, the range of sounds evident in the babbling of infants is wider and includes various CV combinations (e.g., *ma-ga-doo-pee*) instead of repetitions of the same combination. Another interesting aspect of the babbling in this stage is that it takes on the prosodic features of the languages of an infant's caregivers. In other words, infants almost sound as though they are speaking (but no real words are being produced). Within a month or so, however, infants finally begin putting some of the sounds they can produce together to form their first words.

Later Achievements (13 Months to 7 Years)

As might be expected from the earlier discussion of receptive abilities, the development of children's productive competence is far from complete by the time they produce their first words at age 12 months. Studies have shown that the following 11 consonant sounds comprise 90% of the consonant sounds produced by infants at the end of the babbling stage: *huh, wuh, juh, puh, buh, muh, tuh, duh, nuh, kuh,* and *guh* (Locke & Pearson, 1992). Obviously, children have to be able to produce a number of other consonant sounds, as well. In addition, infants tend to produce vowel sounds such as the short /u/ in *but,* the short /a/ in *sofa,* and the short /a/ in *bat* much more frequently than the other 12 vowel sounds that English speakers use (Vihman, 1988). Thus, they need to expand their repertoire of vowel sounds, as well.

By the time most children are 3, however, they can produce all of the vowel sounds and nearly all of the consonant sounds in English, at least some of the time in certain words (Menn & Stoel-Gammon, 2005). Sounds that continue to cause problems for children between the ages of 3 and 7 include: (1) certain liquids such as *luh* and *ruh,* (2) certain fricatives such as *vuh* (when it is part of long words) and the two different /th/ sounds in words such as *thin* and *the,* (3) the glide *yuh,* and (4) various combinations of phonemes at the beginning (e.g., /spr/, /sn/, /tr/) or end of words (e.g., /lps/). Most children master all of these sounds by the time they are 7, however.

Before they do, children in the age range of 2 to 6 tend to make a number of systematic errors. Sometimes, children substitute a closely related sound for the correct sound they cannot make. For example, many children can make the bilabial glide *wuh* before they can make the palatal liquid *ruh* (e.g., 12 months vs. 4 years). Although the mouth movements used to make these two sounds are not identical, the similarities are close enough that children may substitute *wuh* for *ruh* in words (e.g., *wabbit* instead of *rabbit*). Note how children tend not to substitute sounds that use less-similar movements such as *tuh* and *guh* for *ruh* (e.g., *tabbit* or *gabbit* for *rabbit*), even though they can make the sounds *tuh* and *guh* before *ruh.* Thus, there is more to the story than simply the fact that children can already make a sound. Sometimes they substitute *duh* for words that start with *tuh* (e.g., *duh boy* instead of *the boy*), even though they can usually make both sounds. Conversely, some children substitute one later-occurring sound (e.g., *yuh*) for another (e.g., *luh*) when they want to pronounce a word that requires one of the two sounds (e.g., *yap* instead of *lap*).

In addition, children sometimes produce a sound properly when it is part of a duplicated sequence using similar or identical parts of the mouth (e.g., the two /k/ sounds in *cookie*) but not when it is part of a sequence using sounds from different categories that are made using different, spatially separated parts of the mouth (e.g., *tat* instead of *cat*). So, it would be incorrect to say that children cannot make a particular sound given such cases. A more accurate description is that they cannot make a particular sound when it occurs with certain other sounds (Menn & Stoel-Gammon, 2005). To see how spatial distance matters, note that in the word *cat*, the *kuh* sound, which emanates from the back of the mouth (using the velum tissue), has to be combined with the *tuh* sound, which is made near the front of the mouth (using the alveolar ridge). This combination is harder for children than two sounds that both use the alveolar ridge (e.g., *tadaah!*). Similarly, a child may only substitute *wuh* for *ruh* in words that include bilabials in the middle or end of the word (e.g., they might say *wabbit* instead of *rabbit* but might not say *wag* for *rag*). This process of changing one of two sounds to make them more similar (e.g., *tat* instead of *cat*) is called *assimilation*.

In addition to substituting one phoneme for another, children also sometimes substitute phonemes for blends or combinations they cannot yet produce. For example, the combination of the fricative *sss* with the stop consonant *puh* in *spagetti* is difficult for children to produce. When these initial sounds are combined, however, the *puh* tends to get more voicing than it normally gets in other contexts (making it sound more like *buh*). Perhaps this is why many children say *bisketti* for *spagetti* (because *buh* has more voicing than *puh*, and *kuh* and *guh* are both velars).

Besides substitutions, another way children try to solve problems of pronunciation is to omit sounds that they cannot say either alone or in combination with other sounds. Such omissions are called *cluster reductions*. For example, a child who cannot combine the fricative *sss* with stop consonants or with velars might say *pill*, *tore*, and *cool* for *spill*, *store*, and *school* (Menn & Stoel-Gammon, 2005). Or, a child may say *gandma* instead of *grandma*. When words contain a number of syllables, children may also be prone to omit portions of these words. For example, they may say *tehphone* instead of *telephone* or *keenie* instead of *zucchini*. Here, the issue may be an upper limit on working memory rather than an inability to say or combine phonemes together.

By age 7, most children attain most of the receptive and productive phonological skills they will need to perform well in school. They have sizable spoken vocabularies, so they can match whole words to written versions of these words. They can often hear segments of words such as syllables, onsets, rimes, and phonemes, and they can often pronounce many of the common words they will encounter in children's books. Hence, they are in a good position to learn how to read. However, not all children exhibit this kind of developmental pattern. Why is this the case? In the next section, we will examine the factors that produce the age changes described in this section. Insight into these developmental mechanisms will help us understand ways to help all children attain the phonological processing skills they need to have when they begin first grade.

THE DEVELOPMENTAL MECHANISMS QUESTION:
What Factors Promote Changes
in Phonological Processing Competence?

In the previous section, we learned that children's receptive and productive phonological skills change with age. The developmental progression for receptive skills was said to be as follows: (1) At birth, infants can recognize the prosodic features of their native languages; (2) by 4 months, they can discriminate several consonantal and vowel contrasts; (3) by 8 months, they can do three new things: discriminate more subtle or hard-to-detect contrasts, use syllables and rhythmic patterns to parse an utterance stream, and hear individual words in passages; and (4) by 12 months, they can use phonetic, phonotactic, and syllable-stress patterns to parse utterances into individual words. In addition to these developmental increases, however, it was also noted that children seem to become less sensitive to some (but not all) non-native vowel contrasts by 6 months and some (but not all) non-native consonant contrasts by 12 months. Between the ages of 1 and 7, children seem to progress from the ability to recognize whole words to the ability to recognize progressively smaller portions of words (e.g., whole words → then syllables, onsets, rimes, → then eventually phonemes).

The developmental progression for productive skills was said to be as follows: (1) marginal babbling and pronunciation of certain vowels by 7 months, (2) frequent use of 11 consonant and 3 vowel sounds by 12 months (also production of their first word by 12 months), (3) correct pronunciation of nearly all consonants and vowels at least some of the time by age 3, and (4) correct pronunciation of various blends and difficult combinations by age 7.

Why do these changes in receptive and productive skills occur? What factors operating within children or within their environments foster these changes? In what follows, we consider three general classes of explanatory factors or developmental mechanisms: (1) biological, (2) experiential, and (3) motivational.

Biological Developmental Mechanisms

There are four reasons why scientists have appealed to biological explanatory factors to explain some of the developmental trends for receptive and productive phonological skills that were discussed above. The first is that many of these same trends have been found in a number of distinct cultures (Locke, 1993). For example, the *muh* sound is often one of the earliest sounds that infants make in many cultures, and nearly all languages (97%) have this sound in their set of phonemes. Similarly, infants engage in the earliest forms of babbling at similar ages all around the world. Further, the babbling of infants who are deaf is indistinguishable from the babbling of infants who can hear until the point at which infants who can hear start to engage in canonical babbling.

The second reason why scientists appeal to biological explanations is that children's brains are known to go through some of their most significant changes between birth and age 5. (Note, however, that processes such as synaptogenesis and mylenation continue to occur well into adulthood; see Chapter 2). As neural networks in various regions of the cortex become reorganized and myelinated (e.g., the auditory processing cortices in the temporal and frontal lobes; the primary motor cortex), infants may show improvements in their ability to (1) process speech quickly and (2) manipulate various component muscles of their vocal tracts. Skills that appear later may involve brain regions that mature later. In addition, changes in the proportional sizes and shapes of an infant's mouth and tongue could contribute to their emerging ability to create consonantal sounds that use the tongue (Stark, 1986). Further, neuroscientific studies of healthy adults and adults with brain injuries support the idea of distinct neural networks for many of the skills reported earlier (e.g., initial auditory processing of speech, detection of rhymes and phonemes, motor control of the mouth and tongue).

The third reason why scientists invoke biological explanations is that very young infants show some of the same discrimination abilities that adults have, and also seem to quickly form stored representations of novel sounds (even within the context of an experiment). Thus, it would appear that infants are born with the ability to encode important properties of speech, much the same way that they are born with the ability to form representations of people's faces or other objects. As such, many scientists think that it is perfectly reasonable to make assertions such as the following: Infants' brains must be wired, almost at birth, to hear distinctions in sounds and to create sound categories out of variable input (Jusczyk, 1997). In other words, since infants can perform these tasks, we have to assume that their brains are already configured to carry out these tasks.

However, in acknowledging some or all of these points, one need not advocate a strong form of *nativism*. Radical nativists not only assume that children are born with the ability to do certain things (e.g., hear the contrast between *puh* and *buh*), they also assume that children are born with the stored representations for particular sound categories (Jusczyk, 1997). In other words, one would not assume that infants create a neural network that corresponds to a sound like *puh* after many exposures; one would assume instead that the network for that sound is already created before a child is born and exposed to auditory stimuli (i.e., infants know what *puh* sounds like before the first time they hear it). By analogy, a radical nativist account of dancing would invite the inference that a person must already know a particular dance step ahead of time (e.g., the tango) if that person is able to learn that form of dancing from an instructor. In other words, if you can learn it, you must have already known the step.

Scientists used to believe such radical nativistic explanations of the abilities of certain animal species (e.g., song birds or ducklings) until they conducted experiments that showed no evidence that these animals are born already knowing the songs of their conspecifics or knowing what their mothers would look like (e.g., by ablating regions of animal brains known to be involved in learning songs or recognizing conspecifics). Other findings that caused problems for radical nativism pertained to the fact that nonverbal, nonhuman species (e.g., chinchillas) can make many of the same vowel and consonant discriminations that human infants can make (Jusczyk, 1997). People used to think that only humans had such skills because we were the only species to have the spoken language competencies described in Chapter 3.

These days, many scientists advocate a much weaker form of nativism called *innately guided learning* to explain how various species (including humans) learn certain things (Johnson, 1997; Jusczyk, 1997). The basic premise is that many organisms are preprogrammed to learn particular things and learn them quickly. Part of this preprogramming may simply be a bias toward, or strong interest in, particular kinds of stimuli (e.g., speech in the case of humans; songs in the case of song birds). Another part of the preprogramming may be the ability to create and store representations of recurrent stimuli. By orienting a young organism to attend to certain categories of recurrent stimuli, the organism can then extract the kinds of information it needs to adapt to the demands of its environments (e.g., the frequency and phonotactic properties of one's native language).

Advocates of innately guided learning also believe that this approach explains the general pattern of findings reported earlier:

> The picture that seems to emerge from developmental studies of speech perception is that infants begin with a language-general capacity that provides the means for discriminating potential phonetic contrasts in any of the world's languages and then winnow the set of contrasts down to the ones most relevant to their native language. This notion is consistent with learning-by-selection accounts [in the neuroscience literature] . . . where is it claimed that the nervous system begins with an overexuberance of connections that are pared down in the course of development. (Jusczyk, 1997, p. 73)

Discussion Topic: How could biological factors be used to explain why some children come to first grade with deficient phonological processing skills while others come with high levels of phonological skill? Do we have to assume that children with deficits cannot be helped if we assume a role for biology? Why or why not?

Experiential Developmental Mechanisms

The preceding section suggests, then, that biological factors may well contribute to age changes in receptive and productive skills. However, a purely biological account could not explain all of the findings reported earlier. For example, children do not progressively master the phonology of all languages (even those they are never exposed to); rather, they progressively master the specific phonology expressed by others in their rearing environments. Hence, it is exposure to, and internalization of, sound patterns in one's environment that explains why (1) children show a preference for tape recordings of their own mothers' voices, not the voices of strangers (because they were exposed to their mothers' voices in utero); (2) canonical babbling takes on the prosodic characteristics of a child's own native language rather than those of some other language; (3) children who are deaf do not reach the canonical babbling stage; (4) children can use the characteristic syllable-stress patterns, phonetic features, and phonotactic restrictions contained within their native languages to parse an utterance stream into individual words; and (5) children seem to become less sensitive to non-native contrasts over time. The more exposure a child has to the ambient language-related sounds in his or her environment, the more his or her internal representations will eventually correspond to this ambient environment. Note that this correspondence between internal representations and the environment is a central assumption of the connectionist approach discussed earlier in this chapter.

But there are other ways to construe the construct of "experience" besides the idea of passive (yet attentive) exposure to the utterances of others. For example, when children babble, utter a single word, or create multiword utterances, they provide themselves with additional auditory input that they can analyze. In other words, children serve as their own audiences. The quality of this input will, of course, be rather restricted when children are 12 months old (due to their partial mastery of pronunciations), but eventually children will promote growth in their stored representations by exposing themselves to their own utterances. In addition, however, children can use these experiences as feedback regarding their productive attempts. For example, if children want to say *rabbit* and know that adults say *rabbit*, their early flawed attempts (e.g., *wabbit*) can provide them with feedback that can be used to modify how they produce this word. Thus, just as children will never become good at shooting basketballs, writing in cursive, or playing an instrument unless they practice and observe their own mistakes, they will also never become proficient in pronunciation unless they repeatedly try to pronounce a wide range of words.

A third way to view the role of experience is to consider the ways in which adults respond to or interact with children. Researchers have found that infants vocalize more when their mothers are responsive to these vocalizations (Bornstein & Tamis-LeMonda, 1989; Rheingold, Gewirtz, & Ross, 1959). Conversely, infants growing up in impoverished households babble less than infants growing up in households with higher income levels (presumably because the former receive less verbal stimulation than the latter; Ollers, Eilers, Basinger, Steffens, & Urbano, 1995). In older children, experiences such as reading a broad array of books with parents, watching television shows that focus on letters and vocabulary, and playing computer games that focus on prereading skills, all predict the level of rime awareness and phonemic awareness in 4- and 5-year-olds (Foy & Mann, 2003; Scarborough & Dobrich, 1994).

A final way to consider the role of experience is to consider the effect of vocabulary development on children's phonological processing skills. According to Metsala and Walley's (1998) lexical restructuring model, children's phonological representations of words are thought to become more segmental over time as a result of children gaining new vocabulary words. Each time a new word is learned, it has the potential to promote the segmentation of existing representations if the onset, rime, or phonemes in the new word also occur in words that are already in a child's vocabulary. For example, a child who already has the word *snake* in his or her vocabulary might segment the holistic auditory representation for this word into /sn- + -ake/ in response to learning the new word, *rake*.

Because the segmental process is a function of the words already in a child's vocabulary, each new word may or may not promote segmentation. Given the word-by-word nature of this mechanism, the model further suggests that the restructuring process is likely to take many years instead of happening in an all-or-none, abrupt manner. In addition, the model predicts that words that exist in dense neighborhoods (e.g., *hat, mat, cat, rat*) are likely to be more segmented than words that exist in sparse neighborhoods (e.g., *orange*).

Whereas studies have found a consistent correlation between the size of a child's vocabulary and his or her performance on gating tasks (a measure of the degree of segmentation), several studies reviewed earlier in this chapter suggest that older children's representations may not be substantially more segmented than younger children's representations. Thus, although we do know for certain that children's vocabularies increase from one word at around 12 months to as many as 10,000 by first grade (see Chapter 5), we do not know for certain whether the stored representations of first graders are more segmental than those of 12-month-olds. Until the latter uncertainty is resolved in additional experiments, we cannot draw firm conclusions about the implications of the lexical restructuring hypothesis for interventions. For example, there are several programs that are known to increase a child's vocabulary (see Chapter 5); however, we do not yet know whether these programs would also increase the segmentation of children's stored representations.

Discussion Topic: Two children enter first grade with differing amounts of phonological processing skill (e.g., one enters with a high level of skill while the other enters with a low level of skill). How might one appeal to experiential factors (as opposed to biological factors) to explain the different levels of phonological processing skill manifested by these two children? If your experiential explanation is correct, could you design an intervention to eliminate the differences between these children? What could happen at home or at school that would be beneficial?

Motivational Factors

In Chapter 3, it was argued that the human communication system is inherently goal directed. In particular, the claim was that people engage in communicative acts because they want to accomplish particular goals (e.g., get a listener to do something). One of the benefits of viewing communication from the perspective of goals is that additional implications can be derived from the work of scholars who place a heavy emphasis on goals in their theorizing. For example, scholars who study motivation appeal to goals to explain why people differ in their tendencies to initiate certain activities, expend effort in these activities, and persist in the face of failure. (Note: Motivation theorists also appeal to other constructs to explain differences such as values, levels of interest, and levels of self-efficacy; see Chapter 10). Others who emphasize goals are those who study problem solving. These scholars argue that people engage in the following four processes when they try to solve a problem: (1) setting a goal, (2) devising and evaluating alternative ways to accomplish this goal, (3) choosing and implementing the best alternative, and (4) observing the effects of this decision (Byrnes, 1998).

These motivational and problem-solving perspectives help provide insight into two sets of findings that have emerged in the literature on the development of phonological processing skills: (1) individual differences in the level of phonological processing skill manifested by children at particular ages, and (2) individual differences in the phonological processing strategies used by children to solve the same phonological problem. To illustrate the former finding, if one 3-year-old manifests a higher level of phonological skill than another 3-year-old, motivation theory leads one to hypothesize that (1) one child used language to accomplish his or her goals more often than the other child, (2) one child was more interested in engaging in communicative exchanges than the other, and (3) one child was more perfectionistic than the other (and cared whether his or her pronunciations matched those of adults). Motivational theory can also be used to explain why some infants are "intonation babies" who engage in extended bouts of canonical babbling (complete with prosody) while others are "word babies" who produce much shorter babbles (Dore, 1975). Motivational differences may also be at the root of the finding that children who can make the same set of sounds sometimes differ with respect to the frequency with which they make particular sounds (Vihman, 1993). Such differences in the relative frequency of sounds in babbles may reflect personal preferences for making these sounds.

To illustrate the findings regarding strategy choices within problem solving, two equally motivated children may use different strategies to solve the same pronunciation problem. For example, one child may decide to simply not use a hard-to-pronounce word (e.g., *spagetti*) while another may decide to use the word in a reduced form (e.g., *pagetti*). Such individual differences in problem-solving solutions are to be expected according to phonology scholars who advocate a problem-solving perspective. The problem-solving perspective on phonology arose as an alternative to nativist proposals (Menn & Stoel-Gammon, 2005). Instead of observing all children using the same strategy to solve particular phonology problems (as strong forms of nativism would predict), children are found to utilize a variety of creative solutions to the same problem (as problem-solving theorists would predict). In addition, children have been found to progressively master the phonology system little by little as they tackle one problem after another. Nativist accounts have a hard time explaining progressive mastery (they imply faster and more systemwide mastery). Further, children differ in terms of the problems they wish to solve at any point. Some may choose to stop substituting *wuh* for *ruh* sounds while other may focus on correctly pronouncing blends (e.g., *spr-*). Finally, children sometimes show regressions in their pronunciations after they discover a pronunciation rule that they overgeneralize. Such regressions would not be predicted by nativists. Why would children be preprogrammed to first pronounce a word correctly and then pronounce it incorrectly?

Discussion Topic: The discussion questions presented earlier in this chapter asked you to posit biological and experiential explanations of individual differences in the phonological skills children bring to first grade. This time, explain these differences using motivational and problem-solving accounts. Could a child who manifests a high level of skill be more motivated or faced with communication problems more often than a child who manifests a lower level of skill? If there is a motivational basis to individual differences in the phonological processing skills that children bring to first grade, design an intervention to combat this problem in preschoolers.

THE DEFICIENCIES QUESTION: Are There Populations of Children or Adults Who Lack Some or All of the Key Skills of Phonological Processing Competence? Do These Individuals Experience Problems When They Learn to Read or after They Have Learned to Read?

The answers provided to the preceding four questions provide clues as to the kinds of children who might have trouble learning to read. As noted earlier, children will not benefit from formal reading instruction unless they enter first grade with adequate levels of phonological processing skill. In particular, skilled readers need to be able to (1) reflect upon sound segments in words (e.g., onsets, rimes, and phonemes) and (2) map graphemes (i.e., letters or groups of letters) onto these segments. Comprehension is also facilitated when readers temporarily store copies of sentences that have just been read in their verbal working memories; see Chapters 7 and 8. Verbal working memory seems to rely on some of the same brain regions that are utilized when people produce speech (which provides support for the long-standing claim that verbal working memory utilizes an "articulatory loop" to maintain or rehearse information).

This analysis suggests that, on a priori grounds, children who evince problems in either their receptive or productive phonological skills would be likely to experience problems when they learn to read. On the receptive side, it was noted earlier in this chapter that the core deficit of children who are reading disabled or dyslexic derives from their inability to access and manipulate segmented phonological representations for words. But there are other groups of children who would also be expected to be at a disadvantage due to their having underdeveloped phonological representations. Children who are congenitally deaf, for example, do not create phonological representations of words (though they do create gestural representations if they learn sign languages). It makes sense that these children also experience considerable problems when they learn to read (Marschark, Lang, & Albertini, 2006).

Another group would be those children dubbed language learning impaired (LLI) by Tallal and colleagues (e.g., Tallal, Merzenich, Miller, & Jenkins, 1998). Whereas children with LLI can only discriminate between acoustic events if the temporal gap between these events exceeds several hundred milliseconds, children of the same age and intelligence who are not LLI only need tens of milliseconds. This temporal integration deficit interferes with a child's ability to discriminate the brief acoustical cues within syllables and words that distinguish one phoneme from another. The larger the temporal gap needed to distinguish sounds, the larger the degree of receptive language impairment. More important, the extent of the temporal gap deficit during preschool predicts children's later problems in phonological decoding.

On the productive skills side, reading problems seem to be surprisingly less severe. For example, children who have articulation disorders do sometimes experience problems when they learn to read, but they only have marked deficits in their reading when the production deficits are extreme (e.g., as in the case of nonvocal children with cerebral palsy) or when articulation problems are accompanied by semantic-syntactic deficits (Catts, 1993). But even in the extreme case of being nonverbal, reading problems seem to derive from problems in verbal working memory rather than from problems in phonological awareness (Sandberg, 2002). In addition, studies have shown that (1) children who have problems limited to articulation do not differ from controls in reading achievement (Catts, 1993), and (2) training in phonological awareness is more effective than traditional speech-language interventions that focus on improving articulation and language skills (Gillon, 2000). Thus, as long as children with articulation problems are exposed to the correct pronunciations of others, they seem to form representations that they can use to acquire reading skills. In other words, their own mispronunciations may not alter these representations too severely when they hear themselves speak. Similarly, the ability to articulate in any manner may allow a child to make use of the articulatory loop of verbal working memory.

5

The Development of Word
Meaning and Vocabulary

Vignette: Matty told Ms. Melville, her first-grade teacher, "I need to wear my special rainbow today," pointing to the ribbon in her hair. Ms. Melville looked quizzically at Matty and asked, "Why is that a rainbow?" Matty replied, "Because I wear it on rainy days. Tomorrow, if it is sunny, I can wear my sun bow."

MAIN IDEAS OF THE CHAPTER

1. Word meanings involve the concepts or ideas that language users associate with phonological word forms. The collection of pairings between meanings and spoken words is a person's vocabulary. Philosophers and linguists have revealed some interesting puzzles when it comes to explaining what a word means and how words are learned.

2. Teachers should care about the development of vocabulary for three reasons: (a) Reading involves the mapping of printed words onto stored phonological and semantic representations (i.e., meanings) for spoken words; (b) children who enter first grade with larger spoken vocabularies are often the ones who score the highest on reading achievement tests at the end of first grade; (c) children need to have segmented phonological representations of words in order to map sounds onto text when they read. Phonological representations may become segmented each time a child learns a new vocabulary word that has phonemes in common with existing words.

3. Some notable age trends in vocabulary development include the following: (a) Children's first words appear around 12 months of age; (b) by the time children are in first grade, they have 10,000 words in their vocabularies; (c) the rate of word learning seems to speed up after age 3 and then slow down after age 12; (d) there are large individual differences in the size of children's and adults' vocabularies at different ages; (e) there is a preponderance of nominals in the first words of many U.S. children from middle-to high-income homes but not in the first words of middle-

class children from several Asian countries; (f) some children adopt a referential communicational style while others adopt a more expressive style; and (g) word meanings become progressively more elaborated, abstract, and integrated with age.

4. Explaining these age trends has been a challenge because of the arguments of philosophers regarding the nature of inductive inferences. When a new word is used in a situation, how do children figure out what it means when there are endless possibilities? The fact that they do implies they (a) may rely on some learning principles and (b) are able to attribute goals and beliefs to others; in addition, they learn new words because of changes in their receptive phonological skills, productive phonological skills, working memory, and conceptual knowledge.

5. Regardless of whether the source of a small vocabulary is a disability (e.g., Down syndrome), lack of education, or economic disadvantage, it is essentially impossible to become a skilled reader if one has a limited vocabulary.

As noted in Chapter 3, spoken language competence involves both fundamental and advanced skills. The fundamental skills are the kinds of skills that a person has to have before we can reasonably say that he or she "knows" a language. For example, we would only say that a person could speak Russian if that person was able to do at least three things: (1) recognize and pronounce a large number of Russian words correctly (phonological knowledge), (2) understand the meaning of a large number of Russian words (semantic knowledge), and (3) combine Russian words together in grammatically acceptable ways (grammatical knowledge). In Chapter 4, the focus was on the first of these fundamental skills—phonological skills. In the present chapter, we consider the development of the second skill, semantic knowledge, using the same five questions that were utilized in previous chapters.

THE "NATURE OF" QUESTION: What Does It Mean to Say That a Child Knows the Meaning of Words?

This question may seem relatively straightforward, but philosophers and linguists have shown that answers to it can be rather complex and controversial (e.g., Frege, 1975; McNamara, 1982; Quine, 1960). In fact, the scholarly literature on the topic of word meaning is so large that it could fill up many shelves in a standard university library. We do not think it would be beneficial if this chapter were to delve too deeply into many of these abstract theoretical matters, so this section will focus on just those matters that have direct relevance to development and instruction. Following a discussion of these relevant theoretical issues, we will then consider the methods that have been used to reveal semantic knowledge in children and adults.

Theoretical Issues in the Study of Semantics

In Chapter 4, it was noted that competent speakers of a language have stored phonological representations for words (and parts of words) that they match to sounds that they hear. For example, a woman who turns around when someone calls out her name engages in this matching process. She hears her name, recognizes it, and then turns around. But communication of ideas requires other kinds of representations besides phonological representations. To understand what someone is saying to you, you also need to know the meanings associated with particular sound patterns. For example, to respond appropriately to the question, "Can you speak French?" you need to know what *can*, *you*, *speak*, and *French* mean. Contrast your ability to answer such a question with the situation in which someone says to you, "Parlez-vous Français?" Many people have heard this familiar expression before and may even have stored phonological representations for some of the words. However, they may not know the meaning of *parlez*, *vous*, or *Français*. Without stored representations of the meanings of these words, a listener could not provide an appropriate response. Conversely, the tip-of-the-tongue phenomenon demonstrates that people can have an idea that they want to express but sometimes fail to access the phonological word form associated with this idea (Saffran, 2003).

Although most philosophers, linguists, and psychologists have agreed for many years that people need to have stored representations of both phonological word forms (PWFs) and word meanings, there have been many disagreements over the precise nature of the latter. Many scholars have assumed that meaning arises when people map PWFs onto their conceptual knowledge (Bloom, 2000). For example, English-speaking people are said to derive the meaning of PWFs such as *dogs* and *cats* by mapping these words onto their concepts of dogs and cats, respectively. In countries where English is not the native language, of course, different PWFs would be mapped onto these same concepts (e.g., *hunde* and *katzen* in Germany, *chiens* and *chats* in France, and *perros* and *gatos* in Mexico).

Further reflection on this mapping process prompted many scholars to contend that (1) conceptual knowledge seems to be a precondition for learning new words (e.g., children have to have a certain amount of conceptual knowledge of dogs and cats before they can learn the words *dogs* and *cats*) and (2) the connection between word forms and concepts is both conventional (i.e., a community of speakers all agree that a particular word shall be used to refer to a particular concept) and arbitrary (i.e., any PWF could have been used besides the one that happened to have been selected in a given community).

One of the benefits of this conceptual knowledge account of word meaning is that it helps us see that word meaning is more than simply the overt labeling of objects, actions, and properties. To the average person, it certainly seems like we are referring only to a specific dog when we say to a toddler, "Look at that cute doggy!" But in reality, the word also refers to the category of things called *dogs*. In other words, the speaker is really saying, "Look at that thing that is a member of the category of dogs!" In essence, one could say that the referent of the word is not "out there" in the real world per se; rather, it is inside a person's head (though noted philosophers such as Putnam and Quine have vigorously disagreed with this claim). If common nouns do, in fact, refer to members of categories and not just specific individuals, we often do not need to have an actual referent of a noun present in order to have a meaningful conversation about the referent. For example, mothers and children often discuss animals they have seen at the zoo well after the trip to the zoo occurred (Nelson, 1996).

A second benefit of the conceptual knowledge account is that it helps us see that there is nothing in the act of applying a label (e.g., *dog*) to a particular object (e.g., your neighbor's dog) that provides the definition of the word (Pan, 2005). Similarly, there is nothing in the act of describing a particular painting as being *cubist* that is informative as to what it means for a painting to be cubist. Categories are mental representations that specify what members of that category (e.g., dogs) have in common (Smith, 1989). These commonalities might be things that we can detect with our senses (e.g., has four legs, barks, and wags tail), but they might not be. For example, U.S. presidents have applied the term *dictator* to Adolph Hitler, Benito Mussolini, and Saddam Hussein. These leaders are not in the same category because they look alike, sound alike, smell alike, or taste alike; rather, they are in the same category because they ruled with supreme and unrestricted authority. Supreme and unrestricted power is not something that we can sense in the way that we can see that two apples are both red. Note also that the term *dictator* gets part of its meaning through the contrast between that category and the category of leaders who (1) are elected, (2) can be turned out of office without force, and (3) have many of their policies rebuffed or rejected by others who share power with them (e.g., congressional representatives). As the foregoing examples illustrate, meaning often derives from the relations within concepts (e.g., membership relations, similarity relations) and relations among concepts (e.g., contrastive relations such as that between dictators and other leaders, single persons and married persons). In noting that shared commonalities may not be perceptible or visual, we can see that word meaning is not simply the association between a word and a "picture in the head" as the average person tends to assume (Bloom 2000; Pan, 2005).

There are, then, several important benefits that accrue from casting meaning in terms of the mapping between word forms and categorical concepts. However, this account is not without its problems. The first problem is that scholars disagree about the precise nature of categories. According to the classical view of concepts that dates back to the ancient Greeks, membership in a category is determined by a set of necessary and sufficient criteria (Smith & Medin, 1981). In other words, all members of the category have to have these criteria and the condition of having all of them is sufficient grounds for saying that an object is a member of the category. For example, the necessary and sufficient criteria for being a member of the category "square" are (1) having four angles, (2) having angles with 90 degrees, (3) having four sides, and (4) having sides that are all the same length. If we change the number of angles, the size of the angles, the number of sides, or the equilateral criterion, the shape is no longer a square. Note that with such a scheme, categorization is all-or-none. In other words, something either is or is not a member. Moreover, all objects that have the necessary and sufficient criteria are equally good representatives of the category. It would make little sense, for example, to say that one square is a better example of the category of square than another.

Based on both philosophical arguments and empirical research, however, it is now believed that only certain scientific or mathematical concepts are defined through necessary and sufficient criteria (Bjorklund, 2001). The vast majority of our concepts need to be defined in some other way because it is often impossible to come up with necessary and sufficient criteria for these concepts (Rosch, 1975; Wittgenstein, 1953). To illustrate, consider the classic case of the category of "games." What makes something a game versus something else? Does it need rules? Do you have to keep score? Can one person or more than one person play? You could try to develop a set of necessary and sufficient criteria, but you would eventually learn that there are always exceptions. Next, consider the category of "dogs." Do dogs have to be pets or bark? What about wild dogs and species of dogs that do not bark? Once again, the set of necessary and sufficient features for even this familiar category does not exist.

Instead of being defined through necessary and sufficient criteria, most of our concepts seem to be defined through characteristic features (Murphy, 2002; Rosch, 1975). Characteristic features are attributes that many (but not all) members of a category seem to have. For example, most dogs bark and most birds fly. These criteria are pretty good clues to category membership, but an object does not need to have these criteria to be considered members. As such, membership in a category is more graded and probabilistic than all-or-none. In a related way, whereas it does not make sense to say that one member of a classically defined category (e.g., "square") is a better representative of the category than another, it does makes sense to say that a particular kind of dog or bird is a better example or better representative of its category than other kinds of dogs or birds. For example, a terrier seems to be a better example of the category of dogs than a Chihuahua. Similarly, a robin seems to be a better example of the category of birds than an ostrich. The best representatives in a category tend to be those individuals who have more of the characteristic features (e.g., typical size, typical shape, typical behaviors). One would even say that the best representatives are stereotypical or prototypical for the category.

The *prototypes* of a category are said (metaphorically) to reside at the core or center of the category; less typical members are said to reside at the periphery, close to the border with other categories (Murphy, 2002; Rosch, 1975). So, a robin would reside at the core of the category of birds close to other prototypical instances of birds (e.g., canaries, sparrows). Ostriches, chickens, and so on would reside near the periphery. This "distance from the core" metaphor has been used to explain differences in the speed with which people respond to questions such as "Is a robin a bird?" and "Is an ostrich a bird?" People respond much faster to the former question than to the latter. The features of prototypes are also highly correlated. For example, features such as long snout, barking, and tail wagging tend to co-occur a lot. It is thought that these features bundle together in children's minds the way phonemes cluster together in spoken words.

Regardless of whether categories are defined using necessary and sufficient criteria or characteristic features, categories can often be organized into hierarchies (Murphy, 2002). For example, categories such as "dog," "cat," and "cow" are subcategories of the superordinate category "mammal" because dogs, cats, and cows have in common the following features: (1) bear live young, (2) have hair, (3) have mammary glands, and (4) have self-regulating temperature (once called "warm-blooded"). "Mammals" and "reptiles," in turn, are subcategories of the superordinate category of "animals" due to their sharing features common to animals (e.g., locomotion, respiration). The category of "animals," in turn, is itself a subcategory of its superordinate category, "living things." Hence, many categories have subordinate categories beneath them (e.g., "Terriers" and "German Shepherds" in the case of "dogs") but also superordinate categories above them (e.g., "dog" and "cat" have "mammal" over them). This hierarchical arrangement of categories has been used to explain the different speeds in which people answer questions such as "Do birds fly?" and "Do bird breath?" The attribute of flying is thought to be linked to the category of "birds," but the attribute of breathing is thought to be linked several tiers up to the category of "living things" (Rosch, 1975).

In considering the features that define particular levels of a conceptual hierarchy, it has been argued that the basic level might be the most conceptually primitive or easiest to acquire (Mervis & Crisafi, 1982). Why? Instances of basic levels stand out because basic levels maximize within-category similarity (e.g., a dog is more similar to another dog than it is to a cat) as they highlight between-category differences than are not too difficult to detect through visual inspection. In contrast, it can be harder to understand the basis of similarity for superordinate categories such as "living things" (e.g., the similarity between dogs and trees) and harder to see differences between instances of subordinate categories (e.g., the differences between oak trees and maple trees).

The preceding discussion of the classical view of concepts and prototype theory suggests that children know the meaning of various nouns when they map these nouns onto categories that are defined by either necessary and sufficient criteria or characteristic features (depending on the category). In addition, it has been suggested that children's understanding of other types of words (e.g., verbs and adjectives) may also be supported by probabilistic representations. For example, actions such as jumping and pushing can be illustrated through both good and bad examples. Similarly, there are very good examples of the color red and colors that lie more on the periphery of the color category of "red" (as a trip to the paint store can easily demonstrate). The graded quality of membership in such cases suggests that some version of prototype theory may apply to actions and attributes, as well. However, this suggestion has been challenged through counterarguments and by findings that provide less-clear support for a prototype theory of verbs than has been found for nouns (Tomasello & Merriman, 1995).

Hence, the mapping-to-categorical-concepts account seems to work best for nouns that clearly refer to categories of things. What about other common kinds of words such as adverbs? Do we derive the meaning of *quickly* from a mental representation of what all actions done quickly have in common? Probably not. Then, there are determiners (e.g., *the*), prepositions (*to*), and question words (e.g., *what* or *how*) that do not seem to have any kind of meaning associated with them at all. Further, there are other important concepts that are not really categories, such as numerical concepts (e.g., *three*), causal concepts (e.g., *X* caused *Y*), spatial concepts (e.g., *X* is next to *Y*), and temporal concepts (e.g., *X* happened before *Y*). Thus, there must be some sort of mapping between these concepts and word forms, but the concepts are not categories. At present, we know much more about children's understanding of categories and nouns than we know about children's understanding of other kinds of concepts and word forms.

Finally, a good case has been made that meaning usually derives from units of discourse that are larger than individual words (Bloom, 2000). Consider, for example, the sentence about dogs that was utilized above: "Look at that cute doggy!" The part of this sentence that refers is the noun phrase *that cute doggy*. The listener must access his or her knowledge of the category "dogs" in this instance (e.g., in order to know what dogs look like), but to understand the sentence or even the noun phrase, the meaning derived from the category "dog" must be augmented and fixed using the determiner *that* (which points out a specific dog, not just any dog) and *cute* (which describes the dog's attribute and says something about the speaker's attitudes). Thus, it would appear that the acquisition of vocabulary is really part of a larger story of making meaning out of larger units of discourse such as phrases and sentences. By narrowing the study of meaning to just individual words, philosophers, linguists, and developmental psycholinguists may have been "seeing the trees but not the forest." Perhaps this is why words such as *what*, *to*, and *that* have been (wrongly) said to be semantically "empty." They actually contribute to the meaning of larger units such as noun phrases, prepositional phrases, and sentences. In a similar way, it is sometimes the case that the meaning of a whole phrase or sentence is larger or different than the sum of the individual meanings of words. Consider how the individual meanings of *pretty* and *stupid* combine into the phrase *pretty stupid*. The phrase does not mean an attractive but unintelligent person.

In essence, then, it would appear that traditional accounts of semantics have placed too much emphasis on the categories that supply meaning to common nouns. The story that seems to hold true for common nouns may not provide an adequate account of other kinds of words (e.g., verbs, adverbs, adjectives, question words, determiners) or larger units such as noun phrases, verb phrases, or prepositional phrases. The inadequacy of the categorical account does not mean that categories are not involved. Rather, it means that scholars need to develop accounts of other kinds of concepts besides categories that match the categorical account in their level of detail. In addition, scholars need to move beyond the level of individual words to understand how children figure out the meaning of phrases and sentences. In any event, an important aspect of semantic development is children's acquisition of categories and other kinds of concepts.

Methodological Issues in the Study of Semantics

So far, we have considered the "nature of" question primarily at a theoretical or philosophical level. Now we have to take the theoretical definitions of meaning supplied above and consider how a researcher might go about measuring children's semantic understandings and vocabulary. When scientists come up with a way to measure a theoretically defined ability, they are said to supply an *operational definition* of the ability (Mertens, 2005). To illustrate the difference between the theoretical definition of a construct and its operational definition, consider the case of intelligence. Theoretically, we might say that an intelligent person learns things quickly. If so, then operationally, we may measure the level of intelligence in people by asking them to study 80 facts and see how many times they have to study the facts before they get 100% correct on a test of these facts. Or, we might time people to see how long it takes for them to get 100% correct (e.g., 15 min vs. 30 min). Either way, we would say that the fast learners (i.e., those who mastered the facts in relatively shorter times) are more intelligent than the slower learners (i.e., those who mastered the facts in relatively longer times).

One of the keys to making an appropriate translation between a theoretical definition and an operational definition of some construct is to avoid underestimating or overestimating people's ability. When our measurement procedure does a pretty good job of tapping into a construct such as intelligence, we say that it is a *valid measure* (Mertens, 2005). When tests substantially overestimate ability or underestimate it, we say that the measure lacks validity. For example, you may have argued at one time that you have more ability than your IQ scores, achievement test scores, or SAT scores suggest. In saying that any of these tests underestimate your ability, you are questioning the test's validity.

That said, we can next consider the various ways that scientists have measured children's vocabulary to see which methods seem to have more or less validity. This issue is important because we want to be able to make statements later on in this chapter about growth in children's vocabulary. If the methods used to measure vocabulary in most studies are not very good (i.e., they lack validity), the age trends revealed in these studies are not to be believed.

One common way to measure vocabulary is called the *dictionary method* because researchers use a dictionary to sample the words that a child knows (Anglin, 1993; Bloom, 2000). For example, a researcher might ask for the definitions of 10 words that appear on each of 10 random pages in a dictionary. The researcher would then extrapolate from a child's performance on these 100 words to all of the words in the dictionary. For example, if a child could provide the correct definition for 24 of the 100 words (24%), and the dictionary contained 50,000 words, a researcher might then infer that the child knew 12,000 words (because 12,000 is 24% of 50,000).

To get a sense of the validity of this approach, try the following exercise. First, turn over this book and come up with the definition of a common word such as *dog*. Write it down or say it out loud. When finished, turn the book back over and continue reading from this point. Please try this exercise now before reading on.

Finished? Now consider the following definition of *dog* provided in the Oxford Encyclopedic English dictionary: "*n.* (1a) a domesticated flesh-eating mammal, *Canis familiaris*, usually having a long snout and nonretractile claws, and occurring in many different breeds kept as pets or for work or sport. . . ."

It would be interesting to see how many readers of this book had features such as flesh-eating mammal, the Latin species term, or nonretractile claws in their definitions. When does someone get credit for knowing a word (Anglin, 1993)? When most of the definition is provided, or only when all of the definition is provided? Also, is credit only given when a child uses "dictionary-ese" as evident in the example above?

In addition to these areas of slippage, the dictionary method could be criticized for being rather demanding because it requires (1) explicit knowledge of word meaning that has to be recalled from long-term memory, (2) knowledge of dictionary-ese, and (3) knowledge of other words that can be used within the definition (e.g., *domesticated*). Hence, some might argue that the dictionary method is so demanding that it may well underestimate children's vocabulary. Another way it might underestimate the size of a child's vocabulary is that there are many combinations of prefixes, suffixes, and stems that are not included in a dictionary (Anglin, 1993; Bloom, 2000). For example, a dictionary may contain the words *active* and *eligible* but not *inactive* and *ineligible*. Dictionaries may also not contain slang words or words that are newly entered into a culture. Thus, one has to augment the number provided using percentages of a sample of words (e.g., 24% of 100 words) with a figure that takes into account productive combinations and other words. For example, if a child was said to have 12,000 words based on the sample method, we might say that the real figure might be closer to 20,000. Note that there could be considerable errors in this extrapolation method. Different estimates also emerge when one uses abridged dictionaries versus unabridged dictionaries (Anglin, 1993).

One way to lessen the intellectual demands of the dictionary approach is to tap into children's implicit, functional knowledge of word meaning that they may not be able to express. For example, we can ask, "Does the child use the word appropriately in his or her own spontaneous utterances?" Children (and adults) can sometimes use words appropriately in sentences but not provide a very coherent definition. The ability to use dictionary-ese is a metalinguistic skill that appears later in the elementary years (Anglin, 1993). Wouldn't the ability use a word correctly be evidence that suggests that children know a word? A second way to lessen demands is by using a multiple-choice format. In addition to eliminating memory demands (because the choices are right there), the multiple-choice format also obviates the need for knowing dictionary-ese. However, it does not eliminate the need to have other words in one's vocabulary (e.g., synonyms) because these words are often listed as choices.

Whereas these two alternatives to the dictionary method seem to be better approaches, issues of validity are not completely circumvented because new problems are introduced. For example, in the case of the multiple-choice format, a person could guess the correct answer and get a higher score for the wrong reasons. In the case of spontaneous utterances, re-searchers would have to record a rather large corpus of utterances over many months to observe low-frequency words that a child occasionally uses. Moreover, a child may appear to know a word through correct usage but not really know the true meaning (Vygotsky, 1978). For example, many adults believe the word *prodigal* has something to do with returning home after realizing the errors of one's ways (from the biblical story of the prodi-gal son). In reality, however, the word means recklessly wasteful. If a per-son always uses the term to describe people who are both recklessly waste-ful and who return home, we would never know that the person had the incorrect definition.

Another approach to vocabulary estimation that is even less demand-ing than the spontaneous usage or multiple-choice approaches is exempli-fied in the Peabody Picture Vocabulary Test (PPVT). In the PPVT, a child is shown four pictures and asked questions such as, "Where is the *X*?" (e.g., banana). The child merely has to point to the correct picture rather than re-call the object label him- or herself. As such, the PPVT is said to measure *receptive vocabulary* rather than *expressive vocabulary*. The PPVT could be turned into an expressive measure if a researcher pointed to picture and asked, "What's that?" or "What's going on in this picture?" Moreover, the methodology could be made into an even easier receptive measure by seat-ing a child between two video monitors that display different scenes and asking questions such as, "Where is the *X*?" (e.g., doggy). Children get credit if they look longer at the correct monitor than the incorrect monitor (e.g., 15 total seconds vs. 5 total seconds), even if they look at both and al-ternate back an forth. As you may have guessed, the PPVT and video moni-tor approaches have been criticized for potentially overestimating children's vocabulary.

Several final ways to estimate a child's vocabulary do not even involve the child at all. Instead, researchers ask mothers to either keep a diary of all words that their children use or fill out a vocabulary checklist such as the MacArthur Communicative Development Inventories (Fenson et al., 1994). The diary method has been most often used with children between the ages of 12 months and 18 months. Children may only have 50 total words in their vocabularies by 18 months, so they may only say 2 new words per week on average. Many parents are really excited when new words emerge during this time, so they would be inclined to notice new words and write them down. But what if a parent is not especially interested or sometimes does not have paper and pencil handy when the new word emerges? New words could be missed. For similar reasons, disinterested parents might also underestimate their children's vocabularies using the checklist method. However, the opposite problem could occur, as well. Overly eager or com-petitive parents could exaggerate the number of words in their children's vocabularies using either the diary or checklist methods (Tomasello & Mervis, 1994).

In addition, as noted above, children's behavior may suggest that they know a word when they do not (Tomasello & Mervis, 1994). For example, imagine cases in which a mother always says to her daughter, "Do you want some juice?" just before a meal. The child may nod "yes" and run to her highchair. Because of this behavior, the mother may indicate on a checklist that *juice* is in her child's vocabulary. At some point, however, the mother may say, "Come on, sweetie. Let's go to the store. We are out of juice." If the child runs to her highchair, this behavior suggests that the word is a signal that she is about to be fed (much the way the whirring sound of a can opener signals to cats that a meal is coming). Most language researchers and parents can tell of similar instances. Parents who say that their children know the word *juice* in such instances are simply making honest mistakes rather than engaging in competitive exaggerations. Regardless of the source of the overestimation, we can see that diary methods and checklists are not foolproof.

Hence, all of the approaches to estimating vocabulary have validity problems. Whereas some tend to overestimate the number of words in a child's vocabulary, others tend to underestimate vocabulary size. If we are primarily interested in age changes in vocabulary size and not in absolute levels of knowledge, these validity issues may not alter our overall conclusions about age trends. For example, if parents tend to overestimate to the same extent when their children are 2 and 3 years old (e.g., they say that their children have 50% more words than they really have at each age), we can still conclude that vocabulary does increase at a certain rate. To illustrate, imagine a child who really knew 50 words at age 2 and knew 150 words at age 3. This pattern suggests that his or her vocabulary triples in size between age 2 and 3. If the child's parent says he or she knows 75 words at age 2 and 225 words at age 3 (saying that the child had 50% more words at each point than he or she really had), this exaggeration would not hinder us from accurately concluding that vocabulary size triples between age 2 and 3 (225 is three times larger than 75). However, problems of overestimation should cause us concern if we are interested in using parent reports as normative guides. If the average child really only has 50 words at 2 years, but we use a normative guide of 75 (based on parent reports), a new mother might be very concerned if her 2-year-old only had 30 words in his or her vocabulary (i.e., the discrepancy between 30 and 50 is less than between 30 and 75).

In addition, problems of validity mean that we would have to worry about studies that give two conflicting estimates of vocabulary size (e.g., one says the average is 50 words at age 2 while the other says 75) or two different rates of learning if researchers in these studies used different estimation methods (e.g., video monitors vs. checklists). We would also have to worry about comparisons between countries, cultures, socioeconomic groups, and ethnic groups. What if well-educated U.S. parents tend to exaggerate more than less-educated U.S. parents? If a difference in parent estimates arise between cultures or ethnic groups, is this difference real or a function of cross-cultural, ethnic, or socioeconomic differences in the tendencies to exaggerate or the desire to make a favorable impression on researchers?

It is a good idea to keep in mind both the theoretical and methodological issues presented in this section when you attempt to make sense of age trends in semantic development that are reported in response to the developmental trend question below.

THE RELEVANCE QUESTION:
Why Should Teachers Care about Whether Children Know the Meaning of a Large Number of Words?

Teachers should care about semantic development for three primary reasons. First, reading involves the mapping of printed words onto stored phonological and semantic representations for spoken words (see Chapter 7). The printed word *walrus*, for example, has to be mapped to the phonological word form /walrus/ in a reader's memory and also to the person's semantic knowledge of what this word means. If we could somehow take away a person's spoken vocabulary, that person would have a lot of trouble reading (there are no stored words that can be matched to printed words). To get a sense of the connection between spoken vocabulary and reading comprehension, think of a recent time when you tried to read a paragraph in which 5 to 6 words in the paragraph were not in your spoken vocabulary. When this occurs, it is difficult to comprehend the paragraph, is it not? If you are having trouble remembering such an occasion, try out this sentence: *The vituperative vixon vitiated the vapid volume of vermin.* Does this sentence make sense to you? It would not make sense to the average adult (but would make sense to adults with extensive spoken vocabularies). Beyond such anecdotal examples, the empirical evidence for the association between vocabulary and reading comprehension is very strong. In fact, the correlation between scores on a standard vocabulary measure and a standard reading comprehension measure is almost as high as the test–retest reliability for the comprehension measure (Sternberg, 1987).

Second, given the connection between spoken vocabulary and reading, it should not be surprising to learn that children who enter first grade with larger spoken vocabularies are often the ones who score the highest on reading achievement tests at the end of first grade (Snow et al., 1998). This predictive relation makes even more sense when we consider the nature of the most widely used achievement tests. Most of these tests present children with sections that measure their knowledge of 20 to 30 vocabulary words using a multiple-choice format, and also present them with 5 to 6 short paragraphs that are typically followed by four questions. Very often, one of the four questions pertains to a word found in the paragraph (e.g., "Which of the following provides the closest meaning of the word *hazardous* as it is used in line 23?"). Thus, children with poor vocabularies are destined to get 25% or more items wrong on standardized reading tests. In an era of increased accountability through testing, most teachers should be interested in improving scores by 25%.

The third reason relates back to the discussion in Chapter 4 about the connection between vocabulary and phonological processing skills. In that chapter, we learned that children need to have segmented phonological representations in order to map clusters of letters to phonemic segments (e.g., for the printed word *bat*, mapping the B to /buh/ and the -*at* to /-at/). It is widely believed that phonological representations become segmented each time a child learns a new word that is in the same lexical neighborhood as existing words (see Chapter 4). For example, an unsegmented phonological word form such as /rake/ might become segmented into /rrr + -ake/ after a child learns the new word *cake*.

For all of the above reasons, then, school systems should do what they can to make sure that most children enter first grade with large spoken vocabularies. In the following section, we get a sense of how many children do, in fact, enter school with sizable vocabularies.

THE DEVELOPMENTAL TRENDS QUESTION: How Does a Child's Spoken Vocabulary Change over Time?

There are three useful ways to describe developmental trends in vocabulary development. The first is to provide estimates of the average number of words in children's vocabularies at successive ages, and to examine age changes in the rates at which children acquire new words. The second is to describe the content of children's early vocabularies. The final way is to examine general patterns that emerge across all ages. In what follows, each of these approaches is presented in turn.

Age Changes in Vocabulary Size and Rate of Word Learning

Studies using diary methods and vocabulary checklists show that children usually produce their first words sometime around their first birthday (i.e., between 10 months and 15 months of age). By the time the average child is in first grade, however, studies using well-executed versions of the dictionary method suggest that he or she knows approximately 10,000 words (Anglin, 1993). In order for a child's vocabulary to grow from one word to 10,000 words in 6 years, the child has to learn an average of 2,000 words a year, 38 words per week, and 5 to 6 words per day! Given the arbitrary pairing between words and their referents, this amazing feat would be analogous to preschoolers learning a large number of other kinds of arbitrary pairings such as that between U.S. states and their capitals (e.g., Harrisburg and Pennsylvania). Whereas much older children learn the latter through multiple trials of effortful studying (and still sometimes do poorly on tests!), many studies suggest that young children learn words in a seemingly effortless manner through far fewer repetitions (Bloom, 2000).

In fact, some studies have shown that children can learn a word after a single brief exposure (e.g., Carey & Bartlett, 1978). For example, an experimenter might say to a child, "Let's measure the size of this toy using the koba," as she picks up an unfamiliar object and places it against the toy (Markson & Bloom, 1997). When asked a week later or a month later to identify a "koba" among an array of objects, even 3-year-olds could do so at an above-chance rate. This ability to quickly acquire words after a single exposure has been dubbed *fast mapping* by language researchers.

But children do not apparently learn all of their words in such a fast manner. Moreover, careful analysis of vocabulary growth during the preschool period suggests that the average rate of growth discussed earlier (i.e., 2,000 words every year) is a bit misleading. For example, well-designed studies using the checklist method (e.g., Fenson et al., 1994) have revealed the following about the average sizes of children's vocabulary at specific ages:

Age	Vocabulary size
12 months	1 word
16 months	50 words
24 months	300 words
30 months	575 words

As these findings show, children only learn about 300 words between ages 1 and 2 and only about 550 words between ages 2 and 3 (both far less than 2,000). Moreover, given that they only seem to have 850 words by the time they are 3 years old, that means they need to learn something like 3,000 words a year (or 3.6 words a day) for the next few years to get themselves up to 10,000 words by age 6. Hence, by dividing 10,000 by 5 years, we get the false impression that children learn 2,000 words a year in a constant manner. The more accurate description is that they learn relatively slowly for several years and then learn words very rapidly between ages 3 and 6 (Bloom, 2000; Huttenlocher, Haight, Bryk, Seltzer, & Lyons, 1991).

As remarkable as the rate of learning nearly 4 words a day seems to be, studies using the dictionary method suggest that children older than 6 learn words at an even faster rate (Anglin, 1993). For example, children seem to learn nearly 7 words per day between ages 6 and 8 and approximately 12 words a day between ages 8 and 12 (Bloom, 2000). Between age 12 and adulthood, the pace slows down for most people to a still-respectable 8 words a day. By the time students reach early adulthood, they tend to have an average of 60,000 words in their vocabularies.

What is interesting about these age trends is that there does not appear to be a specific time period in which word learning in most children suddenly increases then returns to a slower pace (Bloom, 2000). The apparent absence of this short-term, rapid burst of word learning is puzzling given that many previous reviews of child language studies describe a *word spurt* that is alleged to occur right after children reach the milestone of 50 words, at around 18 months of age (e.g., Hoff, 2001; McCarthy, 1954; Nelson, 1973; Vygotsky, 1978; Walley, 1993). The existence of word spurts also is assumed in a number of empirical articles (e.g., Mervis & Bertrand, 1995; Reznick & Goldfield, 1992). In these studies, a spurt is said to occur when children learn 10 to 12 new words in a 2- to 3-week period (i.e., a new word every other day). Whereas this rate of word learning is impressive, it is far less than what occurs after age 3 when things really pick up (i.e., 4 or more words a day). Given the recent findings from large-scale, normative studies, it seems better to say that the spurt actually occurs well after the 50-word mark and continues for some time (e.g., 3 to 12 years of age). In addition, it is clearly possible that longitudinal studies of individual children would probably reveal patterns in which periodic spurts of rapid word learning are followed by periods in which few words are learned. However, it is also the case that these spurts would probably be found at many ages besides 18 months. Moreover, it is likely (and has been found) that children would differ as to when these bursts occur (Bloom, 2000). In essence, word spurts may well occur, but they do not appear to be restricted to the period right after child have 50 words in their vocabularies.

So far, we have described the course of vocabulary development for the average child. Studies have found, however, that same-aged children can differ considerably in terms of the size of their vocabularies and in the rate at which they acquire new words. To illustrate, consider the findings of Fenson et al. (1994) who subdivided their sample into percentiles. Those at the 90th percentile had larger vocabularies than 90% of all other children in the sample. Hence, they were among the top 10% for vocabulary size. Similarly, those at the median had larger vocabularies than 50% of children in the sample, and those at the 10th percentile were among the bottom

10% for vocabulary size. Fenson et al. found that whereas the bottom 10% had no words at 12 months, those at the median had 6 words, and those at the 90th percentile had around 30 words. By 30 months, these figures were approximately 250 words (bottom 10%), 575 words (median), and 660 words (top 10%). Thus, the top 10% are clearly learning words at a faster rate than those in the bottom 10% given the fact that the former had more than double the number of words than the latter when they were both 30 months old. Another way that this faster rate of learning becomes evident is when we compare the age at which children reach a particular milestone, such as having 250 words in their vocabularies. Whereas the top 10% had 250 words in their vocabularies when they were only 16 months old, the bottom 10% did not reach this milestone until they were 30 months old.

These extreme differences among same-aged individuals are also found in older children and adults. For example, whereas the average adult has 60,000 words in his or her vocabulary, those who read extensively and engage in other activities that expose them to new words may have closer to 120,000 words in their vocabularies (Bloom, 2000).

The Content of Children's Early Vocabularies

A number of studies using the diary method and checklist method have examined the kinds of words that comprise children's first 50 words. In a landmark longitudinal study of 18 children using the diary method, Nelson (1973) found that children's first words could be grouped into six categories:

1. *Specific nominals*: which are names for specific people (e.g., *Mommy, Daddy, Poppy*) or specific things (e.g., pet names such as *Tippy* and *Bootsie*; names of favorite stuffed animals such as *Woody* and *Fluffy*).
2. *General nominals*: which either refer to categories of things rather than individuals (e.g., *doggy, kitty, ball, bottle, milk*), or are generic terms such as *he* or *that*.
3. *Action words*: which are used as part of requests such as *go, up,* and *look*.
4. *Modifiers*: such as *big, mine,* and *all-gone*.
5. *Personal social words*: such as *no* and *please*.
6. *Grammatical function words*: such as *what* and *for*.

However, children's words were not evenly distributed throughout these categories in Nelson's study. Whereas the two nominal categories comprised over 70% of the first 50 words produced (general nominals, 60%;

specific nominals, 10%), each of the remaining four categories accounted for only 8–15% of the total.

Other researchers have found similar results, even when they used different methodologies. For example, Fenson et al. (1994) analyzed the early vocabularies of a larger sample of children (N = 161) using the checklist method and found that the first words of 22-month-olds tended to fall into the following categories:

1. Nouns (63%) such as *dog, ball, baby,* and *book.*
2. Verbs (9%) such as *sit* and *go.*
3. People's names (5%) such as *Mommy* and *Daddy.*
4. Games and routines (7%) such as *bath, bye-bye,* and *patty-cake.*
5. Adjectives (4%) such as *cold, pretty,* and *wet.*
6. Sound effects (6%) such as *uh oh* and *moo.*
7. Other (5%).

When these and related studies of children from middle-income households in the United States were examined for common patterns, it became clear that there was a preponderance of nouns and other nominals in children's first words. This apparent "noun bias" was largely taken for granted and unquestioned for 20 years until researchers started conducting studies in other countries. Interestingly, studies conducted in Asian countries such as Japan, China, and Korea have found no evidence of a noun bias (Gopnik & Choi, 1995; Tardif, 1996). In addition, however, even early studies of U.S. children suggest that children differ in terms of their tendency to exhibit a noun bias. Whereas some children clearly do have a preponderance of nouns in their early vocabularies, other children have a preponderance of words that comprise social interactions, games, and routines (e.g., *bye-bye, peek-a-boo, thank you*). Nelson (1973) called the former orientation a *referential style* of communication and called the latter an *expressive style.* Pinker (1994) called children who adopt the latter style "schmoozers."

Some Additional General Age Trends

There are several other notable changes in children's vocabularies that occur over time. To understand the first of these general trends, we need to probe a little deeper into the question of when children can be said to "know" a word. The fast mapping studies and checklist studies described above merely suggest that children sometimes use a word or can pick out an appropriate referent for a word. This does not mean that children have the full meanings of words that adults might have (Bloom, 2000; Nelson, 1996; Vygotsky, 1978). For example, a young child in a typical middle-income household might be able to point to the monitor of a personal computer when asked, "Where's the monitor?" but have very little conceptual sense of what a monitor is and also not know other meanings of the word *monitor* (e.g., a hall monitor in a high school, a nurse monitoring a patient's blood pressure). Thus, the initial mapping between a word form and a concept might be superficial and based on a single dimension (e.g., what an object looks like). As children learn more about the world and observe others using a word in new ways, these initial semantic understandings become expanded. For example, they might hear a soccer coach use the word *dribbling* to refer to the action of tapping the ball forward with one's foot but then later hear a basketball coach use the same word to refer to an entirely different action involving one's hands. Relatedly, most adults do not know that a worm is a kind of animal (Carey, 1985). If they were to consult a dictionary for the definition of *animal*, however, they would see that a worm fits that definition and would presumably expand the meaning of this word in their own minds.

As children fine-tune their understandings of existing words in their vocabularies, they can be found to make various kinds of systematic but sensible errors. For example, children may define the word *dog* as anything that roughly looks like a dog (including cats, horses, otters, and so on). As a result, they apply the label to too many things. When they do, they are said to make an *overextension* error (Hoff, 2001). Sometimes, however, children may apply labels to too few things. For example, they might resist calling a Chihuahua a dog, or only use the word *car* when looking at cars parked beneath their apartment windows (Bloom, 2000). As noted above, adults can sometimes apply a word to too few things, as well (e.g., not apply *animal* to worms). When children or adults apply labels to too few things, they are said to make *underextension* errors. Studies have shown that the frequency of over- and underextensions in spontaneous speech is highest early on, when children have fewer words in their vocabularies. Related work has shown that (1) children's definitions of various basic-level categories (see prototype theory above) do not always overlap with the basic-level categories of adults (Mervis, 1987), and (2) children's and adults' everyday understandings of words such as *force, temperature*, and *conditioning*, do not always overlap with the scientific meanings of these words (Vygotsky, 1978). Over time, these differences usually become worked out.

The second general trend besides the fact that children increasingly add to, and refine, their understandings is that children's conceptual knowledge and semantic memory gets increasingly integrated and interconnected with development (Pan & Berko Gleason, 2001). Early in the preschool period, for example, children primarily seem to organize their knowledge into separate basic-level categories (e.g., "dogs" vs. "cats"). Later in the preschool period, children begin to show evidence that they organize their knowledge into hierarchies in which several basic-level categories are linked through superordinate categories (e.g., Mervis & Crisafi, 1982). The presence of superordinate categories and superordinate labels becomes increasingly common during the elementary school years (Anglin, 1993; Callanan, 1991).

A superordinate category is more abstract than a basic-level category, so we might say that there is also a trend toward increasingly abstract word meanings with age, as well (Anglin, 1993). Other evidence for this concrete-to-abstract shift comes from studies of the words children know on intelligence tests (Feifel & Lorge, 1950), studies of kinship terms such as *uncle* (Keil, 1989), and studies that show a shift from the use of functional properties (e.g., a shovel is something you dig with) or characteristic properties (e.g., has gray hair in the case of grandparents) in word meanings to the use of more superordinate properties (e.g., a shovel is a gardening tool) and defining properties (e.g., a grandparent is a parent of my parents).

Studies using brain-imaging technologies and studies of brain-injured adults show several other interesting facts about semantic knowledge (Saffran, 2003). First, people's knowledge of living things (e.g., animals) is stored in a different area of the brain than their knowledge of artifacts (e.g., tools). Relatedly, knowledge of concrete objects seems to be stored in a different area than their knowledge of abstract concepts. Finally, knowledge of numbers and number words seem to be stored in areas other than those associated with living things, artifacts, concrete objects, or abstract concepts. Thus, semantic knowledge is widely distributed in the brain.

THE DEVELOPMENTAL MECHANISMS QUESTION:
What Factors Promote Changes in Children's Spoken Vocabulary?

A number of different age trends were reported in the previous section. For expository purposes, it is helpful to subdivide the general "developmental mechanisms" question about why these age trends occur into six more specific questions: (1) Why do children's first words appear around 12 months? (2) Why does the rate of word learning speed up after age 3 and then slow down after age 12? (3) Why are there such large individual differences in the size of children's and adults' vocabularies at different ages? (4) Why is there a preponderance of nominals in the first words of many middle-income U.S. children but not in the first words of middle-income children from several Asian countries? (5) Why do some children adopt a referential communicational style while others adopt a more expressive style? (6) Why do word meanings become progressively more elaborated, abstract, and integrated with age? Before answering each of these questions, in turn, in the present section, we need to first provide an answer to a preliminary question that has puzzled many philosophers, linguists, and developmental psychologists: Why do children learn *any* words at all? As will be come clear, answers to this preliminary question highlight important skills that children need to have. Discussion of this initial question also helps us understand the popularity of certain topics in the literature on semantic development.

Why Do Children Learn Any Words at All?

Children seem to learn spoken language skills so readily that many people mistakenly believe, at first, that it is relatively straightforward for children to learn a language. For example, it is often assumed that all one has to do is show an object to children and provide a label for it. Children then commit the label to memory. No problem, right?

However, philosophers have shown through careful argumentation that such a simplistic conception of language acquisition could not be correct (Bloom, 2000). Some of the problems include the fact that (1) children can learn words even when there is not a strict spatial and temporal cooccurrence between the utterance of a word and an object being present; (2) parents in the United States have been found to label objects but not label actions in the same way (so how do children learn verbs?); (3) children do not need a full complement of sensory abilities to learn words (e.g., consider the case of Helen Keller); (4) children do not need explicit feedback from parents or teachers to learn words; and (5) children do not need ostensive naming to learn labels for objects (Bloom, 2000; Nelson & Kessler, 2002). But, as we shall see, the argument fails to take into account the fact that children may not know at first what it means to label an object.

Whereas the average person would probably not be adversely affected if he or she held misconceptions about the nature of word learning, teachers might be, especially if their beliefs cause them to espouse an instructional program that gets its inspiration from a simplistic or faulty account of language learning. Hence, before we delve into issues regarding developmental mechanisms for specific age trends, we need to first clarify what really is involved when children learn language. Following the lead of philosophers, we will make the key points using several informative analogies.

The first analogy involves a hypothetical English-speaking male adult who travels to another country such as Germany. As he arrives at the Berlin airport, he observes a pair of German citizens making alternating vocal sounds as they face each other. If our traveler were asked, "What are those people doing?" he is likely to say, "They are having a conversation, but I'm not sure what they are talking about. I don't speak German."

This English-speaking tourist obviously knows what a conversation looks like because he has had many conversations himself. In a related way, adults can use their existing knowledge and experiences to recognize other categories of behavior, as well. For example, U.S. adults might be a little confused the first time they observe people playing Irish hurling, Australian football, or jai alai. And yet, it would not take them long to realize that the participants are playing some kind of sport.

In contrast to such cases in which adults are able to discern the general category of behavior that they are observing, there are times when behaviors cannot be readily categorized or judged to be familiar. Generally speaking, such experiences occur when adults observe behaviors that they have never engaged in or seen before. For example, some U.S. adults are unfamiliar with the ancient martial art called t'ai chi that a growing number of people practice in order to work out in a low-impact, meditative way. Certain movements look as if the participant is engaged in a slow, graceful interpretive dance. Other movements suggest that the participant is defending him- or herself in slow motion against an imaginary opponent. If U.S. adults unfamiliar with t'ai chi saw someone practicing it in the middle of a park as they jogged by, these adults might say to themselves, "What in the world is that person doing?"

Philosophers have appropriately pointed out that we do not know what preverbal infants think the first few times these infants observe two adults having a conversation. Do they already know that adults are trying to communicate with each other (as our English-speaking tourist immediately recognized), or is the situation more akin to the t'ai chi example above? If infants immediately or very quickly recognize that the adults are having a conversation, that means the infants already know what a conversation is before they see it. If so, that must mean that the idea of communicative acts is innate. In contrast, if it takes some time for infants to figure out what is going on, such a finding suggests the idea of communication may not be innate (in the way that this term is ordinarily conceived).

But philosophers have not invoked innate ideas simply because of the speed with which infants come to interpret vocal behavior as communication. Their belief in innate ideas also derives from the argument that language learning is a form of induction (Quine, 1960). In contrast to deductive inferences that are logically certain, inductive inferences are probabilistic guesses and extrapolations from specific cases (Byrnes, 2003a). As such, inductive inferences can often be right, but they also can be wrong. An example would be a child inferring that all men hate to shop simply because the child's own father hates to shop.

To understand the connection between induction and language learning, consider again the situation in which an infant observes two people having a conversation for the first time and tries to figure out what they are doing. Just as adults make hypotheses about the behaviors of others (e.g., "I'm not sure what these people are doing, but it seems to be a sport of some kind"), infants are alleged to engage in something analogous to hypothesis-testing, as well. Hypothesis generation is a form of induction because any hypothesis generated is just a probabilistic guess that could be wrong. When two people face each other and make alternating sounds, for example, one hypothesis that fits this situation is that the two individuals are communicating. However, there are many other hypotheses that could be generated, as well. As we saw in Chapter 4, for example, infants love to experiment with sounds (e.g., make raspberries) and seem to have little interest in communicating when they are simply experimenting and amusing themselves. What is to stop an infant from hypothesizing that the adults are experimenting with sounds and playing a game similar to peek-a-boo with each other? Moreover, what infants cannot see or "read" from the situation is that one person is "sending" ideas to another. Sounds are just the medium for the invisible communication of ideas.

If many hypotheses fit the situation and there is nothing in the situation that tells an infant that communication is going on, why, then, do infants eventually hit upon this hypothesis and start communicating themselves? Some scholars argue that the only possible explanation for this outcome is that the idea of communication is innate.

To illustrate this line of reasoning further using a second analogy, we can examine a famous and influential example offered by the philosopher Willard Quine (1960). Quine asks us to imagine ourselves on an exotic and unfamiliar tropical island where we do not speak the language of the people who live there. As we are standing outside of a hut next to a man who speaks the language, we see the man shout "Gavagai!" as he extends his arm and one finger in the direction of a rabbit that is scampering by. What would we make of this behavior? Once again, we could generate a number of hypotheses. For example, it is possible that the man just experienced a gripping abdominal pain or was prone to making random sounds. It need not be assumed that the man was engaged in an act of communication. Quine thinks that it is very telling that adults naturally assume that the behavior is an act of communication (as opposed to something else). He also thinks that it is telling that most adults assume that the man was referring to the rabbit that scampered by (e.g., that *Gavagai* is the local term for rabbit). Once again, though, there are a large number of other hypotheses that could also fit the situation. For example, the man could have been saying the equivalent of "Look at those beautiful flowers over there!" (that happen to be behind the rabbit) or "Look at those long ears!" or just about anything else. The fact that (1) there are a large number of possible hypotheses and (2) not enough information in the situation to help decide among these possibilities, means that such situations represent a real interpretive problem for the observer. Quine dubbed this dilemma the *induction problem*.

How do people solve this problem? Quine (1960) argues that they use their existing knowledge and make certain assumptions to constrain the possibilities. But the main reason he developed this analogy was because he felt that it aptly characterized the task facing young infants who are trying to learn language. How do infants know that their parents are labeling an object when their parents pick up an object and make a sound? Sometimes parents pick up objects (e.g., a stuffed animal) and make sounds such as "Bow wow!" or "Ta-dah!" Parents are not labeling in such instances. Besides, where did children even get the idea of labels that they could insert into their hypotheses? Furthermore, how do infants know that the label applies to the whole object and not to its parts or the substance it is made of? For example, if a parent says, "Look at this cute doggy!" why would an infant assume that *doggy* refers to the whole dog and not his ears or fur?

In the 1970s and 1980s, Quine's arguments influenced a number of child language researchers. These researchers concluded that the only way for infants to decide on correct language-related hypotheses as quickly as they do (e.g., that parental behaviors are acts of labeling and that labels apply to whole objects) is if there were inborn constraints that guide the selection of hypotheses. For example, one such constraint was called the principle of conventionality (Clark, 1991). Here, infants are said to assume (without being directly told) that there is a community of speakers who all agree on the labels that are applied to objects, actions, and so on (e.g., that a dog shall be called *dog* and not something else). Another constraint is represented by the principle of *contrast* in which infants assume that the same label cannot be applied to objects from different categories and that each word form has its own meaning (Clark, 1991). Hence, when they hear a new word for the first time (e.g., *giraffe*), they assume that it cannot be applied to objects that they already have labels for (e.g., dogs). According to the *taxonomic assumption*, children make the inductive inference that common nouns refer to any instance of a category of objects, not just those they saw labeled as such (Markman, 1991). For example, children who hear someone apply the label *dog* to their own dog often assume the label applies to other dogs, as well (e.g., her neighbor's dog). According to the *whole object assumption* (Markman, 1991), labels refer to entire objects rather than parts of objects or the substance that the object is made of. (This assumption played a central role in *Gavagai* example above.)

To see if, in fact, children utilize these assumptions to constrain the possible meanings of words, researchers engaged in a variety of experiments. In most of these experiments, researchers usually set up contrasts between two possible interpretations or inferences. For example, researchers might place a familiar object (e.g., a spoon) and an unfamiliar object (e.g., a garlic press) in front of a child (Bloom, 2000). Before starting, re-searchers check to make sure that the objects are familiar and unfamiliar, respectively, and that the child knows the label of the familiar object. Next, the experimenter says, "Can you handle me the *fendle*?" Children as young as 3 readily hand the garlic press to the experimenter. In doing so, they are said to make use of the principle of contrast (or a related assumption called the *novel-name-nameless-category assumption*; see Golinkoff, Mervis, & Hirsh-Pasek, 1994).

Whereas such experiments generated quite a lot of findings that seemed to indicate that young children do rely on constraints to learn the meaning of new words, the idea of innate constraints has been criticized on a number of grounds (e.g., Nelson, 1988; Kuczaj, 1990). Some scholars, for example, have argued that it is possible to provide equally sensible ac-counts of children's behaviors that do not involve the idea of innate con-straints. Others, however, have taken issue with the suggestion that chil-dren are born with assumptions that are specific to word learning. Bloom (2000) showed how the reasoning used in situations similar to the *Gavagai* and *fendle* examples could be applied to a whole range of situations that do not involve word learning. Still others have conducted experiments show-ing how young children will violate various word-learning constraints. Over time, such criticisms and empirical problems have led to a decreased emphasis on innate constraints such as the whole-object assumption in studies of language development.

Waning interest in constraints, however, does not mean that debates about their existence were futile or that experiments which attempted to demonstrate their usage were conducted in vain. Quite the contrary. These debates and studies made it clear that language learning would never take place if infants and young children did not have the capacity to attribute in-tentions, beliefs, and desires to other people (Bloom, 2000). In other words, infants are still assumed to struggle with the issue of how to interpret the vocal behaviors of others around them, but many scholars question the need to posit language-specific constraints. Instead, it is assumed that in-fants figure out the "language game" by making use of a capacity that is common to all human beings who do not have a disability: their naïve psy-chology or *theory of mind* (Gopnik & Wellman, 1992). For example, in-fants are said to utilize their theories of mind (TOMs) when they realize that there is a community of speakers who agree upon the conventional la-bels for objects.

As we discuss in the last section of this chapter, one way to test the proposal that a TOM is necessary for word learning is to determine the level of language skill evident in individuals who lack a highly developed TOM or in other species that have less-developed TOMs than in the human species (e.g., other primates). It is very interesting that the human species is the only species that has both a highly developed TOM and also the sophisticated language skills that are described in this book. Apes, in contrast, have a fairly rudimentary TOM and develop very modest levels of language skill even in the best of circumstances (e.g., a 300-word sign language vocabulary). The correlation between their TOMs and language is probably not coincidental. Relatedly, there are certain disorders in humans in which TOM is selectively impaired (e.g., autism; see the last section of this chapter). Individuals with autism vary in their level of TOM and in their language. Whereas individuals with autism who are high functioning have both highly developed TOMs and fairly good language skills, individuals who have severe deficits in TOM also tend to be considerably delayed in their language skills. Once again, this correlation between TOM and language skills is probably not coincidental.

Thus, infants learn words because they want to communicate and because they slowly recognize that they can accomplish their goals (e.g., get fed, get a toy out of reach) using language to serve these ends. They further assume that other people have goals and beliefs in their minds, too, thanks to their TOMs. This insight allows infants to progressively understand the communicative intents of others. For example, imagine the case of an infant who has a penchant for touching an electrical outlet. If that infant's parent repeatedly says, "No!" and grabs the infant's arm before the infant touches the outlet, the infant may eventually get the idea that the parent has a desire or goal to stop the behavior and says "No!" as a means to this end.

But a TOM merely helps a child see that a speaker has communicative goals, beliefs, and desires. It does not provide enough information as to the precise mapping between particular words and particular concepts (Bloom, 2000). In the next few subsections of this chapter, we show that establishing the proper mapping between words and their referents requires other cognitive abilities besides a TOM. It is for this reason that a TOM is thought to be a necessary but not sufficient condition for vocabulary development.

Having considered the fundamental issue of why children learn even a single word, we can now turn our attention to the more specific questions that were listed at the beginning of this section on developmental mechanisms. Answers to each question highlight factors that explain why semantic skills change as they do.

Why Do Children's First Words Appear at Around 12 Months of Age?

Given the preceding discussion of TOM, it seems reasonable to hypothesize that the emergence of children's first words probably has something to do with changes that occur in infants' tendency to attribute beliefs, goals, and desires to others. In support of this hypothesis, studies have revealed changes in infants' tendency to follow the gaze of parents (indicating their appreciation for the link between attention and gazes) that occur in the latter part of their first year. Studies have also shown comparable increases in infants' understanding of intended actions that also occur right around their first birthday (Bloom, 2000; Carpenter et al., 1998; Meltzoff, 1995; Moore & Corkum, 1994). These changes are paralleled by significant advances in children's own ability to combine several actions together to accomplish certain goals (Piaget, 1952). This ability is called *means–end reasoning*. Thus, there may be a convergence of infants' own goal-directedness and their understanding of the goal-directedness of others. This analysis suggests that interventions designed to enhance vocabulary skills need to focus on goals and intentions. For example, children may be especially inclined to learn words if these words help them accomplish particular goals or are presented as they are in the midst of pursuing goals. Note how, anecdotally, many people argue that the best way to learn a language such as French is to spend time (e.g., a few months or a year) in a country where people speak French. People who learn languages through conjugation exercises are not learning words for communicative reasons and rarely retain what they have learned over time.

A second possible explanation for the emergence of first words at around 12 months derives from Vygotsky's (1978) claim that parents impose communicative meanings on children's early gestures and sounds. Children have no idea, at first, that their vocalizations and behaviors have any significance. To illustrate, Vygotsky used the example of pointing. Vygotsky correctly noted that infants try to accomplish their own goals (e.g., grabbing an object themselves) before they try to use parents as intermediaries (e.g., asking parents to get an object for them). Vygotsky believed that when infants extend their arms to reach for an object themselves, parents sometimes interpret this behavior as a point rather than as a grab. Children may soon learn that every time they extend their arms to get an object, the parent seems to respond to this behavior by getting the object. Over time, children are thought to slowly understand that pointing and reaching can be used as a signal or sign of desires (e.g., I want that) to others. Infants may not understand at first why parents seem to be able to read their minds, but they nevertheless exploit this situation to have their goals accomplished through pointing.

It has been found that pointing precedes first words in development (Bates, 1976), so perhaps infants generalize their problem-solving strategies from points to words as a means of accomplishing their goals. Note that for Vygotsky, children would never learn language if they did not have adults impose cultural meanings on their behaviors that really are not intended to be meaningful to others. This does not mean, of course, that the child is irrelevant in this process. It is the child's responsibility to slowly internalize and figure out the cultural meanings of gestures and vocalizations. Once again, their TOMs may be used to make sense of the behaviors they evoke from others with their gestures and vocalizations. But this analysis also suggests that teachers need to use words in ways that highlight the embeddedness of word meaning in the larger culture (how the word is normally used, in what kinds of contexts, its connotations, etc.).

A third possible explanation of the emergence of first words at around 12 months was discussed in Chapter 4: Between the ages of 9 and 12 months, children start to use frequency and phonotactic information in the sounds of their native language to parse utterances down into individual words (Jusczyk, 1997). In other words, they start to be able to hear individual words in multiword utterances just before they start using words themselves. This parsing skill is extremely useful considering the fact that parents typically do not yell out single labels such as *Gavagai!* when they talk about objects with children (Bloom, 2000). Instead, they might say, "Look at that doggy. Isn't it cute?" on one occasion, and "Here comes Grandma's doggy!" on another occasion. Hence, the label *doggy* is embedded in larger utterances. Note that this ability to rely on phonotactics to parse utterances is largely a function of children's exposure to their own language (see Chapter 4). Phonotactics derive from the particular correlations among sounds that occur in one's own language (e.g., *buh* often occurs before *ah* or *ih* but not before *puh*). Hence, take away exposure, and infants would not internalize these correlations or be able to parse utterances into individual words.

However, as noted in Chapter 4, infants develop both receptive and productive phonological skills during their first year of life. First words at 12 months are comprised of the sounds infants make when they babble between 6 and 12 months. Thus, it makes sense that children would not produce words until they master production of the component sounds in words. However, this explanation is somewhat less compelling than the other three above because there is still a lag of several months between children's ability to produce sounds that appear in early words and their tendency to use words to communicate. Relatedly, there are other animal species that have the vocal apparatus necessary to produce words (e.g., parrots, certain primates) but nevertheless fail to develop the language skills of humans. Thus, it may be best to think of productive phonological skills as being a necessary but not sufficient condition for producing one's first words (similar to the way both TOM and receptive skills are necessary but not sufficient conditions).

One further necessary change (that may be the most important) pertains to the point made earlier in this chapter that word meaning derives from the mapping between phonological word forms and children's conceptual knowledge. Children cannot engage in this mapping process if they have not yet developed the concepts to which words refer. Studies with young infants show that they have surprising insight into basic-level categories of objects and also certain physical properties of objects (Quinn, 2006; Spelke & Newport, 1998; Younger & Cohen, 1986). Moreover, they seem to be able to form mental representations of correlated features in both real objects and made-up experimental objects (e.g., body type X goes with leg type Y and skin covering Z). Further, infants seem to track the identities of objects over time (even when the objects disappear or are partially occluded). Thus, they typically develop enough conceptual knowledge of objects, properties, and actions by 12 months that they could map phonological word forms onto some of these concepts.

In sum, then, first words are preceded by relevant changes in infants' (1) TOM, (2) receptive phonological skills, (3) productive phonological skills, and (4) conceptual knowledge. Once these changes take place, children have the tools they need to use words to achieve their communicative goals and understand the vocalizations of others. The question remains, however, as to why these antecedent factors change when they do and why children in a wide variety of circumstances and cultures utter their first words around age 1. Some would argue that the regularity with which first words appear at 12 months strongly supports the claim that language skills are innate. One version of this innateness thesis is that all of the age changes that occur between the ages of 6 months and 12 months reflect brain maturation. Once the brain matures to a certain point, all of these skills "come online."

Alternatively, it might be argued that brain maturation is yet one more necessary but not sufficient condition for the emergence of first words. Advocates of the latter perspective point out the indispensable role of exposure to ambient sounds in one's native language, and to the indispensable role of parents in providing cultural meaning to infants' gestures and vocalizations. Take these environmental factors away, and a child with a neurologically mature brain would never acquire a language. However, maturation could play a role in constraining the relative efficacy of inputs and the efficiency with which input is processed. Thus, the compromise position is that there are five factors that conspire together to determine the emergence of first words at 12 months: (1) TOM, (2) receptive phonological skills, (3) productive phonological skills, (4) conceptual knowledge, and (5) brain maturation.

Discussion Topic: A 16-month-old boy has not yet uttered his first word. Take the five possible developmental mechanisms for first words and use them to create hypotheses as to why this child is somewhat delayed (e.g., he may have an underdeveloped TOM because . . . , he may have underdeveloped receptive phonological skills because. . .). Then, create an instructional intervention that would foster word usage in this child.

Why Does the Rate of Word Learning Speed Up after 30 Months and Then Slow Down after Age 12?

There are several things that are true of 3-year-olds that are not true of 1- and 2-year-olds. The first is that 3-year-olds have more knowledge of grammatical constructions than younger children have (Bloom, 2000; see Chapter 6). They can use this knowledge to help them figure out the meaning of words (Brown, 1958). For example, if children in an experiment were shown an unusual-looking stuffed animal and told, "This is Blurpie. He likes to eat chocolate worms," children older than 2 usually assume that *Blurpie* is a proper name, not a name for a category of things. In contrast, if children were told, "This is a Blurpie. Blurpies like to eat chocolate worms," children assume that *Blurpie* is not a proper name, it is the label of a category of things called *Blurpies*. The primary difference between the two descriptions is the presence of the determiner "a" that precedes the name in the second grammatical construction. This determiner is a syntactic signal that the term is a common noun rather than a proper name.

To show whether children can use such cues to draw appropriate inferences, experimenters have presented children with three objects: (1) a stuffed animal that looks exactly like the animal they saw, (2) another that is similar but has a different color, and (3) a distractor object. Children who think *Blurpie* is a proper name only select the identical toy when asked, "Which one is Blurpie?" In contrast, children who think that *Blurpie* is the name of the category will select either of the two similar looking toys (e.g., Gelman & Taylor, 1984; Katz, Baker, & McNamara, 1974; McNamara, 1982). This ability to use syntax to help learn words is evident in even 3-year-olds.

Second, there are a number of conceptual changes that have been observed in children that occur between the ages of 2 and 3, and then again between the ages of 3 and 4. These conceptual advances could be a driving force behind the rapid increases in vocabulary that occur right around the same time. Between the ages of 2 and 3, children show substantial, qualitative changes in their understanding of symbols (DeLoache, Miller, & Pierroutsakos, 1998). Between the ages of 3 and 4, a similar qualitative change has been found in a wide range of abilities. The pervasiveness of this finding across abilities and content areas has prompted some to argue in favor of a generalized "3-to-4" shift in thinking skills (e.g., Acredolo, 1992). One of these changes occurs in children's performance on a popular measure of TOM called the *false belief task* (Wimmer & Perner, 1983). In this task, dolls representing a child and the child's mother are used in conjunction with a doll-sized kitchen. The experimenter creates a scenario in which the child doll places a piece of candy in a drawer of the kitchen. After the child doll leaves the room, the mother doll is brought in and puts the candy in another location (e.g., a cabinet). Then, the mother doll is removed and the child doll is brought back in. When asked, "Where will the child look for the candy?" 3-year-olds are more likely to wrongly say its new location (the cabinet). Four- and 5-year-olds, in contrast, are more likely to say the original location because they are better able to keep in mind the inferred mental state of the child doll. This increase in the ability to understand changes in mental states is often accompanied by increases in the use of mental state terms such as *think* and *know* during the preschool period.

Third, it is also generally the case that people learn more efficiently and effectively when they are highly knowledgeable (Ericsson, 1996). There are a number of studies comparing novices and experts, for example, that show how experts can encode larger segments of a situation than novices. For example, when novices and experts in chess are shown a chessboard with pieces arranged in a certain way and then asked to reconstruct the arrangement of the pieces after the pieces are taken off the board, novices can only correctly replace a few pieces. Experts, in contrast, can replace the vast majority of the pieces. Both groups see the same situation, but experts can encode more of it in memory. Since vocabulary increases with age, older children have more vocabulary expertise than younger children. Hence, it is to be expected that older children would assimilate more words than younger children even when both are exposed to the same number of words in particular situations. To illustrate, imagine the case in which a younger child with a vocabulary size of 200 words and an older child with a vocabulary size of 600 words were each exposed to 6 new vocabulary words in a given day (e.g., during a trip to the zoo). Expertise theory suggests that the younger child would retain fewer of these words (e.g., 2 or 3) than the older child (e.g., 5 or 6). Thus, knowledge tends to "snowball" over time, leading to a faster rate of learning with age.

Fourth, children are more likely to be read to and to read themselves after the age of 3. In the older grades, much of what children learn from school they get from textbooks and fiction written for children. Moreover, it is common for 3-year-olds from middle-income households to spend about 3 half-days in school a week. Five-year-olds, in contrast, typically spend either 5 full days or 5 half-days in school. After first grade, children spend 5 full days in school. This greater amount of time spent reading and learning in school surely relates to increases in children's vocabulary (McKeown & Curtis, 1987).

Finally, as to why the rate of word learning slows down after age 12, Bloom (2000, p. 47) argues that "The reason the rate slows down . . . is that adults have learned all of the words the immediate environment has to offer. Unless we learn a new language, our only opportunities for word learning are proper names, archaic or technical terms, or new words that enter the language."

> *Discussion Topic*: Children from middle-income households show sharper increases in their vocabulary between the ages of 3 and 6 than children from lower-income households. Use the developmental mechanisms for the increases in vocabulary growth (i.e., syntax skills, conceptual-knowledge growth, expertise, reading, and time in school) to explain why this might be the case. Then, design an intervention using these mechanisms to reduce the size of the gap between children from middle-income and lower-income households.

Why Are There Such Large Individual Differences in the Size of Children's and Adults' Vocabularies at Different Ages?

At a basic level, there have to be two categories of explanatory factors to account for individual differences in vocabulary size: (1) characteristics of the environment and (2) characteristics of the child. The most likely environmental cause of individual differences in vocabulary size is differences in the level of exposure to words. Studies have shown, in fact, that whereas children with large vocabularies come from homes in which their parents speak to them a great deal, children with smaller vocabularies come from homes in which the opposite is true (Hart & Risley, 1995; Huttenlocher et al., 1991; Tomasello, Mannle, & Kruger, 1986). But simply talking to a child would not be expected to have much of an effect if parents merely repeated the same, small set of words over and over. Vocabulary growth should only occur if parents introduce new words all of the time. Indirect support for this expectation comes from studies that show how vocabulary growth is associated with the size of a parent's vocabulary and also with parents' level of education (Fenson et al., 1994; Hart & Risley, 1995; Scarr & Weinberg, 1978). Thus, the quality of interactions may matter as much or more than quantity of interactions.

Additional evidence of qualitative effects comes from studies of differences in parental styles of communication. The key finding is that certain styles are associated with more growth than other styles. For example, some studies suggest that parents need to ask a lot of questions in addition to providing elaborative descriptions of situations in order to promote vocabulary growth in their children (Whitehurst, Arnold, Epstein, Angell, Smith, & Fischel, 1994; Hart & Risley, 1995). In addition, there are many things that could be pointed out to a child in a learning situation (e.g., at a museum, while reading a book). Some of these things are more central to the meaning of a word than others. Educated parents not only talk to their children a great deal, they also ask a lot of questions and point out highly relevant things (Hart & Risley, 1995).

And yet, all of the studies that link exposure variables to vocabulary growth also show that exposure variables seem to be less important than characteristics of the child (e.g., Huttenlocher et al., 1991). Parents merely provide the opportunity to learn new words; children have to be willing and able to take advantage of these opportunities. The "willing" part of this propensity to take advantage of opportunities refers to a child's motivation. Children are particularly likely to learn words if these words (1) refer to things that children care about and (2) are related to goals that children are trying to accomplish (Bloom & Tinker, 2001). For example, some infants seem to be particularly interested in social relationships. They get excited when parents, siblings, and grandparents interact with them. Other children may be more interested in playthings (e.g., balls) or pets than other people. The motivational account suggests that if children in these two groups were all exposed to words such as *Mommy, Poppy, ball,* and *Rover,* children in the first group would learn *Mommy* and *Poppy* while children in the second group would learn *ball* and *Rover.*

By implication, the motivational account could be used to explain individual differences in the rate of word learning, as well. Note that any vocabulary measure has test words that pertain to topics that may or may not be of interest to a child. It is possible that children in the top 10% for vocabulary size are more interested in the topics associated with test words than children at the median or in the bottom 10%. In addition, those in the top 10% may be more interested in communicating with others than those at the median or in the bottom 10%. In support of such a motivational account, Crain-Thoreson and Dale (1992) found that children who seemed to be more engaged in book reading with their mothers showed more growth in their vocabulary than children who seemed less engaged. Engagement was a better predictor of growth than the frequency with which children read books with their mothers.

In addition to being willing to take advantage of exposure opportunities, however, a child has to be able to benefit from these opportunities, as well. Which aspects of ability matter? Prior to age 5, it could be expected that children with more-developed TOMs would acquire more words than same-aged peers with less-developed TOMs. Again, this differential rate of learning would be expected even when children are exposed to the same number of new words using high-quality techniques such as question asking, elaborative descriptions, and book reading. A second important ability, however, is verbal *working-memory capacity.* The more working-memory capacity a child has, the greater rate of growth in his or her vocabulary during the preschool period (Adams & Willis, 2001; Avons, Wragg, Cupples,

& Lovegrove, 1998; Gathercole & Baddeley, 1989; Thal, Bates, Zappia, & Oroz, 1996). Two ways to measure this capacity is to ask children to repeat back nonsense words and also a string of numerical digits (e.g., 2, 5, 8, 6). A third ability was implicated earlier in this chapter: existing vocabulary words. If two same-aged children were exposed to the same number of words in a particular learning context (e.g., during book reading), the child with a larger vocabulary would probably learn more of these words than the child with the smaller vocabulary.

In sum, then, individual differences in vocabulary growth seem to be due to differences in exposure variables (e.g., more exposure to high-quality opportunities to learn) and to differences in characteristics of children that predispose them to benefit from exposure in different ways. Preschool children are likely to take advantage of opportunities to learn new words if the children (1) are highly motivated, (2) have highly developed TOMs, and (3) have greater working-memory capacity. In older children and adults, vocabulary growth is also related to exposure (e.g., time spent reading books), motivational variables, and verbal working memory. However, Sternberg (1987) argues that older learners also seem to have the knack for learning words in context using abilities such as selective encoding (deciding which elements of a textual passage are relevant for figuring out the word and which are irrelevant), selective combination (integrating various clues in the right way), and selective comparison (relating the derived definition to existing knowledge). These three abilities are highly correlated with IQ and vocabulary.

Why Is There a Preponderance of Nominals in the First Words of Many Middle-Income U.S. Children?

The preponderance of nominals has been explained in several different ways. Some have argued that objects stand out because they are in the foreground of perception. This "pop-out" quality of objects is largely due to the human visual system that parses the world into objects and backgrounds when objects move against a stationary background (Bloom, 2000). Given the choice of things to attend to in a situation, objects that move frequently would be obvious candidates. One would further predict that children would learn the label for objects that move (e.g., balls, parents, and cookies) before they learn the labels for objects than do not move very often (e.g., end tables, rugs, and walls).

A second explanation for the preponderance of nominals relates to a point made earlier in this chapter that basic-level categories stand out because they are more distinctive than superordinate or subordinate categories. A third explanation is that middle-income U.S. parents spend considerably more time labeling objects than parents from Asian countries do (Gopnik & Choi, 1995; Tardiff, 1996). Many Asian utterances end with verbs, and parents seem to stress verbs in their utterances. Hence, verbs and actions end up being more salient to Asian children than movable objects.

Why Do Some Children Adopt a Referential Communicational Style While Others Adopt a More Expressive Style?

Two explanations of this finding have been proposed and verified in several studies. The first explanation, once again, demonstrates the role of exposure and input (Hoff, 2001): Whereas the mothers of referential children spend a great deal of time talking about objects and their properties, the mothers of expressive children spend proportionately more time encouraging social interactions and games (e.g., waving bye-bye to grandparents, playing peek-a-boo). The second explanation pertains to the children themselves. Some children seem to be more interested in objects and talking about these objects. Other children seem to be more interested in social interaction. Collectively, these findings provide further support for the claim that language is a function of both opportunities (i.e., exposure to certain words) and propensities (i.e., motivation and cognitive aptitudes).

Why Do Word Meanings Become Progressively More Elaborated, Abstract, and Integrated with Age?

The proposed developmental mechanism for elaboration was discussed earlier in this chapter: Children need to observe a word being used in multiple contexts in order to understand the full range of meanings of this word. Many words occur infrequently, so the process of elaboration is likely to take some time and extend through adolescence and adulthood (for words that have a variety of meanings). The principal explanation of the finding that word meanings become increasingly abstract and integrated comes from various constructivist theories of cognitive development, such as those of Piaget (1983) and Vygotsky (1978).

For Piaget, children's knowledge is initially grounded in what one can do with an object and in the appearance and disappearance of objects. Somewhat later in the early preschool period, words map onto mental representations that are closely linked to perception. In other words, things are considered to be in the same category if they look alike. Then, during the elementary years, concepts become somewhat more abstract as children replace perceptual properties (e.g., grandfather = old, gray hair) with more defining properties (e.g., grandfather = male father of one of my parents). Finally, during the adolescent period, children are capable of even more abstract ideas (such as those in high school math, political science, or natural sciences).

The driving forces behind such changes are children's interactions with the environment (including interactions with peers and teachers) and an internal developmental mechanism called *equilibration*. Equilibration is defined as the process by which a balance is restored between *assimilation* and *accommodation*. *Assimilation*, in turn, is defined as the process of finding a place for information in an existing mental structure. The structure does not have to be changed in order for the information to be incorporated and retained. In fact, assimilation can be viewed as the property of knowledge or a "mental force" that resists changes. *Accommodation*, in contrast, is defined as the process of changing a mental structure in response to information that cannot be assimilated using the existing structure. Whereas assimilation resists changes, then, accommodation promotes it.

To illustrate these two opposing tendencies, imagine that a child has categorical knowledge that is arranged into hierarchies. One such category is "whales" and another is "sailboats." If this child is told, "Whales can sometimes be larger than sailboats," the child need not reorganize his or her knowledge to understand or assimilate this information. However, if told, "Whales are mammals just like humans, dogs, and cats," the child may need to reorganize his or her knowledge substantially (especially if whales are misclassified as fish and all categories are based on perceptual properties).

Assimilation and accommodation are always in a kind of tug-of-war. One struggles to keep knowledge the same while the other works to create changes. When too much assimilation has occurred, accommodation reins the process in. When too much accommodation has occurred, assimilation promotes a return to a balance. This process of equilibration is said to promote the development of increasingly abstract and integrated knowledge over time.

For Vygotsky, in contrast, knowledge becomes more abstract, logical, and organized in response to social interactions with more knowledgeable people (especially parents and teachers). Children at first do not understand some of the things they are told by parents and teachers. Unlike Piaget, who suggests that this hard-to-understand information is simply ignored, Vygotsky argues that even difficult, abstract information could be internalized. For example, it could be learned by rote but not understood. Over time, children are thought to slowly understand this information as they participate in culturally relevant activities in school.

Both of these theories, then, assume that development toward more abstract and integrated semantic knowledge takes time. Moreover, experience and education are considered to be indispensable factors that drive such changes. Further, both disagree with the claims of scholars who are more nativist or empiricist in their orientations. Nativists argue that children need not be taught very abstract ideas because they already have access to these ideas even when they are young infants. Empiricists, in contrast, argue that it is possible to teach abstract ideas relatively quickly even at young ages as long as children have sufficient memory capacities.

THE DEFICIENCIES QUESTION: Are There Populations of Children or Adults Who Have Underdeveloped or Impaired Spoken Vocabularies? Do These Individuals Experience Problems When They Learn to Read or after They Have Learned to Read?

As we discuss in Chapters 7 and 8, reading is a complex process that involves component operations related to working memory, grammatical knowledge, phonological skills, semantic skills, orthographic skills, and strategies. To highlight the unique contributions of vocabulary, it would be informative to consider the reading skills of individuals who have problems in semantics but who are relatively unimpaired in all of the other component operations (e.g., working memory, phonological processing). It turns out, however, that most individuals with disabilities who have limited vocabularies (e.g., individuals with autism who are low-functioning, children with Down syndrome) also have problems in areas such as memory and syntax. Thus, when these individuals experience problems reading (which they often do), it is not clear whether their limited vocabularies are to blame or whether the other factors are responsible.

Perhaps, though, it may be unwise to dissociate all of the component operations from one another given the fact that scientists have found that skills in one area seem to be correlated with skills in another. As noted earlier, for example, there is a correlation between the size of children's vocabularies and their phonological processing skill (i.e., children who know more words seem to have more segmented phonological representations). In Chapter 6, you will learn of a correlation between vocabulary size and developments in the area of syntax (i.e., syntax starts to emerge only in children who have 400 words in their vocabularies). Further, studies with individuals who have certain brain disorders suggest that semantic, phonological, and orthographic representations work together and mutually influence each other (Noble, Glosser, & Grossman, 2000). Thus, it is not clear what could be made of the results of studies that considered the reading skills of people who only had deficits in semantics.

A better approach seems to be one that was discussed earlier in this chapter in the "relevance" question. In that section, the strong association between vocabulary measures and reading comprehension scores was highlighted (e.g., people with the highest reading comprehension scores also have the largest vocabularies). This powerful association occurs regardless of whether the source of a small vocabulary is a disability (e.g., autism), lack of education, or economic disadvantage. It is essentially impossible to be a skilled reader if one has a limited vocabulary.

6

The Development
of Grammatical Knowledge

Vignette: "Julia, where did your mommy go? She was here a minute ago," Grandma asks Julia who is playing in the sandbox. "I not know, Grandma," Julia replies. "She gone." "No, she's not gone, honey, she is just in the kitchen and is watching you play through the window." Even though adults speak to children using the correct grammatical structure, children younger than 5 frequently make grammatical errors in their speech by overgeneralizing rules in the English language and omitting obligatory forms (such as the auxiliary "do").

MAIN IDEAS OF THE CHAPTER

1. Grammatical knowledge involves knowledge of open-class words (e.g., *truck*, *hit*, and *red*), closed-class words (e.g., *to* and *for*), and inflections (e.g., *-s* and *-ed*). For English speakers, it also involves knowing the proper temporal order of words within phrases and larger units (e.g., adjectives usually before nouns in the case of English; adjectives usually after nouns in the case of French) and knowing where to place inflections in order to get certain ideas across (e.g., *-ed* is placed on verbs, not on nouns or determiners). Some also argue that grammatical knowledge involves knowledge of grammatical classes (e.g., noun, verb) and rules (e.g., sentence = noun phrase + verb phrase). Grammatical knowledge underlies the ability to combine words and word endings in such ways that communication can be successful.
2. Teachers should care about the development of grammatical knowledge in students because students use their grammatical knowledge when they read texts and when they write. In other words, children could not become good readers or writers if they lacked the grammatical knowledge described in this chapter.
3. Some notable age trends in grammatical knowledge include the following: (a) Between the ages of 15 months and 24 months, most children begin to put two words together; (b) early utterances are telegraphic (i.e., children include only the most

important content words in their utterances and omit inflections and grammatical function words); (c) between 24 and 36 months, children create expressions around focal verbs, place inflections on the ends of words, and acquire words that serve particular grammatical functions; (d) grammatical skills usually begin to appear after children have 400 words in their vocabularies; (e) although children have initial difficulty mastering questions, negation, and complex constructions, they usually demonstrate full mastery by first or second grade.

4. Theories that can explain these age trends can be grouped into categories such as learning theories, nativist theories, constructivist theories, and emergentist theories. Each kind of theory has different implications for instruction.

5. Children with the following diagnoses tend to have deficiencies in their grammatical knowledge and skills: Down syndrome, autism, Williams syndrome, Specific language impairment, and deafness. These same children have later reading difficulties.

In previous chapters, competent speakers of a language were said to have three kinds of fundamental knowledge (and several kinds of advanced skills, as well). Two of the fundamental forms of knowledge (i.e., phonology and semantics) were discussed in Chapters 4 and 5. In the present chapter, the focus is on the third kind: grammatical knowledge. In what follows, information about the development of grammatical knowledge is organized using the now-familiar five guiding questions of this book.

THE "NATURE OF" QUESTION: What Does It Mean to Say That a Child Has Grammatical Knowledge?

Following the lead of previous chapters, this "nature of" question will be addressed by first considering theoretical issues pertaining to the definition of grammatical knowledge, and then by considering methods that have been used to determine the level of grammatical knowledge in children at various ages.

Theoretical Issues

Throughout this book (but especially in Chapter 3), we have emphasized the fact that speakers have goals that they try to accomplish using specific kinds of expressions (Tomasello & Brooks, 1999). For example, when speakers have the goal of informing listeners of something that they believe to be true (e.g., the traits of a friend), they often accomplish this goal using a declarative format that contains an explicit subject (e.g., "Mary" in *Mary is very nice*). In contrast, when speakers want listeners to do something as soon as possible (e.g., move away from something dangerous), they often express this goal using a subjectless imperative format (e.g., *Get out of the way!*). In order for communication to be successful, both speakers and listeners have to be familiar with the conventional formats that are normally used to express various goals. There are, of course, several ways to accomplish the same goal (e.g., using the declarative format, *I wish I knew what time it was*, instead of the interrogative format, *Can you tell me the time?*), but this fact does not undermine the need to know how to create multiword structures that are likely to be interpreted as intended.

Up to this point, we have said that competent speakers know how to produce the phonological word forms of their language (e.g., /fa-ther/) and also know the meanings associated with these phonological word forms (e.g., male caregiver). Whereas having such phonological and semantic knowledge is necessary for successful communication, it is not sufficient. To see this, consider the hypothetical case of an adult male who only had four words in his vocabulary (but could pronounce them perfectly!): *you*, *give*, *money*, and *me*. Imagine next that he wanted his boss to pay him his weekly salary. If he said to his boss on payday, *You give me money*, the boss would probably interpret this utterance to mean that the employee wanted his weekly salary. However, if the employee used the same words but said, *Me give you money*, the boss would probably not hand over the check. In fact, the boss would probably expect that the employee would be handing him money instead. As a second example, consider the case of a woman who was a witness to a criminal assault but only has three words in her vocabulary: *Bill*, *hit*, and *Joe*. When asked by a prosecutor during a trial to describe what happened, it clearly matters whether she says, *Bill hit Joe* or *Joe hit Bill*.

As these two examples illustrate, competent speakers need to know more than individual words. They also need to know how to combine words in ways that are (1) likely to be interpreted correctly by other listeners and (2) judged to be acceptable or well-formed by other listeners. One aspect of this combinatorial knowledge for English speakers is made evident in the examples above: *word order*. Different meanings emerge from different word orders. However, grammatical knowledge involves more than arranging words in conventional orders. It also involves knowing how to (1) add endings onto words (called *inflections*) and (2) insert various *grammatical function words* in appropriate places in an utterance (Bates, Bretherton, & Snyder, 1988; Hoff, 2001; Tomasello & Brooks, 1999). To illustrate the role of inflections, consider our Tarzan-like employee again. Imagine that the next time he saw his boss, he merely wanted to express his delight over getting paid a few days earlier. If he said with a broad smile, *You hand me money!* (to mean, "I like you because you gave me money the other day!"), the boss may incorrectly infer that the employee wanted to get paid again (too soon). It would be useful, then, to know how to indicate additional meanings in some way. One way to convey new meanings in this example would be if the employee inserted tense into his utterance. In English, speakers often indicate tense by adding -ed onto the ending of verbs. Note how the utterance, *You handed me money!* would be interpreted differently by the boss than *You hand me money!* Other important endings include the -s attached to the end of verbs when utterances are about things other than the speaker or listener (e.g., *You walk home once a week but John walks home every day*), the -s attached to the end of nouns when utterances are about several countable entities (e.g., *I have 1 chicken but you have 10 chickens*), and the -ing that is attached to verbs to indicate that the utterance is about an ongoing activity as opposed to something that happened in the past or will happen in the future (e.g., *You are counting chickens*).

Comparison of these four endings (i.e., -ed, third person singular -s, plural -s, and -ing) reveals that whereas some endings add additional meanings to utterances that could probably not be inferred without them, other endings seem to be redundant or unnecessary. For example, one could not take away the -ed or -ing from verbs and know for sure when the event described in an utterance took place. In contrast, listeners often can still understand the main message of an utterance even when speakers leave off the third-person-singular or plural -s (e.g., Q: *How much does this gum cost?* A: *It cost 10 cent*). Most languages have similar kinds of inflections or designations that seem to have little to do with the meaning of the utterance (Maratsos, 1983). For example, Spanish-speaking listeners could probably understand the meaning of *La gato es grande* (i.e., the cat is large) even though the proper wording is *El gato es grande*. Thus, gender is one aspect of grammar that carries little if any meaning. In fact, the connection between gender assignment and meaning has been said to be completely arbitrary. As a result, speakers have to learn gender assignment by rote.

In contrast to gender assignment, most aspects of grammar relate to the overall meaning of a sentence in an important way. In particular, it is sometimes said that grammar pertains to using word order and inflections to describe "who did what to whom" (e.g., Saffran, 2003). In our two examples, this connection between word order and agency in English is apparent. For example, Bill is the hitter in *Bill hit Joe*, but Joe is the hitter in *Joe hit bill*. But there are many languages that rely less on word order and more on inflections to carry information about agency and so on (e.g., Turkish, Russian, and Latin). For example, there would be different endings on the Russian word for *hammer* in a sentence depending on whether (1) it is the subject of the sentence (e.g., *That hammer is rusty*), (2) it is an instrument (e.g., *He hit it with a hammer*), or (3) something is located on the hammer (e.g., *Her coat is lying on the hammer*). Notice how hammer is spelled the same way in English regardless of these differences in the grammatical role of hammer. In contrast, the Russian word might have endings such as *-e*, or *-nim* added to the end of the word. Similarly, in Latin, the word for *father* would be spelled *Pater* when father is the subject of a sentence, *Patris* when some object in a sentence belongs to the father, and *Patrem* when father is the recipient of an action. Use of these endings obviates the need for determiners (*a, the*) and prepositions (*to, of, with*) in Latin and other heavily inflected languages. In addition, one could say the words in any order in heavily inflected languages and still get the proper meaning across (unlike English).

Because English and certain other languages are not heavily inflected, there is a need for determiners, prepositions, and other grammatical function words (also called *closed-class words*). These words contribute to the overall meaning of an utterance but do not themselves have meaning in the way that so-called *open-class words* such as nouns, verbs, and adjectives have meaning (Hoff, 2001). Examples of grammatical function words besides determiners and prepositions include complementizers (e.g., *that*), conjunctions (e.g., *because, and, when*, and *if*), auxiliaries (e.g., *can, do, should*), and question words (e.g., *what, when, how*). The labels "open class" and "closed class" pertain to differences in the size of, and limits on, these two categories (Bates et al., 1988). Whereas children learn nearly all of the limited number of closed-class words that they will ever learn by age 6 or 7, they continue to learn new nouns, verbs, adjectives, and adverbs for the rest of their lives (see Chapter 5).

To see how closed-class terms add to the meaning of an utterance beyond that supplied by open-class terms, compare the following pairs of sentences:

1a. *Hand me an apple, would you?*
1b. *Hand me the apple, would you?*

2a. *Hand me the painting of Bill, would you?*
2b. *Hand me the painting for Bill, would you?*

3a. *You saw a man yesterday. That same man has just arrived.*
3b. *The man that you saw yesterday has just arrived.*

4a. *Today is Tuesday. I have go to class.*
3b. *If today is Tuesday, I have to go to class.*

Speakers say (1a) when there are several apples present and apples have not been the topic of conversation earlier (here, the inference is that any apple will do). In contrast, they say (1b) when a particular apple has been discussed before or when there is only one among other fruits. In (2a), Bill's likeness has been captured in a portrait. In (2b), we do not know the subject of the painting, but we do know that the painting seems to be a gift for Bill. Use of the complementizer in (3b) allows a speaker to say two things about a subject at the same time in the same utterance. In such cases, complements function almost as adjectives by modifying the noun (compare *The tall man* and *The man you saw yesterday*). In (4a), the speaker seems pretty sure about what he or she knows (that it is Tuesday and that he or she has to go to class). In contrast, in (4b), the speaker is not sure about the truth of the first clause (whether it is, in fact, Tuesday). The speaker is, however, sure about the connection between the day and classes held that day.

Thus, grammatical knowledge involves knowledge of open-class words, closed-class words, and inflections. For English speakers, it also involves knowing the proper temporal order of words within phrases and larger units (e.g., adjectives usually before nouns in the case of English, adjectives usually after nouns in the case of French) and knowing where to place inflections in order to get certain ideas across (e.g., *-ed* is placed on verbs not on nouns or determiners). Speakers who have this knowledge and use it to formulate declaratives, imperatives, interrogatives, and so on will be more likely to accomplish their communicative goals than speakers who lack some or all aspects of this knowledge. Consider how beneficial it would be for a female tourist in France to know how to construct expressions such as, *Où se trouve les toilettes femmes?* (*Where is the women's restroom?*).

Implicit in the foregoing discussion of grammatical competence, however, is the idea that adult speakers have knowledge of different *kinds* or categories of words such as nouns, verbs, determiners, and question words. Why is this assumption of *grammatical categories* necessary? Consider the following analogy. When people make themselves sandwiches, they implement a procedure that has steps such as the following. First, they assemble all of the ingredients (e.g., find two slices of bread, some lunchmeat, and mayonnaise). Second, they place the lunchmeat on one slice and spread mayonnaise on the other. Third, they place the slice with mayonnaise on top of the slice with lunchmeat. In order to carry out these steps, the person has to have mental categories of the kinds of ingredients that are normally used to make sandwiches (e.g., bread slices as opposed to chocolate syrup). Moreover, when certain steps are carried out, reference is made to specific categories (e.g., mayonnaise is spread on the bread, not on the lunchmeat). Well, the same applies when people construct sentences and questions. They assemble specific kinds of words and carry out procedures that apply to these specific kinds. For example, to formulate the question, *What did you eat for breakfast?* speakers need to retrieve the proper question word from memory (i.e., *what* rather than *how*) and place it at the beginning of the question. Placing some other kind of word at the beginning (e.g., an adverb) is a little like using two bunches of broccoli to make a sandwich instead of two slices of bread. Second, speakers have to retrieve the proper auxiliary from memory (e.g., *do* rather than *can*), place it right after the question word, and apply tense markings to it (e.g., *did* rather than *do*). Again, placing a word from a different category would either lead to the wrong question being asked (e.g., a preposition would lead to a question such as *What in the world did you eat?*), or to an ungrammatical question (e.g., *What happily did you eat?*). Similarly, applying tense to words other than the auxiliary in the question would be ungrammatical, as well (e.g., *What do you ate?*). Next, the proper pronoun has to be retrieved from memory (e.g., *you* rather than *we* or *they*) and placed next in line, and so on.

Language scholars make use of this assumption of categories and procedures when they argue that language production is highly *generative* or creative (Chomsky, 1965; Pinker, 1994). Just as there are many possible ingredients that can be combined in various ways to make sandwiches (e.g., different kinds of breads, different kinds of dressings, different kinds of filling), speakers can combine words together in productive, creative ways, as well. The only alternatives to the assumption of categories and procedures are proposals that require specific word-by-word constructions to be stored in memory (or stored portions of words, as in connectionist theories). If people stored millions of specific sentences rather than a much smaller number of procedures for making them, doing so would be a little like a chef having hundreds of separate recipe cards that each describe the ingredients for one specific sandwich (e.g., Sandwich 1 = wheat bread + ham + lettuce + mayonnaise; Sandwich 2 = wheat bread + ham + lettuce + mustard; Sentence 3 = wheat bread + ham + lettuce + Russian dressing) as opposed to a single card that lists the possible categories of ingredients (e.g., breads, lunchmeat, toppings, dressing). Moreover, proposals that require highly specific word combinations stored in memory have a hard time explaining people's ability to make *new* statements or formulate new questions that they have never said before.

Note, though, that in saying that speakers (including young children) have knowledge of grammatical categories such as "noun" and "verb," one need not assume that this knowledge is explicit or that speakers use the same category labels as linguists. Most people only become explicitly aware of grammatical categories during school in the following kinds of situations: (1) when their essays are corrected by teachers (e.g., a marginal comment says, "There is no verb in this sentence"), (2) during foreign language instruction when they learn about determiners (e.g., *la* and *le*), verb endings and other inflections (e.g., *-e*, *-es*, *-e*, *-ons*, *-ez*, *-ent*), and so on, and (3) when they are asked to diagram sentences. But note that children can often learn how to perform many things before they know the labels used by experts to refer to specific objects or actions. For example, they might kick a soccer ball for years before their first coach refers to specific kinds of kicks using terms such as *dribble, pass,* and *cross.* If children are observed to always add *-ed* to all regular verbs when taking about past events and never add *-ed* to nouns or adjectives in such situations, it seems reasonable to conclude that they must have at least implicit knowledge of verb-like entities (though this knowledge may be something such as the overly specific notion of "names for actions"). This inference that children have grammatical categories when they add inflections only to the right kinds of words seems particularly warranted when children only hear a specific verb used in the present tense (e.g., a made-up experimental word such as *blick*) but later apply the *-ed* rule to this new term (e.g., *blicked*).

In addition to being a central element in explanations of the generativity of language, however, grammatical categories and procedures are also useful when it comes to understanding the utterances of others. Utterances are easier to understand when groups of words in these utterances are bundled together. For example, when someone says, *The brown dog that you hate is up the street,* it is helpful to subdivide the words in this utterance into two major sections or phrases: (*the brown dog that you hate*) and (*is up the street*). If nothing else, these sections refer to two holistic, component ideas in the utterance (one about the dog and the other about its location). Consider how *parsing* the sentence in this way provides a more direct or efficient mapping to these two ideas than if word meanings for each word in the utterance were retrieved one by one (e.g., *brown + dog + you + hate + is + up + street*). When all of the individual meanings are retrieved, it is not clear how they should be combined. *Brown* and *dog* should go together, but what is to stop *dog* and *you* or *hate* and *street* from being combined when they are accessed in an unbundled manner? Moreover, as discussed in Chapter 5, the individual words in this sentence are not specifically the elements that do the referring; rather, the elements that do the referring are the constituent *noun phrase* (*the brown dog that you hate*) and *verb phrase* (*is up the street*). Thus, it would seem that people have to have some mental processes that help them bundle groups of words into such constituents.

Many common models of language processing assume that people create bundles using *grammatical rules* such as the following:

1. Sentence = noun phrase + verb phrase.
2. Noun phrase = (determiner) + (adjective) + noun.
3. Verb phrase = verb + (noun phrase) + (prepositional phrase).

Whereas the entities that are not in parentheses in each rule are required elements, the entities that are in parentheses are optional. For example, a noun phrase could have both a determiner and an adjective in addition to a noun (e.g., *the big dog*) or it could just have a noun (e.g., *Bill*). The basic idea is that people assign incoming words to phrases based on the grammatical category of each word and the categories that have been already assigned to words that were processed up to that point. For example, when listeners hear the sentence above about the brown dog, they are assumed to start creating a noun phrase using Rule 2 above (e.g., *The . . . brown . . . dog . . .*) because they hear the word *the* first (which is a determiner). They keep building this noun phrase word-by-word until the speaker utters the word *is*. At that point, Rule 3 kicks in and they start to build up a verb phrase. After both phrases have been built, they are combined together using Rule 1 above. Hence, listeners are believed to use such rules to create meaningful bundles of words.

However, not all language scholars advocate the existence of such rules or grammatical categories such as verb and preposition (Tomasello, 1992). Some scholars, for example, advocate mental processes that rely on so-called *argument structures*. In these views, the central element of any expression is a verb. Verbs are the linchpins that describe the relationship between entities that are referred to by other words in an utterance. For example, in the sentence, *Darth Vader is Luke's father*, it is fine to know that (1) *Darth Vader* and *Luke* refer to a particular individuals, (2) *father* means something like "male caregiver," and (3) the *-s* attached to *Luke* is possessive (the parent *of* Luke). But to really understand the meaning of the sentence, the listener has to make the identity connection between the first two words and last two through the verb *is*. Often, advocates of argument structures convey this meaning using formalisms such as (Darth Vader, Luke, father-of, is). The general format is (argument 1, argument 2, . . . , verb). Depending on the theorist or the age of the speaker, these structures might be only somewhat abstract and general (e.g., hitter, person hit, hit) or fairly abstract and general (e.g., agent, patient, action).

Hence, scholars differ in the answers they would provide to the question posed at the beginning of this section regarding the nature of grammatical knowledge. Despite these differences, most would agree that people use their grammatical knowledge to create and interpret multiword utterances that (1) portray the relationships among entities in visible, ongoing situations or in mental "scenes" that they envision (Tomasello, 1992), (2) demand responses on the part of themselves or their listeners, or (3) request information that can be used to clarify relationships among entities. As we discuss in the "developmental trends" section, however, the different models adopted by researchers determine the kinds of skills that they look for at different ages. For example, people who believe in grammatical rules often conduct studies to determine when children seem to have particular rules. In contrast, scholars who advocate argument structures often focus on age changes in verbs.

Methodological Issues

When it comes to measuring the extent of grammatical knowledge at different ages, researchers confront many of the same issues that were discussed in previous chapters on phonological processing and semantics (i.e., Chapters 4 and 5). Perhaps the most common way to assess the level of productive grammatical knowledge in children is to record their spontaneous utterances at regular intervals for 12 months or so and then construct theoretical models of the processes that children might be using to generate these utterances (e.g., Braine, 1976; Brown, 1973; Tomasello, 1992). These models may look something like those discussed in the previous section on theoretical issues (e.g., Rules 1 to 3), but they may not.

Whereas the spontaneous utterance methodology is widespread and very informative, it can be criticized on several grounds. Perhaps the biggest problem is that there are no obvious ways to decide among various theoretical models of children's "grammars" if all of these models fit the data. For example, given two-word utterances such as *Mommy hit*, theorists have proposed that children create such utterances using rules or procedures such as "pivot + word" (Braine, 1976), "agent + action" (Brown, 1973), and "____ + *hit*" (Tomasello, 1992). All of the systems developed to date fit the data fairly well, so which one is to be preferred?

A second problem is that children often understand sentences of a particular type (e.g., *Get me a new diaper please*) before they can express the sentences themselves. Hence, it is possible that children can use grammatical knowledge to interpret the utterances of others before they can use this knowledge to create utterances themselves (Hoff, 2001). It would be wrong, then, to say that children lack certain kinds of grammatical knowledge (e.g., the proper format of questions) because certain constructions are missing in their spontaneous utterances (e.g., well-formed questions).

A second methodological approach is to create experimental procedures as a means of tapping into children's receptive and expressive grammatical skills. For example, Hirsh-Pasek and Golinkoff (1991) paired two video monitors that depicted distinct actions (e.g., an adult in a Big Bird costume and an adult in a rabbit costume spinning together vs. the rabbit grasping Big Bird to make him spin). As children watched, sentences were presented that matched only one of these scenes (e.g., "Big Bird and the bunny are "gorping' "). Using this technique, children are said to demonstrate receptive comprehension of particular grammatical constructions if they watch the correct monitor longer than they if they watch the incorrect monitor (even if they switch back and forth). In contrast to the spontaneous utterance methodology in which underestimation is a possible problem, there is always a possibility of overestimation in the case of the video monitor method.

With older children, researchers might present a story within which a particular kind of grammatical construction is embedded. For example, de Villiers (1991) used a story in which a child was said to have fallen from a tree earlier in a day. Later on, before his nighttime bath, his father noticed a bruise and asked about it. The child responded, "I must have hurt myself when I fell this afternoon." Experimenters were interested in how participants would answer questions such as, "*When did the boy say he fell?*" Would children assume that the question concerned when the character fell (in the afternoon) or when the character described his falling (at night)?

As for experimental studies of expressive skills, a number of scholars have emulated the classic study of Berko Gleason (Berko, 1958). In that study, children were shown pictures of fictitious objects and actions. For example, they were shown a picture of a bird-like creature and told, "This is a wug." Then they were shown a picture of two of these creatures and asked, "Now we have two . . . ?" Children were given points when they responded with a word suggesting that they correctly applied the plural morphological rule "noun + -s" (e.g., *wugs*).

The third way to assess children's grammatical knowledge is to use parental checklists such as those contained in the MacArthur Communicative Development Inventories (Fenson et al., 1994). When parents fill out the CDIs, they indicate whether their children (1) use particular grammatical function words such as question words, determiners, prepositions, auxiliaries, and conjunctions, (2) add -s to the ends of words to indicate plurals and possession, and (3) add -ing and -ed to the ends of verbs.

The portrait of developmental trends that will be described later in this chapter relies on the collection of observational, experimental, and parent-report methods used to date. Before we can make claims that children do or do not have particular kinds of grammatical competencies at particular ages, we have to be confident that the methods used to make these claims are reliable and trustworthy. Because all methods are flawed in some way, the most sensible approach is to (1) draw definitive conclusions about the level of grammatical skill in children of a particular age when multiple methodologies converge on the same conclusion and (2) draw more tentative conclusions when only a few studies support a claim or when researchers using different methods find different results.

THE RELEVANCE QUESTION: Why Should Teachers Care about Whether Children Ever Acquire Grammatical Knowledge?

What should be evident from the prior theoretical discussion of the nature of grammatical knowledge is that the focus is not on "grammar" as this term is usually construed in educational contexts. To be sure, it does not help a child's cause in school if he or she always splits infinitives or writes essays that are full of dangling participles. However, these issues are somewhat tangential to the actual focus of this chapter: the ability to combine words and word endings in such ways that communication can be successful. Communication was said to be successful when people understand what children are saying and when children understand what other people are saying. Whereas a student may not receive an A on an essay if she includes sentences with split infinitives (e.g., *The main character was able to quickly go home*), children who use such constructions in conversations would be likely to get their message across. This communicative ability can be contrasted with our hypothetical examples used earlier in which a man was said to have only four words in his vocabulary and a woman was said to have only three words. Without additional open-class words, grammatical inflections, and closed-class words, these individuals would have a great deal of difficulty getting their ideas across to other listeners. Moreover, they often would fail to understand what others are saying to them.

From an educational standpoint, however, the most relevant concern derives from the fact that students use their grammatical knowledge when they read texts and when they write themselves (see Chapters 7, 8, and 9). In other words, children could not become good readers or writers if they lacked the grammatical knowledge described in this chapter. Thus, it is important for all children to acquire the grammatical competence described in this chapter before they begin formal instruction in reading and writing in kindergarten or elementary school.

THE DEVELOPMENTAL TRENDS QUESTION:
How Does a Child's Grammatical Knowledge Change over Time?

To a nativist such as the linguist Noam Chomsky, this "developmental trends" question is the wrong one to ask (e.g., Chomsky, 1981). Radical nativists believe that children are born with all of the grammatical knowledge they need to create and interpret well-formed expressions. Hence, grammatical knowledge does not really change at all in terms of the amount of knowledge that children have at different ages, or in terms of its nature. How, then, would nativists explain the fact that children progress from producing simple one-word utterances at age 1 (e.g., *Dada*) to complex multiword utterances by age 5 (e.g., *The man that you saw yesterday is here again*)?

As we discuss in the section on developmental mechanisms, some nativists explain this trend by claiming that children do not have enough memory capacity to create multiword expressions (e.g., Fodor, 1975). To get a sense of what is meant by this claim, consider the following analogy.

Imagine that a carpenter had all of the materials and tools needed to construct something (e.g., a cabinet that was 9-ft high × 4-ft wide × 2-ft deep), but was asked to build this structure in a workspace that was too small for the structure (e.g., an open section of a basement that was 7-ft × 3-ft × 1-ft). If the carpenter ended up making something much smaller, it would be wrong to assume that he or she lacked the knowledge, materials, or tools needed to build the larger structure. In a similar way, nativists argue that young children "build" smaller grammatical constructions than they are capable of because the functional capacity of their memory store is too small. As children's memory span increases, they develop the mental "space" they need to build larger expressions.

In contrast, non-nativist developmental psychologists disagree with this account. The latter believe that age differences in the kinds of expressions constructed by children are not simply due to memory increases; rather, these scholars believe that there really are bona fide age changes in children's grammatical knowledge, as well (e.g., Bates et al., 1988; Tomasello, 1992; 2003). As we'll see in "The Developmental Mechanisms Question" section, other differences between nativist and non-nativist accounts emerge when additional explanations of age trends are invoked. For now, it is useful to provide a little more detail about the grammatical skills expressed by children at different ages. For expository purposes, these trends are grouped using the following headings: (1) early grammatical knowledge, (2) questions and negation, and (3) complex expressions.

Early Grammatical Knowledge

As noted earlier, English speakers rely on word order, inflections, and grammatical function words (GFWs) to communicate particular ideas. Thus, a sensible way to study the development of grammatical knowledge in English-speaking children is to find answers to questions such as (1) When do children provide evidence that they use word order to convey particular meanings?, (2) When do children use inflections to convey meaning?, and (3) What kinds of grammatical function words do children use at particular ages?

Prior to age 15 months, most children have 50 or fewer words in their vocabularies (see Chapter 5). In addition, most of their earliest utterances use only a single word such as *Mommy* or *cookie*. Although children's first words are sometimes GFWs or verbs, the vast majority (> 70%) are uninflected common or proper nouns. Collectively, to the non-nativist, these findings suggest that children seem to have very little grammatical knowledge before the age of 15 months.

Between the ages of 15 months and 24 months, however, most children begin to put two words together. For example, they might say *more cookie, more page, Mommy shoe,* or *Daddy sock* at this point. These two-word expressions are used instead of their more adequate multiword counterparts such as *I'd like another cookie please, I'd like you to read another page to me, That's Mommy's shoe,* and *That's Daddy's sock,* respectively. Some scholars have noted that there are two kinds of words in each of these utterances: those that appear in many utterances (e.g., *more* in utterances such as *more cookie, more milk, more page*) and those that appear far less frequently. In addition, researchers found that the frequent words always appeared in the same position in utterances (e.g., *more* is always the first word). As noted earlier, Martin Braine (1976) suggested that these early utterances can be described using grammatical "rules" such as "pivot + open" in which the pivot words are the frequently occurring words that always appear in the same position and the open words are less frequent words that occur in any position that is not occupied by a pivot word.

Other scholars, however, used a more semantic approach in their analysis of two-word utterances. For example, Brown (1973) argued that children's two-word utterances derive from combinations of conceptual categories such as "agent + action" or "possessor + possessed." The "agent + action" combination would be the basis of utterances such as *Baby kiss, Mommy hit,* and *Daddy eat.* The "possessor + possessed" combination would be the basis of utterances such as *Baby cookie, Mommy shoe,* and *Daddy sock.*

Still other scholars, however, argue that there is not sufficient evidence to suggest that children are relying on any kind of abstract rule when they create such two-word utterances (e.g., Bates et al., 1994; Tomasello, 1992). By "abstract" scholars mean that the rule makes reference to general categories such as "pivot," "agent" or "noun" that may be instantiated by specific words. Scholars in this third camp argue that one should only ascribe grammatical competence to children if children use different word orders to convey different ideas. If children always use the same word order when they use certain words in an utterance (e.g., *more milk, more cookie, more page*), this tendency contrasts with the tendency of older speakers to use one order to convey a particular idea (e.g., *Bill hit Joe*) and another word order to convey a different idea (e.g., *Joe hit Bill*). The fact that children do not seem to vary word orders in such ways is taken by some theorists to mean that children may not be relying on grammatical knowledge at all. These scholars argue that more compelling evidence of grammatical knowledge would be children's tendency to (1) add inflections to words, (2) construct expressions around central verbs, and (3) use GFWs within multiword expressions.

Although language researchers disagree about the level of grammatical knowledge evident in early two-word utterances, they all would agree with the assertion that children's early utterances are *telegraphic* (Brown, 1973). By telegraphic, we meant that children include only the most important content words in their utterances and omit inflections and grammatical function words, much the same way that adults tend to omit inflections and grammatical function words when they send messages via services such as Western Union. Adults omit unimportant words because these services charge by the word (e.g., "arrive Tuesday 3 P.M." is cheaper than "I will arrive Tuesday at 3 P.M."). In fictional works and films, two adult characters who regularly use telegraphic speech include Tarzan and George of the Jungle (e.g., *Me Tarzan, you Jane*).

A few months after children start combining two words and speaking telegraphically (between 24 and 36 months), three new developments occur: Children create expressions around focal verbs, they place inflections on the ends of words, and they acquire words that serve particular grammatical functions (Brown, 1973; de Villiers & de Villiers, 1973; Tomasello & Brooks, 1999). In effect, they show an increased ability to convey additional meanings beyond the meanings conveyed in one-word constructions or verbless two-word constructions. Because many of these new meanings are expressed using linguistic forms that have ties to grammatical entities, the new forms were dubbed *grammatical morphemes* (Brown, 1973).

Interestingly, studies have found considerable consistency in the order in which 14 of these grammatical morphemes are acquired (Brown, 1973; de Villiers & de Villiers, 1973). In particular, children tend to acquire the present-progressive ending (-*ing*) first; then the prepositions *in* and *on*; then the plural ending (-*s*); then irregular past forms (e.g., *went*); then the possessive ending (-*s*); then the uncontractible verb *to be* serving as a copula (e.g., *he is a big boy*); then determiners (*a, the*); then the past-tense ending for regular verbs (-*ed*); then the third-person ending for regular verbs (-*s*, as in *she walks, she sits*); then the third-person form for irregular verbs (e.g., *I do → he does; I have → he has*); then the uncontractible auxiliary form of certain verbs (e.g., *I am running, he is talking*); then, finally, the contracted forms of the copula and auxiliaries (e.g., *I'm, he's, you're*).

There are, of course, slight individual differences in the precise order in which children acquire specific grammatical morphemes (e.g., some acquire the irregular past before the plural ending), but a pattern very similar to the pattern above is usually obtained. Another way in which individual differences are evident concerns the ages at which these morphemes emerge and the rate at which they are used consistently and productively in contexts that call for them. Some children show mastery when they are only 24 months old while others do not show mastery until after age 3. Hence, age is not always a reliable guide. Researchers have found, instead, that a child's *mean length of utterance* (MLU) is a better guide (e.g., Brown,

1973). To determine the MLU for a child, one examines a sample of his or her utterances (e.g., the 100 utterances in the middle of an hour-long transcription) and calculates the number of ideas expressed in each utterance. For example, *mommy eat* expresses two ideas (one for mommy, one for the action of eating), so it is said to contain two morphemes (a *morpheme* is a linguistic unit that carries meaning). However, *mommy ate* has three morphemes (one for mommy, one for the action, and one for the fact that it happened in the past). After computing the number of ideas per utterance, one then finds the sum across utterances and divides by the total number of utterances to find the average. It is interesting that children often show full mastery of a particular morpheme not when they reach a particular age but, rather, when they reach a specific MLU (e.g., 3.0). Whereas some children reach an MLU of 3.0 when they are 24 months, others reach an MLU of 3.0 a number of months later.

In a related way, studies using the MacArthur CDIs have found that children begin to express GFWs soon after their total vocabulary size reaches 400 words, regardless of how old they are (Caselli, Casadio, & Bates, 1999). Hence, children do not demonstrate this form of grammatical knowledge because they reach a certain age; rather, they demonstrate the use of GFWs because their vocabulary exceeds 400 words.

Based on several studies using the CDI with large U.S. and Italian samples, Bates and colleagues (e.g., Bates et al., 1994; Caselli et al., 1999) report that the development of grammar seems to proceed through four stages:

1. *Routines and word games*: When vocabulary size is 10 words or fewer, children produce words such as *bye*, *hi*, and *uh-oh* that are not referential per se. Categories such as "noun" and "verb" are probably not operating at this point.
2. *Reference*: By the time vocabulary size is between 50 and 200 words, the majority of words are nominals that establish reference to individuals or categories.
3. *Predication*: Whereas verbs and adjectives comprise less than 5% of children's early words, there is a noticeable increase in these kinds of words after vocabulary size reaches 100 words. This change reflects the emergence of *predication*, or the ability to encode relational meanings. Word combinations are rare before the 50-word milestone but are often produced consistently when vocabularies range between 100 and 200 words.
4. *Grammar*: Whereas GFWs also comprise less than 5% of early words, there is a proportional growth in these words after the 400-word milestone. Moreover, the number of these terms in a child's

vocabulary correlates with various indices of grammatical productivity and complexity. Whereas the median age for attaining the 400-word milestone is 24 months, highly verbal child attain this level 4 months earlier while less verbal children attain this level 6 months later. In addition to GFWs being linked to the 400-word milestone, the percentage of predicates in children's vocabularies reaches a maximum at this point, as well.

Eventually, children use appropriate word orders, GFWs, and inflections in nearly every situation that calls for these grammatical devices. As suggested earlier, it is this regularity in their behavior that has led many language scholars to argue that language is rule-governed. In other words, when children say *walked, talked, kicked, pushed,* and so on, they are thought to be using a rule such as "verb + -*ed.*" When they place -*ed* on the end of made-up words such a *blick* in experiments (e.g., Berko, 1958) and do not place this inflection on other kinds of words in natural speech (e.g., nouns), advocates of rules argue that their position gains further support.

One additional finding is generally taken as yet another form of evidence of rule-governed behavior: the *overregularization* of inflectional and other rules. Before children widely and consistency use a particular inflection, they often show the tendency to use the correct irregular form of a word. Initially, for example, they might correctly say *went* instead of *goed* for the verb *go.* Similarly, they might say *mice* instead of *mouses.* Later, however, after they are found to apply an inflection widely and systematically, they start making overregularization errors such as saying *goed* or *mouses.* Sometime later, they return to using the proper irregular forms again (*went, mice*). This pattern of being correct for a while (*went*) then incorrect due to the overapplication of a rule (*goed*) to finally being correct again (*went*) is called a *U-shaped developmental pattern.* Studies have shown that children's parents are not modeling the incorrect forms for them, so children are not merely imitating what they hear. Rather, they are hearing *went* and *mice* but switch to saying words such as *goed* and *mouses* that they do not hear.

Questions and Negation

As the preceding section suggests, children are well on their way to mastering the grammatical system of their native language by the time they are 30 months or 2½ years old. However, it is not the case that this system is fully mastered by 30 months. Consider the case of questions (e.g., *Where are we going?*) and negated statements (*I do not want to eat my vegetables*). Many children are reported to have question words in their vocabularies by 30 months (e.g., 35% to 45% of U.S. and Italian children have *where* and *why*), but this does not mean that children produce well-formed questions at this age (Hoff, 2001; Klima & Bellugi, 1967). Early on, children create questions by simply giving a rising intonation to a declarative (*We going home?*). Somewhat later, questions contain both rising intonation and certain question words (*Who that?* or *Where ball?*). Somewhat later, questions have rising intonation, question-words, and auxiliaries. However, the auxiliaries and subjects are not correctly inverted (*What mommy is doing?*). Finally, they eventually invert auxiliaries and subjects, and also apply tense to just the auxiliary (e.g., *What did you say?*).

In the case of negation, the word *no* is very common by age 2 (as any parent of a "terrible 2" can attest!). However, children wishing to deny something begin by using an external negative marker (Hoff, 2001). For example, instead of saying, "I don't want to go home now!" a child might say, "No (slight pause) go home!" Somewhat later, children place the negative term inside the main structure but do not include auxiliaries. For example, a child might say, *I not know, Grandma*. Finally, they include both an internal negative term and an auxiliary (e.g., *I do not know, Grandma*). Hence, it takes some time for children to progressively master the syntax required to formulate questions and negated statements after early versions of these constructions appear around age 2. Many children show good control over these forms, however, by the time they are 3 or 4.

Complex Constructions

An utterance is said to be a *complex construction* if it contains two component constructions that would be well-formed and complete if they stood alone. For example, there are several ways to create complex constructions out of the complete components *the floor is wet* and *I fell*. One could say (1) *I fell because the floor is wet*, (2) *The floor is wet, so I fell*, and (3) *The floor is wet and I fell*. Recalling an example used earlier, the components *Today is Tuesday* and *I have class* can be combined using the subordinating conjunction *if* (i.e., *If today is Tuesday, I have class*). Finally, one can use the complementizer *that* to combine component sentences such as *You met a man yesterday* and *A man has just arrived* (e.g., *The man that you met yesterday has just arrived*). Whereas complex constructions are fairly rare in the spontaneous utterances of 30-month-olds, most children use these constructions at least occasionally by the time they are 36 months old and demonstrate full mastery by the time they are 4 or 5 (Bowerman, 1986; Byrnes, 1991; French & Nelson, 1985; Smith, Apperly, & White, 2003). In addition, the usual order of acquisition of conjunctions is often *and* first, then *because*, then *so*, then *if*. Children tend to master *if* and the complementizer *that* between the ages of 3 and 4.

THE DEVELOPMENTAL MECHANISMS QUESTION:
What Factors Promote Changes
in Children's Grammatical Knowledge?

In the previous section, we learned that children progress from using single words to express their communicative goals at age 1, to eventually using the full range of grammatical devices that adults use by the time they are 5 or 6. How can this overall age trend (and the more specific age trends described in the previous section) be explained? In what follows, we consider general classes of explanation in turn.

General Categories of Explanations

Theories of grammatical development can be grouped according to similarities in their core philosophical orientations. Some theories, for example, are grounded in the idea that children learn languages in much the same way that they learn anything else—through observation, imitation, and corrective feedback. In the language development literature, these approaches are often called *learning* theories. Other theories, however, are based on the idea that general, empiricist theories of learning cannot explain the acquisition of language. Moreover, theorists in this camp argue that important aspects of grammatical knowledge are innate. These theories are called *nativist* in their orientation. Still other theories have their origins in attempts to refute both the nativist and learning-theory perspectives. Some of these alternatives place a heavy emphasis on children's agency and conscious problem-solving abilities as they build up their grammatical structures step by step. These approaches are said to be *constructivist* in their orientation. Other alternatives utilize more implicit learning mechanisms that detect statistical regularities in the ambient language environment. Grammar is said to emerge from the collection of these implicit mechanisms working together. As such, these approaches are called *emergentist* in their orientation. In what follows, these four orientations are described and critiqued in turn.

Learning Theories of Grammatical Development

In the 1950s, the predominant views of learning placed a heavy emphasis on the contingencies among environmental stimuli, the behavior of people or animals, and outcomes. At the same time, advocates of these views were extremely reluctant to explain behaviors using mental constructs such as imagery, intentions, concepts, and rules. To illustrate this *behaviorist* approach, consider how theorists in this camp would explain the following behavioral regularity evident in a young, female soccer player: Every time the player has the ball in the corner of the field near her opponent's goal and she sees several teammates standing in front of that goal, she makes a crossing pass to them. The sensory perception of her players in front of the goal would be called a *discriminative stimulus* (or S^d). The crossing pass would be called a *response* (or R). Her teammates scoring off of the pass (or her coach yelling, "Nice cross Julia!") would be called a reinforcer if the frequency with which the pass is executed when the child is in the corner of the field increases over time. To behaviorists, there is no substantive difference between the child's behavior in this situation and the behaviors of other kinds of animals in analogous situations. For example, pet cats often come running (R) when they hear the whirring sound of can openers (S^d) because running is often followed by an outcome that increases the frequency of running (i.e., dinner). Hence, cat food operates as a reinforcer. Similarly, rats can learn that if they press a bar (R) immediately after a green light (S^d) comes on, a food pellet will be delivered into their cage (reinforcer).

Behaviors such as crossing passes, running, and bar presses cannot be considered behavioral reflexes (i.e., hard-wired responses such as knee-jerk reactions), so principles of classical (or Pavlovian) conditioning do not apply. In contrast, principles of operant conditioning (championed by B. F. Skinner (1957) and others) do apply. These principles not only explain the regular, predictable sequence of events in such situations (S^d followed by R followed by reinforcer), they also explain how it is that (1) soccer players progress from never making crossing passes in relevant situations to always making crossing passes in such situations, (2) cats progress from never running to the kitchen when the can opener is operating to running nearly every time, and (3) rats progress from never pressing the bar after the green light comes on to always doing so.

To explain such progressions, behaviorists utilize the construct of *shaping*. Shaping involves the reinforcement of successive approximations to the end behavior. For example, to get a rat to press a bar in a cage to dispense food (end behavior), an experimenter would begin by placing a rat in a cage and waiting for the animal to merely face the bar from any point in the cage. When the animal faces the bar (R), an experimenter makes a food pellet come out of a small opening in the side of the cage (a reinforcer). Normally, the animal runs over to get the pellet but then returns to the same position and faces the bar again (this is called *superstitious behavior*—it is built into animal species). The researcher continues to reinforce this facing behavior for a few trials until it is well-established. Then, the experimenter waits for the animal to not only face the bar but now move a bit closer to it, as well (the next successive approximation). When the animal stumbles across this new behavior (face + move closer), it is reinforced using a food pellet. This process proceeds for a few trials. Next, the experimenter waits until the animal faces the bar and moves even closer before reinforcing, and so on. Eventually, experimenters can get an animal to reliably press a bar in a cage through such reinforcements of successive approximations. Similarly, one would explain the development of crossing passes and running in the same way (successive approximations are reinforced).

After 20 years or so of successful experimentation with both animals and human subjects on a variety of behaviors, prominent behaviorists eventually turned their attention to language. In a 1957 book called *Verbal Behavior*, B. F. Skinner explained the development of language in children using principles of operant conditioning. In particular, Skinner argued that the following progression is a paradigmatic example of shaping: making babbling sounds (*da-da-da-da-ma-ma-ma-ma*) at 6 months, to uttering first words at 12 months (*Mama*), to putting two words together at 18 months (*Mommy kiss*), to putting three words together at 24 months (*Mommy kiss Daddy*), to adding inflections and GFWs somewhat later (*Mommy is kissing Daddy*). In addition, the sight of his or her mother might be an S^d for a child. If the child engages in the behavior of uttering *Mama* after seeing his or her mother (R), and this behavior is somehow reinforced (e.g., the mother looks at or smiles at her child), the label *Mama* would be expected to increase in frequency.

Note that behaviorists would assume that any word or utterance that is used by a speaker is part of that speaker's behavioral repertoire because of a history of reinforcement. According to behaviorists, words and syntactic constructions that are retained in a person's oral repertoire are continually reinforced. Words and constructions that drop out are assumed to be followed by a stimulus that either acts as a punisher or a neutral stimulus (neither a reinforcer nor a punisher).

Note also that reinforcers and punishers are defined by their effects on behavior, not by whether they seem pleasant or negative, respectively. For example, if a parent angrily says, "Stop that!" every time a child touches an electrical outlet, this utterance is only a punisher if the frequency with which a child touches the outlet decreases over time. If the frequency stays the same, the warning is a neutral stimulus. This point is important because critics of the behaviorist account often refer to a study conducted by Brown and Hanlon (1970) as providing evidence against the behaviorist account of language development. Brown and Hanlon found that parents rarely corrected their children when they spoken ungrammatically (e.g., the child says *Her curl my hair* instead of *She is curling my hair*). What's worse, they actually responded to such utterances in a seemingly positive way (e.g., *That's right. She is curling your hair*). Nonbehaviorists argued that if the behaviorist account were correct, the frequency of such ungrammatical utterances should either stay the same or increase over time because these utterances are followed by reinforcements. The fact that ungrammatical utterances become less frequent over time was taken by nonbehaviorists to mean that the behaviorist view was wrong. But note that a behaviorist could easily dismiss this criticism by saying that seemingly positive statements could not be properly viewed as reinforcements since the frequency of ungrammatical utterances did not increase.

A second criticism that is often lodged against the behaviorist account is that it seems to leave little room for novelty. In reality, however, animals (including humans) are alleged to always be engaging in randomly emitted behaviors that possibly involve new combinations of old elements. Just as a rat does not "know" that facing the bar will lead to reinforcement (the rat just randomly does it), humans do not always know that their utterances (e.g., *Mama* or *That dress looks nice on you*) will be reinforced. Note how this unintentional account is the exact opposite of the perspective of this book in which utterances are constructed to fulfill communicative goals and intentions.

A third criticism is that the behaviorist account could not easily explain the U-shaped age trend for over-regularizations that was described earlier in this chapter. Behaviorists would argue that there must be stimuli in the environment that extinguish the proper term (*went*) at a particular point in time, then others that reinforce the incorrect term (*goed*) at a later point in time, and finally others that punish the incorrect term and reinforce the correct term (*went*) at a still later point in time. To behaviorists, the frequency of behaviors does not increase or fall in an unexplained manner. Rather, increases mean that reinforcers are operative; decreases either mean that these reinforcers are no longer present or that punishers are present.

But what about the ability of children to add suffixes to novel words such as *blick*? Doesn't that finding cause problems for behaviorism because it seems to demonstrate the use of cognitive rules? Here, behaviorists would apply the construct of *generalization* (Catania, 1998). If a particular S^d is followed by a behavior and then a reinforcer (e.g., a musical E note corresponding to 440 hz is followed by bar pressing and then food), it is often possible to elicit the reinforced behavior (bar pressing) using S^ds that are similar but not identical to the original (e.g., an E-flat or F note of, say, 400 hz or 500 hz, respectively). The ability of S^ds to elicit the behavior falls off as the similarity between an S^d and the original training S^d decreases (e.g., a C note of 250 hz would not elicit it). So, when children correctly say *blicked*, behaviorists would argue that they are merely engaging in the process of generalization (e.g., *He kicked the ball* got reinforced, so *He blicked the ball* would be reinforced, too).

Many readers may not be persuaded by the foregoing behaviorist account of language development. Certain camps of psychologists tend not to be persuaded either. In the 1960s, a different paradigm that was still within the general category of learning theories emerged to deal with two claims of the operant conditioning account that were judged to be problematic: (1) the idea that behaviors are randomly emitted then reinforced and (2) the idea that all complex behaviors need to be built up through reinforcement of successive approximations. To understand objections to these claims, consider the case of a soccer player who never made a crossing pass in her life but does so right after she observes her coach praising a teammate for making such a pass during a game. Such imitative sequences clearly occur in everyday life. The phenomenon is called *vicarious learning* (the child did not get reinforced herself, but someone the child judges to be similar to herself did). In contrast to radical behaviorists who resist attributing mental constructs to people, *social learning* theorists (e.g., Albert Bandura (1986) in earlier days) argued that imitative behaviors can be explained by appealing to constructs such as goals (e.g., I would like to be praised too). When imitation occurs some time after the observed behavior, theorists in this camp argue that mental imagery needs to be invoked, as well (i.e., one models one's memory of what was observed). Social learning theorists use constructs such as goals, imitation, and mental imagery to explain the development of language in children. Note, though, that they still retain the idea of reinforcement.

Discussion Topic: Use the developmental mechanisms and constructs of behaviorists (i.e., S^d, behavior, reinforcer, punisher) or social learning theorists (e.g., goals, vicarious learning, imitation, reinforcement) to design a preschool intervention to promote the development of grammatical skills in 2- and 3-year-olds.

Nativist Accounts of Grammatical Development

In 1959, Chomsky wrote a scathing review of B. F. Skinner's 1957 book *Verbal Behavior* (Chomsky, 1959). In addition to arguing that constructs such as reinforcement were vague and circular (and, therefore, the existence of reinforcers is unprovable), Chomsky made a case for the generativity of the human language faculty that was widely accepted. As noted earlier, this generativity is said to derive from people's ability to use a finite number of grammatical rules to generate an infinite number of possible sentences. For example, using Rules 1 to 3 that were presented earlier in this chapter, a person could generate an infinite number of well-formed and novel declarative sentences (e.g., *Mary kissed Bill, Bill kissed Mary, Mary ate the food, Bill hit the ball*). Importantly, these novel sentences need not bear any similarity to sentences that have been uttered and allegedly reinforced in the past (e.g., *The green Martian tackled the fine young Republican motorist*).

The ability to utter novel sentences that are very dissimilar to sentences said in the past causes problems for behaviorist explanations such as those involving generalization.

Whereas many scholars readily accepted the validity of Chomsky's critique of behaviorism and the notion of rule-based generativity, some of these scholars found it difficult to accept another claim that he made: Children are innately endowed with grammatical knowledge. Why did Chomsky (1957, 1965) and many others after him (e.g., Fodor, 1983; Gleitman, 1990; Pinker, 1994) adopt a nativistic stance? Some of their reasons include the following:

* *The poverty of the stimulus argument*: Inasmuch as young children demonstrate generativity and systematicity in their utterances, it is reasonable to assume that they have knowledge of grammatical and morphological rules. However, children only hear or experience the surface form of sentences produced by others; the underlying rules that others use to generate these utterances are neither observable nor directly taught to children. Moreover, the utterances of parents are not terribly complex (in grammatical terms) and often contain errors, omissions, and slips of the tongue. Taken together, these claims about language imply that simplistic notions of imitation could not be correct. Whereas one could get children to parrot complete utterances such as *Je m'appelle Jacques*, this ability to mimic a continuous string of unparsed sounds would not allow children to create similar sentences in a productive manner on their own (e.g., *Il s'appelle Bernard*, *tu t'appelles Bernice*). If it is the case that (1) children do not learn rules via observation and imitation and (2) they nevertheless use rules to produce sentences, it follows that they must already know these rules or at least know the key elements of these rules. In other words, grammatical knowledge must be innate.

* *The parsing problem*: Before children can create grammatical constructions (i.e., strings of words), they have to have stored representations of individual words (as argued in Chapters 4 and 5). After all, words are the building blocks of sentences. Unfortunately, parents do not talk to their children using single-word constructions such as *Bottle?* Instead, they use multiword, seamless constructions such as *Doyouwantyourbottle?* To create building blocks for themselves, children have to parse these seamless sentences down into individual words (i.e., *Do/you/want/your/bottle*). How do they do this? Some nativists argue that children can use their innate knowledge of grammatical categories to map portions of input onto these categories (e.g., *dog* onto noun, *bark* onto verb). Hence, grammatical categories and rules (e.g., Rules 1 to 3 above) help children solve the parsing problem (Fodor, 1975; Pinker, 1989).

* *The inadequacy of domain-general developmental mechanisms*: To

develop the structure of language that is evident in well-formed expressions, children need two things: (1) richly structured and systemic input from adults and (2) a developmental mechanism that is capable of fostering the development of language-specific structure. On the basis of the poverty of the stimulus argument above, nativists argued that the first condition is never met for most children. As for the second condition, Chomsky (1980, pp. 33–34) argued that domain-general mechanisms such as Skinner's operant conditioning or Piaget's equilibration are not specific enough or consistent enough across children to generate language-specific knowledge and structures:

> Were it not for [children's] highly specific innate endowment, each individual would grow into some kind of an amoeboid creature, merely reflecting external contingencies, one individual quite unlike another, each utterly impoverished and lacking intricate special structures that make possible a human existence and that differentiate one species from another.

• *The universality and species-specificity of language*: Whereas other species such as crickets, birds, whales, apes, and bees engage in bona fide forms of communication, no other species communicates using the complex pragmatic, semantic, and grammatical knowledge utilized by humans. For example, bees can only communicate about the location of pollen using a very circumscribed dance system. Humans, in contrast, can talk about anything they want in various ways. Moreover, there is a fair amount of consistency in the ages at which children master particular milestones across all cultures (e.g., babbling at 6 months, first words at 12 months, two-word combinations at 18 months). If people are willing to admit that physical milestones such as walking or puberty are encoded in the genes to emerge at particular ages, why not language? Further, there appear to be dedicated systems in the brain for language functions (see Chapter 2). Damage to these areas in adults often produces language problems that are difficult to overcome. Together, the findings of species specificity, regular developmental sequences, and brain regions for language are taken by nativists to mean than there is a "language module" in the brain that matures over time.

• *The relative speed and ease with which children acquire language*: Language scholars spend a great deal of time reading works that describe complex grammatical rules and systems (e.g., Chomsky, 1965). Many scholars are struck by the fact that children master this complex system between the ages of 1 and 5. All one has to do is converse with children and they seem to pick up the skills they need. Moreover, whereas very young children learn grammatical rules relatively quickly and tend to make very few errors once they do, much older children take much longer to learn most other topics and tend to make many errors, as well. For example, whereas 3-year-olds never apply the "verb+ -ed" rule to nouns by mistake, 8-year-olds often misapply addition rules for whole numbers to fractions (e.g., $\frac{1}{2} + \frac{1}{4} = \frac{2}{6}$). The latter error continues well into adolescence despite low grades on tests.

• *No one has come up with a better explanation*: In a famous debate with noted developmentalist Jean Piaget, Noam Chomsky (1981) argued that explanations of language development differ in terms of their adequacy. Whereas nativist accounts are not perfect and leave many questions unanswered, Chomsky argued that no one has proposed a better alternative. Until that alternative is proposed, he argued that it is reasonable to maintain the nativist perspective.

In sum, then, nativists have generated a number of arguments against the viability of seemingly simplistic accounts that appeal to constructs such as imitation and reinforcement. Moreover, they have supplied a number of arguments in favor of the idea that children are born with considerable insight into the nature of language. But to be useful to practitioners, nativists have to propose specific kinds of developmental mechanisms that explain the age trends reported earlier in this chapter. For example, they need to supply viable answers to questions such as, Why do children progress from (1) one-word utterances to (2) two-word utterances without inflections to (3) multiword utterances with inflections, and so on?

As noted earlier in this chapter, some nativists have appealed to the construct of working memory to explain such progressive changes in children's grammatical competence (e.g., Fodor, 1975). In particular, as children mature, they slowly develop the processing capacity needed to build increasingly large and complicated structures in their minds. By analogy, imagine the kinds of structures that a carpenter could build as he or she moved from a 3′ × 3′ workroom to a 10′ × 10′ workroom to a 20′ × 20′ workroom.

But a viable account must involve more than working memory increases. If there is only room to build two-word constructions, why choose nouns and verbs and not nouns and GFWs? Moreover, children do not utter just any word at 12 months; they utter words from the language in their ambient environment. Similarly, they do not acquire just any grammatical system; they acquire the system utilized by their caregivers (e.g., English in the case of U.S. children; Russian in the case of Russian children). Thus, exposure to language is a second element of any viable nativist explanation. Inasmuch as a child's rearing environment could not be "known" or anticipated by their genetic endowment in advance (and it would make little sense for evolution to promote the encoding of this information), it is unlikely that children have specific words or specific grammatical systems encoded in their genes. For example, U.S. children do not have Rules 1 to 3 encoded in their genes. Similarly, Russian children do not have knowledge of the specific system of Russian inflections encoded in their genes. What if a Russian newborn were adopted by an English-speaking U.S. family (or vice versa)? Instead, children must have innate knowledge that would help them learn any language. This knowledge (called *universal grammar*, or UG) must specify the elements or concepts that are common to all languages. For example, nearly all languages utilize grammatical categories such as "noun," "verb," and "adjective." Thus, these categories are good candidates for being elements of the innate UG. In addition, most languages have ways to specify agents, actions, and patients (patients = things acted upon). These grammatical roles would be good candidates for UG, as well.

Other forms of innate knowledge become candidates when one considers factors that would make it difficult for children to learn language. Some nativists have argued that the task of language learning would be far simpler if children also knew the possible ways that languages could map words and inflections onto grammatical categories or grammatical roles (Pinker, 1989). As noted earlier, for example, some languages (e.g., English) specify grammatical roles using word order (e.g., *Bill* is the patient in *Mary kissed Bill*). Other languages (e.g., Turkish), however, specify these roles using inflections. Some nativists have proposed that children implicitly "know" these two possibilities in advance. They merely need to be exposed to their native language to discover which system (i.e., word order or inflections) is utilized. Explanatory accounts that make use of the idea that children know the possibilities in advance and then select one possibility after exposure have been called *parameter setting* accounts (Hyams & Wexler, 1993; Maratsos, 1998).

Discussion Topic: If nativists are correct in their explanation of language development (i.e., innate knowledge of grammatical categories and roles; parameter setting; working memory increases), what should parents and preschool teachers do in order to make sure that children have the grammatical skills they need before they start formal reading instruction in first grade? What if parents and teachers behave as you say, and children do not acquire sufficient levels of grammatical skill? Or, what if children differ in the level of grammatical knowledge they manifest even though they were treated similarly? What would such findings mean for nativism?

Constructivist Alternatives to Learning Theories and Nativistic Accounts

There are two ways to provide support for one's theoretical perspective: (1) using logical argumentation to support particular claims and (2) gathering data to test hypotheses (Kuhn, 1992). Analysis of the language development literature reveals that nativists have relied more on the former approach than the latter (Hoff, 2001). In other words, instead of providing empirical evidence (i.e., data) against the proposals of learning theorists, nativists have primarily provided theoretical critiques and logical argumentation. Similarly, instead of using data to confirm the hypothesis that children have knowledge of grammatical rules and categories, nativists have primarily developed lines of logical argumentation to support this claim.

As suggested in the previous section of this chapter, the logical structure of one of the core nativistic arguments is as follows:

Premise 1: Adults use rules to generate the sentences that children hear; these rules refer to abstract grammatical categories (e.g., "noun") and roles (e.g., "agent").

Premise 2: The rules used by adults are not observable; only actual words are observed.

Premise 3: Children use the same rules as adults when they produce their own sentences.

Conclusion: Therefore, knowledge of grammatical categories and roles must be innate.

Various alternatives to the nativistic perspective reflect differences of opinion regarding two things: (1) the truth of Premises 1 to 3 and (2) the extent to which the conclusion above follows from these premises. For example, whereas constructivists tend to agree with Premises 1 to 3 (e.g., Tomasello & Brooks, 1999), they generally disagree with the claim that these premises (and other ancillary premises) imply that knowledge of grammatical categories and roles must be innate. They argue instead that this knowledge is the end product of a slow, progressive abstraction process.

Moreover, a key difference between constructivists and nativists pertains to their level of conservatism (and skepticism) regarding the need to attribute competencies to young children. Whereas nativists tend to be generous in their attributions (even when the competencies of newborns are at issue), constructivists tend to be more minimalistic. In other words, the latter only attribute competencies and knowledge when the evidence strongly supports this attribution.

To illustrate the general approach of constructivists, consider the account of grammatical development proposed by Tomasello and Brooks (1999). These authors argue that there are three basic components of the ability to communicate: (1) mental representations of "scenes," (2) communicative goals regarding aspects of these scenes, and (3) linguistic devices for accomplishing communicative goals. Scenes are schematized representations that involve multiple participants (e.g., people, inanimate objects) that are related to one another in clearly differentiated ways. The participants may be visible in the immediate environment or may be part of a child's memory of an event. In addition to specifying the roles of participants, children's representations of scenes may also take into account various perspectives (their own, that of the listener, or that of one of the participants). The theory assumes that children are motivated to talk about these scenes by commenting on them, requesting or demanding changes in them, or asking for more information about them. These goals are accomplished through the use of word order, inflections, GFWs, and intonation.

For example, given a scene involving a manipulative activity (e.g., a parent knocking over a small tower of blocks), children may partition this scene into participants that play respective roles (e.g., the parent is the agent, the action is knocking over, the patient is the tower of blocks). In addition, children may decide to highlight the outcome rather than the action or the agent (i.e., children may take the perspective of the blocks). If so, they may decide to accomplish this descriptive goal using the passive construction (e.g., *The blocks were knocked over by Daddy*). On another occasion, the child may decide to highlight the agent using the active voice (e.g., *Daddy knocked over the blocks*). On yet another occasion, the scene may represent an unexplained outcome that motivates the goal of finding out the person responsible for this outcome. When such a goal arises, a child may try to fulfill it by asking a question about the scene (e.g., *Who knocked over my blocks?*). With age, children are argued to acquire increased ability to use language to (1) partition scenes into objects and their roles and (2) highlight individual components of scenes. Which participants and perspectives are highlighted in speech is a matter of a child's communicative goals. As goals change, children discover the need to expand their repertoire of structures and linguistic devices.

After reviewing the evidence regarding age changes in children's grammatical knowledge (see the "development trends" section of this chapter), Tomasello and Brooks (1999) argued that children progress through four major levels:

1. During the *holophrase level*, children between the ages of 12 and 17 months use single linguistic symbols and intonation to express declarative and imperative goals. These symbols (e.g., *Jenna!*) are distilled from the larger expressions used by their caregivers (e.g., *Here comes Jenna!*). Which symbols are distilled depends on issues such as the salience of referents in particular scenes, the frequency of terms in discourse, and the phonological stress placed on these symbols in the ambient language. For example, first words tend to be nouns in U.S. homes but tend to be verbs in many Asian homes (see Chapter 5). Inasmuch as children do not use word order or in-

flections in a productive manner at this level (e.g., they do not always add the plural -*s* to nouns where appropriate), there is no need to attribute grammatical categories to children.

2. During the *word-combination level*, children between the ages of 18 and 23 months accomplish their communicative goals using two-word utterances. These utterances often partition scenes into two components. Observational and experimental studies show that children combine words using the same word orders utilized by adults in their environment. For example, if they hear adults say *That's Daddy's shoe*, they tend to say *Daddy shoe* rather than *Shoe Daddy*. Moreover, the existence of consistent patterns of "pivot-word" combinations (e.g., *More* + ____) suggests that these combinations are productive and that children are starting to form the grammatical categories of "noun" and "noun phrase." Because children do not generally demonstrate similar kinds of productivity with verbs, there is no need to assume that they have created the grammatical category of verb as yet. Similarly, inasmuch as they do not contrastively use alternative word orders or inflections to denote distinct grammatical roles (e.g., "agent," "patient"), there is no need to posit knowledge of these roles either.

3. During the *verb-island-construction level*, children between the ages of 24 months and 35 months use word order, verbs, and inflections to explicitly indicate several participant roles in scenes but do so in a scene-specific and verb-specific manner. If there were an overall, organized system of verbs, one would expect similar levels of complexity and productivity across all verbs. What is observed, however, is a pattern in which some verbs occur in a single, simple frame (e.g., *Cut* ____) while others occur in a variety of more complex frames (e.g., *Draw* ____; *Draw* ____ *on* ____; *Draw* ____ *for* ____). Similarly, prepositions such as *by* only occur with certain instrument verbs, not all of the instrument verbs that appropriately use this preposition. Thus, the words that can fill particular slots in instrument verbs are better captured by concrete categories such as "things to draw with" rather than the more abstract grammatical category of "instrument." Experimental studies (e.g., Akhtar & Tomasello, 1997) reveal findings that are consistent with this interpretation of spontaneous speech data. For example, children who are taught novel verbs create constructions with these verbs that closely mirror the learning context. In other words, they do not generalize across scenes to syntactically mark similar participant roles in similar ways without having heard those participants marked in such ways by adults. If there were a productive category of verbs, and generalized usage of inflections to mark the roles associated with verbs, children would not restrict their usage in such ways. In contrast, training studies with same-aged children on novel nouns reveals that children do generalize their training in productive ways across scenes. From a minimalist perspective, then, one would argue that children in this age range seem to have an

abstract category of "noun" as part of their grammatical knowledge but do not seem to have an abstract category of "verb." Similarly, they seem to have knowledge of specific grammatical roles such as "hitter," "thing hit," and "thing hit with," rather than more abstract categories such as "agent," "patient," and "instrument."

4. Finally, during the *adult-like construction level*, children who are 36 months old and older accomplish their communicative goals in ways that suggest they have knowledge of abstract grammatical categories and roles. They engage in discourse about scenes using a range of grammatical devices that partition these scenes into two or more participants. Moreover, there is clear evidence of productivity and systematicity in their spontaneous use of word order, inflections, and GFWs across verbs, as well as evidence of generalization across categories of scenes. The most compelling evidence, however, for the claim that children have moved beyond the verb-island level is in their occasional overgeneralizations and performance in experimental training studies. In the case of overgeneralizations, a child may say (1) *He falled me down* when constructing simple transitive expressions of the form NP – Verb–NP (e.g., *Julia kicked the ball*); (2) *I spilled it of orange juice* when constructing three-argument locative expressions of the form NP_x – Verb – NP_y – locative–NP_z (e.g., *The farmer loaded hay onto the wagon*); (3) *I'll brush him his hair* when constructing dative expressions of the form NP_x – Verb – NP_y – NP_z (e.g., *Grandpa gave Julia some money*); (4) *I'll capture his whole head off* when constructing resultatives of the form NP_x – Verb – NP_y – Adj (e.g., *The busboy wiped the table clean*); and (5) *It was bandaided* when constructing passives of several different forms (e.g., *Bootsie got hit by a car; The wood was chopped in the yard*). For each of these grammatical forms, experimental studies show that it is not until children are 3 to 5 years old that they generalize and show productivity across contexts in their use of focal types of expressions that have been trained.

However, as was argued in the prior section on nativist approaches, the constructivist account can only be useful to teachers if it gives a sense of developmental mechanisms. What factors cause children to progress through these four levels of grammatical knowledge? Can these factors be manipulated by teachers in the classroom? At present, comprehensive and detailed models of developmental mechanisms have not been proposed by constructivists who study language development (Tomasello & Brooks, 1999). Tomasello and Brooks (1999), however, speculate that children may eventually acquire abstract grammatical categories and roles in the same way that they form schemas, event representations, and categories in other domains: by "extracting commonalities of both form and function" (p. 179). For example, children might notice that for all of their transitive constructions, the participant responsible for an action or state is in the preverbal position and the participant being affected is in the postverbal position. Given the variety of verb islands that children create, the extraction of commonalities and construction of abstract categories would be expected to take some time.

Other possible factors that could promote the development of abstract grammatical categories and roles include frequent adult modeling of structures in joint-activity or joint-attention situations (e.g., talking about the same scene) and children engaging in frequent discussions about similar scenes. Moreover, the literature on transfer (e.g., Singley & Anderson, 1989) suggests that people are likely to transfer the same solution to a problem across different situations when their goals are the same in the two situations (e.g., situation 1: locking one's keys in one's own car; situation 2: locking your parent's keys in their car). If adults talk about scenes in similar ways (e.g., highlighting similar aspects of the scene such as facial expressions, clothing), they provide models that can be imitated. Similarly, if adults ask children to comment in similar ways across scenes (e.g., ask how the person is feeling), adults may evoke similar communicative goals in children. In general, however, constructivists need to devote considerable energy to the problem of developmental mechanisms before this perspective can be practically and systematically implemented in the classroom.

Before moving on to the final perspective on grammatical development (i.e., emergentism), it is important to note that nativists have not been swayed by the arguments and evidence marshaled by constructivists. Nativists argue that there is an important problem with the claim that children progress from concrete notions such as "hitter" and "thing hit" to more abstract notions such as "agent" and "patient" by noticing commonalities evident in all transitive constructions. In order for children to notice commonalities, nativists claim that children have to know what they are looking for in advance (Fodor, 1975). In other words, children could not realize that "hitters" and "kickers" are both agents unless they already knew what agents were. However, if they know what they are looking for in advance, this fact implies that they are not really learning anything and that their pre-existing knowledge must be innate. Until constructivists figure out how to counteract the claim that children need to know what they are looking for in advance in order to abstract commonalities, such nativistic arguments remain compelling. Nativists, however, have to solve their own problems caused by studies of overgeneralization errors and experimental studies. Why would children be innately programmed to make grammatical errors? What purpose would that serve? Also, why do children have to be at least 42 months old before they productively generalize certain syntactic constructions that are taught to them in experimental training studies? If grammatical knowledge is there from the beginning, 30-month-olds should perform no differently than 60-month-olds.

Discussion Topic: If it is true that children progress through four levels of grammatical competence, what does this mean for early-childhood curriculums? Also, what can teachers do to promote the development of more abstract grammatical knowledge in children? Would it be enough to simply converse with children as the nativists say, or should teachers be more systematic and focused?

Emergentist Perspectives on the Development of Grammatical Knowledge

In the previous section on the constructivist perspective, it was noted that constructivists tend to agree with three premises of a core nativist argument (e.g., that adults and children use rules to create novel expressions) but disagree with the conclusion that grammatical knowledge must therefore be innate. Emergentists, in contrast, disagree with both the premises and the conclusions of that nativistic argument. In particular, emergentists believe that they have found a way to explain regularities and novelties in people's linguistic behavior without appealing to constructs such as grammatical rules or abstract grammatical categories (MacWhinney, 1998, 2006). Historically, this discovery was taken to be a noteworthy development given the intrinsic relationship between grammatical rules, grammatical categories, and nativism. If it is true that people do not use rules to generate or interpret language, certain nativist arguments immediately evaporate (e.g., the poverty of the stimulus argument).

In the earliest manifestations of the emergentist perspective that arose in the 1980s, theoretical models of linguistic behavior were grounded in the connectionist paradigm (e.g., Rumelhart & McClelland, 1986). As discussed in Chapter 4, connectionists create computer simulations involving inputs (e.g., the sound pattern corresponding to the word *bottle*), hundreds of interconnected "units" that process these inputs, and outputs (e.g., the person recognizes the word as being /*bottle*/). To illustrate how connectionists model grammatical processing, we can consider an example from MacWhinney et al. (1989). These authors designed a computer simulation to explain how German children might learn to select one of the six German definite articles. In the first layer of the model, some of the 176 input units are activated if the input contains certain configurations of phonological elements, meaning elements and case clues. For example, given an input such as *Der Mann gab ____ Frau einen Löffel* (The man gave the woman a spoon), the sounds associated with these words, the meanings of these words, and the fact that *Frau* is a direct object activates certain input units but not others. The input units, in turn, are connected to 37 hidden units that are arranged in a second and third layer of the model. The hidden units, in turn, are connected to 6 output units corresponding to each of the six possible definite articles (i.e., *der*, *die*, *das*, *des*, *dem*, *den*).

When the input layer units are activated, they send their activation to the hidden units, which in turn send their activation to output units. If the connection weights among all of the units are set properly, an input frame such as ____ *Löffel ist Silber* (The spoon is silver) should produce the correct output, *Der* (the correct choice when the noun is singular, masculine, and the subject of the sentence). If the input frame is ____ *Gabel ist Silber* (The fork is silver), the output should be *Die* (the correct choice when the noun is singular, feminine, and the subject). At first, the outputs generated by the simulation are not correct because the connection weights among units are initially set at the same arbitrary figure (e.g., 0.5). Through a mechanism called back-propagation, the incorrect output (e.g., *Der*) is matched to the correct answer (e.g., *Die*). The computer automatically adjusts weights slightly after each error such that, eventually (after hundreds of attempts), the simulation outputs the correct choice.

After training on an initial set of 102 nouns, MacWhinney et al. (1989) found that the simulation outputted the correct choice 98% of the time. In a later part of the study, the input was slightly altered such the training nouns were placed in new case roles (e.g., the direct object if they had always been subjects during training). This time, the simulation provided the correct output 92% of the time. Finally, when given a completely novel set of nouns, the simulation correctly predicted the article 61% of the time (which is well above the chance level of 17%). Thus, the simulation demonstrated a high degree of systematicity, regularity, and generalization to new cases. It did so, moreover, without having explicit rules built into its system.

In more recent versions of emergentism (e.g., MacWhinney, 1998), connectionist systems that rely solely on linguistic cues are said to be part of a larger system in which other kinds of cues and pressures are said to be operative, as well (e.g., sociolinguistic cues, pragmatic cues, intonation cues). Collectively, the entire set of cues and pressures are argued to lead to the kinds of behavioral regularities and structured expressions that prompted nativists to posit the existence of rules and abstract grammatical categories. Instead of arguing that people use rules to create well-formed expressions, emergentists argue that a well-formed expression is an emergent property of a system of components. When we say that something is an emergent property, that means the property is not given in advance; the property only emerges after the quantitative and qualitative relationships among components in a system are worked out.

To illustrate this idea of emergence through more familiar examples, MacWhinney (1998) refers to several outcomes that also emerge from systems of forces working together rather than from a set of rules intrinsic to these systems: (1) the fact that lines at a grocery store often have the same number of people in them (e.g., 6 in each rather than 10 in one and 2 in another), (2) the hexagonal shape of honeycombs, and (3) the particular pattern of stripes on a tiger. In the case of grocery-store lines, people do not follow store rules such as, "All lines have to have the same number of people in them." Rather, people have goals such as "get out of the store as quickly as you can." A group of people who have this rule will eventually form lines of similar lengths. Similarly, honeybees do not have blueprints for honeycombs encoded in their genes, nor do they follow the rule, "Honeycombs must be hexagonal in shape." Rather, the hexagonal shape is an emergent property of the fact that small balls of honey form this shape when they are incidentally packed together. As for the stripes on a tiger, individual patterns emerge from the timing of the expression of a pair of competing genes for color that operate within a developing tiger embryo.

In essence, then, emergentists take issue with the nativistic claims that (1) children are born with knowledge of grammatical categories and roles, and (2) children and adults uses rules to produce and interpret language. However, the fact that emergentists dispute certain nativistic claims does not mean that emergentism is entirely incompatible with nativism (MacWhinney, 1998). To be tenable, all perspectives on grammatical development have to admit some innate capacity to children. In the case of emergentism, a basic assumption is that children are born with a preconfigured neural substrate that makes possible a representational system that can process language-relevant cues in the manner described above. After processing this input for some time, children produce outputs that mirror the structures evident in their ambient environment. It is in this way that grammatical knowledge emerges from a history of changes within an organized system of interlocking components. Presumably, emergentists could develop a similar proposal to explain how it is that children progress from the verb-island level to adult-like construction level (as constructivists contend).

As was noted in the previous section on the constructivist perspective, however, nativists and other language scholars have not been swayed by the arguments and evidence marshaled by emergentists. For example, some have alleged that emergentists have not really done away with rules in their simulations. These scholars contend that it is always possible to take a real rule that people do follow and build an apparently "rule-less" connectionist system from it. For example, Catholics are supposed to not eat any meat on Fridays during the religious season of Lent. This rule can be expressed as such: If it is Friday, no meat can be eaten; if it is not Friday, it is OK to eat meat. A computer model (see below) could be built in which cues in the environment tell input units what day it is (e.g., one sees the word *Friday*

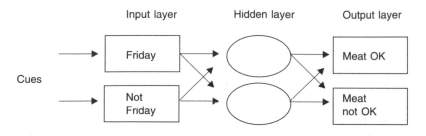

on a calendar). These input units then pass on their stimulation to a layer of hidden units, which in turn send their activation to an output layer. This system seems to work without rules, but the people who build this system know the rule. Moreover, they arrange the units in ways that it would eventually follow the rule through training.

Other critics of connectionism have argued that the simulations to date have only successfully learned small aspects of grammar (Hoff, 2001). Moreover, a prominent figure in the emergentist movement has argued that a three- or four-layer system that utilizes back-propagation could never simulate the U-shaped developmental pattern discovered for the past tense and other aspects of grammar (MacWhinney, 1998). Finally, the systems developed to date generally rely on a large number of learning trials and corrective feedback. Observational studies of children suggest that children need fewer trials to learn and often do not experience corrective feedback on their grammar.

As for developmental mechanisms that could explain the age trends described in the "developmental trends" section of this chapter, emergentists would appeal to such factors as (1) exposure to language and situational cues and (2) children making multiple attempts at constructing expressions. Most simulations have taken into account the relative frequencies of cues in the environment. Hence, emergentists could explain the following outcomes that reflect environmental frequencies: (1) why it is that nouns predominate in U.S. children's first words but not in Asian children's first words, (2) why German children overgeneralize the definite article associated with female gender (i.e., *Die*) because it is the most frequent article in the ambient environment, and (3) why Turkish children sometimes use inflections during the one-word stage, but U.S. children never do (Turkish is a heavily inflected language). However, the emergentist perspective would have a harder time explaining the overall progressive set of changes (e.g., consonantal babbling at 6 months, first words at 12 months, two-word combinations without inflections at 18 months), and would also have trouble explaining commonalities in the milestones reached by children who are reared in different language environments.

Discussion Topic: Imagine that you are an expert on emergentism and are called to testify before Congress. How would you respond when asked the following questions during your testimony? Why is it that low-income and affluent children enter first grade with different levels of language and literacy skills? What can be done to eliminate these entry-level differences? Remember to use the emergentist perspective.

THE DEFICIENCIES QUESTION:
Are There Populations of Children or Adults Who Have Underdeveloped or Impaired Grammatical Knowledge? Do These Individuals Experience Problems When They Learn to Read or after They Have Learned to Read?

Given the interesting linkage between the size of the lexicon and grammatical competence that was discussed earlier in this chapter (i.e., GFWs start appearing soon after children's vocabulary reaches 400 words), it may come as no surprise to learn that many of the same subgroups of children who were said to have underdeveloped vocabularies in Chapter 5 also have underdeveloped grammatical competencies. In particular, studies show that children with the following diagnoses tend to have deficiencies in their grammatical knowledge and skills: Down syndrome, autism, Williams syndrome, and specific language impairment (Bernstein Ratner, 2005; Fowler, Gelman, & Gleitman, 1994; Karmiloff-Smith et al., 1997; Leonard, 1998). In addition, one other group of children that was not mentioned in Chapter 5 has also been found to have difficulties in the grammatical area: children who are deaf (Quigley & Paul, 1987).

However, children in these diagnostic categories differ with respect to the kinds of errors they make and the extent to which grammatical problems resolve over time. For example, studies suggest that high-functioning children with autism are initially delayed in their grammatical development relative to their nondisabled peers but eventually catch up by early adolescence. In contrast, the grammatical deficiencies of children with the following diagnoses persist into adulthood: lower-functioning children with autism, children diagnosed with Down syndrome, and children diagnosed with specific language impairment (SLI). In addition, whereas the grammatical problems of children diagnosed with Down syndrome tend to be rather broad-based, those of children diagnosed with Williams syndrome and SLI tend to be limited to problems such as omitting obligatory inflections and certain GFWs (e.g., past tense, plurals).

Despite such differences in the durability and nature of grammatical deficiencies, children with all of these disabilities demonstrate problems with their reading comprehension and writing. However, given that children in most of these groups also have problems in working memory and vocabulary, their comprehension and writing problems cannot be said to derive solely from their difficulties in the area of grammatical processing. What can be said is that grammatical deficits certainly contribute to their reading and writing difficulties.

A similar argument can be made for adults who have sustained injuries to certain areas of their brain. When adults sustain injuries that involve Broca's area and surrounding areas in the left frontal lobe, they often lose the capacity for fluent speech (Saffran, 2003). The slow, halting speech that these individuals produce is often telegraphic in the sense that it omits inflections and GFWs. Moreover, when asked to read or listen to sentences, these individuals cannot tell the difference between sentences such as *They fed her dog the biscuits* and *They fed her the dog biscuits* (Carpenter & Just, 1987). Further analysis of their error patterns suggests that these individuals use a word-order strategy rather than phrasal strategy that relies on GFWs. Given that these individuals often shift from being good comprehenders to poor comprehenders after sustaining their injuries, such findings provide further support for the centrality of grammatical processing in reading comprehension.

When the findings about individuals with brain injuries first appeared in the scientific literature, it seemed as though there were certain areas of the brain that were devoted to specific components of language (e.g., grammatical processing) and others devoted to other components of language (e.g., semantic processing). Nativists argued that the specificity of such deficits supported their claims that there are inborn language modules in the brain. However, subsequent research revealed that the same deficit can arise (e.g., problems of grammatical processing) even when damage is sustained in a number of different locations (Dick et al., 2001). In addition, grammatical-processing errors can be produced in nondisabled adults who are placed in experimental conditions that place stress on linguistic processing. These findings greatly undermine the idea of language modules.

The Development
of Reading
and Writing Skills

7

Beginning Reading

Vignette: Olivia, a beginning first grader, is reading Dr. Seuss's *Green Eggs and Ham* to her teacher, Ms. Julia. "I do not like them in a box. I do not like them with /f/, /f/ fry?" Ms. Julia says, "Let's look at the word more closely. You are right that it begins with the /f/ sound. It looks like the word you just said" (pointing to *box*). Olivia begins, "/f/, /f/ 'f box'; /f/ ox; fox. It's *fox*. The word is *fox*." "Yes," said Ms. Julia. Olivia begins to read the sentences from the beginning. "I do not like them in a box. I do not like them with a fox."

MAIN IDEAS OF THE CHAPTER

1. Reading is traditionally divided into "learning to read" and "reading to learn" phases. The former phase is also called beginning reading (the focus of this chapter). How do children learn to decode all of the words in a single sentence and construct a meaningful representation of it?
2. Two models of beginning reading skill include the connectionist model and the simple view of reading. Both emphasize the importance of meaning and the processing of sounds, letters, and grammatical relationships.
3. Teachers should care about the development of reading skills because there is a direct and strong connection between reading skills and the level of academic and professional success enjoyed by an individual in his or her lifetime.
4. Throughout the preschool period leading up to first grade, children acquire emergent literacy skills, which include the knowledge and attitudes that are presumed to be developmental precursors to conventional forms of reading and writing. Several aspects of emergent literacy are highly predictive of later reading (i.e., concepts of print, knowledge of letters, phonemic awareness); other strong predictors of early reading are socioeconomic status, the ability to recall sentences, and the ability to rapidly name objects.
5. Research has also revealed several general trends in acquiring beginning reading skills. First, children rely less on context to figure out words and more on automatically recognizing and interpreting words as they become more skilled; second, al-

though early phonological processing skills predict later reading skills, acquiring reading skill promotes increases in phonological processing; third, children pass through four phases in their ability to decode words that range from partially identifying letters to systematic and fluent decoding.

6. These age trends can be explained by noting that children who become skilled readers were not only provided with more opportunities to engage in prereading and reading activities (e.g., book reading, rhyming games, exposure to print) than less-skilled readers, they were also more prone to take advantage of these opportunities because they had the prerequisite skills (i.e., larger vocabularies) and motivation to do so.

7. There are three core differences between skilled and struggling readers: (a) Skilled readers are better at recognizing words automatically (i.e., they do not have to pay attention to the decoding process); (b) skilled readers are better at rapidly recognizing words and subword units; and (c) skilled readers are better at recoding print items into a phonological representation.

This chapter marks a transition between the previous chapters that have focused on spoken language competence and the next three chapters that will focus on reading and writing skills. However, as noted several times in Chapters 1 to 6, there is considerable overlap in the component skills that are needed to comprehend and produce spoken and written language (as well as unique, nonoverlapping components). So much is known about reading that we need to examine it in two successive chapters. We follow the convention in the literacy field of dividing reading competencies into the distinct tasks of "learning to read" (i.e., beginning reading; the focus of this chapter) and "reading to learn" (i.e., reading comprehension; the focus of Chapter 8). Beginning reading skills are applied to the task of reading single words or single sentences. In nondisabled readers from middle-income households, beginning skills are often mastered by the end of third grade. Chapter 8 focuses on additional skills related to comprehending larger segments of text. The latter skills are progressively mastered after the fourth grade. As was the case for previous chapters, the now-familiar five questions are used to organize the presentation of information.

THE "NATURE OF" QUESTION: What Does It Mean to Say That a Child Has Beginning Reading Skills?

In order to know how to help children become good readers, we first need to know what good reading entails. The task of defining good reading is approached in three ways. First, we consider a consensus view of reading that emerged from a panel of experts convened by the National Research Council (NRC) (Snow et al., 1998). Then, we discuss an influential model of proficient reading that emerged in the 1980s and still plays a prominent role today (i.e., Seidenberg & McClelland's (1989) connectionist model).

Finally, we examine a model that demonstrates the inherent connection between spoken language and reading.

A Consensus View

The field of reading research has been continually plagued by deep divisions among camps of researchers who hold diametrically opposed perspectives. Given this history, one would think that it would be impossible to come up with a consensus view of reading on which most scholars could agree. In the late 1990s, however, a group of 17 experts on reading did just that (Snow et al., 1998). Although these experts approach reading from a variety of perspectives, they readily agreed that, at a general level, reading should be defined as "a process of getting meaning from print, using knowledge about the written alphabet and about the sound structure of oral language for purposes of achieving understanding" (p. vi). What should be noticed about this definition is the combined emphasis on (1) meaning and understanding (as opposed to an exclusive focus on sounding out words), (2) knowledge of alphabetic characters (as opposed to suggesting that letter knowledge is less important than whole, undifferentiated words), and (3) knowledge of sounds (as opposed to minimizing the role of these sounds). The expert panel, in conjunction with a number of reviewers and consultants, elaborated on this general definition by suggesting that skilled readers:

- Rapidly and automatically identify written words through visual processes, phonological decoding processes, semantic processes, and contextual interpretive processes.
- Use their general world knowledge and extensive sight vocabulary to comprehend texts literally and draw inferences.
- Demonstrate the ability to accurately assess and monitor their own understanding.
- Use a common set of syntactic and inferential processes to comprehend both spoken language and text, as well as text-specific processes to comprehend texts.

The second way to understand the nature of skilled reading is to examine contemporary theoretical models of this ability. Although there are a number of such models in existence (Coltheart, Curtis, Atkins, & Haller, 1993), it is most efficient to examine just two of these models here for illustrative purposes. Both have had considerable impact on reading research, and both highlight important constructs. The first is Seidenberg and McClelland's (1989) connectionist model (see Chapters 4 and 6 for discussions of connectionism). Whereas this model has been strongly endorsed in several influential publications (e.g., Adams, 1990; Pressley, 1997), certain kinds empirical problems have caused it to be refined over the years (Brown, 1998). Figure 7.1 depicts the key elements of the original model. The second model is the simple view of reading proposed by Gough and his colleagues (e.g., Gough, Hoover, & Peterson, 1996).

A Connectionist Model of Reading

Connectionist models are based on the idea that when people read, they process many different types of information (e.g., letters, word meanings, syntax). More important, the model shown in Figure 7.1 implies two things: (1) that processing is *divided* among relatively autonomous subsystems that perform their own tasks (indicated by the ovals), and (2) that each subsystem *sends* what it "knows" or has "figured out" to at least one other subsystem (indicated by the arrows). The former point means that readers have many different clues they can use to make sense of a sentence. The latter point means that one processor can send its clues to other processors to help them make sense of their own clues; that is, the processors work *interactively* with one another (Perfetti, 1985). With this in mind, let's

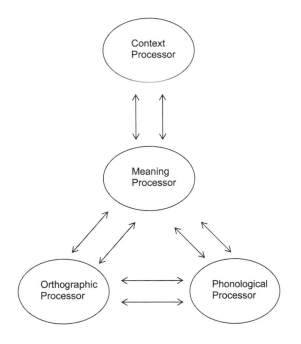

FIGURE 7.1. The four processors of the Seidenberg–McClelland model.

examine the jobs performed by the orthographic, meaning, phonological, and context processors in turn.

The Orthographic Processor

Orthographic knowledge consists of knowing the individual symbols of a written language. For example, a U.S. child who knows the letters of the English alphabet has orthographic knowledge, as does a Chinese child who knows all of the logographic characters of Chinese. The orthographic processor shown in Figures 7.1 and 7.2 can be thought of as a storehouse of orthographic knowledge. The single oval for the orthographic processor in Figure 7.1 is shorthand notation for the more detailed set of connections shown in Figure 7.2. More specifically, the orthographic processor has the job of processing and recognizing strings of letters (i.e., words). It accomplishes this feat by means of small *units* that recognize individual letters and parts of letters (McClelland & Rumelhart, 1981; Seidenberg & McClelland, 1989). As noted above, the system is designed according to connectionist principles.

Word recognition occurs when the units for each letter of a word attain a sufficient degree of activation. The main way that each unit becomes activated is through direct perception of the letter it represents in the mind. Using the model in Figure 7.2, for example, any of the units in the lowest row (representing portions of letters) become activated when a reader perceives any of the individual portions in text in front of them. The second

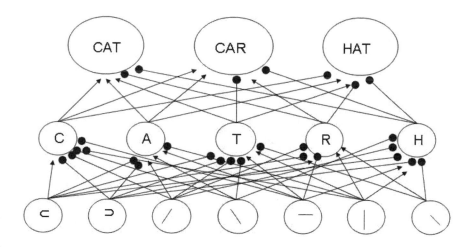

FIGURE 7.2. A connectionist model of the orthographic processor.

way that units can be activated is through *spreading activation*. A unit can spread its activation to another unit if the units are linked in an associative relationship. Associations form between units when certain letters (e.g., *q*) frequently co-occur with other letters (e.g., *u*). Any unit that has been partially activated by spreading activation turns on faster than it would have if the letter were presented alone. Memory researchers refer to this process as *priming*. For example, when someone sees a *q* while scanning a word left to right and then sees a *u* next, the unit for *u* is turned on faster than it would have been if *u* were perceived alone. Thus, associations and spreading activation promote faster reading.

In connectionist models, moreover, units spread their action either to increase the activation of units they are connected to (the lines with arrowheads in Figure 7.2) or to decrease or inhibit the activation of units they are connected to (the circular ends of connecting lines in Figure 7.2). For example, since a slanted vertical line (/) is part of the letter *A*, its unit is connected to the unit for *A* with a connection ending in an arrowhead. Since a completely vertical line is not part of the letter *A*, the link between the two units has a circular (inhibitory) end to it.

Any familiar word, then, is really a highly associated pattern of letters, and each letter in the word primes the perception of the others. As a result, the entire word is recognized very quickly and automatically as a result of perceiving every one of the letters.

After many years of research using sophisticated technology, we now have a better sense of how the orthographic processor works in skilled readers. Here are some of the findings:

1. Contrary to a common belief held among nonscientists, skilled readers process the individual letters of the words they are reading. They are not aware of this because word recognition has become automatic and subconscious for them. However, skilled readers do not recognize the letters of a word independently of one another. Rather, after many years of reading, associations form between the units for one letter in a word and the units for other letters. As a result, a familiar word is perceived as a whole.

2. The strengths of the association between the units for letters reflect the frequencies with which these letters co-occur in written texts. For example, when the letter *t* occurs as the first letter of a three-letter word, it is extremely likely that the next letter will be an *h* (Adams, 1990). People who read a lot develop mental associations between letters. Once associations form, they allow the activation from the units for one letter to "spread" to the units for another. As a result, skilled readers recognize familiar words very quickly and automatically. In contrast, someone who has never read a book and

only knows letters would not recognize words as fast as a skilled reader because no associations have formed among the units for letters. Such a person would, however, recognize isolated letters as fast as a skilled reader.

3. Letter associations also help skilled readers process the proper order of letters in a word (e.g., *the* vs. *hte*), as well as perceive association-preserving pseudowords (e.g., *Mave* and *Teel*). A pseudoword is a made-up word created by researchers. It uses combinations of letters that appear frequently in real words (e.g., the *-ave* in *Mave*).

4. Finally, letter associations also help a reader divide a word into syllables. For example, whereas *dr* is an acceptable combination of letters that maps onto the sounds of spoken English (e.g., the /drrr/ sound in the word *drive*), *dn* is not. As a result, a skilled reader who encounters the word *midnight* would visually divide this word into *mid* and *night* (splitting between the *d* and *n*, which do not make a combined sound like *dr*). In contrast, skilled readers would not visually divide *address* into *add* and *ress*. Moreover, a skilled reader implicitly knows that vowels seem to "pull" their adjacent consonants into a cluster of association patterns. For example, the *a* in *party* perceptually pulls the *p* and *r* toward itself. This fact combined with the fact that *rt* is an unacceptable spoken combination means that *party* would be divided into *par* and *ty* (Adams, 1990).

It is interesting to note that, historically, written language did not use spacing and punctuation to delineate words (Just & Carpenter, 1987). As a result, readers had to exclusively rely on their orthographic knowledge to make sense of a sentence. To see how this might work, consider the following sentence: *Thattoywaslost*.

The Meaning Processor

Of course, comprehending a sentence requires far more than the ability to determine whether letter strings are orthographically acceptable or familiar. For example, the pseudosentence, *Trat distle quas*, contains combinations of letters that appear in real words (e.g., the *tr-* in *trat* also appears in *truck* and *tree*), but it is meaningless. Similarly, the sentence *The octogenarian insinuated himself into our organization* would be meaningless to a person who knows that he or she has seen the written words *octogenarian* and *insinuated* before, but cannot remember what they mean. Thus, sentence comprehension requires both an *orthographic* processor to recognize letter strings and a *meaning* processor to access word meanings.

Several views have been proposed regarding how meanings are assigned to words. According to the *lexical access* view, for example, entire word meanings are stored in a *lexicon*. The lexicon is a hypothesized mental "dictionary" that organizes word meanings in terms of lists of attributes or schemata. When a written word is perceived, its meanings are accessed if the resting activation levels of these word meanings are high enough (Just & Carpenter, 1987). Moreover, the higher the resting activation level, the faster a word meaning will be retrieved. Word meanings attain a high activation level if the words to which they are attached occur frequently. Thus, the meanings of frequent words are accessed faster than the meanings of infrequent words. For example, whereas common words like *man* might have their meanings accessed in 250 ms, uncommon words like *propensity* might take 750 ms or longer (Carpenter, Miyake, & Just, 1995).

Other models of meaning include recent connectionist theories. According to connectionist views, word meanings are represented in the meaning processor as associated sets of primitive meaning elements, in the same way that spellings of familiar words are represented in the orthographic processor as associated sets of letters and parts of letters (Adams, 1990). A person's experience determines which meaning elements are associated and stored for a given word (Hintzman, 1986). For example, a child who hears the word *dog* applied to a specific dog in a specific context might associate the whole experience with the word *dog*. The next time he or she hears the word *dog* applied, however, it might be with a different dog in a different context. According to the connectionist view, those aspects of the second context that are similar to aspects of the first context (e.g., both dogs had a flea collar) would become associated and stored with the word *dog*. Over time, a consistent set of meaning elements would be distilled from these repeated encounters with dogs. Each element would be highly associated with the others and would, therefore, prime one's memory for the others. Moreover, some aspects of the meaning of *dog* would be more central to its meaning and reflect consistent correlations of attributes (e.g., "has fur" and "barks"). Such attributes would be accessed the fastest when the single word *dog* is read. Other meaning elements that are somewhat less central (e.g., "has an owner") would also be accessible but would be accessed more slowly, if at all, when the word is read in isolation.

As Figure 7.1 shows, the meaning processor is directly linked to the orthographic processor. This means that the output of each processor can help the other do its job better. In support of this claim, Whittlesea and Cantwell (1987) found that when a pseudoword is given a meaningful definition, subjects perceived this word faster than they did when it lacked a definition. This improved perceptibility lasted for at least 24 hours, even when the supplied meaning had been forgotten. Thus, the meaning processor helped the orthographic processor do its job better. But the reverse can happen, as well. As we show in the section on the development of reading ability (Developmental Models and Trends, p. 187), students who frequently read text with new words can dramatically increase the size of their vocabularies. Thus, orthographic knowledge can improve the capacity of the meaning processor.

The Phonological Processor

Analogous to the orthographic and meaning processors, the phonological processor consists of units that form associations with each other. In this case, however, the basic units correspond to phonemes in the reader's spoken language. As noted in Chapter 4, phonemes such as "ba" and "tuh" can be combined into syllables such as *bat* and also into words such as *battle* (phonologists and linguists prefer the convention of encasing sounds in a pair of backslashes and representing these sounds with a set of symbols such as /θ/, which represents the sound corresponding to *th*). A word can also be composed of an initial sound (*onset*) and final sound (*rime*) that it may have in common with other words. For example, the rime of *cat* and *hat* is -at while the onset of these words are /k/ and /h/, respectively. The auditory representation of a word, syllable, onset, rime, or phoneme is composed of an activated set of specific units in the phonological processor (Adams, 1990). Figure 4.1 is an example of a connectionist model of the phonological representation of sounds (see Chapter 4).

Recent studies suggest that phonemes and larger sound units take on different levels of importance in reading and oral language. In particular, Treiman and colleagues have found that many words seem to be represented in terms of an onset and a rime, perhaps because certain vowel–final–consonant combinations occur in texts more often than chance (Kessler & Treiman, 1997). Both children and adults make fewer errors and respond faster when they utilize onset–rime information in words (especially rime information). They appear to be less reliant on the more specific connection between graphemes and individual phonemes (Treiman, Mullennix, Bijeljac-Babic, & Richmond-Welty, 1995; Treiman & Zukowski, 1996). In a related way, other studies suggest that the level of the syllable often overrides the level of the phoneme in early writing (Treiman & Tincoff, 1997).

When skilled readers see a written word, they do not have to translate it phonologically in order for its meaning to be accessed. Many studies have shown that meaning can be accessed simply by a visual pattern of letters (Adams, 1990; Seidenberg & McClelland, 1989). And yet, skilled readers of a variety of languages often *do* translate words phonologically when they read. This tendency to create phonological representations even occurs in languages such as Chinese that use logographic symbols that do not map onto sounds the way English graphemes do (Chow, McBride-Chang, & Burgess, 2005). Why would people perform some operation when they do not have to? The answer seems to be that the phonological processor provides a certain degree of redundancy with the information provided by the other processors. This redundancy can be quite helpful when the information provided by the other processors is incomplete, deceptive, or weakly specified (Stanovich, 1980; Adams, 1990).

More specifically, the phonological processor seems to provide two important services to the overall reading system. In the first place, it provides an alphabetic backup system that may be crucial for maintaining fast and accurate reading (Adams, 1990). This backup system exists mainly because the orthography of written English largely obeys the *alphabetic principle*: Written symbols (i.e., graphemes) correspond to spoken sounds (i.e., phonemes). Although this grapheme–phoneme correspondence is not one-to-one or perfectly regular, it is nevertheless fairly predictable (Brown, 1998; Just & Carpenter, 1987; Treiman et al., 1995). As a result, the phonological processor could provide helpful information in a variety of situations. For example, consider the case in which a reader knows the meaning of a spoken word but has never seen it written down. There would be no direct connection between (1) the units corresponding to the letters of this word in the orthographic processor and (2) the units corresponding to the meaning of this word in the meaning processor. There would, however, be a connection between the phonological processor units and the meaning processor units for this word. If the word obeys the alphabetic principle fairly well, readers would be able to "sound it out" and hear themselves saying the familiar word. This pronunciation, in turn, would access the meaning of the word. Over repeated readings, the two-way association between the phonological processor and meaning processor units for this word would become a three-way association between the orthographic, meaning, and phonological units. The basic premise, then, is that good readers mentally represent the statistical properties of the relations between graphemes and sound patterns that appear in texts (Brown, 1998). Words are read more quickly and accurately if they contain graphemes that are consistently related to particular sound patterns (e.g., the *-ave* rime in *gave*, *save*, and *rave*).

The second service provided by the phonological processor has to do with readers' memory for what they have just read. Memory researchers appeal to the construct of *working memory* to explain many phenomena including retention during reading. Working memory is related to the concept of short-term memory in that both forms deal with temporarily-holding information (e.g., a person hears a phone number said to him or her for the first time). Within working memory, research has revealed a "phonological loop" in which verbal information is rehearsed for later processing (Baddeley, 1990). In order for readers to make sense of what they are reading, they have to take all of the words in a sentence and put them together into a meaningful whole (Caplan & Waters, 1999; Just & Carpenter, 1987). This integration requires a certain degree of memory because when readers read from left to right, only one or two words fall within their visual-fixation span. That is, all of the words to the left of a visual-fixation point must be retained in working memory until the person reaches the end of a sentence. The phonological loop plays the crucial role of keeping a record of all words in a sentence in order that all of their meanings can be integrated together. If this integration does not take place within 2 s, the reader has to go back and reread the sentence. Such findings demonstrate the importance of reading fluency (i.e., reading rapidly and automatically). In addition, the phonological processor must be intimately connected to the phonological loop because adults with certain brain injuries show a marked inability to retain words that they just read. One proposal based on studies of individuals with brain injuries and individuals without brain injuries suggests that there may even be a subsystem of working memory that is uniquely specialized for syntactic processing (Caplan & Waters, 1999).

The Context Processor

The context processor has the job of constructing an online, coherent interpretation of text (Adams, 1990). The output of this processor is a mental representation of everything that a reader has read so far. For example, upon reading the sentence, *When Queen Elizabeth entered the chamber, the MPs all rose*, the context may be a mental image of Queen Elizabeth walking up to the podium in the British House of Commons. Whereas some researchers (e.g., Just & Carpenter, 1987) call this image a *referential representation* of the text, others (e.g., van Dijk & Kintsch, 1983) call it a *situation model*. For simplicity and consistency with other chapters, we shall use the latter term.

Semantic, pragmatic, and syntactic knowledge all contribute to the construction of a situation model (Seidenberg & McClelland, 1989). For example, when skilled readers encounter the sentence, *John went to the store to buy a ___*, they use their semantic knowledge to access the meanings of all of the words in the sentence. In addition, they use their pragmatic knowledge to expect that John will buy something that people usually buy at stores. If the blank were filled in by *savings bond*, readers would likely be surprised when their eyes reached the word *savings*.

Syntactic knowledge also prompts the reader to form certain expectations about what will occur next (Garrett, 1990; Goodman & Goodman, 1979; Just & Carpenter, 1987). To see how the syntactic "parser" operates, it is useful to describe the notions of grammatical rules and tree structures.

In some circles of linguistics and psychology, scholars argue that language comprehension and production are guided by a set of grammatical rules (Lasnick, 1990). That is, there are certain *types* of sentences and each type can be produced using a specific set of rules. For example, each of the following sentences can be produced by using the same three rules:

1. *The tall boy hit the round ball.*
2. *The girl chewed an apple.*
3. *A man drew a picture.*
4. *A woman dropped the cup.*

These rules are:

R1. Sentence = Noun Phrase + Verb Phrase (i.e., S → NP + VP)
R2. Verb Phrase = Verb + Noun Phrase (i.e., VP → V + NP)
R3. Noun Phrase = Determiner + (optional adjective) + Noun (i.e., NP → Det + (adj)+ N)

To depict the hierarchical arrangement of a set of rules, linguists have used *tree structures*. Figure 7.3 depicts a tree structure for the three rules above. By nesting one component (e.g., a determiner) within another (e.g., a noun phrase), the structure shows how the former is part of the latter. It should be noted, however, other kinds of syntactic theories besides those that entail rules have been proposed (including connectionist models; Caplan & Waters, 1999). The rule-based ones are presented here for illustrative purposes, but other kinds of models would also provide the basis for grammatical expectations.

Given a specific input sentence and knowledge of grammatical rules, the human mind is thought to build up a particular tree structure for the sentence, component-by-component. For example, upon reading the word *the*, the rule for producing noun phrases is elicited. Implicitly, the mind says "OK. A noun phrase must be starting." Given that a determiner has already been encountered, Rule 3 (above) sets up the expectation that either an adjective or a noun will be encountered next. When the word *tall* is next read in sentence 1, it is assigned the slot for adjective. Having organized the words *the* and *tall* together, Rule 3 now sets up the expectation that the next word will likely be a noun (to complete a noun phrase), and so on. In order for this system to work, written words (e.g., *tall*) have to be mentally associated with grammatical classes (e.g., adjective) in addition to word meanings.

Over the years, various researchers have doubted the existence of a mental parser, grammatical rules, and grammatical classes. Although these doubters have made some good points, there is considerable evidence that syntactic knowledge is an important aspect of sentence comprehension (regardless of whether the parser relies on rules or others kinds of representa-

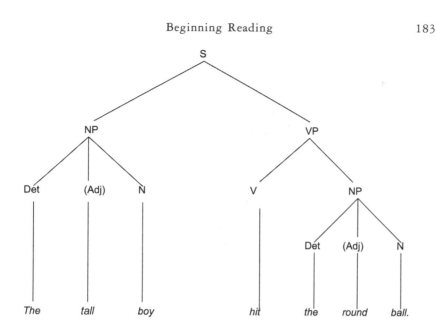

FIGURE 7.3. Tree diagram for the sentence *The tall boy hit the round ball.*

tions). In the first place, there is the syndrome called *Broca's aphasia* that results from injury to the Broca's area of the cerebral cortex (located in the left frontal lobe; see Figure 7.4). Individuals who have this disorder are able to comprehend the meanings of individual words but have trouble with the syntax of sentences (Caplan & Waters, 1999; Just & Carpenter, 1987). For example, they see no difference between the following two sentences:

    1. *They fed her the dog biscuits.*
    2. *They fed her dog the biscuits.*

Although these two sentences have the same words, they have different tree structures and, therefore, different meanings.

    In addition, there are many well-known "garden-path" sentences such as the following:

    3. *The old train the young.*
    4. *Since Jay always jogs a mile seems like a short distance to him.*
    5. *The horse raced past the barn fell.*

Note that there are no typos in sentences 3 to 5. If you read a few words of each and then said, "Huh?" at some point, that is because your syntax analyzer started to construct one kind of structure until it met a particular

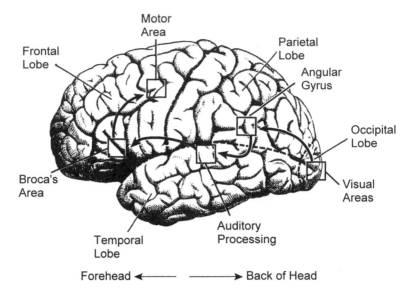

FIGURE 7.4. Brain areas corresponding to the Geschwind–Galaburda model. From Byrnes (2001b). Copyright 2001 by The Guilford Press. Reprinted by permission.

word that violated expectations (e.g., the second *the* in sentence 3, and *seems* in sentence 4). A sentence such as *the old train blew its whistle* would probably be more consistent with expectations than that listed as sentence 3. In sentence 4, a comma after *jogs* would have helped you create the right tree structure.

Further, there are studies that show how syntax affects both the meaning and pronunciation of a word that is encountered. For example, read the following sentences:

6. *John said, "Does are in the park, aren't they?"*
7. *Tomorrow was the annual one-day fishing contest and fisherman would invade the place. Some of the best bass guitarists in the country would come here.*

In sentence 6, grammatical rules suggest that *Does* is an auxiliary verb. Instead, it turns out to be the plural noun referring to female deer. The noun and the auxiliary have different pronunciations and meanings. In sentence 7, grammatical rules and prior context suggest that *bass* is a noun that labels a type of fish. Instead, it turns out to be an adjective in this instance that modifies a type of guitar. The noun and adjective have different meanings and pronunciations.

Finally, grammatical relations are evident when a reader encounters ambiguous sentences such as:

8. *Visiting relatives can be a nuisance.*
9. *The burglar saw the cop with binoculars.*

Does sentence 8 mean that it can be a bother to go see your relatives, or that relatives who come to see you can be a bother? Theoretically, the only way someone could "see" the multiple readings of these sentences is if he or she constructed multiple syntactic structures for each one.

In sum, then, syntactic, pragmatic, and semantic knowledge all contribute to the construction of a situation model. Once in place, this model prompts a reader to form expectations about what will occur next in the text. As each new segment of text is encountered, skilled readers interpret what is read in a way that makes it consistent with the current situation model.

The model of proficient reading in Figure 7.1 shows the two-way relationship between the context and the meaning processor. The model implies that the prior context can influence the meaning assigned to a word and that current meanings influence the construction of a situation model. Thus, when skilled readers process the sentence *John removed the thorn from the rose*, they assign a different meaning to *rose* than they would if they read the sentence *The crowd rose to sing the national anthem.*

However, research has shown that the context-meaning effects are weak relative to the orthography-meaning effects. That is, readers are much better at predicting possible meanings of a word based on its perceived spelling than they are at predicting which word will follow a preceding context (Adams, 1990; Snow et al., 1998). When context-meaning links conflict with orthography-meaning links, the latter wins. Thus, skilled reading consists, first and foremost, of learning the correspondences between written words and their meanings. Context effects occur *after* words are perceived and various possible meanings are accessed. But overall, context, orthography, meanings, and phonology all work in concert to help a reader construct the best possible interpretation of a text.

The Simple View of Reading

The second theoretical perspective, the simple view of reading, begins with the insight that reading comprehension and listening comprehension have much in common (Gough et al., 1996). For example, the same lexicon is used when reading and listening; sentences or words that are ambiguous in one modality (e.g., reading) are often ambiguous in the other modality (e.g., listening); both modalities rely on sequential processing (one word at a time) and on word order to compute syntax (at least in English); and the same background knowledge supports the interpretation of both printed and spoken words. These commonalities suggest that reading can be subdivided into two parts: that which is unique to reading (i.e., *decoding* or translating text into sounds) and that which is shared with listening (i.e., comprehension).

This suggestion can be integrated with the connectionist model by noting that listening comprehension involves the context, meaning, and phonological processors of the connectionist model in Figure 7.1. Reading skills are made possible by "grafting" the orthographic processor onto the other three processors. Decoding is represented by the links between the orthographic and phonological processors.

We know that decoding and comprehension are separable because a typical 5-year-old or older child with a reading disability can comprehend spoken language but cannot decode. Conversely, there are conditions such as hyperlexia in which an individual can decode but not comprehend (Gough et al., 1996). To be able to read, then, a student has to be skilled at both decoding and comprehending. To capture the fact that decoding and comprehending are both necessary but not individually sufficient for reading, Gough and colleagues proposed a multiplicative hypothesis. If reading skills (r), decoding skills (d), and comprehending (c) skills can be placed on three hypothetical continua that range from 0 to 1 (e.g., someone who has more skill would receive a score closer to 1), reading must be the product of decoding and comprehension and not simply the addition of these components, as the formula $r = d \times c$ suggests. Both decoding and comprehending have to be greater than 0 for reading to take place. In their studies, Gough and colleagues found that the correlations between reading scores (r) and the product of scores for decoding and comprehending ($d \times c$) were higher (r's = .84 to .91) than the individual correlations between decoding and reading or between comprehension and reading. Decoding was measured by having students read pseudowords. Listening comprehension was measured by having students listen to stories and answer questions about these stories. Reading was measured using standardized reading tests.

Summary

Collectively, the definitions of reading evident in the conclusions of the NRC, connectionist models of reading, and the simple view of reading all emphasize the importance and integration of orthographic skills (including decoding), language comprehension skills (phonological processing, semantics, syntax), and background knowledge. When do these skills emerge in development, and when does their integration seem evident? We address these developmental trends questions in a subsequent section. For now, we can briefly consider the relevance question.

THE RELEVANCE QUESTION: Why Should Teachers Care about Whether Children Acquire Beginning Reading Skills?

Unlike other topics explored so far, it is relatively easy to convince educators, policymakers, and parents of the importance of reading skills. There is a direct and strong connection between reading skills and the level of academic and professional success enjoyed by an individual (Snow et al., 1998). By definition, skilled readers perform very well on reading achievement tests. In addition, however, they also show higher levels of problem-solving success in mathematics and higher levels of achievement in science and social studies. Conversely, less proficient readers struggle a great deal academically and are more likely to experience negative outcomes such as dropping out of school or incarceration (Malmgren & Leone, 2000). Unless reading problems are detected and corrected early in a child's schooling, the gap between their performance and their more proficient peers grows steadily each year (Stanovich, 1986).

THE DEVELOPMENTAL TRENDS QUESTION: How Do Beginning Reading Skills Change over Time?

Now that you know what skilled reading involves and why it is important, you have sense of the "endpoint" of reading development (but, of course, reading always improves a little with continued practice and experience). The beginning point of reading development is that point in a child's life when he or she has no idea what reading involves (e.g., infancy). In this section, we discuss how children progress from the beginning point to the endpoint of reading development, and proceed as follows. In the first subsection (Emergent Literacy), we examine a collection of skills that progressively appear prior to the onset of formal reading instruction in first grade. In the second subsection (Factors Predictive of Reading Success), we examine the characteristics of preschool children that seem to predict their ability to read well by the end of first grade. In the third subsection (Explaining Predictive Relations), we consider explanations of the predictive links between certain factors and reading success and put the predictors together in a coherent story. When you know why certain children become skilled readers, you gain insight into how to help all children become skilled readers. In the fourth subsection (Precocious Readers), we examine the incidence and causes of precocious reading in preschoolers. In the fifth and final subsection (Developmental Models), we consider some general or global trends in the development of reading skills.

Emergent Literacy

Whitehurst and Lonigan (1998, p. 849) suggest that *emergent literacy* "consists of the skills, knowledge, and attitudes that are presumed to be developmental precursors to conventional forms of reading and writing . . . and the environments that support these developments." The construct of emergent literacy was originally proposed in the 1980s as an alternative to the idea of *reading readiness* that has existed in educational circles since the early 1900s (at least). According to the latter concept, it is not possible to teach reading to children until they are maturationally "ready" to benefit from this instruction. Some researchers went so far as to use IQ tests to determine when the brain was ready (Morphett & Washburn, 1931). Notwithstanding the merits of this brain-based proposal, a readiness conception implies an all-or-none dichotomy between readers (i.e., first graders who are ready) and nonreaders (i.e., preschoolers who are not ready). The emergent literacy conception, in contrast, implies a *continuum* of skills that have their origin well before formal reading instruction begins in first grade (Teale & Sulzby, 1986). Some examples of such skills include knowing that (1) the words in a book tell the story, and the pictures are an accompaniment to the words, (2) English readers read words from left to right and lines of words from the top of a page to the bottom, (3) written words correspond to spoken words, (4) one reads all of the words on a page before reading the words on the next page, (5) pages are read in a specific order from the first to the last page, (6) there is someone (i.e., the author) who had the story in his or her mind and decided to write it down so that children could know the story too, and (7) writing is like speaking because it is way of communicating ideas (Clay, 1985; Sulzby, 1991; Teale & Sulzby, 1986; Whitehurst & Lonigan, 1998). The advocates of the emergent literacy perspective argue that such ideas are just as important as knowledge of the alphabetic principle for beginning reading.

Whitehurst and Lonigan (1998) elaborated on the original conception of emergent literacy to suggest that it also involves other kinds of skills such as an oral vocabulary, knowledge of syntax, knowledge of letters of the alphabet, metalinguistic knowledge of sounds in words, the alphabetic principle, pretend reading, reading motivation, and verbal processing skills (e.g., rapid naming and verbal working memory).

Predicting Reading Success

From the standpoint of No Child Left Behind (NCLB) legislation, there are two main categories of first-grade students: those who acquire the reading skills they need to be successful in later grades and those who do not. NCLB legislation is designed to put pressure on schools to increase the number of children in the successful category. To accomplish this goal, school officials should begin by gathering data to answer the following question: What is true of the successful students that is not true of the unsuccessful students? When children attend the same schools and experience the same curriculum, it would seem that the difference in reading achievement between successful and unsuccessful students is probably not due to instructional variables. Rather, the main reasons for the differing levels of reading achievement probably derive from characteristics of students themselves. To test this assumption, a standard methodology involves collecting data on children when they are in preschool or kindergarten and then seeing which variables predict who eventually becomes a good reader. By revealing the ways in which successful and unsuccessful students differ as preschoolers, school systems may gain insight into how to elevate the performance of the less-successful students by conducting early intervention.

Before describing the findings, it is helpful to make a few preliminary points about the statistical concept of correlation because predictive studies report correlations. Correlations can range between −1.0 and +1.0, with numbers closer to −1.0 or +1.0 indicating a stronger predictive relation. If, for example, the number of books in a home is found to correlate $r = .60$ with later reading success, that means an increase in books is associated with higher reading scores. However, the fact that the correlation is less than 1.0 means that there may be cases in which there were many books in the home but the child did not end up being in the category of successful readers at the end of first grade (and vice versa).

However, as the old adage goes, "Correlation does not imply causation." Simply finding a correlation does not mean that one could make sure that all children become successful readers by increasing the level of the predictive factor. Continuing the previous example, children's reading achievement would not necessarily improve if the government were to buy a lot of books for families that have very few. Other problems with correlational studies include spurious correlations and age changes in the predictive power of certain factors. A *spurious correlation* exists when two variables are linked through some other variable. In effect, the linkage is illusory. To illustrate such a correlation, consider the fact that there is an association between the number of physicians who work in a geographic area and the infant mortality rate in that area (the more doctors there are, the higher the infant death rate). This spurious correlation can be explained as follows. There tend to be more physicians and more low-income people living in urban areas than in rural areas. The infant mortality rate tends to be much higher among the poor than among the rich, so the infant mortality rate tends to be higher in the cities than elsewhere. Hence, the number of doctors has nothing to do with the infant mortality rate, but a correlation computed between these two factors makes these variables appear to be related somehow. In this case, their apparent linkage is explained by other variables, such as a common geographic area and poverty. Applied to the case of reading success, there are a number of factors that are correlated with reading success (see below). Before we can understand the differences between successful and unsuccessful readers, we will first need to determine which of these correlations are real and which are spurious.

Besides spurious correlations, another interpretive problem has to do with the fact that predictive relationships may be more complicated than the "more of X yields more of Y" variety (e.g., more literacy experiences yields more readiness to benefit from instruction). Some activities or skills may be prerequisites for others and fall away in importance as time goes on (de Jong & van der Leij, 1999). The correlation between such prerequisites and later reading scores may be low, but it would be wrong to assume that the factor is not important. Relatedly, some correlations may involve thresholds in which there has to be a minimum level of some experience to have an effect (e.g., you have to read to children at least 10 min a day). Any amount over that minimum has no added benefit. When a threshold effect occurs, lower correlations ensue because correlations only are large if an increase in one factor (e.g., minutes read to each day) continues to produce increases in another (e.g., first-grade reading scores) at all levels of the first factor.

With these caveats in mind, we can now look at the list of factors that have found to be correlated with reading success in the first grade. After presenting this list, we will attempt to reduce the number of factors down using tests for spurious correlations. Factors are presented in a rank-order, starting with those that (1) have been found to have the highest correlation with being ready to benefit and (2) have the most studies supporting the linkage.

School Readiness

There are widely used measures of overall school readiness that tap into a number of component skills such as knowledge of the alphabet, knowledge of numbers, the ability to follow directions, and visual memory for drawings (e.g., the Metropolitan Readiness Test). There are also other more specific measures that are alleged to tap into readiness to read. Five studies found fairly high correlations between overall school readiness measures and first-grade reading scores that ranged between .34 and .76. The average correlation across these studies was $r = .62$ (Bolig & Fletcher, 1973; Gordon, 1988; Nagle, 1979; Randel, Fry, & Ralls, 1977). In a related way, 21 studies using the more specific reading-readiness measures generated an average correlation of $r = .56$ (Snow et al., 1998). Thus, children who had higher readiness scores in preschool showed the highest reading achievement scores at the end of first grade.

Socioeconomic Status

Socioeconomic status (SES) refers to such things as income level and parent education. In their meta-analysis of the correlations between SES and various indices of school achievement, Iverson and Walberg (1982) reported an average correlation of $r = .57$ between SES and reading scores (across 8 studies). Other researchers concur that children from higher SES households demonstrate higher levels of reading readiness and emergent literacy than children from lower SES households (Adams, 1990; Baker, Fernandez-Fein, Scher, & Williams, 1998; Bowey, 1995; Snow et al., 1998).

Letter Knowledge

Starting with Chall (1967) and Bond and Dykstra (1967), a number of studies have shown that children's knowledge of letter names is a very good predictor of their beginning reading achievement (Adams, 1990). Thus, children who enter school knowing that B is called "Bee" and T is called "Tee" perform better than children who lack this knowledge on end-of-year reading achievement tests in first grade. The correlations tend to hover around $r = .53$ (Snow et al., 1998).

Memory for Stories, Memory for Sentences, and Working-Memory Span

Children's ability to repeat sentences or stories that were just read to them is a better predictor of their reading achievement than other kinds of memory measures such as digit span (i.e., repeating a list of numbers that was just called out). Across 11 studies, the median correlation between memory for stories or sentences and reading achievement was found to be $r = .49$ (Snow et al., 1998). However, recent studies that have investigated the role of working-memory span as opposed to short-term memory storage have found correlations that rival the findings for memory for stories and sentences (e.g., Bayliss, Jarrold, Baddeley, & Leigh, 2005; Gathercole, Alloway, Willis, & Adams, 2006; Swanson, 2003; Swanson, Sáez, Gerber, & Leafstedt, 2004). Working-memory-span tasks require children to listen to a list of sentences and try to remember the last word of each sentence.

Concepts of Print

In the earlier discussion of emergent literacy, we saw that concepts of print involve such things as knowing that one reads from left to right. Across seven studies, the average correlation between measures of concepts of print and reading achievement was found to be $r = .49$ (Snow et al., 1998).

Phonemic Awareness

Phonemic awareness is the ability to reflect on, manipulate, and discriminate among phonemes. It can be assessed by asking children to delete certain sounds (e.g., "How would *pink* be pronounced if the last sound were eliminated?"), tap the number of sounds in a word, and so on. The average correlation between measures of phonemic awareness and reading achievement is $r = .42$ (Adams, 1990; Snow et al., 1998; Tunmer, Herriman, & Nesdale, 1988; Vellutino & Scanlon, 1991). In recent formulations, it has been argued that phonemic awareness is just one of a set of *phonological processing* or phonological sensitivity abilities that predict reading success (Anthony & Lonigan, 2004). Children who can recognize the global similarity between words such as *beach* and *dish*, or identify words that rhyme such as *beach* and *teach*, are also more likely to be skilled readers than children who cannot perform these tasks well (Carroll & Snowling, 2001). Interestingly, a number of studies have also found cross-linguistic transfer in phonological processing skills in bilingual children. For example, preschool children who have good phonological processing skills in their first language (e.g., Spanish) often become good readers in elementary school even when books are written in their newly acquired second language (e.g., English) (Chow et al., 2005; Lesaux & Siegel, 2003; Lindsey, Manis, & Bailey, 2003).

Rapid Automatized Naming

Measures of rapid automatized naming (RAN) ask children to name a series of letters or objects as quickly as they can (Compton, 2003). Typically, the score reflects the number of items correctly named in 60 s. Scarborough (1998) reported that the median correlation between RAN measures and subsequent reading measures is $r = .40$.

Language Skills

Children enter first grade with a variety of oral-language abilities. Studies have shown that correlations range between $r = .24$ to $r = .49$, depending on the language skill in question (Hammill & McNutt, 1980; Snow et al., 1998; Vellutino & Scanlon, 1987). Across 59 studies, Scarborough found that the average correlation was $r = .38$ between oral-language skills and reading achievement in school. Whereas the most predictive language skill was the ability to name a series of pictures ($r = .49$), the least predictive skill was the ability to point to pictures named by the tester ($r = .33$). Thus, it clearly matters whether one uses a measure of receptive vocabulary or productive vocabulary. Researchers have also found that (1) the correlations tend to be higher when one uses an aggregate score of multiple language abilities (e.g., vocabulary, semantics, and syntax) rather than a single score that represents a single aspect of language (e.g., vocabulary), (2) whereas vocabulary scores assessed before first grade sometimes predict the ability to sound out real words or pseudowords, broader measures of language are better predictors of reading comprehension (Muter, Hulme, Snowling, & Stevenson, 2004; National Institute of Child Health and Human Development (NICHD) Early Child Care Research Network, 2005), and (3) the match between a student's dialect and the language of books is important. For example, children who predominately speak African American Vernacular English showed lower reading achievement than their peers who were more familiar with the Standard English used in school textbooks (Charity, Scarborough, & Griffin, 2004).

Syntactic Awareness

Syntactic awareness is the ability to judge the grammatical acceptability of sentences. A child is said to possess syntactic awareness if he or she can tell the difference between an acceptable and unacceptable construction. In most studies, unacceptable constructions are formed by violating word order. For example, a child would be asked to listen to ill-formed sentences such as *Made cookies Mom* or *Why the dog is barking so loudly?* and asked to either say whether it is acceptable or not (Bialystok, 1988; Bowey & Patel, 1988; Tunmer et al., 1988). The results of these studies show that the ability to detect grammatical violations as a preschooler tends to correlate about $r = .37$ with first-grade reading scores.

Intelligence

Recall that the readiness construct was partially based on the finding that one could use a child's mental age on an IQ test to predict readiness to read (Adams, 1990; Just & Carpenter, 1987; Stanovich, Cunningham, & Feeman, 1984). While it is true that a child's preschool IQ is correlated with later reading success, this correlation is not as high as the mental-age hypothesis would predict. For example, the average correlation between IQ and reading scores for children below the fourth grade is about $r = .45$ (Stanovich et al., 1984) and the median correlation is $r = .34$ (Stanovich, 1988b). Given that IQ is moderately correlated with working-memory span, it is possible that the correlation between IQ and reading really reflects the working-memory loads of IQ tests.

Operativity

Finally, several studies have shown that concrete operational skills (the third level of thought in Piaget's stage theory) are correlated with first-grade reading performance (Arlin, 1981; Tunmer et al., 1988). The kinds of skills measured in these studies include classification, seriation, and conservation. The correlations between operativity and reading skills range between .21 and .48 (mean = .33).

Analysis of the Evidence

Before making too much of any one of these correlations, we need to consider the extent to which they are inflated or even spurious. What we really want to know is whether a predictor remains a strong predictor after one controls for other variables. There are two approaches to test for the unique predictive value of a factor. One approach, called *regression*, can be illustrated with the following example. Imagine that we gave just two measures to ten 5-year-olds: an IQ test and a measure of their letter knowledge. Then, we came back a year later and measured their reading skills in first grade. The fictional table below shows how the data turned out:

Name	IQ at 5	Letters at 5	First-grade reading
Matt	High	High*	Very good
Ryan	High	High	Poor
Steven	High	Low*	Poor
Chris	Low	Low	Very good
Tom	High*	High*	Very good
Kristen	Low*	Low*	Poor
Tiffany	High	High	Poor
Julia	High*	High*	Very good
Tara	High	Low*	Poor
Amanda	High*	High*	Very good

If IQ is a good predictor, then every child who has a high IQ at 5 years of age should be a skilled reader by the end of first grade (like Matt above; read his data across the top row). Conversely, every child with a low IQ should be a struggling reader by the end of first grade (like Kristen above). The table shows that IQ is not a perfect predictor because only 4 of 10 children show the right low–low or high–high pattern (Note: Children fitting the pattern have an asterisk next to their IQ outcome.) Nevertheless, these data would probably generate a correlation of about $r = .30$. As for letter knowledge, a perfect correlation would ensue if every child with high letter knowledge at age 5 was a skilled reader at the end of first grade and every child with low letter knowledge was a struggling reader at the end of first grade. The table again shows that letter knowledge is not a perfect predictor, but 7 out of 10 children fit the pattern. This fictional data for letter knowledge might generate a correlation of $r = .60$. Comparing the data across the two factors, it is better to know someone's letter knowledge because it predicts success or failure better than IQ. If we had no other information but IQ, however, we would see that it correctly predicts outcomes for some of the children. However, you should also see that when you know both IQ scores and letter-knowledge scores, IQ scores add very little new information. The same four children who fit the IQ pattern (Tom, Kristen, Julia, and Amanda) also fit the letter-knowledge pattern. Therefore, knowing their IQ is redundant information for these four children. Note further that we pick up three additional children by knowing their letter knowledge (who would have been missed by using just IQ). Finally, note that IQ is highly correlated with letter knowledge (those high on one are high on the other). If we entered these data in a statistical procedure called *regression*, the procedure would tell us which factors are unique, nonredundant predictors and which are merely correlated with the better predictors. In this case, regression would tell us that letter knowledge is a unique predictor and IQ adds no new information beyond letter knowledge.

A second way to discriminate between authentic predictors and spurious predictors is to use partial correlations instead of raw correlations. When a partial correlation is computed, one sees whether the original correlation maintains its numerical value when the effects of other variables that might be involved are mathematically eliminated. For example, let's say that the correlation between letter knowledge and reading achievement is $r = .53$. If this correlation shrinks down to a figure close to 0 (e.g., $r = .05$) when the effects of IQ are subtracted out in a partial correlation computation, it is probably a spurious correlation. However, if it stays roughly the same size after the effects due to IQ are subtracted out (e.g., $r = .46$), then it is probably not spurious (at least with respect to the variable of IQ).

What happens when regression and partial correlation approaches are applied to the list of 10 predictors above? The best way to answer this question would be to assess the 10 factors in the same set of preschool children and see how well they read in first grade. When all factors are considered at once, the genuine predictors will remain significant and the spurious predictors will no longer be found significant. Unfortunately, researchers have generally not taken such a comprehensive approach to date. They have, however, assessed 3 or 4 of the 10 factors in the same study. One exception to this pattern is Schatschneider, Fletcher, Francis, Carlson, and Foorman (2004) who assessed the role of 6 categories of factors. As might be expected from the size of the correlations reported above, studies that have assessed at least 3 factors show that SES, letter knowledge, sentence memory, concepts of print, RAN, and phonological processing all retain their predictive power even when one subtracts out the effects of other variables. In contrast, factors such as receptive vocabulary, syntactic awareness, IQ, and operativity all lose their predictive powers when one controls for one or more of the 6 factors that are unique predictors (e.g., phonemic awareness and letter knowledge). It is also worth noting that the school- and reading-readiness measures contain many items tapping into such things as letter knowledge.

Explaining Predictive Relations

How can we explain the fact that SES, letter knowledge, sentence memory, concepts of print, RAN, and phonemic awareness all retain their predictive power after the effects of other variables are controlled? The first thing to note is that some of these correlations may still be illusory even though they retain their value after statistical techniques are applied. The only way to know for sure whether a correlation reflects a causal relation between a predictor and outcome is to experimentally manipulate the predictor to see if changes then occur in the outcome variable. The second point to make is that some of the predictors may be proximally related to reading achievement (e.g., letter knowledge) while others are more distally related (e.g., SES). To be able to tell the difference between proximal and distal causes, it is helpful to ask a series of "why" questions. Proximal causes are usually answers to the first "why" question one asks (e.g., Question 1: Why are some children ready to read at the start of first grade? Answer: They have knowledge of letters). In contrast, distal causes are usually answers to the second or third "why" questions that follow on the first one (e.g., Question 2: Why do some children have more knowledge of letters when they start first grade? Answer: They have well-educated parents who taught them letter names).

Our first task, then, is to consider whether any training studies have been conducted to demonstrate a causal relation between the six unique predictors and reading achievement. It is not really feasible to manipulate SES (i.e., it is not ethical to randomly give a high-paying job and college education to the parents of children in one group but not give the same things to children in another group) or sentence memory (this may be a fairly stable individual difference trait), so we need to determine whether researchers have tried to teach letter knowledge, concepts of print, RAN, or phonemic awareness to preschool children. With respect to letter knowledge, early studies suggested that reading scores do not improve when one provides direct instruction in letter names to preschoolers. However, these studies have been criticized for being too short in duration and for using symbols other than real letters. Later studies that addressed these concerns showed that letter knowledge is both a prerequisite to later skills and a bridge to phonetic decoding (Adams, 1990). With respect to phonemic awareness, a meta-analysis of 34 training studies showed that interventions designed to increase phonemic awareness regularly lead to substantially enhanced reading skills (Bus & van IJzendoorn, 1999). As for concepts of print, no experimental investigations seem to have been conducted at this writing (though there are many studies looking at the natural correlates of concepts of print, such as preschool curriculum and style of mother-child interaction).

Hence, there is good reason to suspect that letter knowledge and phonemic awareness are causally related to a children's ability to benefit from formal reading in first grade. Why might this be the case? With respect to letter knowledge, some have argued that simply knowing letter names is not enough (Adams, 1990). Children who learn to read well are also *fast* and *accurate* in their letter naming; that is, they are highly familiar with this information (as assessed by RAN letter tasks). As a result, they are free to use their attentional resources to think about other things. In addition, 6-year-olds who are fluent in letter names must differ in important ways from 6-year-olds who are not. Fluency only comes from a lot of repetition. Someone (e.g., a parent or preschool teacher) must present letter names to children in daily interactions, and this same person might also engender a budding "emergent literacy" in them, as well (Goodman, 1991). But it is important to note that the predictive relation between RAN and reading not only holds for letters but also for rapidly naming colors, numbers, and objects (Compton, 2003). Thus, the connection is not purely due to repetition-based fluency with letters.

A second possibility is that children who know letter names may use this information to discover the alphabetic principle (Adams, 1990; Treiman, Tincoff, & Richmond-Welty, 1996). In particular, many letter names sound like how a letter is pronounced. For example, the name of B is "Bee," and it is pronounced "buh." Children may exploit this similarity to induce symbol–sound correspondences. Thus, the key to the process may not be letter names per se, but the recognition of the connection between letter names, pronunciations, and the alphabetic principle (i.e., that there is a systematic correspondence between letters and sounds). Treiman and colleagues have provided considerable support for the idea that letter names help children come to appreciate the alphabet principle (Treiman et al., 1996; Treiman, Weatherston, & Berch, 1994). To illustrate one key finding, many preschoolers spell words that start with *w* using *y*. The name of *y* is "Wei," and this name is close to the "wuh" sound made at the beginning of words like *woman*.

The story for phonemic awareness is similar. Children cannot appreciate the alphabetic principle until they can "hear" the component sounds of words and map these sounds onto letters and groups of letters (i.e., graphemes). Early in the preschool period, children cannot say which words rhyme and whether a string of words all start with the same initial sound. To be able to perform these tasks and map sounds onto print, two things have to occur. First, children need to have segmented mental representations of words (Metsala, 1999). In such representations, a sound of a word is stored as an interconnected pattern of component sounds. At first, the phonetic representation of a word is stored as an undifferentiated whole (e.g., *bat* as /bat/). Over time, it subdivides into components (e.g., *bat* as /b- + -at/). The primary factor thought to precipitate these changes is the acquisition of new vocabulary words—especially words that have onsets or rimes that are similar to already-stored words (Metsala & Walley, 1998). For example, when a child already has /bat/ stored, her learning of the words *cat, hat,* and *rat* could prompt all these words to be stored as segmented representations with different onsets but a common rime. The second thing that has to occur is that children have to be able to consciously reflect on these segmented representations. In development, many skills start out at the implicit, nonconscious level but eventually become accessible to consciousness (Karmiloff-Smith, 1995).

In sum, then, we now know that training can produce enhancements of letter knowledge and phonemic awareness. Given the paucity of training studies for concepts of print, it is not yet known whether this factor is also causally related or simply a correlate. Whereas future studies can resolve this issue, we may never know the true causal status of SES or sentence memory because these factors cannot be experimentally manipulated.

Nevertheless, the information as a whole permits the following tentative explanation of the differences between successful and unsuccessful children. Here, we can appeal to the distinction between proximal causes and distal causes that was alluded to earlier. The three proximal causes of group differences include sentence or story memory, letter knowledge, and phonemic awareness. Children who are found to be skilled readers at the end of first grade (successful children) have greater sentence or story memory, letter knowledge, and phonemic awareness than children who are found to be less competent in reading at the end of first grade (unsuccessful children). Why? Successful children have an extensive productive vocabulary that contains numerous segmented representations of words, as well as the ability to consciously reflect on these representations. In addition, they have had extensive practice recognizing letters, writing letters, and trying out invented spellings. Further, they have had many stories read to them, causing them to create mental schemata for stories (schemata = mental representations of what most stories have in common), which in turn help them to remember stories. They have also been spoken to a great deal and asked to express themselves on numerous occasions. Why would only the successful children have an extensive productive vocabulary, practice with letters, stories read to them, and regular conversational encounters? Because they come from high SES households. Children who come from high SES households tend to (1) be exposed to numerous books, (2) have parents who have advanced language skills and who intentionally expose them to letters and writing, and (3) attend high-quality preschools and kindergartens that further engage the children in language games (e.g., nursery rhymes and songs) and emergent literacy activities (Sénéchal & LeFevre, 2002; Snow et al., 1998).

Further evidence of the role of SES comes from several additional sources. Studies of disadvantaged children show that these children have considerable difficulty "hearing" the individual sounds in words as first graders (Adams, 1990; Wallach, Wallach, Dozier, & Kaplan, 1977). One could interpret this finding as evidence that there is a higher incidence of reading disability in disadvantaged children than in advantaged children, or that these children have not had the relevant formative experiences described above. The latter seems more likely, given the success of various tutoring programs that have brought many disadvantaged children "up to speed" in a matter of months (Vellutino et al., 1996). Relatedly, studies suggest that middle-income parents often read to their preschoolers about 10 min a day. By the time these children reach their sixth birthday, then, they will have been exposed to 300 hr of book reading (Adams, 1990). Children in low-income households that do not emphasize reading, in contrast, might accumulate only about 40 hr or less of book reading by the time they are 6 years old (Heath, 1983; Teale, 1986). Note that the average child receives about 360 hr of reading instruction in first grade (Adams, 1990), which might be enough to get a low SES child, by the end of first grade, up to the point a high SES child was at the *start* of first grade.

Overall, then, we see that the research on skilled readers squares nicely with the research on predictive factors and that it is easy to develop activities to promote important prerequisite skills. The curious thing about the research on predictive factors, however, is the fact that skills such as phonemic awareness and syntactic awareness are not only prerequisites for learning to read, they also seem to *improve* after a child learns to read! That is, children who have been reading for several years (e.g., third graders) show more phonemic awareness, syntactic awareness, and naming speed than children who are just starting to read (Adams, 1990; Compton, 2003; Snow et al., 1998; Stanovich, 1988b). Moreover, having phonemic awareness, syntactic awareness, and insight into the alphabetic principle is a large part of what it means to know how to read. Thus, the research seems to say that children learn to read well in the first grade only if they already know much about reading when they enter first grade (Adams, 1990; Goodman, 1991)! The lesson to be learned from these studies is that reading skills tend to "snowball" over time (Stanovich, 1986).

Precocious Readers

It is common for teachers and parents to report that most preschoolers vigorously resist being taught to read. In addition, experimental and informal attempts to teach young children how to read have generally failed when children are younger than 5 (Feitelson, Tehori, & Levinberg-Green, 1982; Fowler, 1971). There are, however, documented cases of precocious readers who ranged in age from 2 to 5 when they began reading (Fowler, 1971; Goldstein, 1976; Jackson, 1992), as well as a few experimental programs that have been seemingly successful with 4- and 5-year-olds (Feitelson et al., 1982; Fowler, 1971). If we combine this evidence with the fact that it is often straightforward to teach (nondisabled) 6-year-old children from low- and middle-income households to read (Snow et al., 1998), the data as a whole can be interpreted in two ways. According to the reading-readiness view, there is a neurological basis to being ready and willing to read. According to a motivational view, the age trends reflect normative trends in reading motivation.

With regard to the reading-readiness view, it was noted earlier that well-controlled studies have found that age alone is not a very good predictor of responsiveness to reading instruction when factors related to knowledge and experience are taken into account (Adams, 1990; Bryant, MacLean, Bradley, & Crossland, 1990; Stanovich & Siegel, 1994). Early studies (e.g., Fowler, 1971; Morphett & Washburn, 1931) showed that it was a child's *mental age*, not his or her chronological age that mattered (e.g., a 2-year-old who could answer questions for 5-year-olds on an IQ test could learn to read better than a 5-year-old who could only answer questions for 4-year-olds). Moreover, mental age and intelligence were soon replaced in later studies with better predictors such as letter knowledge and phonological processing. Children are clearly not born with knowledge of letters, and they need to acquire a substantial productive vocabulary (through experience) to create the segmented, phonetic representations of spoken words that were described earlier (Metsala, 1999). Segmented representations, in turn, are required for creating links between graphemes and phonemes. Thus, a lack of receptivity to instruction could reflect a lack of exposure to relevant information. Similarly, it is no coincidence that precocious readers usually come from affluent, well-educated households and that 4-year-olds who learn to read have unusually high levels of letter knowledge for 4-year-olds (e.g., Fowler, 1971).

Thus, it would appear that age constraints on reading instruction reflect the fact that it takes time for children to acquire important kinds of knowledge (i.e., knowledge of letter names and segmented phonetic representations of words). This knowledge, however, must be embodied in the form of neural assemblies (i.e., clusters of neural groups that have formed synaptic connections with each other). In order for neural assemblies to form, there has to be a sufficient number of neurons located in certain regions of the brain that have matured to the point that they can form synaptic connections with neighbors. Studies of brain development suggest that only the neurons in the frontal lobe continue to develop substantially beyond infancy (Byrnes, 2001b), so the primary temporal constraint related to maturation may well be the time it takes for synapses to form after repeated encounters with the same kind of stimulation (e.g., the sight of a given letter). Conversely, it is possible that skills like phonemic awareness and decoding are subtended by areas in the frontal lobes (Shaywitz et al., 1998). If these areas take some time to finish their development, there may be two kinds of factors that explain why it is hard to teach children below the age of 4 to read: (1) experiential factors (e.g., insufficient exposure to letters and spoken words) and (2) maturational factors (e.g., continued development of frontal brain regions). Again, however, we cannot discount the potentially important role of motivation. Children who read early have an unusually strong desire to read as preschoolers.

Developmental Models and Trends

In the previous sections, we examined reading development from infancy to the point at which children enter the first grade. In this section, we extend this analysis somewhat. In particular, this section begins with a description of some general developmental trends in performance, and then describes a developmental model of early decoding skill.

The general developmental trends can be understood with reference to the model of proficient reading described earlier. In the earliest phases of reading development, children have very little orthographic knowledge but considerable knowledge of meaning–sound relations (i.e., oral vocabulary). Moreover, as mentioned above, successful readers also enter first grade with phonemic awareness, syntactic awareness, the ability to rapidly name letters, and knowledge of the alphabetic principle. Early reading development consists of putting all of this entering knowledge together with written words; that is, it can be characterized as the progressive acquisition of letter–sound correspondences, as well as word-meaning correspondences.

Because word recognition is slow and effortful in the beginning, beginning readers rely heavily on prior context to help them guess words rather than read them phonetically. With much repeated practice, word recognition eventually becomes automatic, thereby indicating that the connections between words and meanings are firmly established. Whereas prior context and the pronunciations of words are still involved in reading, they are no longer essential for the beginning reader. Rather, they now serve as backup systems to the primary links between the orthographic and meaning processors. Thus, with age, children rely more on letter–meaning connections and less on prior context and pronunciations (Adams, 1990; Snow et al., 1998; Stanovich, 1986). Furthermore, children who enter first grade with phonemic awareness and syntactic awareness dramatically increase these skills as they read more and more. Finally, rapid, efficient word recognition allows readers to attend to meaning more closely and to develop a variety of comprehension strategies (see Chapter 8; Stanovich, 1986).

In addition to these general trends, early reading development can also be cast in terms of Ehri's (1995) phase model. To begin with, Ehri notes that mature readers have at least four ways to read words. For unfamiliar words, they can use *decoding* (i.e., transforming graphemes into phonemes and blending the phonemes into pronunciations), *reading by analogy* (i.e., using already-known sight words to pronounce new words that share letter clusters), and *reading by predicting* (i.e., making educated guesses about words based on context clues or initial letters). For familiar words, however, they tend to use *sight-reading* because it is fast and automatic. The goal is to become a reader who shifts from relying mostly on the first three approaches to relying primarily on sight-reading. When readers acquire an extensive sight vocabulary, they can allocate most of their cognitive resources to tasks such as accessing word meanings and creating mental models. Sight vocabularies are acquired through extensive reading and repeated exposure to the same words. In effect, connections form between printed words and their meanings, spellings, and pronunciations, and the sight of a word triggers rapid retrieval of the latter four kinds of information (Ehri, 1995).

After conducting numerous longitudinal studies with young children that extend from the preschool period to the point many children are fluent readers in the third grade, Ehri suggests that the connection-forming process proceeds through four phases: prealphabetic, partial alphabetic, full alphabetic, and consolidated alphabetic. The term *alphabetic* is used to denote the fact that (1) words consist of letters and (2) letters function as symbols for phoneme and phoneme blends in words. During the *prealphabetic phase*, "beginners remember how to read sight words by forming connections between selected visual attributes of words and their pronunciations or meanings and storing these associations in memory" (p. 118). For example, they may see the tail of the letter *g* in *dog* and associate it with real dogs, or see the two humps in *m* and associate *camel* with real camels. This phase is called prealphabetic because children are not really focusing on letters and their association to phonemes. This is also the phase when children engage in reading environmental print such as stop signs and fast-food symbols. During the *partial-alphabetic phase*, "beginners remember how to read sight words by forming partial alphabetic connections between only some of the letters in written words and sounds detected in their pronunciations" (p. 119). For example, they might recognize the *s* and *n* of *spoon*, associate these two letters with their names (not their sounds) and retrieve the word *spoon* based on prior encounters (e.g., the last few times *s* and *n* co-occurred this way, the word was, in fact, *spoon*). Relatedly, they might pronounce the letter string KDN as *garden* because *k* and *g* are articulated using the same region of the mouth. During the *full-alphabetic phase*, "beginners remember how to read sight words by forming the complete connections seen in the written forms of words and phonemes detected in their pronunciations" (p. 120). For example, in reading *spoon*, a child in this phase would recognize that the five letters correspond to four phonemes and that the double *o* corresponds to the sound /u/. Finally, in the *consolidated-alphabetic phase*, growth in a child's sight word vocabulary produces fully connected spellings for an increasing number of words. After this occurs, letter patterns that recur across different words become consolidated. For example, the connection between the -*at* in *bat*, *cat*, and *hat* and the common rime of these words prompts a consolidation of that pattern. Consolidation of many such patterns helps a reader become facile with multiletter units that correspond to morphemes, syllables, and subsyllabic units. Studies suggest that second grade may be the time when many children's sight vocabularies are large enough to support the consolidation process (Ehri, 1995).

THE DEVELOPMENTAL MECHANISMS QUESTION:
What Factors Promote Changes in Beginning Reading Skills?

In the previous section on developmental trends, we learned the following: (1) Children progressively acquire emergent literacy skills (e.g., concepts of print, phonological awareness) between birth and age 5; (2) six factors assessed in kindergarten (i.e., SES, letter knowledge, sentence memory, concepts of print, RAN, and phonemic awareness) predict how well children learn to read in first grade even after controls; (3) there seem to be maturational, experiential, and motivational obstacles to getting children to read prior to age 4; and (4) children progress through four phases in their decoding skills (i.e., prealphabetic, partial alphabetic, full alphabetic, and consolidated alphabetic). The developmental mechanism question focuses on the factors that could explain these age trends. For example, what factors could explain the shift from the prealphabetic to partial-alphabetic stage? Why do children from middle-income households progress from not having concepts of print at age 2 to having rich concepts of print at age 5?

The most obvious answer to such questions is that children progress when they are provided with repeated *opportunities to learn* about books, letters, and printed words at home or at school. They may also play games that promote phonological processing skills. However, children necessarily bring certain *propensities* to these opportunities that influence the amount of learning that takes place (see Chapters 10 and 11; Byrnes & Miller, 2007). One of these propensities is children's current level of understanding of literacy. As articulated in various constructivist theoretical approaches (e.g., Piaget's theory, Vygotsky's theory, Schema theory; see Byrnes, 2007a), children's current level of knowledge and insight serves as a foundation on which new knowledge can build. With each pass through a literacy experience, children can detect and assimilate new items of information (e.g., notice that *cat* and *cut* differ in the middle letter). The knowledge snowballs over time. Parents and teachers can accelerate this detection and build-up by pointing things out to children and using routines and repeated readings of the same books. A second kind of propensity relates to children's motivation. Children can be engaged motivationally by (1) using books that are appealing and interesting and (2) asking children to perform tasks that are within their ability level but slightly challenging at times. A third kind of propensity has to do with children's spoken language competencies. As the simple view of reading states, reading skills intersect with spoken language skills as children read. Moreover, children with larger spoken vocabularies are more likely to have segmented phonological representations than children with smaller vocabularies. Large spoken vocabularies also provide an assimilative base for sight vocabularies. A fourth aspect of propensity may be constraints imposed by brain development. For example, working memory and RAN skills may increase as the brain develops across the preschool period. As a result, a 2-year-old and 4-year-old may get very different things out of the same literacy experience.

> *Discussion Topic*: Given the preceding discussion of developmental mechanisms, design a home literacy intervention for low-income mothers that would attempt to replicate the literacy experiences of children from middle-income households. What would these mothers need to be told? What resources would need to be provided? What would a mother of a 2-year-old be told to do? What would a mother of a 4-year-old be told to do?

THE DEFICIENCIES QUESTION: Are There Populations of Children or Adults Who Lack Some or All of the Beginning Reading Skills? Do These Individuals Experience Problems When They Learn to Read or after They Have Learned to Read?

In what follows, we answer the deficiencies question by examining and then explaining the core differences between skilled and struggling readers.

Core Differences between Skilled and Struggling Readers

With respect to cognitive processes, there are a number of ways in which skilled readers could conceivably differ from struggling readers. On the one hand, they could differ in terms of general processing factors such as intelligence, working memory capacity, perceptual ability, rule induction, and metacognition. On the other hand, they could differ in terms reading-specific processes such as word recognition, use of context, phonemic awareness, and comprehension strategies. It turns out that significant differences have been found between skilled and struggling readers for all of these variables (Stanovich, 1980, 1986, 1988a). The question is, however, which of these variables seem to most clearly distinguish skilled readers from struggling readers.

Careful reviews of the literature have revealed three particularly important differences between skilled and struggling readers. First, skilled readers are better than struggling readers at recognizing words *automatically* (i.e., they do not have to pay attention to the decoding process). When word recognition is automatic, a reader can focus his or her attention on higher-level sentence integration and semantic processing (in the same way a skilled driver can drive a car and have a conversation at the same time). However, automatic recognition is most important in the first and second grades because most high-frequency words are automatized to adult levels by the third grade (Stanovich, 1980). Beginning in the third grade, the second and most important difference between skilled and struggling readers emerges: Skilled readers are able to *rapidly recognize* words and subword units (de Jong & van der Leij, 1999). Speed is important because readers need to be able to operate on information in working memory before it dissipates. The third important difference between skilled and struggling readers concerns the ability to recode print items into a phonological representation (de Jong & van der Leij, 1999). *Phonological recoding* facilitates reading by (1) providing a redundant pathway for accessing word meaning and (2) providing a more stable code for the information that is held in working memory (Adams, 1990; Stanovich, 1980).

At one time, the ability to use prior context was also thought to be a major difference between skilled and struggling readers. After many years of research, however, this proposal turns out to be incorrect. In fact, struggling readers use prior context as much if not more than skilled readers and are likely to make many substitution errors when they encounter an unfamiliar word (Adams, 1990; Stanovich, 1988b). Skilled readers rely much more heavily on direct connections between orthography and meaning than on context. Context only exerts an experimental effect on skilled readers when the text is artificially doctored or degraded. Thus, whereas skilled readers rely on context less and less as they get older, struggling readers do

not show a similar kind of decreasing reliance on context presumably because they have so much trouble recognizing and deciphering a word. Of
course, this is not to say that context is irrelevant to skilled readers. As
mentioned earlier, context serves as an important backup system to the
connections between text and meanings.

Explaining Core Differences

Why are skilled readers better at automatic and fast recognition and pronunciation of words than struggling readers? From what we know about
the nature of skill acquisition and the formation of associations, it seems
clear that skilled readers have had considerably more practice at recognizing and pronouncing words than struggling readers. A likely cause of practice differences could be the fact that children are grouped by reading ability starting in the first grade. Children in higher-level groups are given more
opportunities for practice than children in lower-level groups, and the initial gap between groups widens with age (Stanovich, 1986).

However, it would also appear that there are fairly stable individual
differences in the core phonological processes of reading ability (Stanovich
& Siegel, 1994; Torgesen & Burgess, 1998). One study, for example,
showed that the longitudinal correlations between phonological processing
abilities in successive years in school ranged from a low of .62 to a high of
.95 (mean = .81). Hence, it would appear that children's relative ranking in
terms of their phonological processing skills remains fairly constant over
time. In further support of this claim, another study of readers with disabilities showed that children who scored at the 10th percentile for phonological skills at the start of school ended up no higher than the 30th percentile
by the end of fifth grade, even after being provided with remediation services (Torgesen & Burgess, 1998).

The stability of individual differences and apparent intractability of severe reading problems has led many to wonder whether reading skills have
a neuroscientific basis. Several lines of neuroscientific research are informative in this respect. To begin with, studies of adults with brain injuries have
revealed a number of distinct (but sometimes co-occurring) deficits in their
reading skills. At one time, the typical approach was to classify collections
of deficits in terms of syndromes (e.g., dyslexia with dysgraphia vs. dyslexia
without dysgraphia). Since the 1960s, information-processing and other
psychological accounts have prompted investigators to subdivide acquired
reading problems into two general classes: (1) those related to visually analyzing the attributes of written words (*visual word-form dyslexias*) and (2)
those related to presumed later stages of the reading process (*central
dyslexias*) (McCarthy & Warrington, 1990).

Visual word-form dyslexias include spelling dyslexia, neglect dyslexia, and attentional dyslexia (McCarthy & Warrington, 1990). *Spelling dyslexia* is manifested in adults with brain injuries who read letter by letter (e.g., when they see *Dog* they say, "*D, O, G* spells *dog*"). Such individuals may have normal spelling and writing ability, but cannot read back what they have written. The tendency to spell is a strategy that these individuals seem to use to overcompensate for an inability to recognize words as units. In most cases, individuals with spelling dyslexia have lesions located near the junctions of the occipital, temporal, and parietal lobes (the left angular gyrus). *Neglect dyslexia* consists of omitting or misreading the initial or terminal parts of words (e.g., *his* when confronted with *this*; *wet* when confronted with *let*; *together* when confronted with *whether*). Case studies reveal that whereas the left (initial) portion of words is neglected when there is damage to the right parietal lobe, the right (terminal) part of words is neglected when there is damage to the left parietal lobe. Adults with *attentional dyslexia* can read individual letters quite well (e.g., *A*) but have significantly more difficulty when they have to read individual letters that are flanked by other letters in the visual field (e.g., the *A* in *K A L*). The few individuals who have had attentional dyslexia have had large tumors that occupied posterior regions of the left hemisphere and extended into subcortical structures. The rarity of the disorder makes the precise location of damage difficult to specify at present.

In contrast to visual word-form dyslexias, central dyslexias are thought to include reading processes that occur after the initial visual processing of words (McCarthy & Warrington, 1990). The two major types of *central dyslexias* include reading by sound (*surface dyslexia* or phonological reading) and reading by sight vocabulary (with a corresponding inability to sound out words). Surface dyslexia is a problem because of the abundance of English words that defy the rules of regular letter–sound correspondences (e.g., *yacht, busy, sew*). Because of their over-reliance on pronunciation rules, individuals with surface dyslexia are likely to pronounce irregular words in predictable ways (e.g., *sew* as "sue") and also pronounce phonologically regular pseudowords quite well (e.g., *blean*). Anatomically, surface dyslexia has been associated with a wide range of lesion locations but usually tends to involve damage to the temporal lobes in conjunction with damage to other areas.

The second type of central dyslexia consists of being able to read using one's sight vocabulary but losing the ability to read by sound. In contrast to individuals with surface dyslexia, individuals with central dyslexia struggle with reading pseudowords that obey the spelling–sound rules of their language (e.g., *blean* or *tweal*). In addition, individuals with the latter disorder may also have difficulty reading function words (e.g., *if, for*), grammatical morphemes (e.g., *-ed* or *-ing*), or abstract words (e.g., *idea*), and they sometimes make semantic errors, as well. The co-occurrence of pronunciation difficulty and difficulty with abstract words has been called *deep dyslexia*. Case studies of such individuals reveal no consistent pattern of localization (McCarthy & Warrington, 1990).

The late Norman Geschwind tried to summarize the literature on acquired dyslexias in the form of the anatomical model presented in Figure 7.4 (e.g., Geschwind & Galaburda, 1987). As can be seen, this model suggests that a written word is first registered in the primary visual areas of the occipital lobe. Activity in the visual areas is then relayed to the angular gyrus, which is thought to play an important role in associating a visual form with a corresponding auditory representation in auditory processing areas (e.g., Wernicke's area). Activity then passes from Wernicke's area to Broca's area by way of a bundle of fibers called the *arcuate fasciculus*. If the person is reading aloud, signals are then sent from Broca's area to the primary motor cortex, which controls the movements of the lips, tongue, and so on.

What can be made of the aforementioned findings on the reading problems of adults with brain damage? Two conclusions seem warranted. First, reading consists of multiple tasks that are performed in concert. For example, there are processes related to (1) perceiving letters and groups of letters, (2) pronunciation of word and letter strings, (3) syntactic processing related to function words and word endings, (4) semantic processes related to retrieving word meanings, and (5) conceptual processes related to the abstract–concrete continuum. Second, these processes seem to be at least weakly modular and redundant (Kosslyn & Koenig, 1994). That is, individuals with dyslexia can read some words at least some of the time despite their problems (e.g., individuals with surface dyslexia can read phonologically regular words). Moreover, what they can do can overcompensate for what they cannot (Stanovich & Siegel, 1994).

The findings from studies of children with dyslexia (using standard laboratory tasks) and studies of nondisabled adults using positron emission tomography (PET) scans tend to corroborate and extend the findings from studies of adults with brain injuries. In particular, a large number of studies have revealed that the vast majority of children with dyslexia have the following characteristics: (1) They have a great deal of difficulty pronouncing pseudowords, (2) they have difficulty on phonological tasks that do not require overt pronunciation, and (3) they show relative strength in orthographic processing skill (Stanovich & Siegel, 1994). Hence, they are more like adults with brain injuries who have deep dyslexia than adults who have surface dyslexia.

Given the nature of children's problems, it is not surprising that neuroscientists who study developmental dyslexia have tried to identify morphological abnormalities in areas of the left temporal lobe that seem to be responsible for phonological processing (Hynd, Marshall, & Gonzales,

1991). It should be noted, however, that classification systems that are used for acquired dyslexias might not be appropriate for developmental dyslexias (Rayner & Pollatsek, 1989). With acquired dyslexias, there are known sites of brain damage; the existence of damage in developmental dyslexia remains speculative (Reschly & Gresham, 1989). In addition, the practice of superimposing the categories of acquired dyslexia onto individuals with developmental dyslexia can hinder the discovery of the problems and mechanisms that are unique to developmental dyslexia (Raynor & Pollatsek, 1989). Further, it was noted earlier that deep dyslexia has not been associated with damage to particular sites in the brains of adults. If deep dyslexia in adults is, in fact, similar to developmental dyslexia in its manifest symptoms, it is not clear why developmentalists would expect to find abnormalities in particular sites in the brains of children.

Notwithstanding these caveats, Shaywitz and colleagues have used fMRI technology to determine whether different patterns of brain activity can be observed in the brains of children with dyslexia and nondisabled children when they read (e.g., Shaywitz et al., 1998). Focusing on the regions identified by Geschwind (see Figure 7.4), they found that brain activations differed significantly between the two groups, with dyslexic readers showing relative underactivation in the striate cortex (in the primary visual areas), angular gyrus, and Wernicke's area, and relative overactivation in Broca's area. Whereas these authors suggest that this pattern of activation might be a "signature" for dyslexia, it should be noted that involvement of left frontal areas is also indicative of task difficulty and working memory (Barch et al., 1997). To show that the aforementioned pattern really is a sign of functional disruption in the reading circuitry, these researchers would need to demonstrate at least two additional things in future studies: (1) that the pattern is not observed in nondyslexic children who are given a task that is hard for them and (2) that the pattern in not found in nondisabled children who are just beginning to read (who might have as much trouble pronouncing new words as older children who have dyslexia).

With respect to PET scan studies of normal adults, Posner, Peterson, Fox, and Raichle (1988) and Petersen, Fox, Snyder, and Raichle (1990) have found that passively looking at real words (e.g., *board*), pseudowords (e.g., *floop*), nonwords (e.g., *jvjfc*), and strings of letter-like fonts all activate the same portions of the occipital lobe. However, real words and pseudowords also activate portions of the occipital lobe that are not activated by nonwords and false fonts (the extrastriate cortex). Recall that damage to occipital regions often produces the visual word-form dyslexias that were described earlier. Whereas presentation of real words and being asked to define words activates regions of the left frontal lobe, presentation of pseudowords does not activate these regions. Finally, auditory and phonological processing seem to activate regions of the left temporal and lower parietal cortices, near regions of interest to individuals who study developmental dyslexia.

Collectively, then, various neuroscientific studies have supported the idea that there are specific brain regions associated with orthographic, phonological, semantic, and syntactic processing. Orthographic processing seems to be centered in the primary visual area and extrastriate area. Phonological processing seems to be associated with the superior temporal lobes and the angular gyrus (though Shaywitz and colleagues have also found frontal activation for rhyming tasks). Semantic processing has been associated with two regions in the left hemisphere: Broca's area (frontal lobe) and areas in the medial temporal lobe.

So, reading disabilities may reflect some underlying disruption in the normal circuitry for reading. What caused this disruption? At present, it is hard to know because we still do not know whether there is something wrong with the brain of a child who is reading disabled and what the nature of this problem is if the circuitry has been disrupted. A further problem is that there is often slippage in the definition of *reading disabled*. For example, most school systems assign the label "reading disabled" when there seems to be a discrepancy between a child's intelligence and his or her reading level (i.e., normal IQ but reading 2 years behind grade level). In recent years, this discrepancy approach has been found to mix together two very different groups of children: those who have an actual reading disability and those who have been dubbed "garden variety" struggling readers (Stanovich, 1988a). Whereas the latter can be brought up to speed through a short period of intense tutoring (e.g., 6 weeks), the former cannot (Vellutino et al., 1996). Further, comparisons of these two groups show marked differences in their phonological-processing skills but no substantial differences in their visual, semantic, or syntactic skills (Stanovich & Siegel, 1994; Vellutino et al., 1996). The key problem here is that the discrepancy approach is not sensitive enough to pick up this phonological core deficit. In addition, use of this approach in longitudinal studies (e.g., Shaywitz et al., 1992), reveals four kinds of children: (1) those who meet the discrepancy criterion at both of two testings (2%), (2) those who meet the criterion at the first testing but not the second testing (6%), (3) those who are said to be nondisabled at the first testing but reading disabled at the second testing (7%), and (4) those found to be nondisabled at both testings (85%). If the discrepancy approach were sufficiently accurate, the second group should not appear. After all, a child who catches up after a few years of instruction is probably not really disabled.

In the literature, some researchers have taken pains to make sure that their sample only includes children with authentic reading disabilities. Most others, however, have relied on the discrepancy criteria employed by children's school systems. This difference in definitions makes comparisons across studies difficult. To believe that some set of findings (e.g., that children with dyslexia demonstrate less blood flow to a certain region of the brain than skilled readers), we have to believe that the labels applied to children in a given study (i.e., "dyslexic" versus "skilled reader") are accurate.

In addition, if the neuroanatomy of reading really is a system of interdependent parts, problems could conceivably arise if something were wrong with any (or several) of the brain regions described above (in the same way that a tight-knit, interdependent baseball team might start to lose if any of its starters were to be injured). Thus, the search for *the* key area of disruption may be misguided. In addition, the idea that there seems to be built-in redundancy in the reading system suggests that more than one area would have to be affected in order for an intractable reading problem to emerge.

With all of these issues of definition and anatomy in mind, we can now examine several recent proposals regarding the etiology of reading disabilities from a more informed perspective. The first proposal arose in response to three sets of findings: (1) a higher incidence of language problems in boys, (2) symmetry or reversed asymmetry in the size of certain brain areas in children with dyslexia, and (3) unexpected empirical links between left-handedness, language disorders, and immune disorders (Geschwind & Behan, 1982; Geschwind & Galaburda, 1985). To explain all of these findings, Geschwind and colleagues proposed the following. During prenatal development, testosterone levels affect the growth of the left cerebral hemisphere in such a way that an anomalous form of dominance develops. Instead of being right-handed and having language lateralized in the left hemisphere (the most common kind of dominance pattern), affected individuals become left-handed with language lateralized in the right or both hemispheres. This altered physiology, in turn, leads to problems such as developmental dyslexia, impaired language development, and autism. Testosterone levels also affect the thymus, resulting in disorders of the immune system (e.g., allergies and colitis).

In early formulations, the elevated level of testosterone was thought to retard the development of the left hemisphere such that it fails to show the typical pattern (in 66% of people) of growing larger than the right hemisphere. In later proposals (e.g., Galaburda, 1993), however, the suggestion of retarded growth of the left hemisphere was replaced with the idea that something interferes with normal *reductions* in the size of the right hemisphere (e.g., testosterone inhibits the process of cell death). Either way, both proposals were meant to explain the finding mentioned above that 66% of children with dyslexia tend to have either symmetric brains or reversed asymmetry (right larger than left). The region of particular interest in these studies was the *planum temporale* (located bilaterally at the posterior portion of the superior surface of the temporal lobe). The location of the plana suggested that this region might have something to do with phonological processing, a particular problem for children with dyslexia and language delay.

Although the Geschwind–Behan–Galaburda (GBG) proposal showed some early promise, comprehensive meta-analyses have recently revealed numerous anomalies in the literature (Beaton, 1997; Bryden, McManus, & Bulamn-Fleming, 1994). The first problem is that the incidence of reading problems may not be really higher in boys than in girls. Boys are simply more likely to be referred for services than girls, reflecting a bias of teachers and other school personnel (Shaywitz, Shaywitz, Fletcher, & Escobar, 1990). Second, studies that have tried to show the three-way relation between left-handedness, immune disorders, and dyslexia have failed to find this relation. Third, the asymmetry of the plana may have more to do with handedness than with language lateralization. Finally, there is no hard evidence that sex hormones affect human brain structure in humans. Problems such as these led Bryden et al. (1994, p. 155) to conclude their review of the literature on the GBG model by saying, "All things considered, we find the evidence to support the [GBG] model lacking and would suggest that psychologists and physicians have more useful things to do than carry out further assessments of the model."

However, if the GBG model is incorrect, what else could explain the hard-to-remediate problems of children with dyslexia? In other words, if symmetry or reversed symmetry in the plana is not the problem, what is wrong with the reading circuitry of children with dyslexia, and how did it get that way? Several groups of researchers have begun to explore the possibility that reading problems are genetically determined. Studies suggest that 23–65% of children who have a parent with dyslexia also have the disorder. The rate among siblings can run as high as 40% (Shaywitz, 1996). In a longitudinal study of twins, DeFries et al. (1993) found that 53.5% of identical twins were concordant for reading problems, compared to just 31.5% of fraternal twins. Subsequent linkage studies have implicated loci on chromosomes 6 and 15 (Gayan et al., 1999).

Although these findings are intriguing, it is important to note that all of the aforementioned studies relied on evidence such as school records and self-reports to indicate the presence of reading problems within families. It is not clear how many of the children and adults in these studies were truly dyslexic and how many were simply "garden variety" struggling readers. Second, estimates of the heritability of reading problems suggest that nongenetic (i.e., environmental) factors account for more than half (56%) of the variance (DeFries et al., 1993). Third, reading problems may not be encoded in a person's genes per se. Instead, there may be a genetic susceptibility to problems in translating genetic instructions into a specific anatomy. Finally, the fact that reading has a genetic component tells us nothing about the nature of the neurological underpinnings of dyslexia. In other words, we still do not know what is wrong with a dyslexic individual's neural circuitry and how it got that way. Moreover, the fact that the concordance rate for reading problems in identical twins is less than 100% implies that epigenetic and environmental factors must be also involved.

8

The Development
of Reading Comprehension

Vignette: Tommy, a fourth grader, was reading a story along with his teacher, Ms. LaPorte, during small-group instruction. The story was about a boy named Scott who moved to a new school. At one point in the story, Scott said to himself, *"Today I am going to have the courage to invite a friend over to my house. There is David. He seems nice."* So, Scott walked over to David and said, *"Hi David. Can you come over my house on Saturday? We could skateboard or play video games. Whatever you want."* David said, *"Ahh . . . sorry, I can't. I'm going to Tim's birthday party. Everyone is going."* Scott paused for a second and replied quietly, *"Oh. I, um, did not know about the birthday party. Okay. No problem."* At that point in the lesson Ms. LaPorte asked Tommy, "What did Scott try to do that was brave?" Tommy replied, "Ask a friend over." Ms. LaPorte said, "That's right. How do you think Scott felt when Tim said he could not come over?" Tommy replied, "I don't know. The book did not say. He seemed OK, I think."

MAIN IDEAS OF THE CHAPTER

1. Reading comprehension pertains to a "meeting of the minds" between an author and a reader; comprehension ensues when readers' mental representations of what they have read matches the conceptual relations intended by authors. Comprehension is greatly aided when readers (a) set goals for understanding, (b) have declarative and conceptual knowledge of the topic, (c) have adequate working-memory capacity and knowledge of the different types of texts (i.e., narrative and expository), (d) have linguistic knowledge and metacognitive knowledge of reading, and (e) employ a variety of online processes such as inference making, inhi-

bition, identifying the main idea, summarizing, predicting, monitoring, and back-tracking.

2. Teachers should care about reading comprehension because much of the information that students acquire in the later grades is acquired via reading textbooks and works of fiction. Thus, students could not be successful in school or in life if they lacked comprehension ability.

3. Research shows that older children demonstrate better reading comprehension than younger children because the former are more likely than the latter to: (a) have more working-memory capacity, (b) have more declarative and conceptual knowledge of topics, (c) have structural knowledge of the different kinds of texts (e.g., stories and expository texts), (d) engage in functional processes that enhance comprehension such as inference making, inhibition, and comprehension monitoring, and (e) have had more extensive practice reading.

4. The developmental mechanisms responsible for growth in reading comprehension include extensive practice reading narratives and expository texts (with regular assessments and feedback to students about their comprehension) and explicit instruction regarding reading strategies and the structure of different types of texts.

5. Skilled readers show better comprehension than same-aged struggling readers because struggling readers (a) have less working-memory capacity than skilled readers, (b) have less knowledge of the structure of stories and prose passages than skilled readers, and (c) are less likely to have or use reading strategies than skilled readers. Struggling comprehenders also show problems in inhibiting inappropriate construing of words and interpretations of text.

In Chapter 7, we examined "beginning reading" and characterized it in terms of the skills needed to process individual words and sentences. In this chapter, we examine how readers comprehend larger segments of text such as paragraphs, chapters, and books. Before proceeding further, however, it should be noted that the distinction between "beginning reading" and "reading comprehension" is somewhat artificial and was made for expository purposes only. Although it has been traditional to characterize the former as "learning to read" and the latter as "reading to learn" (e.g., Chall, 1983), this characterization might prompt someone to draw two unwarranted conclusions: (1) that beginning reading never involves the extraction of meaning or information from text and (2) that beginning reading only involves the proper pronunciation of words. Teachers and publishers who have drawn these conclusions have sometimes assumed that young readers do not have to read meaningful text in order to learn how to read (i.e., any text or string of words will do). In contrast, one of the major premises of contemporary approaches to reading is that any form of reading can, and should, be meaningful. We share this view, but note that certain skills arise in the context of reading full paragraphs and stories that do not arise when single words or sentences are read. We examine these emergent skills and consider what happens after many children gain fluency in the second and third grades through assessing the literature on multisentence reading comprehension using the five questions.

THE "NATURE OF" QUESTION: What Does It Mean to Say That a Child Has Reading Comprehension Skills?

A useful way to describe reading comprehension is to first give an overall sense of what it entails, then describe some of its structural and functional aspects. The structural aspects of some system pertain to the parts of this system and their interrelations. In the case of reading, such aspects would emerge in response to questions such as, "What do proficient readers know, and how does this knowledge affect their reading?" Functional aspects, in contrast, pertain to the goal-directed or processing aspects of a system. In the case of reading, the latter aspects would emerge in questions such as, "What do proficient readers do when they read?"

To get an initial sense of what reading comprehension entails, it is helpful to examine the three-way relation between writers, written language, and readers. Writers usually begin with the goal of creating certain ideas in their readers' minds. To fulfill such a goal, writers ask themselves questions such as, "If I want my readers to have such-and-such thoughts, what words can I use?" Writers choose certain words, phrases, and sentences based on their beliefs about conventional ways to say things and presume that their readers know these conventions. Thus, if the conventional way to state a prediction is to use an "if–then" construction and writers want their readers to know their prediction, they will use an if–then construction to make this prediction in print (e.g., *If the Iraq war continues, the next president will be a Democrat*). We can say that readers comprehend some written text when they understand what the writer was trying to say (Graesser, Millis, & Zwaan, 1997). In a sense, then, when a reader comprehends a writer, there is a "meeting of minds." Relatedly, we can say that comprehension involves knowing what is going on in some extended portion of text.

In contemporary theories, readers are assumed to achieve this kind of understanding by mentally representing text at five different levels of analysis (Graesser et al., 1997). The first level is called the *surface-code level*. Here, readers temporarily store a verbatim trace of some segment of text. How do we know? Studies show that readers can tell the difference between actually presented text and paraphrases, as long as test items are presented shortly after test takers read a segment of text. The second level is called the *textbase level*. Here, readers represent the content of text in a stripped-down format that preserves meaning but not the exact wording or syntax. The textbase may also include a small number of inferences that are generated to create coherence between a pair of successive sentences (see below). The third level, called the *situation model*, "refers to the people, spatial setting, actions, and events" of a mental microworld that is "constructed inferentially through interactions between the explicit text and background world knowledge" (Graesser et al., 1997, p. 167). The fourth level is called the *communication level*. Here, a reader represents the author's communicative intent (e.g., "She is probably telling me this now to throw me off the trail of the killer"). The fifth and final level is called the *text-genre level* because it reflects a reader's ability to categorize texts into different types (e.g., newspaper article, expository text, fiction). The operation of all five levels is essential for achieving a higher-level or "deep" understanding of text.

One further way to describe comprehension at a general level is to note that textual interpretation is very much a process of creating a coherent representation of the ideas contained in a passage or book (Carpenter et al., 1995; Graesser et al., 1997). Psychologists argue that there are two kinds of coherence: local and global. *Local coherence* refers to an integrated representation of the ideas contained in a pair of adjacent sentences. *Global coherence*, in contrast, refers to an integrated representation of ideas that appear across widely dispersed segments of a text (e.g., ideas in the first and last chapters of a book).

Structural Aspects of Comprehension

Structural aspects of comprehension pertain to aspects of the mind related to either processing capacity or the knowledge possessed by readers. Structural aspects provide the parameters within which the functional aspects of reading can operate. As we discussed later in this chapter, the functional aspects refer to the processes that readers perform when they read (e.g., inference making, reading strategies). As noted above, then, structural aspects largely pertain to what readers know; functional aspects pertain to what readers do. Readers who have limitations in their structural aspects (e.g., they have low working-memory capacity or low knowledge) will be hampered in their ability to carry out functional aspects such as implementing a reading strategy. In contrast, readers with enhanced structural aspects have the resources they need to carry out the functional aspects effectively. Two important kinds of structural aspects are discussed next in turn: memory-related and knowledge-related.

Memory-Related Structural Aspects

Working memory is considered a short-term, transient form of memory that places an important structural limitation on the processing that occurs when people read or engage in other kinds of mental activities. In the same way that a large workshop enables a skilled craftsperson to complete a wider array of projects than a very small workshop, the mind can carry out more elaborate cognitive operations when it has access to greater working-memory capacity than when it has access to less working-memory capacity. Working memory acts as a buffer to temporarily retain previously read successive items of information until the integration of these items can occur (Cain, Oakhill, & Bryant, 2004). In addition, however, skilled readers constantly update their working memory by (1) adding or retaining items of information that are particularly relevant to understanding the text as a whole and (2) deleting items that are no longer relevant (Carretti, Cornoldi, De Beni, & Romano, 2005). They also adjust their level of processing, depending on the purpose of reading, by expending more effort and resources when reading to study versus reading for entertainment (Linderholm & van den Broek, 2002).

Knowledge-Related Structural Aspects

Reading scholars often characterize knowledge in terms of cognitive structures called *schemata* (singular = *schema*). A schema is a mental representation of what multiple instances of some type of thing have in common. For example, a schema for a house specifies the things that most houses have in common, and a schema for birthday parties specifies the things that happen at most birthday parties. Besides having schemata for types of objects and events, it has been claimed that skilled readers and writers have schemata for specific types of texts, too. Reading-related schemata are thought to support the ability to create global coherence (Carpenter et al., 1995; Graesser et al., 1997). The two main schemata that have been examined closely are those for *narrative* and *expository texts*, although there are also schemata for other genres such as essays. In what follows, we discuss how schemata for specific topics (e.g., houses), narratives, and expository texts help students comprehend and remember what they are reading, and then examine several other kinds of knowledge that are important for skilled reading.

TOPIC KNOWLEDGE

When people read, they bring their existing knowledge to bear on a particular passage. This pre-existing knowledge is often called *prior knowledge*, *background knowledge*, or *world knowledge* by text-processing researchers. These researchers argue that a significant portion of this knowledge is represented in the form of schemata. When readers have schematized knowledge for objects and events, they are better able to assimilate the information presented in some text than when they lack this knowledge. In particular, when readers try to process some text, their minds try to find mental "spots" for each successive idea that is expressed in the text. For example, consider the truncated schema for a concept of "dog" below. If you

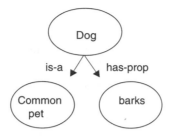

are reading a passage that says, *Dogs are one of the most common pets*, your mind might metaphorically say, "I knew that because my 'dog' node is attached to a 'common pet' node by way of a 'is-a' link." However, if you next read the line *Dogs were first domesticated by ancient peoples*, your mind might say, "I didn't know that; let's add that piece of information to my 'dog' schema."

In addition to providing an assimilative base for incoming information, schemata for topics also help readers make inferences when things are not explicitly stated by an author. For example, if you read the line *The suspect handed Ralphy a 'milk bone'* . . . , you would probably use your "dog" schema to make the inference that "Ralphy" is a dog. Similarly, if you were to read the line *Nobody came to Mary's birthday party*, you might use your knowledge of people to infer that "Mary" became sad as a result.

This schema-theoretic description of topic or background knowledge has been extended in recent years by considering other forms of declarative and conceptual knowledge that could enhance comprehension. Schemata correspond to an important form of conceptual knowledge (i.e., categorical relations among types of things or events), but there are other kinds of conceptual knowledge that could influence comprehension, such as the core principles of some domain (e.g., adaptation, in the case of biology), causality, temporal relations, spatial relations, mathematical relations, and so on (Guthrie et al., 2000). Causality, explanations, and core principles tend not to be modeled via schemata these days. Instead, researchers posit structures such as naive or expert theories in readers' minds, or even connectionist node-link structures (see Chapters 4 and 7 for examples of connectionist models).

Regardless of the theoretical model used, most scholars argue that prior knowledge promotes more extensive processing during reading (Miller, Stine-Morrow, Kirkorian, & Conroy, 2004). Evidence for this claim comes from the fact that high-knowledge readers allocate more time to conceptual integration during "wrap up" and to global inference making. Wrap up is the term for the processing that takes place at major syntactic constituent boundaries such as clauses and sentences.

SCHEMATA FOR NARRATIVE TEXTS

Authors of narratives attempt to communicate event-based experiences to their readers. In most narratives, there are (1) *characters* who have goals and motives for performing actions, (2) *temporal* and *spatial placements* in which the story takes place, (3) *complications* and *major goals* of main characters, (4) *plots* and *resolutions* of complications, (5) *affect patterns* (i.e., emotional and other responses to the storyline), (6) *points*, morals, and themes, and (7) *points of view* and *perspectives* (Graesser, Golding, & Long, 1991).

One tradition within the text-processing literature assumes that authors of narratives have schematized knowledge of the above components of a story and rely on this structure to "fill in" the components as they write a particular story. It is further assumed that an author does so with the expectation that his or her readers have this schematized knowledge, as well. As each part of a story unfolds, readers rely on their narrative schemata to form expectations as to what will come next. Skilled writers play off these expectations to occasionally surprise readers or "leave them hanging" (as cliff-hangers do). Schemata may be responsible for the feeling that readers may get after reading any of the individual portraits of characters in James Joyce's book *Dubliners* (i.e., wishing that each of the short stories did not end where they did, unfinished). Moreover, readers are thought to use their schemata for narratives to help them judge whether a story is a good one and also to create a *situation model* of what they have read.

SCHEMATA FOR EXPOSITORY TEXTS

Whereas the main goal of narratives is to tell a story to entertain readers, the main goal of expository texts is to provide information so that readers can learn something (Weaver & Kintsch, 1991). Thus, *Snow White* or any of the *Harry Potter* books are examples of narrative texts; this textbook is an example of an expository text.

Just as skilled writers and readers are thought to have schemata for narrative texts, they are also thought to have schemata for expository texts. The two most cited theoretical models of expository schemata are those of Meyer (1985) and Kintsch (1982). In Kintsch's (1982) model, there are three main relations that make up the schemata for expository texts: (1) *general–particular relations* that have to do with identifying, defining, classifying, or illustrating things (e.g., "A schema is a mental representation . . . "), (2) *object–object* relations that have to do with comparing or contrasting things (e.g., "Working memory differs from long-term memory in that . . . "), and (3) *object–part relations* that have to do with causal relations, how the parts of something are put together, and how the parts work individually and collectively (e.g., "There are three types of memory: short-term, working, and long-term . . . ").

In Meyer's (1985) model, the ideas in a passage are also said to stand in certain relations to each other. Analyses of many common expository texts show that writers arrange their ideas into five common relations:

1. *Collection*: a relation that shows how things are related together into a group (e.g., *There are seven types of vehicles on the road today. First, there are . . .*).
2. *Causation*: a relation that shows how one event is the antecedent cause of another event (e.g., *The tanker spilled all of its oil into the sea. As a result, the sea life . . .*).
3. *Response*: a relation that shows how one idea is a problem and another is a solution to the problem (e.g., *A significant number of people who are homeless have a substance abuse problem. It should be clear that homelessness will not diminish until increased money goes to treatment of this addiction . . .*).
4. *Comparison*: a relation in which the similarities and differences between things are pointed out (e.g., *Piaget and Vygotsky both emphasized egocentric speech; however, Vygotsky viewed it more as . . .*).
5. *Description*: a relation in which more information about something is given such as attributes, specifics, manners, or settings (e.g., *Newer oil tankers are safer than they used to be. These days they have power steering and double hulls*).

Because these relations pertain to how the ideas are arranged in some text, they are said make up the *prose structure* of the text. Writers hope that the arrangement of ideas in their readers' minds is the same as the arrangement of ideas in the text.

According to schema-theoretic models of comprehension, an individual who writes an expository textbook has schematized knowledge of the relations identified by Kintsch (1982) and Meyer (1985) and also knows the conventional ways of communicating these relations. The most common way to prompt readers to recognize a relation is to place sentences close together. When one sentence follows another, skilled readers try to form a connection between them (Carpenter et al., 1995; Graesser et al., 1997). If a writer fears that his or her readers will not make the connection even when sentences are placed in close proximity, he or she can use various *signaling devices* to make the connection explicit. For example, to convey Meyer's (1985) comparison relation, a writer might use the words "In contrast" To signal causal relations, he or she might use the words "As a result" Of course, readers do not always need signals to make the connection. Consider the following two passages:

1. *There are two main causes of heart disease. Fatty diets promote the formation of plaque deposits on arteries. Cigarettes enhance the formation of plaque by constricting blood vessels.*
2. *There are two main causes of heart disease. First, fatty diets promote the formation of plaque deposits on arteries. Second, cigarettes enhance the formation of plaque by constricting blood vessels.*

For most people, the words *First* and *Second* in the second passage are not needed in order for a reader to connect the ideas in the three sentences into Meyer's (1985) "collection" relation. However, reading times are enhanced in low-knowledge readers when such devices are used (Graesser et al., 1997).

Over time, it is assumed that readers gain knowledge of the common relations found in expository texts, such as collection, causation, response, comparison, and description. In a sense, their mind unconsciously says, "OK, how is this sentence related to the one(s) that I just read? Is it a causation relation? A comparison?" If the closest sentence does not provide an immediate fit, people read on until they find a sentence that does.

In addition to helping readers form expectations, knowledge of prose structure is thought to help readers comprehend and retain more of what they read (Meyer, 1985; Weaver & Kintsch, 1991). In particular, the five relations identified by Meyer often serve as an author's main point or thesis. Main ideas are connected by one of these five relations, and lesser ideas are subsumed beneath this overall relation. People who first encode the main point and then attach additional ideas to the main point demonstrate superior comprehension and memory of the ideas in a passage. People who treat paragraphs as a string of individual ideas show inferior comprehension and memory.

OTHER KINDS OF KNOWLEDGE

Three other kinds of knowledge that have been shown to be predictive of comprehension include knowledge of vocabulary, knowledge of acceptable grammatical structures, and metacognitive knowledge of reading (Cain et al., 2004; Proctor, Carlo, August, & Snow, 2005; van Gelderen et al., 2004). The predictive links between reading comprehension and the two aspects of linguistic ability (i.e., vocabulary and grammatical knowledge) are certainly consistent with the simple view of reading presented in Chapter 7 (i.e., that reading consists of listening comprehension skills combined with decoding skills). Metacognitive knowledge of reading pertains to knowing correct and incorrect ways of approaching the task of reading (e.g., recognizing the utility of using context to figure out the meaning of unfamiliar words).

Functional Aspects of Comprehension

In addition to having structural knowledge of topics and the various kinds of texts (e.g., narrative vs. expository), readers also need to engage in a variety of online processes in order to enhance their reading comprehension (Graesser et al., 1997; Paris, Wasik, & Turner, 1991; Pressley et al., 1994; Pressley & Hilden, 2006). For descriptive purposes, these processes can be organized into three main clusters: orienting processes, coherence-forming processes, and reading strategies. Let examine each of these clusters in turn.

Orienting Processes

The first thing that people have to do before they read is orient their cognitive processing toward some textual passage. For example, they need to engage their attentional mechanisms and, hopefully, motivational components such as interest, as well (see Chapter 10 for more on reading motivation). Next, they have to *set a goal* for reading (Pressley et al., 1994). Reading is a *purposeful* activity in that we read things for different reasons (Paris et al., 1991). For example, whereas we usually read a newspaper to find out what is happening in the world, we read spy novels simply to be entertained or take our minds off work. Similarly, sometimes we only want a rough sense of what an author is trying to say, so we only skim the pages for major points. Other times we really want to process everything that an author says, so we read every line very carefully (e.g., as when we read a textbook right before a test). Goal setting is crucial because the goals we set can either enhance or limit what we get from reading. For example, if someone sets the goal of "pronouncing all of the words correctly" but does not set the goal of "learning something," he or she is unlikely to engage in any of the reading strategies that are described later in this chapter and, therefore, will not comprehend very much of what he or she reads.

Coherence-Forming Processes

Recall that a central goal of reading is to create a coherent mental representation of the ideas in a passage. There are several key processes that facilitate the construction of coherent representations, though *inference making* is probably the most widely studied of these processes (Graesser et al., 1997; Paris et al., 1991). Readers make inferences in order to (1) elaborate on the meaning of an individual sentence and (2) integrate the meanings of several sentences in a text (Alba & Hasher, 1983). For example, when readers encounter sentences such as *The man stirred his coffee*, many of them elaborate on the ideas presented by inferring that he used a spoon. In addition, when presented with a pair of sentences such as *Joe smoked four packs a day. After he died, his wife sold her Phillip Morris stocks*, many readers infer that smoking caused Joe to die. Thus, the two ideas of smoking and dying are integrated together through a causal relation. Moreover, inferences play an important role in the construction of readers' situation models for the text they are reading. As mentioned above, the principal source of inter- and intrasentence inferences is a reader's knowledge of topics such as "coffee" and "cigarettes." The second source is the reader's knowledge of text structures and genres.

Why do readers make inferences when they read? It seems that a reader's mind is always trying to make sense of what it is encountering. One way of making sense of things is to make the information presented more concrete and specific. So, when people read the sentence above about stirring, their minds naturally ask questions such as, "What kind of thing do people usually use to stir their coffee?" Notice that the inference that a spoon was used is merely probabilistic. People sometimes use whatever is handy, such as the handle of a fork.

As to why we make intersentence inferences, it is helpful to repeat a point made earlier: It seems that the mind is always asking, "How does this new sentence relate to the sentences that I already read?" When two events co-occur close in time, it is natural to think that the prior one caused the later one (Bullock, Gelman, & Baillargeon, 1982; Graesser et al., 1997). For example, by stating the first sentence above about smoking and then the second one about dying right after it, it is natural to assume that smoking killed Joe. Similarly, if one reads *The floor was just mopped. I fell*, it is natural to assume that the speaker slipped on the floor. It is possible, however, that smoking did not kill Joe and that the person fell because of something else (e.g., tripping over a bucket). Thus, once again we see that inferences are not necessary conclusions; they are merely probabilistic guesses.

In addition to causal connections, various other intersentence connections could be inferred on the basis of one's knowledge. These include inferences regarding (1) the goals and plans that motivate a character's actions, (2) the traits or properties of characters or objects, (3) emotions of characters, (4) the causes of events, (5) the likely consequences of actions, (6) spatial relationships, (7) the global theme or point, and (8) the attitude of the writer (Graesser et al., 1997). Do readers make all of these inferences? It depends on whom you ask. Some "minimalist" theorists believe that only causal inferences are made routinely (e.g., McKoon & Ratcliff, 1992). Other more "constructionist" theorists believe that readers usually make inferences related to character goals, inferences as to why certain events occurred, and inferences that establish coherence at the local or global levels (Graesser et al., 1997).

As one further illustration of an inference-based coherence process, note that readers naturally link up a pronoun in a second sentence to a person's name in a first sentence (e.g., *Mary saw the doctor. She said* ...). Similar to causal inferences, such *anaphoric inferences* about pronouns are also probabilistic (i.e., the doctor could be a woman). Anaphoric expressions are one kind of class of textual entities called *referring expressions* (Gernsbacher, 1996). Other types include *cataphoric expressions* that refer to future text elements and *deitic expressions* that refer to things in the world. Writers and readers recognize that referring expressions conform to a small set of rules. For example, when a new entity is first introduced in a text, the referring expression usually contains an indefinite determiner (*a* or *an*), a richly specified noun, and a descriptive set of adjectives or prepositional phrases (e.g., *A massive man with a bushy mustache*). The next time this entity appears, however, it usually contains a definite determiner and just the noun (e.g., *the man* ...).

The final way that coherence is established and maintained is by making use of *inhibition* processes that suppress ideas that are incompatible with the current situation model (Gernsbacher, 1996). When words are read in succession, the multiple meanings of each word are temporarily activated. For example, when people read *The woman smelled the rose*, they temporarily activate meanings such as "thorny flower with soft petals" and "stood up" when they reach the word *rose*. However, only the former meaning is compatible with the overall meaning of the sentence. To achieve coherence, readers need to suppress or deactivate the inappropriate meanings.

Reading Strategies

So far, we have seen that readers set goals for reading and engage in processes such as inference making and inhibition to create a coherent situation model. One further way readers enhance their understanding is to apply a number of *reading strategies*. Most theorists argue that a strategy is a deliberate, goal-directed operation that is directed at solving a problem (Bjorklund, 2004). In the case of reading, the "problem" to be solved is achieving a deep and accurate understanding of some text. To say that a strategy is deliberate implies that a reader has some control over it. In other words, he or she intentionally tries to apply it and decides when and where to do so. The converse would be reading processes that happen automatically or implicitly, such as inhibition. Some of the reading strategies that have been investigated include identifying the main idea, summarizing, predicting, monitoring, and backtracking, though there has been some debate as to whether all of these processes are under a reader's control (Magliano, Trabasso, & Graesser, 1999; Rosenshine & Meister, 1994). Inference making has been called a reading strategy, too, and there is evidence that it is partially under a reader's control (Magliano et al., 1999). It was discussed in the prior section because it is so central to the coherence-forming processes. Rather than engage in unproductive taxonomic debates regarding which processes are strategies and which are not, it is best to think of strategies and processes being arrayed along a continuum of deliberateness and explicitness, with some being more deliberate and explicit than others. We now consider those strategies and processes that are perhaps farther along the continuum than others.

In order to *identify the main idea* of some passage, readers need to assess the relevance of each idea in the passage and then rank ideas in terms of their centrality or importance (van Dijk & Kintsch, 1983). Consider the following paragraph taken from George Lakoff's (1987) book *Women, Fire, and Dangerous Things*:

> Most categorization is automatic and unconscious, and if we become aware of it at all, it is only in problematic cases. In moving about the world, we automatically categorize people, animals, and physical objects, both natural and man-made. This sometimes leads to the impression that we just categorize things as they are, that things come in natural kinds, and that our categories of mind naturally fit the kinds of things that are in the world. But a large proportion of our categories are not categories of *things*; they are categories of abstract entities. We categorize events, actions, emotions, spatial relationships, social relationships, and abstract entities of an enormous range: governments, illnesses, and entities in both scientific and folk theories, like electrons and colds. Any adequate account of human thought must provide an accurate theory for *all* our categories, both concrete and abstract. (p. 6)

What is the main idea of this paragraph? Is it contained in the first sentence? The last? The fourth? How do you know? If this were an item from the verbal section of the SAT, one of the questions about this paragraph would ask which was the main idea. Apart from the practical reality that important standardized tests require the ability to identify the main idea, readers also need this skill in order the construct the prose structure for a text (see the previous section on Structural Aspects). George Lakoff rank-ordered the ideas in his paragraph in a particular way (in his own mind), and he wanted you to get his point about categorization. To say that you comprehended his paragraph is to say that you rank-ordered ideas the same way that he did.

In addition to determining the prose structure of a passage, a second way to identify main ideas is to locate various signals in the text. Sometimes signals are graphic (e.g., italics), sometimes they are lexical (e.g., using the word *essential*), and sometimes they are semantic (e.g., explicit topic sentences). Readers expect that the main idea will occur early in a paragraph, but location is not always a very good predictor. In fact, studies have shown that as few as 25% of children's textbooks have main ideas located near the beginning of paragraphs (Garner, 1987). Thus, it may be a better idea to rely on prose-structure relations and prior knowledge to find the main idea than to rely on text signals.

Besides being central to comprehension, an additional reason why identifying the main idea is an important strategy is that it is a prerequisite skill for performing the second important reading strategy: *summarizing*. In order to create a summary, you need to be able to delete unimportant ideas and retain just the "gist" of what is written. The gist, in turn, comprises mostly the main ideas.

To see this, consider the five rules for forming a good summary proposed by Brown and Day (1983). The first two rules specify that readers should delete trivial, irrelevant, or redundant information. The third rule suggests that readers should find a superordinate term for members of a category (e.g., "cars" for Buick, Dodge, and Toyota). Rules 4 and 5 specify that readers should find and use the main ideas of a passage in their summary. If main ideas are not explicitly provided by an author, readers should construct their own main ideas. Thus, one could not construct a good summary without being able to identify main ideas.

Studies suggest that readers adopt different strategies when asked to read a passage and write a summary of it from memory (Hyönä, Lorch, & Kaakinen, 2002). Whereas some readers skim quickly through the passage, others read more slowly or reread portions of the text. The best summarizers have been found to be students who (1) have greater working-memory capacity and (2) spend a good deal of time processing topic sentences.

The third important reading strategy is *predicting*. Predicting consists of simply forming expectations regarding what will happen next in a narrative story or anticipating what the author of an expository text will say next. Good writers are skilled at helping readers make predictions and also skilled at violating expectations in such a way that it is entertaining. To illustrate, consider the following passage taken from the book *Dave Barry Slept Here* written by columnist Dave Barry in 1989:

> While the United States was struggling to get out of the Depression, the nations of Europe were struggling to overcome the horror and devastation and death of World War I so they could go ahead and have World War II. By

the 1930s, everybody was just about ready, so Germany, showing the kind of spunky 'can-do' spirit that made it so popular over the years, started invading various surrounding nations. Fortunately these were for the most part *small* nations, but Germany's actions nevertheless alarmed Britain and France, which decided to strike back via the bold and clever strategy of signing agreements with Adolf Hitler. (p. 117)

Dave Barry's sarcasm works well because readers expect him to say one thing, and he frequently says another.

The fourth reading strategy is called *comprehension monitoring*. Simply put, comprehension monitoring is the ability to "know when you don't know"; that is, it is the ability to detect a comprehension failure (Markman, 1981). As was discussed in Chapter 7, reading does not consist of simply knowing how to sound-out words. Rather, reading consists of extracting meaning from texts. If a portion of a text does not make sense, readers should recognize that the main goal of reading (i.e., extracting meaning) has not been met.

When readers recognize that something they just read does not make sense, they have two options: (1) They could simply read on, or (2) they could decide to do something about their lack of comprehension. The latter option brings us to our fifth and final strategy, *backtracking*. Backtracking consists of rereading a portion of a text when a lack of comprehension occurs. Garner (1987) suggests that readers backtrack in response to four judgments and beliefs:

1. They do not understand or remember what they just read.
2. They believe that they can find the information needed to resolve the difficulty in the text.
3. The prior material must be scanned to locate the helpful information.
4. Information from several prior sentences may need to be combined and manipulated to resolve the comprehension problem.

Summary

In contemporary reading theories, it is assumed that reading comprehension is greatly aided when readers (1) set goals for understanding, (2) have declarative and conceptual knowledge of the topic, (3) have adequate structural capacity and knowledge of the different types of texts (i.e., narrative and expository), (4) have linguistic knowledge and metacognitive knowledge of reading, and (5) employ a variety of online processes such as inference making, inhibition, identifying the main idea, summarizing, predicting, monitoring, and backtracking.

THE RELEVANCE QUESTION: Why Should Teachers Care about Whether Children Acquire Reading Comprehension Skills?

As noted in Chapter 7, it is relatively easy to defend the claim that reading skills are extremely important to academic success and success in the work world, as well. The nuance in the case of the reading comprehension skills discussed in this chapter is that so much of the information that children acquire in the later grades comes by way of reading narrative and expository texts. Even when children have adequate decoding skills, they can, and often do, stumble at the level of comprehension. Most middle schools, high schools, and universities have staffs devoted to helping older students overcome their comprehension problems. The information in this chapter could be used by instructional support staffs to create interventions that target specific deficiencies.

THE DEVELOPMENTAL TRENDS QUESTION: How Do Reading Comprehension Skills Change over Time?

As a means of summarizing the development of reading comprehension skills, we first examine the research concerned with developmental differences in structural aspects of reading comprehension, then the developmental research related to functional aspects, and finally the research related to the role of extensive reading in the development of reading skills.

Development in Structural Aspects

In discussing the development of structural aspects of reading comprehension, one asks questions such as "How do the schemata of younger children differ from those of older children?" and "Do older children have more conceptual knowledge than younger children?" We attempt to answer such questions by focusing first on research pertaining to the development of working-memory capacity, and then consider research on the development of schemata for specific topics, schemata for stories, and schemata for expository texts.

Working-Memory Capacity

Studies have shown that there are monotonic increases in the capacity of working memory that occur between the ages of 5 and 25 (Swanson, 1999). In addition, children show increased ability to update working memory and inhibit the activation of irrelevant information. These increased abilities in memory have been found to be associated with improved reading comprehension skills (Cain et al., 2004; Carretti et al., 2005).

Topic Knowledge

Reading theorists assume that a substantial portion of children's knowledge of various topics (e.g., "animals," "fractions," "baseball") is arranged into schemata. Thus, their knowledge of "birds" might be represented by a node for "bird" connected to a node for "canary" by a "is-a" link, and so on. With age, experience, and increased education, children's schemata for various topics become more and more elaborate. Relatedly, other forms of conceptual and declarative knowledge increase with age as well (Case, 1998). This increased topic knowledge greatly facilitates children's comprehension.

Story Schemata

Although several theoretical models of schemata for stories have been proposed over the years (Graesser et al., 1991), the models that have generated the most developmental research are those based on the story grammars proposed by Mandler and Johnson (1977) and Stein and Glenn (1979). In Stein and Glenn's (1979) classic account, a *story grammar* is a theoretical description of what most stories have in common. It is not intended to reflect an actual knowledge structure in a young reader's mind. Rather, it is a representation of an *expert's* knowledge of what all stories have in common (Stein, 1982). To get a sense of the formal, abstract character of a story grammar, consider the following example: If an adult were to sign up for a writing workshop to learn how to write a book for children, he or she would probably be presented with some form of a story grammar by the workshop leader. The workshop leader would say things like, "Any successful story has seven parts. The first part is. . . ."

Although children do not start out with a formal, explicit story grammar in their minds, it has often been said that they do develop *story schemata* in response to listening to and reading many stories. A story schema contains personalized, implicit knowledge about what most stories have in common (Stein, 1982). Given the personalized nature of story schemata, any two children could develop different schemata if they listened to very different types of stories during their lives. However, as children read more and more stories and gain increased knowledge about people, their story schemata should become more similar to a formal story grammar.

The original story grammar proposed by Stein and Glenn (1979) specified that stories have seven main components: (1) a *major setting* that includes the introduction of characters (e.g., "Once upon a time, there was a beautiful young woman called Cinderella"), (2) a *minor setting* that includes a description of the story context (e.g., "She lived in a modest house with her stepmother"), (3) *initiating events* that include changes in the environment or things that happen to main characters (e.g., "One day, the prince invited everyone to a ball"), (4) *internal responses* that include the characters' goals, plans, and thoughts that arise in response to the initiating events (e.g., "Cinderella said, 'Oh, I want to go the ball too!'"), (5) *attempts* that include the characters' actions to fulfill the goal (e.g., "So she started to fix an old gown to make it more presentable"), (6) *direct consequences* that specify whether the goal was attained (e.g., "But her stepmother made her clean the castle instead of fix her gown"), and (7) *reactions* that include the characters' feeling or thoughts about the direct consequences (e.g., "When it came time to go to the ball, Cinderella was sad because she could not go"). The first two elements are usually grouped together to form what is called the "setting" part of a story, and the last five elements are grouped together to form what is called the "episode" part of the story. Hence, prototypical stories contain both a setting and at least one episode.

Research has shown that when stories conform to the canonical structure specified above (i.e., they have all seven of the components arranged in the same order as above), few developmental differences emerge. In particular, even 4- and 5-year-olds show good recall of the events in a story when it has all of the components outlined in Stein and Glenn's story grammar. Older children do, however, recall more information in the story than younger children and also make more inferences than younger children. The majority of these inferences seem to be attempts to fill in category information that was missing in the actual text (Stein, 1982). For example, if the "reaction" portion of a story was missing, older children tend to fill in this component through inference. In addition, some studies suggest that whereas children are likely to recall the action elements of a story schema (part of the "attempts" node), adults are more likely to recall internal responses such as a protagonist's goals and the events that initiated these goals (van den Broek, Lorch, & Thurlow, 1996).

When noncanonical stories are used, developmental differences become even more pronounced. For example, when a story is artificially disorganized (e.g., the "initiating event" is placed after the "direct consequence"), older children are more able to recover the canonical structure of the story in their retellings than younger children (Stein, 1982). Similarly, when children are given the initial portions of a story and asked to complete it, older children are more likely than younger children to add the components that the story grammar would suggest are missing (Eckler & Weininger, 1989). Finally, when presented with stories that are missing some of the components specified in the story grammar (e.g., "direct consequences"), older readers (who have well-developed story schemata) are more likely than young readers to say that the story was not a good one (Stein & Policastro, 1984).

Thus, developmental differences are most pronounced when children are asked to comprehend a story that does *not* conform to a story grammar. It would seem that a canonical story minimizes the amount of processing that has to be done in order for the story to be comprehended. The argument is that this minimization would only occur if children had something like a story schema in their minds. Since older children tend to have greater processing capacity than younger children, the former can take a noncanonical story and mentally fill in components or rearrange them to make it into a more canonical story.

In sum, then, story schemata have been thought to play two important roles. First, they minimize the processing that has to occur when a story is read. When presented with a canonical story, readers need not devote all of their mental resources to comprehending the basic facts in the story. Instead, readers can use any additional processing resources to perform other mental tasks such as inference making (Stein, 1982) and metaphor comprehension (Waggoner, Messe, & Palermo, 1985). Second, story schemata set up expectations as to what will occur next in a story. For example, if the "initiating event" component has just occurred in a story, readers tend to expect that the "internal response" component will be encountered soon. Although older students can make better use of the two roles played by story schemata than younger students, even preschoolers seem to have a rudimentary story schema. In most cases, however, it is necessary to use auxiliary pictures and probing questions to reveal a story schema in children below the age of 6 (Shapiro & Hudson, 1991).

Many school systems have incorporated the story grammar model into their reading curriculum. In fact, it is often the case that teachers frequently ask students to identify the parts of a story that they just read (e.g., "Who can tell me what the setting is?" "What is the initiating event?"). Thus, students learn the parts and then get a lot of practice finding the parts in actual stories. If the schema theory is correct that the mind "naturally" abstracts common elements on its own, perhaps this explicit instruction would not be necessary. And yet, at the very least, we would expect that this practice would certainly help students acquire a story schema faster than they would on their own. Research supports this expectation, especially for younger students or students with disabilities (Dimino, Taylor, & Gersten, 1995; Lauren & Allen, 1999; Pressley, Johnson, Symons, McGoldrick, & Kurita, 1989).

Schemata for Expository Texts

In its purest form, a developmental study of prose structure would take groups of children at two ages and give them well-organized and poorly organized expository passages to recall (e.g., Danner, 1976). In such a study, one could examine (1) whether older children are more likely than younger children to "use the author's prose structure" to help their recall (i.e., to find the author's main thesis and use it to organize their recall of subordinate ideas), (2) whether older children are less likely than younger children to need explicit text signals to derive the prose structure, and (3) whether older children are more likely than younger children to derive the prose structure in poorly organized passages. All of these findings would support the idea that, with age and increased reading opportunities, children acquire schemata for expository texts.

Unfortunately, such "pure" developmental studies are hard to find. Instead of using multiple age groups, many researchers have used just one age group. In addition, many researchers seemed to be more interested in reading ability than age because when they compared children of two age groups, they usually added reading ability as a variable (e.g., they compared fifth-grade, struggling comprehenders to third-grade, skilled comprehenders). Further, many researchers provided instruction on how to derive prose structure to see if children's comprehension could be improved. As a result, few of the existing studies can be used to say whether children "naturally" acquire schemata for expository texts simply by reading many of them (as seems to be the case for story schemata).

Nevertheless, the existing research suggests that the derivation of prose structure is often not an easy task for children at any age. Meyer, Brandt, and Bluth (1980), for example, found that when given four well-organized passages to remember, only 22% of ninth graders consistently used the strategy of using the author's main thesis to organize their recalls. More than 50% of these students did not use the strategy even once. As a result, even the best readers recalled 70% or fewer of the ideas in the passages. Similarly, Zinar (1990) found that fifth graders only recalled about 20–25% of the content of short prose passages, suggesting that they too did not use the prose structure to guide their recall.

This is not to say, however, that children's performance is always so deficient. For example, Garner et al. (1986) found excellent knowledge of prose structure in a group of seventh graders. In particular, 75% could provide a meaningful description of a paragraph, 98% could exclude topically unrelated sentences from a paragraph, 87% knew where to place a topic sentence in a paragraph, and 87% could arrange a set of sentences into a cohesive whole. Similarly, Spires, Gallini, and Riggsbee (1992) found that fourth graders in a control group recalled 60% or more of the content of expository passages arranged in the form of problem–solution or compare–contrast formats.

The finding that children can perform both extremely well and extremely poorly suggests that something other than schemata for expository texts might be at work. One possible explanation for such variable performance is children's knowledge of the passage topic (Roller, 1990). For very familiar passages, being aware of common formats such as problem–solution or compare–contrast may add little to one's knowledge of the topic. That is, a reader might show excellent comprehension of a familiar passage even when he or she lacks knowledge of common formats (i.e., lacks a schema for expository passages). For example, a young child who is enthralled by dinosaurs might show very good comprehension of a passage about the extinction of dinosaurs even though this child lacks knowledge of the format in which the ideas are arranged (e.g., "causal" relations). Conversely, a reader may show very poor comprehension of an unfamiliar passage even when he or she has knowledge of common formats. For example, an adult who is unfamiliar with computers but familiar with compare–contrast formats might show poor comprehension of a passage about the similarities and differences between two kinds of computers.

If both prior knowledge and schemata for expository texts affect comprehension, the effects of schemata for expository texts should be most pronounced when readers are only moderately familiar with a topic. In reviewing the literature on prose structure, Roller (1990) found two findings in support of this notion: (1) presenting disorganized paragraphs has its strongest effects when readers are moderately familiar with the topic, and (2) providing instruction of the different types of prose structures (e.g., problem–solution) has its strongest effects when readers are moderately familiar with a topic. When readers are either very unfamiliar or very familiar with a topic, these effects are considerably weaker.

In sum, then, there is evidence that children in the later grades have at least implicit knowledge of various prose structures. Whether they make use of this structure to aid their comprehension and recall seems to depend on their familiarity with a topic. Because most studies in this area have neither controlled for familiarity nor used a "pure" developmental design, it is hard to say what the "natural" developmental course of schemata for expository texts is. Nevertheless, a number of studies have shown that when children are told about the various types of relations in prose passages and asked to identify these relations (e.g., "Look at this paragraph. Where is a collection relation? How about a cause–effect relation?"), they show improved comprehension. So, just as teaching story grammar elements can help improve children's comprehension of stories, teaching children the common expository elements can help them better comprehend expository passages. However, given the role of familiarity, it would make sense that pointing out expository relations should only be done when the passage contains content that is moderately familiar to students. It would be a waste of time for content that is either highly familiar or highly unfamiliar. One way a teacher could check the familiarity of a topic is to have students generate a group concept map or web prior to reading (Guthrie et al., 2000). Here, students would say everything they know about a topic, and the teacher would depict this knowledge using a node-link schema on the board.

Development in Functional Aspects of Reading

In what follows, the developmental research on the three categories of functional aspects (i.e., orienting processes, coherence-forming processes, and reading strategies) will be described in turn.

Orienting Processes

Research shows that young children do not set optimal reading goals for themselves. For example, instead of reading something to increase their knowledge about the topic or be entertained, young readers say that the goal of reading is to "pronounce all of the words properly." Other students act as if their goal is to simply "get the assignment done" (Paris et al., 1991; Paris, Byrnes, & Paris, 2001). With these goals, students who read all the words properly and finish reading an assigned passage will not be bothered if they do not comprehend what they read. Over time, children replace their suboptimal goals with more appropriate ones regarding meaning. Typically, however, this shift takes too many years to complete. It should be clear that teachers need to help students set goals that are more appropriate for themselves early on in the elementary grades.

Coherence-Forming Processes

Given the fact that (1) declarative and conceptual knowledge underlies inference making and (2) declarative and conceptual knowledge increases with age, it should not be surprising to learn that many studies have found that children in the later grades (e.g., fourth, fifth, and sixth grades) are more likely to make inferences than children in the earlier grades (Paris et al., 1991; van den Broek, 1989). For example, when reading the sentence *The soldier stirred his coffee*, older students are more likely than younger students are to infer that the soldier used a spoon (Paris, 1978). Inference making, in turn, predicts degree of comprehension even after controlling for other factors such as working memory (Cain et al., 2004).

However, the common finding of developmental differences in inference making should not imply that younger children are incapable of making inferences. Some studies have shown that young children demonstrate very good inference-making skills when they are presented with stories about very familiar topics or are given instruction on how to make inferences (Dewitz, Carr, & Patberg, 1987; Paris et al., 1991; Wasik, 1986). Thus, the "natural" course of inference making can be altered by way of instruction or by using highly familiar content.

One good way of eliciting inferences is to stop in the middle of stories whenever an inference is required and ask questions. For example, when students read the popular "Miss Nelson" stories (about a teacher named Miss Nelson), they need to make the inference that a mean substitute teacher in the story, named "Viola Swamp," is really Miss Nelson in disguise. Throughout the book, subtle clues are left to help readers make this connection. Young readers often miss these clues, so it would be helpful to ask questions such as "What is Viola Swamp's dress doing in Miss Nelson's closet?" Given the centrality of explanations in the comprehension process, "why" questions would also be extremely helpful (Magliano et al., 1999). Over time, repeated questions that require inferences would ultimately help children make inferences on their own. However, since older students seem to make inferences without much prompting, focused instruction on inference making might be best for kindergartners through fourth graders. The combination of increased working-memory capacity, knowledge growth, teacher guidance, and changing goals for reading (see above) should lead to the spontaneous tendency to generate inferences.

Other kinds of coherence-forming processes besides inference making (e.g., anaphora and inhibition) have received very little attention from developmentalists. At present, for example, only one study has shown that it is possible to improve the comprehension of anaphora in third graders through direct instruction (Baumann, 1986). Similarly, there are only a handful of developmental studies of the role of inhibition in reading. One study found that (1) seventh graders demonstrated a greater ability to inhibit distracting information than fifth graders, and (2) the ability to inhibit irrelevant information was strongly related to reading comprehension scores (Kipp, Pope, & Digby, 1998). Another study of 6- to 11-year-olds found that inhibitory skills predicted reading comprehension after controlling for age, intelligence, and level of attentional problems (Savage, Cornish, Manley, & Hollis, 2006). Why age changes in inhibition might occur is still something of a mystery. Some have speculated it has to do with the development of the frontal lobes (Dempster, 1992), but connectionist modeling studies suggest it may have to do with the elaboration of neural nets associated with the reading system (e.g., the addition of inhibitory connections).

Reading Strategies

Children in the elementary grades have difficulty recognizing, recalling, and constructing the main idea in passages (Baumann, 1981; Johnston & Afflerbach, 1985; Paris et al., 1991). Moreover, there is evidence that this skill improves throughout the adolescent and early adult years. Once again, however, the identification of main ideas is more likely when familiar content is used (Sternberg, 1985) and when students are directly taught how to perform this strategy (e.g., Baumann, 1984).

As might be expected given the findings for identifying the main idea, there are clear developmental trends in the ability to provide a good summary. Whereas younger students (e.g., fifth graders) tend to create summaries by simply deleting statements and using the author's words, older students (e.g., high school students) tend to combine and reorganize ideas using their own words (Brown & Day, 1983; Paris et al., 1991; Taylor, 1986).

As was found for both inference making and identifying the main idea, however, preadolescent children can be taught how to provide a good summary (Brown, Day, & Jones, 1983; Palincsar & Brown, 1984; Rinehart, Stahl, & Erickson, 1986). In the Rinehart et al. (1986) study, for example, children were taught four rules for summarizing over the course of five 1-hr lessons: identify the main information, delete trivial information, delete redundant information, and relate main and supporting information. The teacher modeled each strategy and then asked students to practice the modeled strategy. They worked first at the paragraph level, and then moved up to combining paragraph summaries into a single summary for the whole text. When training was over, the researchers found that trained children showed better memory for what they read than untrained children.

With respect to predicting, studies have shown that although many students do not spontaneously make predictions when they read, they can be taught to do so. In support of the claim that good comprehenders make predictions when they read, these studies also show that children's reading comprehension improves after being told how to make predictions (Fielding, Anderson, & Pearson, 1990; Hansen & Pearson, 1983; Palincsar & Brown, 1984; Pearson & Fielding, 1991).

One way to improve student predictions is to have them first look at the cover of a book and make a prediction about what the book will be about after examining the title and cover illustration (Pressley et al., 1994). Then, in the midst of reading the work, children can be asked to stop and make additional predictions as they read. Finally, after the reading is completed, children can be asked to examine their original predictions to see whether they were right. Pressley and his colleagues have shown that whereas first graders need a lot of prompting to make such predictions, older students need much less prompting after 3 years of such instruction.

As noted previously, the essence of reading comprehension is the extraction of meaning; that is, one reads *in order to* gain an understanding of a story or some topic area. If students read a story or an informational passage and do not come away with a good understanding of what they read, that means that they did not attain the central goal of reading (Baker & Brown, 1984; Paris et al., 1991). If it were to be found that many children do not detect their comprehension failures or do not try to fix a comprehension failure when it occurs, that would mean that reading instruction is seriously deficient. To see this, consider an analogy. What would we think about a vocational school that constantly produced car mechanics who could not detect or repair problems with a malfunctioning automobile? Just as the essence of car repair involves knowing the difference between a well-functioning and malfunctioning car (and knowing how to fix the latter), the essence of reading involves knowing the difference between adequate and inadequate comprehension (and knowing how to fix the latter).

Unfortunately, many studies have shown that children in the early elementary and middle school years have difficulty detecting their own comprehension problems (Baker & Brown, 1984; Garner, 1987; Paris et al., 1991). For example, in a classic study, Markman (1979) showed how even sixth graders can fail to detect logical inconsistencies in expository passages. In one passage, several lines pointed out that there is no light at the bottom of the ocean and that it is necessary to have light in order to see colors. After these lines were presented, the very next line stated that fish who live at the bottom of the sea use color to select their food. Even with explicit instructions to find such problems in passages, a sizeable number of sixth graders could not find them. Using similar materials, this finding has been replicated many times with other age groups (e.g., Baker, 1984). Even college students, for example, fail to accurately recognize that they have not fully comprehended passages they have read (Thiede, Anderson, & Therriault, 2003). One way to improve self-assessments of comprehension is to delay asking students for their assessments until a few minutes have passed. When asked to provide assessments immediately, information from the passage and the ideas evoked by this information may still be available in working memory. Having access to seemingly large amounts of information in working memory may lead readers to wrongly conclude that they learned something from it.

Overall, the developmental research on monitoring has revealed the following trends: (1) In the elementary grades and somewhat beyond, children often operate on "automatic pilot" when they read and seem oblivious to comprehension difficulties (Duffy & Roehler, 1987); (2) whereas younger readers tend to use a single standard for judging the meaningfulness of what they have read (e.g., problems with a single word), older readers use multiple standards for judging meaningfulness and consistency (Baker, 1984; Garner, 1981); and (3) older students are more likely to construct coherent representations of texts and benefit from instruction that helps them form such representations (Paris et al., 1991).

In her review of the literature, Garner (1987) argued that backtracking develops substantially between the 6th and 10th grades. There are at least three reasons why younger readers tend not to reread a portion of text: (1) They sometimes think that it is "illegal" to do so; (2) they may not realize that they have a comprehension problem (see the prior paragraph on "monitoring"); and (3) they are often unfamiliar with text structure and cannot, therefore, use text structure to help guide their search for clarifying information. In addition, since many young readers think that the goal of reading is not to construct meaning but to "sound-out words properly," they would not be troubled by a comprehension failure (Paris et al., 1991). Thus, if some meaningless portion of a text were sounded-out properly, there is no need to reread it.

Collectively, the shortcomings in children's structural and functional aspects of reading suggest that they often do not construct adequate situation models in their minds. That is, their mental representation of what is going on in a text does not match the one that the author hoped to create in their minds. To help promote more complete and accurate situation models in young readers, Glenberg, Gutierrez, Levin, Japuntich, and Kaschak (2004) created an intervention in which they used concrete props that corresponded to items in stories (e.g., a toy barn and toy farm animals). Compared to a condition in which children merely reread passages, first and second graders who either manipulated the props or imagined themselves manipulating the props showed markedly improved comprehension.

The Role of Extensive Reading

Studies have consistently shown that students who read frequently tend to have higher scores on reading achievement tests than students who read less frequently (e.g., Cipielewski & Stanovich, 1992; Greany, 1980; Greany & Hegarty, 1987; Nell, 1988; Walberg & Tsai, 1984). How should this finding be interpreted? One approach is to accept the correlation at face value, assume a causal relationship between frequent reading and reading achievement, and infer that a good way to raise test scores is to have students read more often. Another approach, however, is to examine the evidence more critically before drawing any instructional implications from it. The latter approach is adopted here.

The first way to critically evaluate the link between frequent reading and reading development is to ask the following question: "Is the correlation credible?" As noted in Chapter 7, a good way to assess the credibility of a correlation is to see if it is spurious. Could the correlation between frequent reading and elevated reading scores be due to some other variable that tends to be associated with both frequent reading and high test scores? One obvious "other variable" would be reading ability (Cipielewski & Stanovich, 1992). Motivation theorists recognize that people are more likely to engage in some activity if they feel self-efficacious (see Chapter 10). Moreover, they have shown that talented individuals tend to feel more self-efficacious than their less-talented peers. If so, then it would be expected that skilled readers would tend to read more than struggling readers. In addition, skilled readers, by definition, have higher test scores than struggling readers. Hence, it is entirely possible that the correlation between frequent reading and reading achievement is spurious.

As noted earlier, researchers determine whether correlation is spurious by seeing if it maintains its numerical value when the effects of other variables that might be involved are mathematically eliminated. Studies have shown that the correlation between frequent reading and reading achievement does shrink somewhat when the effects of reading ability and other possible factors (e.g., socioeconomic status) are subtracted out, but it does not shrink to zero (Anderson, Wilson, & Fielding, 1988; Cipielewski & Stanovich, 1992; Heyns, 1978; Taylor, Frye, & Maruyama, 1990; Walberg & Tsai, 1984). Thus, the correlation between frequent reading and higher test scores does not appear to be spurious.

However, statistics alone cannot determine the meaning of a mathematical relationship or the direction of causality. There has to be a well-regarded theory to lend further support to an assumed connection between two factors. It turns out that there are theoretical grounds for assuming that frequent reading promotes the development of reading skills. However, the links between frequent reading and skill development are more complicated than they would first appear.

Contemporary theories of cognition suggest that one of the best ways to become more proficient in some activity is to practice regularly and extensively (Anderson, 1995; Ericsson, 1996). In fact, some studies show that a minimum of 4 hr per day of practice is required for someone to attain the highest level of expertise in domains such as tennis, piano, or chess. However, research on the "Power Law of Learning" suggests that practice is particularly important during the earliest stages of skill acquisition. After a certain point in time, practice provides diminishing returns. To illustrate, consider the case of a first grader who makes pronunciation mistakes about 30% of the time in September, but only 15% of the time after 9 months of regular reading in school (a 50% reduction in errors). During the 2nd and 3rd grades, however, the student may find that his or her error rate is reduced down further from 15% to just 10% and 8%, respectively, after 2 more years of practice. The latter represent reductions of only 33% and 20% in the student's error rate, respectively. Thus, the notion of diminishing returns suggests that increased practice would be most beneficial to individuals who are in the earliest stages of learning to read (e.g., 1st through 3rd graders) and least beneficial to individuals who are in the latter stages (e.g., 9th through 12th graders). If so, then a uniform policy that mandates an increase in reading for all students (e.g., all students should read 15 min more per day) would have a greater effect on younger readers than on older readers.

In a related way, the idea of diminishing returns suggests that there would be a higher correlation between frequent reading and test scores in younger children (e.g., second and third graders) than in older children (e.g., fifth or sixth graders). It is notable that most of the studies that have investigated the role of frequent reading have focused on children in the fifth grade or older (presumably because many younger children are not yet fluent, independent readers). However, if practice has its strongest effects early in the process, then the correlations generated from studies of fifth graders may underestimate the potential value of frequent reading for younger children.

One further theoretical point relates to "Matthew effects" (Stanovich, 1986). Cognitive psychologists have shown that the comprehension of sentence-length constructions requires the ability to process and hold in working memory the meaning of all of the words in the sentence (Carpenter & Just, 1987). As your eyes fixate on each word in a sentence, all preceding words in that sentence must be retained and maintained in working memory before this information fades. If any obstacle to comprehension is encountered before the information starts to fade (about 2 s), comprehension processes usually falter (Baddeley, 1990). One such obstacle is the presence of an unfamiliar word. Whereas highly familiar words can be processed in .25 s or less, unfamiliar words can take considerably longer to process. With only 2 s to process all of the words, then, unfamiliar words pose quite a problem. However, if a person reads many different types of works and does so on a regular basis, that person tends to convert words that used to be unfamiliar into familiar words (in the same way that unfamiliar faces can become quickly recognized through repeated encounters). Over time, the troublesome words soon become processed nearly as quickly as other words, and comprehension problems are no longer disrupted (Perfetti, 1985). However, an important caveat in this account is that children differ in their ability to use contextual cues to acquire new vocabulary words from text. Children with greater working-memory capacity acquire new meanings from context more readily than children with less working-memory capacity (Cain, Oakhill, & Lemmon, 2004). Thus, wide reading is more likely to increase the processing speed of the high-capacity children than the low-capacity children.

The most significant consequence of this increase in processing speed is that the reader now has better access to the knowledge contained in the texts that he or she is reading. Acquiring more knowledge, in turn, helps the reader make new inferences that further enhance the comprehension process (Pearson & Fielding, 1991). Other benefits of wide reading include

(1) the acquisition of new vocabulary words and grammatical constructions that are normally not acquired in conversation (Stanovich & Cunningham, 1992) and (2) enhanced phonemic awareness that can be used in the decoding process (Stanovich, 1986).

Thus, regular reading has the potential to increase one's reading speed, vocabulary, knowledge, and phonemic awareness. Such changes, in turn, make one a better reader still. In effect, reading skills tend to snowball over time. This analysis implies that if two individuals were to start out at roughly the same place in the first grade, but only one were to read extensively, it would be expected that the extensive reader would show faster growth in reading skills than the less extensive reader. Moreover, if we were to plot their reading scores as a function of time, we would see a widening gap between their respective "learning curves" over time. Stanovich (1986) labeled this phenomenon the "Matthew effect" after the New Testament author who refers to the rich getting richer (i.e., Matthew).

However, it is important to note that Matthew effects would not be expected to occur if children were to read exactly the same (unchallenging) works again and again. Similarly, little growth would be expected if children were to read new books each time but select books that contain many of the same words and ideas. Thus, researchers would tend to find a higher correlation between extensive reading and reading achievement in a study if they asked questions such as "How many different books did you read last year?" than if they asked "How many minutes do you spend reading each day?" In addition, the idea of Matthew effects suggests that the causal relationship between frequent reading and reading achievement is more appropriately viewed as reciprocal than unidirectional (i.e., frequent reading causes higher achievement, which in turn promotes more frequent reading). However, in general, there does appear to be a solid theoretical basis for assuming that frequent reading would promote higher levels of reading achievement.

So far, then, we have seen that the correlation between frequent reading and reading achievement is probably not spurious and makes sense theoretically. However, one further issue relates to the typical size of the correlation. If frequent reading is authentically connected to reading achievement, but the relationship is relatively weak, why should a teacher allocate more instructional time to silent reading (or assign more of it as homework)? Researchers who focus on such issues have approached the idea of magnitude in several ways. One approach consists of assigning the label "small" to correlations in the range of $r = 0$ to .30, "moderate" to correlations between .30 and .80, and "large" to correlations greater than .80 (Cohen, 1992). Then, greater weight is given to correlations in the moderate and large ranges than to correlations in the small range.

Studies show that the correlation between frequent reading and reading achievement typically range between $r = .10$ and $r = .40$ (e.g., Anderson et al., 1988; Cipielewski & Stanovich, 1992; Greany, 1980; Heyns, 1978; Taylor et al., 1990; Walberg & Tsai, 1984). According to the labeling approach above, these correlations would be considered "small" and, perhaps, not given very much consideration in instructional decision making.

In recent years, however, it has been argued that the conventional labeling approach is not especially helpful when the practical value of some sort of intervention is under consideration. A better approach is to convert the correlation to something called a "binomial effect size display" (Rosenthal, 1994). The details of this conversion are less important than the bottom line that "small" correlations (e.g., those found in studies of reading frequency) can be shown to have nontrivial practical implications. For example, let's assume that the average correlation between frequent reading and reading achievement is $r = .24$. Expressed in the form of a binomial effect size display, a correlation of .24 suggests that an intervention designed to increase reading would tend to produce growth in reading skills in 62% of students as opposed to just 38% of students who do not increase their reading. At the school level, this difference in success rate would mean that a school of 500 students would show growth in 310 students instead of 190 students (i.e., 120 additional students). At the aggregate level across all of the schools in the United States, this analysis suggests that additional reading would have a noticeable effect that would be clearly worth the effort.

However, a reflective practitioner might still wonder why the correlations seem to vary so much across studies. Which of the respective values is closest to the truth? One reason for the variability was alluded to earlier. Some researchers subtracted out the effects of other important variables such as reading ability and socioeconomic status, while others did not. Uncorrected, the correlations are closer to $r = .40$. With the corrections, they drop down into the range of $r = .10$ to .25.

A second important reason for the variability is the precision and accuracy with which reading frequency has been assessed in each study. If someone asked, "How many books did you read last month?" or "How often do you read books?" you might give a less accurate answer than if you kept a daily journal of your reading for a month. Imprecise measurement tends to lead to smaller correlations than precise measurement, so one would expect that the journal approach would generate higher correlations than the questions approach. Studies generally confirm this expectation. Whereas researchers who used the journal approach have tended to find uncorrected correlations in the .30–.40 range (e.g., Anderson et al., 1988; Greany, 1980; Taylor et al., 1990), those using the questionnaire approach have found much smaller correlations (e.g., Walberg & Tsai, 1984).

However, the journal approach is not without its problems. Apart from the fact that it is labor-intensive, there is also the issue of social desirability. People (especially children) may be inclined to report more reading than they actually do in order to make a favorable impression on researchers. In addition, whereas the journal approach taps into current reading habits, it does not assess children's prior reading habits that contributed to their current level of skill. Further, in most studies that utilized the journal approach, researchers chose to focus on the average number of minutes per day spent reading. As noted earlier, the amount of time spent reading may matter less than the type and diversity of books read. To address all of these problems, Keith Stanovich and colleagues created a technique that taps into a variable called *print exposure* (e.g., Cipielewski & Stanovich, 1992; Stanovich & Cunningham, 1992). In this technique, people are presented with names of authors (e.g., Stephen King), books (e.g., *The Grapes of Wrath*), and magazines (*Cosmopolitan*) and are asked to say if they recognize these names. Mixed within the list of actual names are foils (e.g., names of the consulting editors of journals in educational psychology). Note that this measure seems to tap into both the extent of reading *and* the diversity of reading. That is, someone who never reads or who only reads the same three authors would tend to recognize fewer names than someone who reads widely. In addition, people who are inclined toward social desirability would tend to check more names, even the foils. Researchers can use the selection of foils to adjust scores down to a more accurate figure.

Aware of the fact that any correlation between print exposure and reading skills might be spurious (e.g., intelligent people tend to read more and also know more names of authors), Stanovich and colleagues were careful in each of their studies to control for general intelligence (using IQ tests) and aptitude (using various measures of reading comprehension and reading-specific skills such as decoding). Across a series of studies, results showed that print exposure was highly predictive of: (1) college students' orthographic (i.e., spelling) knowledge, (2) children's phonological coding, spelling, vocabulary, verbal fluency, and general knowledge, (3) college students' vocabulary, reading comprehension, knowledge of history and literature, spelling ability, and verbal fluency, (4) children's reading comprehension and reading rate, and (5) college students' and older adults' cultural knowledge (e.g., Stanovich & Cunningham, 1992; Stanovich, West, & Harrison, 1995). On average, the corrected correlations clustered near the value of $r = .28$, suggesting that extensive and diverse reading is associated with growth in reading skills and knowledge. In addition, these studies illustrate how a more precise measurement technique can yield a higher and more accurate indication of the degree of relationship between two factors than less precise techniques.

One final way to address the magnitude question is to consider the likely consequences of increasing reading by a certain amount each day. An

interesting aspect of correlational studies is that one can create mathematical formulas that allow one to say how much one factor might increase if
the other factor were increased by a certain amount. In the case of reading,
several researchers have attempted to determine how much test scores
would increase if children were to read a certain amount more. In one
study, for example, researchers showed that a unit increase in minutes of
book reading would be associated with a 4.9% gain in reading comprehension as measured by a standardized test (Anderson et al., 1988). To illustrate such an increase, a child at the median for book reading in their study
(i.e., about 5 min per day) would have to increase his or her reading by just
9 min more per day (i.e., 13 min per day) to show a 4.9% gain. Another interesting aspect of their data was that increases in book-reading time produced diminishing returns. For example, a child who went from no reading
per day to 6 min per day would move from the 40th percentile for reading
comprehension to the 60th percentile. In contrast, a comparable 6-min shift
from 6 min per day to 12 min per day would move a child from the 60th
percentile to just the 64th percentile.

Summary

In sum, we now have a good sense of the developmental trends in reading
comprehension: Children seem to develop both structural and functional
competencies with age that help them process what they are reading. In
particular, research shows that older children demonstrate better reading
comprehension than younger children because they are more likely than
younger children to: (1) have more working-memory capacity, (2) have extensive declarative and conceptual knowledge of topics, (3) have structural
knowledge of the different kinds of texts (e.g., stories and expository texts),
(4) engage in functional processes that enhance comprehension such as inference making, inhibition, and comprehension monitoring, and (5) have
had more extensive practice.

THE DEVELOPMENTAL MECHANISMS QUESTION:
What Factors Promote Changes in Reading Comprehension Skills?

With respect to developmental mechanisms that could explain these age
trends, three themes emerge from the research on schemata and strategies.
First, it takes considerable time for children to develop schemata and strategies on their own. In the absence of explicit instruction, many middle
school and high school students (who have been learning to read for more
than 5 years) do not make use of schemata and strategies to guide their
comprehension. Second, certain kinds of instruction can substantially de-

crease the amount of time it takes children to develop schemata and strategies. In particular, a large number of instructional studies have shown that explicit instruction on schemata or strategies can improve the comprehension of even elementary students. Third, children's prior knowledge of a topic can influence the degree to which they use their schemata or strategies to enhance their comprehension. Familiarity can compensate for a lack of knowledge of prose structure and can also enhance the chances that strategies will be deployed. Indeed, a variety of studies of adults who are struggling readers show that people who are very knowledgeable about some topic (e.g., baseball) can show excellent comprehension of a passage on that topic (Recht & Leslie, 1988; Walker, 1987). But reading many diverse books instills the broad topic knowledge that can promote comprehension, inference making, and predictions. In essence, then, the primary developmental mechanisms include extensive reading and explicit instruction in strategies.

THE DEFICIENCIES QUESTION: Are There Populations of Children or Adults Who Lack Some or All Reading Comprehension Skills? Do These Individuals Experience Problems When They Learn to Read or after They Have Learned to Read?

Researchers who have investigated individual differences in reading comprehension have attempted to answer questions such as: (1) Why do certain children in a particular grade obtain higher scores on standardized comprehension tests than other children in the same grade? and (2) Do skilled and struggling comprehenders in the same grade differ in terms of working memory and their schemata for narratives, schemata for expository texts, and reading strategies? The goal of this section is to try to provide answers to these questions.

　　If the theory presented near the beginning of this chapter is correct (i.e., that adult readers have reading strategies as well as schemata for topics and various types of texts), then it would be expected that (1) struggling comprehenders would have less working-memory capacity than skilled comprehenders, (2) struggling comprehenders would have less knowledge of the structure of stories and prose passages than same-aged "skilled" comprehenders, and (3) "struggling" comprehenders would also be less likely to have or use reading strategies than same-age "skilled" comprehenders.

　　For the most part, the research confirms these expectations. For example, in terms of story schemata, Montague, Maddux, and Dereshiwksy (1990) found that when given narratives to recall, mid- to high-achieving students from three grades recalled more total ideas and more internal responses of characters than same-aged students with learning disabilities (LD). In terms of expository texts, Meyer et al. (1980), Taylor (1980), and McGee (1982), all found that skilled comprehenders not only recalled more ideas than struggling comprehenders, the former were also more likely to organize their recalls in terms of top-level (i.e., superordinate) ideas. Finally, there are a wealth of studies which show how struggling comprehenders are less likely to have knowledge of and use reading strategies than skilled comprehenders (Paris et al., 1991).

More support for the claim that struggling comprehenders are deficient in their structural and strategic knowledge comes from a variety of instructional studies. In the case of narratives, Dimino, Gersten, Carnine, and Blake (1990) found that the comprehension level of ninth-grade, struggling comprehenders could be improved by teaching them how to identify the main components of a story. Gurney, Gersten, Dimino, and Carnine (1990) had similar success with students with LD in high school. In the case of expository texts, Geva (1983) and Slater, Graves, and Piche (1985) found that teaching students with low abilities how to identify certain text structures improved their comprehension. In the case of reading strategies, it has been shown that struggling readers can be successfully taught how to: (1) make inferences (Hansen & Pearson, 1983), (2) identify the main idea (Schunk & Rice, 1989), (3) summarize (Palincsar & Brown, 1984), (4) predict (Fielding et al., 1990), (5) monitor (Miller, Giovenco, & Rentiers, 1987), and (6) backtrack (Garner et al., 1984).

One particularly powerful approach to teaching strategies is the approach called reciprocal teaching (Rosenshine & Meister, 1994). In the latter approach, a teacher subdivides his or her class into small reading groups that are matched for ability. The teacher and students all read the same materials and take turns "playing the teacher." The actual teacher begins by reading a passage and modeling the to-be-learned strategy (e.g., summarizing). Then, a student takes a turn playing the teacher by reading a new passage and attempting to model the strategy. At first, students are not terribly good at modeling the strategy, so the teacher provides corrections and clarifications. Over time, however, as the group cycles through attempting the strategy, most students internalize the strategy and eventually perform it well. As they gain proficiency, the teacher "fades" by providing less and less prompts and corrections.

Finally, it is important to note that while it is true that skilled and struggling readers differ in terms of schemata and strategies, it is best to think of these differences as a *consequence* of earlier reading problems rather than as the primary cause of their later reading problems. As discussed in Chapter 7, the primary variables which distinguish between skilled and struggling readers in the elementary grades are the abilities to (1) recognize words automatically, (2) recognize words quickly, and (3) interrelate graphic representations together with phonemic representations (Stanovich, 1986). Whereas skilled readers gain mastery over these abilities by the end of the third grade, struggling readers do not. As a result, only the former are given multiple opportunities by their teachers to read longer segments of text, and only the former have the experiences necessary to acquire higher-level schemata and strategies. Hence, we see the Matthew effect in operation again.

9

The Development
of Writing Skills

Vignette: The following paragraph was written by Sam, an eighth grader, for his English class, where they use the *Writer's Workshop* approach. This approach includes a conferencing component in which the teacher asks student-authors questions about their writing to help them reflect on the process:

> I love skateboarding. It makes me feel free. I like the way I can jump off the board into the air. I like the way that I can see the board flip up and land back on the wheels, and I use my skateboard like other kids use bikes, to get from place to place and skate up and down the street in town, skating on the sidewalks and using the curbs to do grinds. I skate down the street and pop my board when I do an ollie.

TEACHER: Sam, can you tell me how you came up with this idea for this story?

SAM: Well, it's one thing that I know about and do well.

TEACHER: Can you tell me how you decided to get started?

SAM: Well, I just sat down and started to write about what I knew about skateboarding.

TEACHER: I see from reading your paragraph that you have a lot of ideas, and they are good. However, there doesn't appear to be any specific order to your ideas. You are being asked to write a five-paragraph essay; have you thought about what the next paragraphs will contain? This can be great essay, but we will need to work on it. What do you want the reader to know?

SAM: I want them to know lots of things. That I like skateboarding, that I know a lot about it, and that I am good at it.

TEACHER: Great, just for a start could each of those ideas be a paragraph?

MAIN IDEAS OF THE CHAPTER

1. The degree of writing competence manifested by a student depends on certain environmental factors (e.g., using a computer vs. pen and paper) and on certain aspects of the student such as (a) the student's motivation, (b) forms of knowledge held in long-term memory (e.g., knowledge of genres and audiences), (c) writing-specific cognitive processes (e.g., text production), and (d) components of working memory.

2. Even though writing skills rival reading skills in their importance to being successful in school and in life, recent national studies show that less than one third of students in the 4th, 8th, and 12th grades score in the proficient level for writing. Thus, teachers should have a stake in improving the writing performance of their students.

3. Most students, even in the high school levels, have difficulty writing stories, expository reports, and argumentative essays. When development occurs, it is usually in the form of the increased use of key elements of a particular genre, greater cohesion, and provision of details. Older children show better writing skills than younger children because older children have greater knowledge of topics, genres, audiences, and language than younger children. However, the major change that seems to occur is children's ability to consciously reflect on and manipulate this knowledge. In particular, children are often found to know more than they demonstrate in writing. In particular, children generate less content than they know, comprehend texts of a particular type (e.g., stories) earlier than they can write texts of that type, and produce or recognize well-formed syntactic constructions before they can write such constructions themselves. Writing also improves with age because older writers are more likely to plan, set goals, and revise than younger writers.

4. In terms of developmental mechanisms, these age changes are probably due to (a) increases in working-memory capacity that may have a neurological basis, (b) writing frequency and practice, (c) extensive reading, and (d) instructional techniques that specifically teach children effective writing strategies.

5. Comparisons of same-aged skilled and struggling writers reveal that better writers (a) can manipulate verbal information better than struggling writers, (b) write and spell more quickly than struggling writers, (c) are better readers than struggling writers, (d) are more likely to use effective memory-search techniques than struggling writers, (e) have a larger repertoire of linguistic constructions at their disposal than struggling writers, (f) spend more time organizing their thoughts, planning, and goal setting than struggling writers, (g) engage in more substantial, nonsuperficial forms of revision than struggling writers, and (h) are more able to consciously reflect on their goals, knowledge, and writing processes than struggling writers. Similar differences appear when students with learning disabilities are compared to their nondisabled peers.

This chapter on writing is the third in the series of chapters on literacy skills. To truly understand the nature of literacy, all three chapters should be considered collectively. There are many connections across the chapters that should be identified (e.g., writers rely on the same schemata to write their own works and comprehend the works of others). To help foster this integration, you will be presented with a group activity at the end of this chapter that asks the participants to identify common constructs and themes across the three chapters. Performing this task will be facilitated if you try to identify connections to other chapters as you read this chapter. The material will be presented via the five questions.

THE "NATURE OF" QUESTION: What Does It Mean to Say That Someone Has Writing Competence?

The goal of this section is to provide a reasonably complete answer to the following question: "What are the component processes involved in writing?" The best way to answer this question is to examine influential models of writing (e.g., Hayes, 1996; Hayes & Flower, 1986; Scardamalia & Bereiter, 1986) and distill major components from these models. At a global level, these models suggest that there are two kinds of variables that affect the writing process: those that pertain to characteristics of *writing environments* and those that pertain to characteristics of *individual writers* (Hayes, 1996). In what follows, these two types of variables are discussed in turn. Then, we briefly consider some of the neural correlates of writing.

Characteristics of the Writing Environment

When people write, they write in particular contexts or situations. For example, whereas some do their writing on a computer in a secluded cabin in Vermont, others do their writing in the midst of a classroom full of peers using a pencil and paper. Similarly, whereas some are attempting to write to a large, popular audience (e.g., a novelist), others may be writing to a single person (e.g., a teacher, a peer, or a pen pal). As a writer moves from one context to another, it is typically the case that the audience, medium (i.e., computer vs. paper), and individuals who are present in that context change, as well. Such contextual variations are thought to affect the writing process in important ways (Hayes, 1996). With respect to the shift from paper to computer, for example, a meta-analysis of 32 studies showed that word-processing packages help all writers (especially weaker writers) to produce higher-quality pieces (Bangert-Downs, 1993). Other significant contextual variations include the text that has already been produced and the availability of collaborators. Obviously, the task of adding the last line to a five-line paragraph is different than the task of adding the very first line to a blank page. Moreover, studies show that writers continually reread what they have already written in order to set the stage for the next portion of text (Graham, 2006; Hayes, 1996). As such, a change in the initial portion would lead to a change in the portion added on. In addition, having a collaborator changes the writing process significantly, as well. For example, children write very differently when they collaborate with a teacher than when they collaborate with a peer (Daiute, 2002), and peers can be helpful resources in the revision process (Atwell, 1987; Graham, 2006).

Characteristics of an Individual Writer

Psychological theories typically explain changes in behavior by appealing to changes in some mental entity. For example, if a person performed Behavior X at one time (e.g., study really hard) but now performs Behavior Y (e.g., not study at all), psychologists usually appeal to changes in mental entities such as concepts, values, and beliefs to explain this behavior change (e.g., he or she no longer believes that studying is effective). Relatedly, psychologists often explain differences in behavior across two individuals (e.g., one studies but the other does not) by appealing to the same sorts of mental entities. To explain variations in the outputs of the writing process (e.g., a well-written essay vs. a poorly written essay), psychologists have appealed to four clusters of person-related variables: (1) motivation factors, (2) forms of knowledge held in long-term memory, (3) writing-specific cognitive processes, and (4) components of working memory (Graham, 2006; Hayes, 1996). Let's examine each of these four kinds of variables in turn.

Motivational Aspects of Writing

People engage in writing for particular reasons. Whereas some write for pleasure, others write because they have been given an assignment by a teacher or an employer. Regardless of whether people write because they want to or have to, it is clear that writing is very *goal-directed* (Hayes, 1996). This analysis suggests that a change in goals would lead to a change in writing output. Notice how a goal such as "I want to write a summary of current research on learning" would lead to a different paper than a goal such as "I want to critically evaluate current theories of learning."

More generally, however, one of the primary aims of education is to produce students who habitually engage in literate activities such as reading and writing (Anderson et al., 1988). Hence, it has been of interest to determine the factors that cause students to regularly engage in writing on their own (Hayes, 1996). Inasmuch as most prolific writers find the writing process intrinsically satisfying, they engage in it as often as possible. Whereas it is relatively easy to get students to write by giving them an assignment, it is quite another to get them to write frequently on their own (or select an occupation because it requires regular writing). In order for students to make the latter kinds of choices, they need to hold positive attitudes toward the writing process and themselves as writers. Moreover, they need to believe that writing affords more benefits than costs. Whereas the tendency to write a particular assignment relates to specific goals, the tendency to write frequently might be called a predisposition to write (Hayes, 1996). However, it is important to note that writing is a difficult task even for the most accomplished writers (Graham, 2006). Interest in writing and the topic of an assignment certainly helps and has been found to predict writing quality (Hidi & Boscolo, 2006), but the difficulty of writing implies that other characteristics of motivation such as self-efficacy and values would matter as much if not more (Graham, 2006; Hidi & Boscolo, 2006). In other words, in order to succeed, writers have to believe that they have the skills and persistence needed to accomplish their goals.

Knowledge Structures in Long-Term Memory

Of course, a well-written document would not be produced if a person merely had the motivation to write. Such a person also needs certain kinds of writing knowledge and skill. Writing researchers have argued that there are five main types of knowledge that successful writers store in their long term memories: (1) knowledge of task schemas, (2) knowledge of topics, (3) knowledge of audiences, (4) knowledge of genres, and (5) knowledge of language (Glover, Ronning, & Bruning, 1990; Graham, 2006; Hayes, 1996; Scardamalia & Bereiter, 1986). Contemporary theories suggest that an alteration in one of these kinds of knowledge (e.g., an absence of topic knowledge in one person vs. its presence in another) would lead to outputs that differ in their quality (e.g., one writes a good essay but the other does not).

Task schemata are mental representations of writing tasks that a person regularly encounters. They include global parameters regarding deadlines and length, as well as stored strategies that were successful in the past (e.g., clarifying things with an instructor first, starting at least 3 weeks early, focusing on familiar topics). As noted in Chapter 8, schemata help people accomplish tasks efficiently. Writers who lack schemata need to reinvent the wheel each time they are given a particular task.

As for knowledge of topics, you may have noticed that it is much easier to write a paper when you know a lot about the topic than when you know very little about it. The same is true for even the most skilled writers. Knowledge helps you generate ideas and organize them effectively. To see this, imagine that you were given the assignment of writing an essay on the nature of writing. It should be clear that you would have an easier time writing such a paper after you read this section than before you read it (unless you were already familiar with the literature on writing!). As another example, imagine that you were writing an essay regarding an unfair grade for a friend. If you did not take the class with the friend and experience things the way he or she did, it would be harder to write the essay than if the unfair grade were given to you. Good writers understand the importance of topic knowledge, so they usually do a great deal of research before they attempt to write about an unfamiliar topic. James Michener, for example, usually researched a topic for about 3 years before he wrote one of his tomes.

However, whereas topic knowledge is necessary for writing a good piece, it is not sufficient. Writers also have to be able to "get inside their reader's minds" in order to be successful. That is, they need to be able to answer questions such as "What do my readers already know?" "What do they want to hear?" and "How would they probably react to my statements?" In the extreme, writers who do not understand what their readers know and believe could produce a variety of unwanted responses in their readers. For example, poor writing could make readers of this work feel: (1) confused (if the level is too high), (2) belittled or bored (if the level is too low), or (3) angry (if the author's stance runs contrary to their beliefs). In most cases, readers want to learn something new or form a "connection" with something they read. Readers will not learn anything new if the material is either too familiar or too unfamiliar, and they may not have their beliefs confirmed by someone who challenges their opinions. Moreover, readers will gain very little from a piece if they are unable to draw inferences that connect sentences and paragraphs together into a coherent whole (see Chapter 8). When writers egocentrically assume that their readers know what they know, they do not provide enough clues in the text to support required inferences. Thus, *knowing your audience* is a key to being a skilled writer. Note that the element of the task environment related to audience (see above) pertains to who the audience is. Here, the issue concerns a writer's knowledge of that audience.

To appreciate the utility of the next kind of knowledge, consider the following question: If someone asked you to write an argumentative essay, a textbook, a story, and a poem, would you know how to write something in each of these *genres*? As we have seen in Chapter 8, genres have their own distinctive structures that skilled readers come to know. For example, we saw that stories have a narrative structure involving components such as settings, characters, and outcomes. Given the fact that there are "standard" ways of organizing ideas in specific genres, and that readers come to expect this standard format when they read a work in that genre, writers need to stick close to this standard format in order to maximize the chance that their readers will like and comprehend what they have read. Of course, the task of writing something in a particular genre is made easier when a writer has a *schema* for that type of work.

Finally, although having knowledge of topics, audiences, and genres is important to writing well, an absolutely indispensable component of good writing is knowledge of your audience's native language. Writers need to know how to place specific words in specific grammatical constructions in order to convey just the right meaning. That is, writers need to have (1) a good vocabulary, (2) knowledge of grammatical rules, and (3) knowledge of the *pragmatics* of a language (e.g., knowing how to be polite, sarcastic).

To see how important *knowledge of language* is, consider the following example: Imagine that a French psychologist who is editing a book on cognitive theories asks a U.S. expert on Piaget's theory to contribute a chapter about Piaget to this volume. The U.S. expert is told that the readers of this book will be non-English-speaking French undergraduates. Even if the expert knew a lot about Piaget's theory (i.e., had topic knowledge), had been asked to write chapters many times before (i.e., had a task schema), knew a lot about how French undergraduates think (i.e., had knowledge of the audience), and also had a schema for expository chapters (i.e., had knowledge of that genre), it should be obvious that he or she would be unable to write a good chapter if he or she were not sufficiently fluent in French.

Writing-Related Cognitive Processes

In his reformulation of the seminal Hayes and Flower (1980) model, Hayes (1996) suggests that there are three important cognitive processes that help writers translate their knowledge and motivation into action: text interpretation, reflection, and text production. *Text interpretation* refers to a set of processes that are used by a writer to create mental representations of linguistic and graphic inputs. These processes include reading, listening, and scanning graphic images. *Reflection* refers to a set of processes that function to transform one internal representation into another. Examples include problem solving, decision making, and inference making. These three processes were included as replacements for the planning component in the original Hayes and Flower 1980 model. *Text production* refers to a set of processes that are used when a writer translates internal representations into written, spoken, or graphic outputs.

This revised model places reading skills at the center of effective writing. However, Hayes (1996) makes a distinction between reading to comprehend and reading to evaluate. As noted in Chapters 7 and 8, readers engage in the following sorts of processes when they read to comprehend: decode words, apply grammatical knowledge, apply semantic and schematized knowledge, draw inferences about instantiations and the author's intentions, and construct a summary. The output of such processes is a representation of text meaning. When people read to evaluate, however, they read with an eye toward problems inherent in the current draft of a document that they have written or someone else has written. Instead of simply decoding words, for example, they also look for spelling errors. Similarly, instead of simply applying grammatical knowledge to form a mental representation of "who did what to whom," they also look for grammatical faults. Components such as semantic knowledge, inference making, schemata, and consideration of audience needs help writers look for unwarranted inferences, schematic violations, incoherence, and inappropriate tone or complexity.

Thus, to revise a document, writers have to engage in (1) critical reading of what they have written, (2) problem solving and decision making (i.e., identification of a problem, consideration of alternative ways to fix it), and (3) text production (i.e., translating these intentions into revised text). These three processes are best coordinated if a writer has a schema for the task of revision. This schema might include a search for common kinds of problems, strategies for locating problems (e.g., not looking at a draft for a few days before returning to it), and so on. In addition, carrying out the three core processes of writing requires the capacity resources afforded by working-memory and knowledge resources contained in long-term memory.

Using this overall framework, a researcher could explain differences between more experienced and less experienced writers. For example, one study showed that college freshmen tend to focus their revisions at or below the sentence level (e.g., fix spelling or substitute a single word). More experienced writers, in contrast, tended to focus on both local and global problems (Hayes, Flower, Schriver, Stratman, & Carey, 1987). Why might this be the case? One place to look might be a difference in the ability or inclination to detect problems in texts. Conceivably, skilled writers could be better readers than struggling writers. Another place might be working-memory differences. A third might be a lack of revision schemata in inexperienced writers. A fourth might be lack of knowledge of good solutions to writing problems that are identified (e.g., "I know it reads sort of choppy but I don't know how to fix it"). A fifth might be differences at the level of production. Skilled and struggling writers might be similar in their ability to read critically and detect problems, but different in their ability to translate their plans into effective text. Studies have shown, for example, that skilled writers produce segments of sentences that are 53% longer than those of struggling writers (Hayes, 1996).

Thus, the model is useful to locating numerous possible differences between skilled and struggling writers. Are any of these differences particularly crucial? Hayes (1996) suggests that reading skills are important for reasons other than the fact that they help a writer identify problems in a draft. For example, reading skills help writers gain accurate topic knowledge as they do research. In addition, readers often formulate a representation of the author of some work (including such things as the author's personality traits and political orientation). Collectively, these representations help a skilled writer create and revise documents in ways that are different from the methods used by struggling readers and writers.

Components of Working Memory

Kellogg (1996) proposed a model that is similar to that of Hayes (1996) but emphasizes the significance of working memory to a greater extent. In Kellogg's model, the text production process consists of three subcomponents: formulation, execution, and monitoring. When in the *formulation phase*, a writer plans what he or she is going to say and then translates this plan into an intention to write down a specific segment of text. When in the *execution phase*, the motoric and related responses needed to carry out this intention are put into play. Note that this process is relatively straightforward for someone who has been writing longhand or typing for years. For the beginning or struggling writer, however, effortful execution could disrupt the flow of ideas from mind to paper. In other words, a slow writer or typist could forget the exact phrasing that emerged during the formulation phase. During the *monitoring phase*, the writer reads and edits the text that has been produced. Working memory could affect such processes, as well.

Neuroscientific Basis of Writing

To round out the discussion of writing processes, it is useful to consider the implications of brain research in this area. For over 100 years, clinicians have observed curious deficits in the writing skills of adults with brain injuries. Analysis of numerous case studies suggests that handwriting is a complex cognitive and motoric process that consists of a number of component operations (Rapcsak, 1997). When an individual attempts to write a word, for example, he or she first retrieves an abstract representation of letter forms from memory. Next, this information is fed to a motor-response program that attempts to carry out the movements necessary to write the word in a particular manner. Success requires that the words are of the right case (lower vs. upper), script (block letters vs. cursive), size (all of similar size) and spacing (not too far apart or on top of one another). Studies show that lesions in the left parietal-occipital area (put your finger just behind and above your left ear) cause problems in retrieving the abstract letter forms. Lesions more in the parietal area proper and motor centers of the frontal lobe cause problems in the motor-output functions. Motor problems have also been caused by lesions in the same subcortical structure affected in Parkinson's disease (the basal ganglia) and in the cerebellum. Of course, the motor- and word-knowledge systems are part of the larger system of writing described earlier (involving goals, knowledge, and so on). Thus, writing involves multiple areas of the brain that work in concert to produce skilled performance. Given the complexity of this system, " . . . it is perhaps not altogether surprising that writing takes a long time to master and that it remains a fragile skill highly susceptible to disruption by brain damage" (Rapcsak, 1997, p. 166).

THE RELEVANCE QUESTION: Why Should Teachers Care about Whether Children Acquire Writing Skills?

The need to understand the nature and development of writing has never been so pressing given that the most recent reports of the National Assessment of Educational Progress (NAEP) for writing in 2002 showed that only 28% of 4th graders, 31% of 8th graders, and 24% of 12th graders performed at or above the proficient levels (Troia, 2006). These findings are troubling because writing skills rival reading skills in their connection to academic success and success in the work world.

THE DEVELOPMENTAL TRENDS QUESTION: How Do Writing Skills Change over Time?

The developmental research on writing skills is organized as follows. First, we will examine the early emergence of writing during the preschool period. Then, we will consider developmental studies that used the original model of Hayes and Flower (1980) as their guide. For simplicity, the latter studies are grouped according to whether they examined the knowledge needed for writing or the writing processes.

Early Writing Skills

Consistent with the literature on emergent literacy (see Chapter 7), a number of studies have shown that children develop conceptions of the writing process well before they are exposed to formal writing instruction in kindergarten and first grade (Brenneman, Massey, Machado, & Gelman, 1996; Gombert & Fayol, 1992; Share & Levin, 1999). To assess what preschoolers know, researchers sometimes dictate words to children and ask them to write these words down. Other times, researchers may present a picture and ask children to write the word for it. Studies have shown that children progress through a series of approximations to writing between the ages of 3 and 5. For example, they may begin with scribbles but then progress to wavy lines and pseudoletters.

After reviewing studies of this sort that were conducted in various countries, Gombert and Fayol (1992) proposed that children progress through three phases in their early writing attempts. In Phase 1 (approximately age 3), children produce nonfigural graphics such as scribbling and wavy lines. These markings usually obey principles of writing such as unidirectionality and also sometimes have features characteristic of mature writing such as linearity, vertically short traces, and discrete units. Notably, children do not confuse writing with drawing even at this beginning level.

During Phase 2 (between ages 3 and 4), children's writing may consist of strings of circles or pseudoletters. The distinct characteristic of this phase is the very clear existence of discrete units. These units, however, are used to correspond to verbal dictations in nonphonemic ways. For example, children tend to write longer sequences for words for large things (e.g., an elephant) than for small things (e.g., a mouse). Relatedly, they may write these units using the same color as the object (e.g., a red marker for *apple*; a yellow marker for *lemon*). Near the end of this phase, however, children may start matching sequence strings to phonemic information (e.g., longer sequences for multisyllable words).

During Phase 3 (between ages 4 and 5), children start to produce writing samples that contain actual letters that they know. In most cases, these letters come from children's own first name, but slowly new letters are added. Unlike earlier phases, children no longer attempt to match sequences to dictations in either semantic or phonological ways. The absence of such matching may reflect their having to allocate considerable attention to the task of writing unfamiliar letters (Gombert & Fayol, 1992). With continued practice, however, these matchings reappear, but only in terms of phonological features. For example, they may write KGN for kindergarten. Interestingly, however, many of the oldest children begin refusing to participate, arguing that they do not know how to spell particular words. This three-phase account is consistent with the findings of Levin and Bus (2003) who found that the drawings and writings of preschoolers become increasingly differentiated with age (i.e., writing looks more like writing; drawing looks more like drawing).

Soon thereafter, children enter kindergarten and receive instruction on writing all letters of their native alphabet or idiographies. In first grade and beyond, many children also receive instruction in spelling and in the alphabetic principle (see Chapters 7 and 8). Of course, good writing involves more than spelling. As noted earlier, writers set goals, rely on schemata, revise, and so on to draft stories, informative passages, and argumentative essays. In the next two sections, we consider children's abilities in these areas during elementary and secondary school.

Further Developments I: Structural Aspects of Writing

In line with the distinction between structural and functional aspects of reading comprehension that were discussed in Chapter 8, it is helpful to consider the development of structural and functional aspects of writing, as well. The structural aspects pertain to developmental changes in working-memory capacity and knowledge resources. The functional aspects involve changes in writing processes.

It has already been noted that there are monotonic increases in the capacity of working memory from early childhood to young adulthood (Swanson, 1999). Such increases provide a processing space within which effortful tasks such as planning and critical reading can take place (McCutchen, 2006). In addition, fluency at the level of text generation helps writers overcome the limits of working memory. As for knowledge-related structural aspects, large- and small-scale studies have found that children become better writers with age (e.g., Applebee, Langer, Mullis, & Jenkins, 1990; Greenwald, Persky, Campbell, & Mazzeo, 1999; Scardamalia & Bereiter, 1986). One reason why older students write better than younger students is that they have more of the knowledge needed for writing. As we have seen, writers can have knowledge of such things as topics, genres, audiences, and language. Let's now examine the developmental literature to see whether there are age differences in these forms of knowledge.

Topic Knowledge

When asked to write a paper on some topic, younger children tend to generate fewer ideas than older children and adults (Scardamalia & Bereiter, 1986). This age difference in the amount of ideas generated derives, in part, from the fact that younger children usually have less topic knowledge than older children and adults. Sometimes age differences are even found within samples of students who are labeled "experts" on some topic. For example, in her study of the effects of knowledge on writing, McCutchen (1986) found that even in a group of children labeled "high-knowledge," her high-knowledge eighth graders still had more pertinent knowledge than her high-knowledge fourth or sixth graders. Thus, it is usually safe to assume that for any given topic, older children will know more than younger children. As a result, the latter will have a greater resource of ideas to tap into.

However, studies have also shown that children seem to generate fewer ideas than their knowledge would warrant. In particular, researchers have found that simply prompting children to think of additional ideas causes them to generate many more things to say (Graham & Harris, 1996; Scardamalia, Bereiter, & Goelman, 1982). Why do children generate fewer ideas than they are capable of? The first reason seems to be that whereas younger students use a somewhat random method of *associative thinking* to generate ideas, older students use a *heuristic search* to guide their generation of ideas (Hayes & Flower, 1986; Scardamalia & Bereiter, 1986).

The difference between associative thinking and heuristic searches can best be described by way of an analogy. Imagine that your knowledge is stored in the form of a mental "filing cabinet" and that each piece of your knowledge (e.g., the fact that dogs bark) is a "folder" in the cabinet. Imagine next that if two ideas are highly associated, their folders are connected by way of a fairly strong string. If you pull out one idea (i.e., folder 1), it pulls out the other idea (i.e., folder 2). Ideas that are weakly associated are connected by weak strings. In an associative memory search, you go to some "main" folder for a topic and pull it out. As you do, you find that you pull out all of those ideas that are connected by strong strings, one-by-one, until there are no more folders attached by strings or until some of the weak strings break (leaving their folders behind). For example, if children are asked to write an expository essay about dinosaurs, the term *dinosaurs* may be associatively linked to people they know who love dinosaurs (e.g., a brother) and to cavemen. Their essays will contain just these associated ideas.

In a heuristic search, in contrast, you first think about *categories* of information and then go to sections of the "cabinet" to pull out an entire set of "folders" for all of the ideas related to specific categories. For example, if you are writing an essay about the status of U.S. education and you are trying to think of things to say, you might locate a section of your mental "cabinet" which groups together "folders" on the problems with the education system. Or, you might think of your ideas as indexed in some way (e.g., metaphorical red dots on folders for things you are good at) and your heuristic search uses this indexing to find specific folders (e.g., "Let's see, let me think of all of the things I'm good at"). Thus, a heuristic memory search is neither random nor purely associative; rather, it is logical and *goal-directed*. Of course, heuristic searches can also be supplemented by associative thinking, and such associations help add additional things to say (Scardamalia & Bereiter, 1986).

The second reason why younger students generate fewer ideas than they are capable of is that they tend to retrieve only those ideas at the highest levels of hierarchically arranged knowledge (McCutchen & Perfetti, 1982; Scardamalia & Bereiter, 1986). When writing about "animals," for example, younger writers might generate ideas immediately connected to the top-level node "animal" and fail to retrieve ideas below that level (e.g., information associated with different types of animals such as dogs and cats). Prompting seems to move them farther down a hierarchy to retrieve more detailed information (e.g., asking "What can you tell me about different types of animals such as dogs or cats?").

Knowledge of Genres

In Chapter 8, we learned that extensive reading seems to cause children to acquire schemata for various types of texts (e.g., stories and expository texts). If children do acquire such schemata over time, it would be expected that when they are asked to write something in a particular genre, older children would be more likely than younger children to write something that conforms to the "ideal" structure for that genre.

The literature on story writing, however, suggests there is a developmental lag between being able to recognize a good story and being able to write one. In particular, even though 5- and 6-year-olds seem to have good knowledge of the canonical structure of stories (Stein, 1982), studies show that much older students (e.g., fourth, fifth, & eighth graders) sometimes have trouble composing stories that conform to this canonical structure. For example, in the 1990 NAEP report for writing, 65% of fourth graders were found to have an understanding of the basics of storytelling, but only 15% were able to write well-developed stories that had both a setting and at least one episode (Applebee et al., 1990). In the 1998 assessment of over 17,000 students, a similar finding emerged (Greenwald et al., 1999). Here, only 38% gave a "sufficient" response to story prompts in which they produced a clear but underdeveloped story with few details. Only 20% attained the "skillful" or "excellent" ratings for well-developed, detailed, and coherent stories. It is important to note, however, that students were only given 25 min to compose each of their stories.

In a study in which children were given several class periods to compose and potentially revise their stories, Freedman (1987) found that there was development between the 5th and 12th grades in the degree of realization of the "ideal form" of a story. In the 5th and 8th grades, only 34% and 45% of children, respectively, wrote stories about true personal experiences that included some setting information and at least one complete episode. When asked to invent a story, however, these percentages rose to 55% and 70%, respectively. Finally, Langer (1986) found that whereas there were few differences between the stories of 8- and 14-year-olds in terms of structure, the stories of the 14-year-olds were more elaborated than those of the 8-year-olds. Comparing the NAEP studies with the Freedman and Langer studies, then, we see that the size of the age difference can be large or small, depending on the nature of the writing task. But even in the best of circumstances, there still seems to be a lag of 3 to 4 years between using schemata to comprehend stories and using them to write stories. Further support for the idea that children need to gain independent, explicit control over their genre knowledge comes from the finding that the quality of writing improves when teachers provide scaffolds for children (Donovan & Smolkin, 2006) such as an outline with question prompts.

With respect to expository writing, we would expect an even larger developmental lag because of the findings for reading comprehension that show that children seem to comprehend stories better than they comprehend expository texts (see Chapter 8). Several studies support this expectation of relatively poorer performance for expository writing. For example, Langer (1986) found a more marked difference between 8- and 14-year-olds for expository writing than for story writing. At both grades, however, performance on the expository task was generally unimpressive. Similarly, in a highly structured task in which students were asked to complete a paragraph that already contained key elements (e.g., topic sentences and signals), Englert, Stewart, and Hiebert (1988) found that whereas sixth graders performed significantly better than third graders in the generation of textually consistent details (40% vs. 37%, respectively) and main ideas (35% vs. 22%, respectively), students at both grade levels tended to perform poorly on both of these expository writing tasks.

In summarizing the 1990 NAEP results for expository writing, Applebee et al. (1990) reported that

> about two-thirds of the eleventh graders were able to write from personal experience and supply adequate information for a job application, but only slightly more than half were able to write an adequate newspaper report from given information. . . . For fourth and eighth graders . . . , the simpler and clearer the information provided, the more successful students were in summarizing and presenting it. More complex material required more complex writing strategies, which the majority of students seemed to lack. (p. 25)

Again, the results for the 1998 assessment were similar (Greenwald et al., 1999). Only 38% gave "sufficient" responses to informational writing prompts (e.g., designing a television show). Children in this category used simple sentences that conveyed information in a clear, sequential but sparsely developed manner. Only 11% received ratings of "skillful" or "excellent."

Across all grades, studies show that children are most successful when they write expository texts in the simple description format (i.e., taking information and summarizing it). They have much more difficulty writing essays in the compare–contrast format or other formats that require them to *analyze* information rather than simply *report* it (Applebee et al., 1990; Englert et al., 1988). Moreover, their passages need work with respect to organization, development, transitions, and grammatical complexity (Greenwald et al., 1999).

Although most developmental researchers have focused on narrative and expository writing, a few have also examined argumentative writing. Argumentative writing is a form of writing in which an author adopts the goal of convincing his or her readers that a particular point of view is a good one (Applebee et al., 1990; Greenwald et al., 1999). For example, a student engages in argumentative writing when he or she writes an essay about deserving an "A." In judging the quality of an argumentative essay, researchers look for the presence of the key elements of a well-structured argument such as claims, data, warrants, recognition of an opposing point of view, and rebuttals (e.g., Knudson, 1992; McCann, 1989). Most developmental studies have shown that children write better argumentative essays with age.

For example, McCann (1989) asked 6th, 9th, and 12th graders to write argumentative essays and found that the essays of the 9th and 12th graders not only had more overall quality than those of the 6th graders, they also contained significantly more claims and warrants. No significant grade differences emerged for the use of data to support a claim, however. In a similar study, Knudson (1992) found that 4th and 6th graders used significantly fewer claims, data, and warrants than 10th and 12th graders. Thus, both studies showed that children are more likely with age to include the elements of good arguments.

However, the increased use of such elements does not imply that older students always produce high-quality arguments. In particular, the 1990 NAEP report for writing showed that only about 20% of students in each of the 4th, 8th, and 11th grades wrote argumentative essays that were judged to be at the "adequate" level or better (Applebee et al., 1990). On the 1998 assessment, these figures (for the "skillful" or "excellent" levels) were 12% (4th grade), 14% (8th grade), and 22% (12th grade). These figures should not imply, however, that little development occurred. The raters used more stringent criteria for assigning the highest two levels for the 8th and 12th graders and also gave different writing prompts. But overall, most children demonstrated only a basic kinds of proficiency in argumentative writing.

In sum, then, most students, even in the high school levels, have difficulty writing stories, expository reports, and argumentative essays. When development occurs, it is usually in the form of an increased use of key elements of a particular genre, greater cohesion, and additional details. In the case of stories, older students are more likely than younger students to include both a setting and a major episode in their stories. In the case of expository reports, older students are more likely to use superordinate structures (e.g., main ideas and supportive details) than younger students.

In the case of argumentative essays, older students are more likely to use claims, data, and warrants than younger students. Although even elementary students have been found to use some structure in their writing, older students use more structure and tend to elaborate that structure more extensively. In addition, the quality of argumentative essays of college students can be significantly enhanced by simply giving them goals to include counterarguments and rebuttals (Nussbaum & Kardash, 2005).

Knowledge of Audiences

A major difference between writing and having a conversation is that when you have a conversation, you have an actual person to whom you speak. This individual reacts to your statements with facial expressions and also helps keep the conversation going by saying things back to you. When you write, however, you have no one to play these roles for you. As a result, you need to create your own imaginary audience and hypothesize about how these people would probably respond to your statements. Moreover, you need to be able to think about what you have written objectively to see whether someone else might have trouble understanding what you are trying to say. Writing, then, poses greater cognitive demands than having a conversation. If so, then young children may be less-effective writers than older children because the former have a harder time creating and writing to an imaginary audience than the latter (Bereiter & Scardamalia, 1982; Knudson, 1992).

In one of the few studies which investigated possible developmental differences in children's knowledge of how audiences affect what is written, Langer (1986) found that both 8- and 14-year-olds realized that a text would have to be modified if an audience were to change. However, whereas the younger children said that a shift in audience would mean that there would be different requirements regarding neatness and length, the older children argued that the changes would be reflected in terms of language and form. Obviously, more studies are needed to reveal the existence of other age differences in knowledge of audiences.

Knowledge of Language

Perfetti and McCutchen (1987, p. 130) define writing competence as "productive control over the grammatical devices of language in the service of some communicative intent." This definition nicely captures the central role played by a writer's knowledge of language. In order to have productive control over one's language and convey exactly what one wants to convey, a writer needs to have a good vocabulary and good command of syntax. Is there evidence that older students have larger vocabularies and greater command of syntax than younger students?

In the case of vocabulary, school children add about 3,000 new words to their vocabularies each year (Adams, 1990). Thus, the notion of "choosing just the right word" is more applicable to older children than younger children since only the former are likely to have the range of words necessary to engage in such a selection process.

In the case of syntax, Loban (1976) and Hunt (1970) found that there is development in syntactic maturity throughout the school years. By "syntactic maturity," we mean that older children are more likely than younger children to group separate clauses together into single, more complex constructions. For example, instead of writing the three separate sentences in sentence 1 below, older students are more likely to write the single construction in sentence 2:

1. *Philadelphia has a great baseball team. Philadelphia has a great football team. Philadelphia does not have a good basketball team.*
2. *Philadelphia has a great baseball team and a great football team, but it does not have a very good basketball team.*

Moreover, even 9-year-olds seem to know that sentence 2 is more acceptable than sentence 1 when asked which is better. However, these same students could not imitate the constructions such as Sentences 1 or 2 when given parallel content (Scardamalia & Bereiter, 1986). Other researchers have found that high school students could not deliberately replicate the very same grammatical errors that they had made on a prior writing assignment. On the 1998 NAEP study for writing that included grammatical complexity, grammatical variability, and word choice in its rating scale, only 27% of 12th graders attained the highest two ratings overall (Greenwald et al., 1999). Recall that children needed to write well in a short period of time. Thus, one could summarize such studies by saying that syntactic development during the school years seems to be the progressive attainment of *fluency and conscious control over complex grammatical constructions.*

A final aspect of language knowledge that seems to develop with age is the ability to use cohesive devices, which include such things as (1) using pronouns in one sentence to refer back to individuals named in earlier sentences and (2) using the same or related words in several successive sentences. Sentence 3 below illustrates both of these devices. The words that create ties are in bold:

3. *Mary was known as a popular girl. **She** was so **popular**, in fact, that **she** was named class president.*

A variety of studies have shown that older children are more likely to use cohesive devices than younger children. McCutchen (1986), for example, found differences in coherence between younger students (i.e., fourth graders) and older students (i.e., sixth and eighth graders) even when their knowledge of the topic was statistically controlled.

Summary

Across a variety of studies, older children were found to demonstrate greater knowledge of topics, genres, audiences, and language than younger children. The major change that seems to occur is not so much the acquisition of these forms of knowledge as children's ability to consciously reflect on and manipulate this knowledge (Perfetti & McCutchen, 1987; Scardamalia & Bereiter, 1986). In particular, with the exception of knowledge of audiences, children were always found to know more than they demonstrate in writing. In particular, children were found to generate less content than they know, comprehend texts of a particular type (e.g., stories) earlier than they can write texts of that type, and produce or recognize well-formed syntactic constructions before they can write such constructions themselves.

Further Developments II: Functional Aspects (Writing Processes)

The improvements in the structural aspects of writing (i.e., working memory and knowledge) provide the resources that help children carry out the functional aspects of writing more effectively. In the original 1980 model of Hayes and Flower, writers were said to engage in three main processes: planning, translating, and revising. The questions that have captured the interest of developmental researchers include, "Are older children more likely to carry out these processes than younger children?" and "If so, do older children carry out these processes more effectively?" In what follows, we will examine the developmental literature to see what the answers to these questions are. Note that the revised model of Hayes (1996) that emphasizes such things as social relations, motivation, and reading skills has not received much attention from developmentalists to date.

Planning

Most developmental studies of writing show that children give very little evidence of explicit planning (McCutchen, 2006; Scardamalia & Bereiter, 1986). Although young writers may at times "rehearse" what they will eventually write in the form of partial or full sentences, these notes are probably early drafts of eventual lines rather than plans per se.

Instead of forming goals and writing to these goals, children are more likely to engage in what has been called "knowledge telling" (Scardamalia & Bereiter, 1986). Writers who engage in "knowledge telling" write down everything they know about a topic, in the order that ideas come to mind. Knowledge-tellers stop writing when they feel that they have written everything they know.

Because children do not write from goals and plans, they tend to generate ideas by way of associative thinking rather than heuristic searches and often do not organize these ideas in any way. As a result, their stories, essays, and arguments often lack conceptual coherence let alone rhetorical coherence.

Translation

In the earlier section of the development of writing knowledge, we learned that younger children have smaller vocabularies, a smaller repertoire of syntactic structures and cohesive devices, less fluency, and less conscious control over these language forms than older children. As a result, they are less equipped for translating their personal meanings into precisely interpretable texts. That is, they tend to produce "writer-based" texts rather than "reader-based" texts (Perfetti & McCutchen, 1987). Writer-based prose is "full of idiosyncratic phrases that are loaded with semantic content for the writer—meaning that is not, however, articulated for the reader" (Perfetti & McCutchen, 1987, p. 126). In reader-based prose, in contrast, ideas are well-articulated and there is little ambiguity and a great deal of intersentence cohesion. In fact, the meaning is so well specified that most people who read a segment of the text would come away with the same interpretation of it.

Although few studies have shown that increases in vocabulary and syntax skills with age directly contribute to the production of reader-based prose, several studies have shown that older children are more likely to use a variety of intersentence cohesion devices than younger children. Moreover, the tendency to create more cohesive texts seems to increase linearly with age between the third grade and adulthood (Garner et al., 1986; McCutchen, 1986; Wright & Rosenberg, 1993). These findings are reflected in some of the age trends reported in the 1998 NAEP report.

Revising

The literature on developmental trends in revising has revealed four main findings. First, children, adolescents, and inexperienced college students do very little of it (Fitzgerald, 1987; Graham, 2006; Scardamalia & Bereiter, 1986). Second, when students do revise, the vast majority of changes are superficial rather than conceptual or organizational. That is, students are more likely to focus on specific words, spelling, or grammar than on deeper issues such as goals, plans, and overall intended meanings (Fitzgerald, 1987; Graham, 2006; McCutchen, 2006; Scardamalia & Bereiter, 1986). Third, the main reason why children tend not to revise is that they have trouble detecting problems in the first place—especially in their own writings (Bartlett, 1982; McCutchen, 2006). When problems are pointed out to them, children can at times be quite good at making appropriate changes (e.g., Beal, 1990), although some studies have found that the changes do not always improve the quality of the text (Scardamalia & Bereiter, 1986). Fourth, a further constraint on children's revising may be that they lack sufficient memory capacity for dealing with multiple issues of content and quality at the same time. When an adult guides them through revisions in a "scaffolded" way, the quality of revisions improve (Scardamalia & Bereiter, 1986).

Summary

In sum, then, children not only gain more working-memory capacity and writing knowledge with age, they also engage in writing processes more effectively. These structural and functional aspects, of course, play equally important and interactive roles in the development of writing skills. For example, as children gain more knowledge of their language, they are more equipped for performing the process of translation effectively. Similarly, as they gain more knowledge of audiences, they become more skilled at detecting and correcting possible ambiguities in what they have written. Thus, it is best to think of the development of writing ability as the coalescing of knowledge and processes, rather than the acquisition of separate components.

According to Berninger, Mizokawa, and Bragg (1991), there are three types of constraints that affect the rate at which writing knowledge and processes coalesce. First, there are neurodevelopmental constraints that influence young children's writing by affecting the rapid, automatic production of letters and hand movements. These low-level constraints are thought to constrain the "transcription process" (i.e., writing down symbols) but not the central "translation processes" (i.e., converting ideas into potential text). After transcription processes have been mastered and automatized, linguistic constraints on words, sentences, and schemata have their effects. Finally, after transcription and translation processes have been sufficiently mastered, cognitive constraints on planning and revising may become evident. Thus, whereas neurodevelopmental constraints have their strongest influence on young writers, older children are influenced mostly by linguistic and cognitive constraints.

THE DEVELOPMENTAL MECHANISMS QUESTION:
What Factors Promote Changes in Writing Skills?

So, we know that the core processes and knowledge of writing change with age, but we still do not know much about the developmental mechanisms responsible for these changes. Several likely sources of improvement include (1) increases in working-memory capacity that may have a neurological basis, (2) writing frequency and practice, (3) extensive reading, and (4) instructional techniques. In particular, practice is likely to engender fluency and the automatization of writing skills. If working memory is freed up to attend to goals and meaning, writing is likely to improve, as well. Extensive reading is likely to help because children would be exposed to new vocabulary terms, styles, genres, and syntactic constructions (Stanovich et al., 1995). To make this information explicit, however, children would need to engage in a form of literary criticism. As for instructional techniques, it should be noted that children historically have not been asked by their teachers to write extensively. Moreover, they tend to get very little feedback on their writing and are rarely asked to submit multiple revisions of their work. Thus, the children who improve may have a natural gift for, and love of, writing. They may also get feedback from sources other than their teachers (e.g., parents).

THE DEFICIENCIES QUESTION: Are There Populations
of Children or Adults Who Lack Some or All Writing Skills?
Do These Individuals Experience Problems When They Learn
to Write or after They Have Learned to Write?

Having completed our discussion of how older students differ from younger students in their writing ability, we can now move on to the question, "How do individuals of the same age differ from one another?" In what follows, we answer this question by comparing skilled and less skilled writers of the same age.

Comparisons of Skilled and Less Skilled Writers

The major findings of the studies which have compared same-aged skilled and less skilled writers are as follows:

1. Although skilled writers and less skilled writers do not differ in terms of grade-point averages (GPAs), achievement test scores, and short-term memory capacity, the former are better at manipulating verbal information than the latter (Benton, Glover, Kraft, & Plake, 1984). In particular,

a study of college students showed that when students were asked to (a) re-order strings of letters into alphabetical order, (b) reorder words into a meaningful sentence, or (c) reorder sentences to make a meaningful para-graph, those students who showed skilled writing ability were faster and more accurate than their peers who wrote less well. Cognitive and educa-tional psychologists have referred to such abilities as being indicative of a large working-memory span for verbal information (Kellogg, 1996; McCutchen, Covill, Hoyne, & Mildes, 1994; Ransdell & Levy, 1996).

2. In elementary school children, the mechanics of writing (i.e., hand-writing and spelling) contribute significantly to both fluency and overall quality (Graham, Berninger, Abbott, Abbott, & Whitaker, 1997; Green-wald et al., 1999). Skilled writers are able to write and spell more quickly than less skilled writers.

3. Skilled writers tend to be better readers than less skilled writers (Abbott & Berninger, 1993; Englert et al., 1988; Hayes, 1996; Langer, 1986; Perfetti & McCutchen, 1987). In particular, studies show that there is a high correlation between a student's reading scores and his or her writ-ing scores. Moreover, the same students who use their knowledge of the structure of genres to guide their reading comprehension, also use this knowledge to help them write something in that genre (Scardamalia & Bereiter, 1986; Wright & Rosenberg, 1993). Writing and reading are not, of course, the same, but they do seem to rely on the same central knowl-edge structures (Perfetti & McCutchen, 1987). But again, there is a differ-ence between reading for comprehension and evaluative reading (see above). Skilled writers are better at both kinds of reading than less skilled writers (Graham, 2006; McCutchen, 2006).

4. Just as older writers are more likely than younger writers to use heuristic (i.e., goal-directed) searches to retrieve ideas from long-term mem-ory, skilled writers of a particular age group are also more likely to use heu-ristic searches than less skilled writers of that age group (Scardamalia & Bereiter, 1986) and also likely to engage in incomplete searches (Graham & Harris, 1996). When good writers lack knowledge on a particular topic and cannot retrieve information from memory, they may also use their heu-ristic search methods to delve into the published literature to find what they need (Glover et al., 1990). Few studies, however, have demonstrated this phenomenon. Finally, whereas expert writers usually elaborate on an as-signment by building in issues, themes, and constraints, novice writers stick very close to the assignment (Scardamalia & Bereiter, 1986).

5. In terms of language competence, expert writers mainly differ from novice writers in three ways: (a) whereas handwriting, spelling, punctua-tion, and grammar are largely automatized in the former, these processes are still somewhat effortful in the latter; (b) the former have a larger reper-toire of sentence constructions and grammatical devices than the latter; and

(c) skilled writers add larger segments to their sentential constructions than less skilled writers (Greenwald et al., 1999; Hayes, 1996; Norris & Bruning, 1988; Perfetti & McCutchen, 1987; Scardamalia & Bereiter, 1986).

6. Whereas skilled writers spend a great deal of time creating goals and organizing their ideas before they write, less skilled writers show little evidence of explicit planning and goals. As a result, they tend to "jump right into" the task of writing, and their work demonstrates less sophisticated organization (Graham, 2006; Scardamalia & Bereiter, 1986). Experts are also more likely to comment on how their goals and plans change in the midst of writing.

7. Because expert writers are more likely than novices to create explicit goals and subgoals, the former are more likely to revise than the latter. Why? Deep-level revisions take place when one realizes that a segment of text does not meet the goals set for that segment (Scardamalia & Bereiter, 1986). For example, if you were writing to a friend to explain that he or she does something offensive, and you had the goal of being polite, you might say in response to reading a draft, "Oh, that's no good. He or she might be offended by this." In contrast, people who do not write from goals have nothing to compare the text to and will not, therefore, see the need to revise anything. Skilled writers are also better at revising than less skilled writers because the former tend to have greater topic knowledge (McCutchen, Francis, & Kerr, 1997), greater executive control over revising (Graham, 1997), and greater sensitivity to their audience (Graham, 1997).

Furthermore, because skilled writers often change their goals and plans as they write, they will have a tendency to review what they have written and delete those portions that do not fit with the new plans and goals. Because less skilled writers tend not to change goals while writing, they will not engage in such wholesale revisions.

8. Finally, many of the aforementioned differences really concern a difference in *metacognition* between skilled and less skilled writers. It is probably incorrect to say that less skilled writers do not have goals when they write or that they have little knowledge of genres or language. Instead, it is more correct to say that whereas skilled writers can consciously reflect on and manipulate their goals and knowledge, less skilled writers do not have the same conscious access to their goals and knowledge (Scardamalia & Bereiter, 1986).

All of the aforementioned differences between same-aged skilled and less skilled writers are magnified when we look specifically at children who have learning disabilities. Children with learning disabilities are significantly less likely to (1) plan, (2) generate adequate content, (3) revise, (4) translate content into text, and (5) recognize the deficiencies of their writing than their nondisabled peers (Troia, 2006). The serious difficulties faced by these children as they write, combined with repeated experiences with failure, inevitably lead to serious motivational problems as well. What is particularly unfortunate is the finding that a sizable portion of regular classroom teachers (42%) reported in a national survey that they often do not adapt their instruction to meet the needs of writers with LD (Graham, Harris, Fink-Chorzempa, & MacArthur, 2003).

Discussion Topic: Earlier we said that younger students and less-skilled, older students had the following deficiencies that seem to lie at the heart of their writing problems: (1) a lack of explicit knowledge about the structure of specific genres, (2) inadequate knowledge of topics as well as ineffective strategies for retrieving the knowledge they do have, (3) a small vocabulary and a lack of awareness of grammatical structures and devices, (4) a failure to set goals or formulate plans, and (5) a failure to revise in more than a superficial way. Based on this diagnosis, create an intervention or curriculum sequence that would improve the writing of all students.

Major Project: Identify common themes and constructs across Chapters 7, 8, and 9. How is beginning reading related to reading comprehension and writing? How is writing related to reading comprehension?

PART  IV

Individual and Group Differences in Language and Literacy

10

Motivational Issues in Speaking, Reading, and Writing

Vignette: Across the span of a year when Julia was 9, she and her father read every one of C. S. Lewis's *Narnia* tales together. At the end of one book that she particularly liked, she hugged the book, kissed C. S. Lewis's picture on the back, and said "I love you, C. S. Lewis!"

MAIN IDEAS OF THE CHAPTER

1. Motivation is a theoretical construct that is used to explain the initiation, direction, and intensity of an individual's behavior in a particular situation; in this book, it is also used to explain why some students do not learn as much as they can even though they are given excellent opportunities to learn language and literacy skills.
2. If we want to fully explain students' motivation to learn language and literacy skills, we need to appeal to their (a) goals, (b) knowledge of how to meet these goals, (c) personal standards for what is good enough, (d) beliefs about their abilities and possible emotions, (e) interests, and (f) values.
3. Students who are intrinsically motivated to learn literacy skills engage in literacy tasks as an end in itself; students who are extrinsically motivated engage in these tasks as a means to an end.
4. Because of a variety of factors that conspire together, older children tend to have less achievement motivation for literacy tasks than younger children.
5. Within any language arts classroom, individual differences can be found along any of the aspects of motivation. Students differ in terms of their goals, tendency to monitor, personal standards, ability beliefs, interests, and values; these differences greatly affect how hard students try, how long they persist, and the emotions they feel when confronted with tasks.
6. Teachers and classroom environments can affect student motivation in significant ways. When instruction is meaningful, challenging, and affords a degree of choice, students are more likely to be engaged than when instruction lacks these features. In addition, students are more likely to participate when they establish positive social relationships and feel valued.

As argued in Chapter 1, it is extremely useful for teachers to have knowledge of normative age trends in the development of language and literacy skills. When teachers are knowledgeable about these age trends and also have insight into the factors that promote growth in skills (i.e., developmental mechanisms), teachers can tell the difference between instructional techniques that are likely to foster literacy skills in their students and instructional techniques that are unlikely to foster these skills. Hence, such information helps teachers make better instructional decisions. However, it is also true that teachers need to know more than normative age trends and developmental mechanisms if they want to be successful with *all* of their students (even those who do not fit the norm). Seasoned teachers know that there are always students who do not benefit from, or respond positively to, the best instructional approaches that have been developed to date. In this chapter and the next, we consider some of the reasons why some students seem to benefit more from learning opportunities than others. As a preface to these discussions, it is helpful to briefly examine a theoretical framework that integrates accounts of student achievement in a coherent manner.

AN OPPORTUNITY–PROPENSITY MODEL
OF STUDENT ACHIEVEMENT

Perusal of the vast literature on student achievement reveals that researchers have identified quite a number of factors associated with learning outcomes. These factors include a variety of family variables (e.g., parent income, parenting style, parent involvement), student characteristics (e.g., motivation, intelligence, gender, ethnicity), and school variables (e.g., curriculum, instructional practices). For example, researchers have found that students demonstrate higher levels of achievement if (1) their parents are highly educated, (2) the students are highly motivated to learn course material, and (3) teachers cover the material found on achievement tests. Considered separately, the distinct literatures on predictive factors are difficult to integrate.

Fortunately, however, several theorists have recently attempted to integrate all of the findings together into a single, comprehensive account (e.g., Byrnes, 2003b; Corno et al., 2002). Despite several differences in their approaches, these integrative accounts have in common the claim that students are likely to attain high levels of achievement in a particular domain (e.g., reading) when two necessary conditions are met: (1) They are regularly exposed to genuine opportunities to enhance their skills in that domain (the *exposure condition*), and (2) they have the propensity to take advantage of these opportunities (the *propensity condition*). With respect to the exposure condition, the assumption is that children would not be expected to demonstrate high levels of reading skill as fourth graders if they were rarely asked to analyze sounds (e.g., play rhyming games), learn their letters, practice decoding, or read for comprehension during their prior years at home and school. Reading is a skill that must be acquired and practiced; it is not an innate competence. However, we would also not expect children to show high levels of reading skill if they did not take advantage of any opportunities that may have arisen. For example, some 3- and 4-year-olds may often decline offers from parents to read books together. Such children may demonstrate lower levels of prereading skills than their peers who regularly take advantage of similar opportunities. In subsequent chapters, we describe (1) what it means for a child to have a genuine opportunity to learn language and literacy skills (Chapter 12) and (2) why some children have more opportunities to learn than others (Chapter 11). Here we focus on the following question pertaining to the propensity condition: Why are some children more likely to take advantage of opportunities to learn literacy skills than others?

Contemporary accounts suggest that there are two component aspects of the propensity to take advantage of learning opportunities: a motivational component and an ability component. Informally, one could characterize the roles of these two components by saying that students will only benefit from opportunities to enhance their skills if they are both willing and able to benefit from these opportunities. Students who are willing to benefit from opportunities have a high degree of motivation to learn the skills in question (e.g., reading skills). Students who are able to benefit from learning opportunities have a certain level of prerequisite skill.

To get a sense of the importance of prerequisite skills, consider the case of a bright 8-year-old who has little background in physics but is given the opportunity to attend classes in a college-level physics course. Clearly, this child would not benefit from this learning opportunity because most of the content would pass right over the child's head. In contrast, consider how the same child would get a lot more out of this experience if he or she were older (e.g., 17 years old) and already had a physics course in high school. Chapters 3 through 9 provided detailed descriptions of the set of skills that children need to benefit from high-quality reading instruction in kindergarten through third grade (e.g., phonological processing, vocabulary). Hence, you have already read what it means to be *able* to benefit from learning opportunities for literacy skills, and, this information will not be repeated here. In contrast, little was said about motivation in previous chapters. In the remainder of this chapter, we consider what it means to be motivated or willing to benefit from opportunities to learn literacy skills.

THE NATURE OF MOTIVATION

Motivation is a theoretical construct that is used to explain the initiation, direction, and intensity of an individual's behavior in a particular situation (Stipek, 1993; Wigfield & Eccles, 1992). Thus, the notion of motivation is useful for answering questions such as the following:

- Why do students pick up books and read?
- Why do students choose to read a book in a particular way (e.g., scan it) instead of reading it in another way (e.g., read it more deeply)?
- Why do students prefer to read certain authors and genres over others?
- Why do students differ in the amount of independent reading they do per day (e.g., 10 min vs. 1 hr)?
- Why do certain students expend a great deal of effort and persist when they read a difficult passage, while others expend very little effort and give up easily?

This standard definition of motivation has been augmented in recent years to include the construct of *engagement* (Eccles, Wigfield, & Schiefele, 1998; Wigfield & Eccles, 2000). A child who is engaged in a classroom activity is an active, attentive, curious, and willing participant. The opposite would be a disengaged, inattentive, and even resistant student. For obvious reasons, most teachers would love to have a classroom full of engaged students. What does it take to transform this dream into reality?

In attempting to answer questions such as these, motivation theorists have identified a large number of constructs. Instead of examining these constructs one by one, we examine them in three groupings: goal-related constructs, knowledge-related constructs, and metacognitive constructs. Then, we will gain closure on the description of motivation by considering the importance of social relationships to motivation, and by drawing the distinction between intrinsic and extrinsic motivation.

Figure 10.1 helps you understand how all of the parts of motivation fit together. For simplicity, this figure shows a timeline ranging from before, during, and after a child engages in a communicative or reading-related action. Each of the parts of motivation (e.g., goals, ability beliefs) is placed along the timeline at a spot that illustrates the role this part plays in motivation.

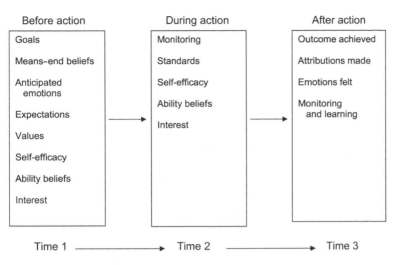

FIGURE 10.1. The timeline of motivational processes.

Goals

We examine goals in three parts: the nature of goals and how they relate to student motivation, the various types of goals, and finally, the effects of goals on student motivation and learning.

The Nature of Goals

Goals have to do with the *reasons why* people do what they do. More specifically, goals specify something that a person would like to accomplish by engaging in a particular activity (Stipek, 1993; Wentzel, 1991). In specifying how things should turn out (e.g., "I would like to finish this book by the end of vacation"), goals tend to direct or guide behavior (e.g., the goal-setter does things to reorganize activities such that more reading can get done).

Goals are inherently *cognitive* in that they are mental representations of some future state of affairs (Bandura, 1986). Thus, motivation theorists who espouse goals tend not to be strict behaviorists because they argue that people control their *own* behavior by thinking about some desirable outcome and then performing actions that might bring about this desired outcome. However, goals are not purely cognitive because they typically refer to outcomes that are likely to affect us positively or negatively. The major determinant of the valence of an outcome is the emotional state it might produce (Frijda, 1994). Hence, goal-directed behavior has both cognitive and affective components. Given the a priori character of goals, they are shown in Figure 10.1 at the very start of the timeline.

Types of Goals

An examination of the research on motivation shows that researchers have proposed four dichotomies and one trichotomy of goal types. The first dichotomy is the "learning versus performance goal" dichotomy (Dweck & Leggett, 1988; Stipek, 1993; Wentzel & Wigfield, 1998). People who have *learning* goals (also called "mastery" or "task" goals) engage in behaviors in order to understand something, gain mastery over a skill, enjoy themselves, or feel competent. In contrast, people who have *performance* goals (also called "ego" goals) engage in behaviors in order to gain the approval of others, look better than others, gain rewards, or avoid criticism.

The second dichotomy of goals pertains to the distinction between proximal and distal goals (Bandura & Schunk, 1981; Schunk, 1991). *Proximal* goals are short-term goals such as "I want to finish this chapter before dinner." *Distal* goals are long-term goals such as "I want to read three books by the end of summer." In information processing theory terms (e.g., Siegler, 1983), proximal goals can be said to be subgoals of an overall, superordinate goal. In effect, they seem to be steps along a longer path. Distal goals, in contrast, tend to be of the superordinate variety.

The third dichotomy has to do with the distinction between *academic* and *social* goals (Wentzel, 1991; Wentzel & Wigfield, 1998). Research shows that in addition to having academic goals such as being a successful student, learning new things, understanding things, doing the best you can, and getting things done on time, students also have social goals such as earning approval from others, having fun, making friends, helping others, being dependable, and being responsible.

The fourth dichotomy concerns the distinction between *process* goals and *product* goals (Schunk & Ertmer, 1999). Students who adopt process goals focus on the techniques or strategies that one can use to attain goals. Students who adopt product goals, in contrast, focus on the outcomes of their efforts (e.g., a completed assignment).

In addition to the dichotomies of goals described above, there is also a trichotomy of goals that comes from the work on the cooperative learning approach (e.g., Johnson & Johnson, 1987). Advocates of this approach suggest that classrooms can have one of three *goal structures*: individualistic, competitive, and cooperative. When a language arts classroom is arranged in such a way that anyone has the opportunity to get the rewards of the classroom (e.g., good grades), students tend to set the goal of doing as well as they can (an individualistic goal structure). Such students are often indifferent about how well other students do (e.g., "As long as I get my A, who cares!"). When only a certain number of students can get the best grade (e.g., just the top 10), students start thinking about doing better than other people in class (not just about doing generally well). Moreover, they want other students to perform poorly. Both of these desires reflect a competitive goal structure. When a classroom is arranged such that the assignment of rewards is based on how well a small group of students perform as a whole, students not only want themselves to do well, but they also want the other students in their own group to do well (a cooperative goal structure).

Effects of Goals on Motivation and Learning

Researchers have discovered five main ways that goals affect student behavior. As we will see, three of these outcomes derive from the research on the "learning versus performance goal" dichotomy, one outcome derives from the research on the "proximal versus distal goal" dichotomy, one outcome derives from the "academic versus social goal" dichotomy, and the final one derives from cooperative learning theory.

First, whereas students who have learning goals seek challenging tasks that help them develop their competencies, students with performance goals choose tasks that will make them look competent to others (Dweck, 1986; Nicholls, 1983; Wentzel & Wigfield, 1998). In order to look good all of the time, of course, you need to do things that you are already good at. Thus, students with performance goals would be expected to rarely challenge themselves and to develop expertise in an area at a slower rate than students with learning goals.

Second, whereas students with learning goals see their teacher as a resource or guide, students with performance goals see their teacher as an evaluator who will either reward or punish their behavior (Stipek, 1993). Thus, it would be predicted that students with learning goals would seek help from their teachers more often than students with performance goals. Inasmuch as teachers can be a valuable resource for information and strategies, it would be further expected that students who seek help appropriately would show greater achievement than students who do not (Wentzel, 1991).

Third, goals can affect what students pay attention to in a learning situation. Students who care more about how they look than what they are learning will tend to learn less than students who are mastery oriented. In support of this claim, research shows that students do not process information at a "deep" level when they are overly concerned about evaluation or looking bad (Graham & Golan, 1991; Nicholls, 1983; Stipek, 1993; Wentzel & Wigfield, 1998). Thus, students reading aloud in class may attend to what others are thinking of them rather than on what they reading.

Fourth, research has found three ways that proximal goals help students more than distal goals: (1) proximal goals provide more frequent and continual feedback; (2) the feedback provided when proximal goals are met gives students a constant sense of progress and mastery (Schunk, 1991); and (3) it is easier to keep proximal goals in mind than distal goals (i.e., students are more likely to forget distal goals).

Fifth, social goals such as being helpful, responsible, and compliant have been found to be strongly related to academic achievement (Wentzel, 1989, 1991). Why should this be the case? It seems that students who know how to get along with others and who are helpful, responsible, and compliant have more frequent and positive interactions with their teachers and peers. The more interactions one has with teachers and competent peers, the more likely one is to achieve (Vygotsky, 1978; Wentzel, 1991). Of course, not all social goals relate to success in school. For example, students who strongly endorse the goal of having fun in school have been found to have low GPAs (Wentzel, 1989).

Finally, the type of goal structure fostered within individual classrooms has predictable consequences on student learning and achievement. Whereas student achievement is higher when cooperative learning programs have both cooperative and competitive elements, competitive goal structures discourage students from helping each other, set up a "pecking order" in the classroom, and create a situation in which low achievers have little chance of success (Ames, 1986; Johnson & Johnson, 1987). In thinking about the type of classroom they would like to design, teachers have to decide whether the higher achievement fostered by competition outweighs its negative consequences.

Knowledge

Although goals are crucial to "getting the ball rolling," there are several other factors that help you attain your goals. For instance, in addition to knowing what you want (e.g., to comprehend a story), you also need to know how to get what you want (e.g., using reading strategies that promote comprehension). That brings us to the second key component of motivation: knowledge.

In several contemporary motivational accounts, beliefs related to "how to" knowledge have been called *means–end beliefs* (e.g., Skinner, Chapman, & Baltes, 1988). Because means–end beliefs have to do with knowing how to do things to reach certain goals, mean–end beliefs pertain to beliefs about the utility of various kinds of *strategies*. Thus, beliefs about how to add fractions, conduct an experiment, and write a summary are all examples of means–end beliefs. Examples in the social realm include knowing how to make friends or persuade others.

In support of the hypothesized linkage between goals, strategies, and outcomes, Elliot, McGregor, and Gable (1999) found that college students used different learning strategies depending on whether they had mastery goals, performance goals, or learning-avoidance goals. Learning-avoidance goals pertain to fear of failure and the possibility of negative outcomes. Students who had mastery goals demonstrated greater persistence and effort and, eventually, showed better grades. Those with performance-avoidance goals, in contrast, showed more strategic disorganization (e.g., strongly agreeing with items like "I find it difficult to organize my study time effectively"). In a related way, Schunk and Ertmer (1999) and Zimmerman and Kitsantas (1999) found links between process-product goals, self-regulatory strategies, and performance in a computer course and writing unit, respectively.

So far, then, we have accumulated two possible explanations of someone's behavior. In particular, in response to motivation-related questions such as, "Why is she taking notes on that chapter?" we can say such things as, "She wants to understand it better and remember the material" (referring to her goals) or "She thinks that underlining is a good way to promote understanding and retention" (referring to her means-ends belief). Similarly, we can account for someone's lack of motivation for something (e.g., not finishing high school) by arguing that he or she lacks certain goals or lacks appropriate procedural knowledge.

Metacognitive Processes

The research on motivation reveals that people engage in a variety of monitoring and appraisal activities. Given the self-reflective quality of both monitoring and appraisal (Bandura, 1986), these activities are grouped under the single heading "metacognitive processes" in this book. We examine three aspects of metacognition related to motivation: (1) monitoring of progress, (2) appraisal of actions, and (3) appraisal of outcomes.

Monitoring of Progress

Although some goals can be attained quickly with a single action (e.g., scratching one's head to relieve an itch), many other goals involve a series of actions and take some time to fulfill. As a result, it is often necessary to examine how far one has progressed toward one's goals (Bandura, 1986, 1997). To see the utility of occasionally taking stock of one's progress, consider the case of a dieter who sets the goal for himself of losing 5 lbs by the time he goes to his 10-year college reunion (2 months away). After seeing several glowing endorsements by celebrities, he decides to use a popular low-carbohydrate diet to achieve this goal (a means–end belief). It should be obvious that in order to maximize his goal of losing the 5 lbs within 2 months, our dieter should weigh himself occasionally to see whether the liquid diet is working. By engaging in monitoring, he could switch diets in sufficient time to lose the weight if he finds out early on that the low-carb diet is not working (i.e., he could "switch to Plan B").

In a sense, then, humans have the capacity to envision a "path" leading from where they currently are (e.g., 5 lbs too heavy) to some ultimate goal state (e.g., 5 lbs lighter). The "path" is a set of intermediate states of affairs that connect the initial state to the goal state (Newell & Simon, 1972). Apparently, this path is a natural consequence of setting a goal and deciding on a particular strategy for attaining the goal. Without this capacity for creating mental paths, we would have no way of knowing how far we have progressed in some endeavor.

Appraisal of Actions

The use of the term *appraisal* is meant to capture notions such as evaluation and estimation. Thus, when we speak of the appraisal of actions, we are referring to the processes of (1) evaluating actions that have been already performed (e.g., they were performed well; what I am doing is working; I am enjoying myself) and (2) estimating the likelihood that actions will be performed in a particular way in the future (e.g., it is likely that they will be performed well; it is likely that such-and-such strategy will work; it is likely that I will enjoy myself).

The appraisal of past and future actions often occurs in the midst of monitoring your progress. Whenever you pause to reflect on your progress, you think about what you have done and whether it is a good idea to continue that course of action. Thus, appraisal is often what we do when we monitor our progress. Having said that, let's now examine four types of beliefs that play an important role in the appraisal process: personal standards, control beliefs, self-efficacy beliefs, and ability beliefs. Then, we discuss an additional dimension along which we judge actions: interest.

Personal Standards

Personal standards refer to beliefs about what is "good enough." Recall that when you monitor your progress, you stop and think about how well things are going. In order to form such a judgment, you have to compare your actual progress to some standard (Bandura, 1986). Let's say that you are dieting and you find that you have lost 1 lb a week for the last 3 weeks. Is that good enough? Is it too fast? Is it too slow? Or, let's say that a student is writing an essay and finished the first draft. The student reads the draft and compares it to an internal standard to say whether it needs to be revised. The student may also consider how much time he or she has spent and will need to spend to make a revision. Thus, standards have to do with issues of quality and often involve considerations of rate of change or progress. Obviously, one's standards play an important role in the process of deciding whether to continue a course of action or switch to a new one.

Control Beliefs

An obvious aspect of goal pursuit is the belief that you have control over outcomes. If a student feels that his or her grade is entirely up to a teacher (and in no way related to his or her own actions), for example, that student would probably not engage in a specific course of action to attain a good grade. Student beliefs about controllability of actions have been found to relate to their motivation levels and achievement (Eccles et al., 1998; Wentzel & Wigfield, 1998). The term *agency belief* refers to the belief that one has control over certain outcomes (Skinner et al., 1988).

Self-Efficacy Beliefs

Self-efficacy pertains to an individual's belief that he or she can succeed on a particular type of task (Bandura, 1986, 1997). In order to feel self-efficacious about something, the individual must first know which actions to perform to do well (a means–end belief) and also how well these actions need to be performed by anyone. But self-efficacy has to do with the person's belief that he or she has the ability to perform these actions well enough to succeed. For example, in the midst of a basketball game, a person might know that he or she would have to shoot a basketball through the hoop in order to earn the 2 points that his or her team needs to win (a means–end belief), but nevertheless believe that he or she lacks the skill necessary to make that shot under pressure. Bandura's (1986) notion of self-efficacy is quite similar to Skinner et al.'s (1988) notion of *agency beliefs*.

How would self-efficacy beliefs affect the monitoring and appraisal processes? Consider our dieting and studying examples again. If our dieter tried extremely hard to lose weight and discovers that he lost 3 lbs in 3 weeks, his decision to stay on the low-carb diet would be affected by his sense of self-efficacy and by his standards. If he has high self-efficacy about dieting (i.e., he thinks that he has the self-control and pain tolerance needed to diet), and he is dissatisfied with his weight loss, he would be expected to find an even stricter diet. If he has low self-efficacy, however, he would be expected to discontinue dieting altogether.

Similar predictions could be made about studying or reading a particular book. Someone with high self-efficacy about his or her ability to study who got disappointing midterm grades would try to find better study habits and expend more effort next time. Someone with low self-efficacy, in contrast, would tend to lose interest in studying. Relatedly, someone with high self-efficacy would choose a challenging book to read and persist through it even when passages that are difficult to understand are encountered.

In a variety of laboratory studies, researchers have shown that self-efficacy relates to effort, persistence, and quality of problem solving on tasks (Bandura, 1986, 1997; Bandura & Wood, 1989). In addition, studies of school children show that about 14% of the variance in academic achievement is accounted for by self-efficacy (Berry & West, 1993). Thus, it is very important to engender a sense of self-efficacy in readers and writers.

Ability Beliefs

Ability beliefs are closely related to, though somewhat distinct from, self-efficacy beliefs. Whereas a self-efficacy belief is a judgment about your ability to be successful on a particular task in a particular situation, an ability belief is a general sense of your skill in an area or set of areas (Berry & West, 1993; Stipek, 1993; Wentzel & Wigfield, 1998). Thus, whereas an example of a self-efficacy belief would be "I can understand this chapter in this science textbook," an example of an ability belief would be "I'm a pretty good reader" or "I'm a very good student."

Most students have a large number of ability beliefs about school subjects, sports, social relations, and their appearance. Researchers have found that the ability beliefs that comprise a student's *self-concept* seem to be mentally arranged into a hierarchy. At the top of the hierarchy, there is a general self-concept that is an overall sense of how competent one feels, or a general sense of self-worth (e.g., "I feel good about myself"). Just below the general self-concept, beliefs subdivide into academic and nonacademic self-concepts (e.g., "I do pretty well in school" vs. "I make friends easily"). Then, the academic self-concept is further divided into lower-level beliefs about abilities in specific subjects (e.g., math, science, English), and the nonacademic self-concept is further divided into social, emotional, and physical self-concepts (Harter, 1985; Marsh, 1989). Support for this hierarchical framework comes from studies that show that people who generally feel good about themselves can nevertheless feel that they are not very good in certain things (e.g., reading). Similarly, researchers have found a near-zero correlation between verbal and math self-concepts (Feather, 1988; Marsh, 1989).

Recent studies have suggested that the original multidimensional model proposed by Marsh and others needs to be refined further. For example, Lau, Yeung, Jin, and Low (1999) found that the English self-concept could be decomposed into ability beliefs about one's listening skills, speaking skills, reading skills, and writing skills. Other studies revealed the need to expand the number of domains.

In most studies in this area, a skill is decomposed into its components and attitudes toward these components are assessed. Another approach consists of looking at different kinds of motivation within a particular domain. To illustrate, Baker and Wigfield (1999) examined the structure of reading motivation in fifth and sixth graders. They found evidence for the following kinds of reading motivation: (1) self-efficacy (e.g., "I know I will do well in reading next year"), (2) challenge (e.g., "I like difficult, challenging books"), (3) work avoidance (e.g., "I don't like reading something when the words are too difficult"), (4) curiosity (e.g., "I like to read about new things"), (5) involvement (e.g., "I like mysteries"), (6) importance (e.g., "It is very important to me to be a good reader"), (7) recognition (e.g., "I like hearing the teacher say, that I read well"), (8) grades (e.g., "I read to improve my grades"), (9) competition (e.g., "I like being the best at reading"), (10) social (e.g., "My friends and I like to trade things to read"), and (11) compliance (e.g., "I read because I have to").

In addition to discovering that people have specific and general beliefs about their abilities in academic subjects, researchers have also found that students develop one of two conceptions of their intelligence. Students who hold an *entity view* of their intelligence believe that (1) intelligence is a fixed capacity that does not increase or decrease over time and (2) intelligent people learn things effortlessly and rarely make errors. In contrast, students who hold an *incremental view* of their intelligence believe that intelligence is not a fixed capacity. In fact, they feel that each time one learns a new skill, one becomes that much smarter. Moreover, they recognize that when one is learning a new skill, expending effort and making mistakes are all part of the game (Cain & Dweck, 1995; Dweck & Elliot, 1983).

In sum, then, we have very specific beliefs about our abilities in certain areas (e.g., reading, math, sports, social relations), as well as more general conceptions about our overall abilities and intelligence. How do these ability beliefs affect our motivation? It seems that ability beliefs play a role in the appraisal process similar to that played by self-efficacy beliefs. In particular, people who feel good about their ability and who have an incremental view of their intelligence would be expected to expend more effort and persist after failure than people with less positive views of their skill, or people who hold an entity view of their intelligence.

But in addition to affecting the way people behave "midstream" in their quest for goals, ability beliefs and views of intelligence also affect the initial goals people set for themselves. For example, when given a choice between easy and hard tasks in an area (e.g., science), people who feel more competent about their skill in that area would be more likely to choose the harder task than people with less positive views of their skill. Thus, similar to students who have learning goals (see above), students who have positive views of their ability and who hold an incremental view of their intelligence would be more likely to challenge themselves than students with less positive views of their ability, or students with an entity view of their intelligence (Dweck & Elliot, 1988). Thus, Figure 10.1 placed such appraisals midway through the goal-pursuit process, but they could also be placed near the beginning, prior to goals.

Interest

A final factor that plays a role in the process of appraising actions is interest. Interest is conceptualized as a quality of a person–object interaction that can "show itself" in the form of prolonged, relatively effortless attention and feelings of pleasure and concentration (Eccles et al., 1998; Renninger, Hidi, & Krapp, 1991). Thus, interest involves a blending of cognitive processes (i.e., attention) and emotional processes (i.e., feelings of pleasure and enjoyment). Interest has been viewed both as a trait-like tendency of individuals (e.g., having a long-standing interest in reading books), as well as a property of objects that captures the attention of most people (e.g., a novel that most people find interesting).

Similar to ability beliefs, interest can affect both "early" and "midstream" processes in the motivation system. Early on, interest can affect the choices people make and goals they set for themselves (Wigfield & Eccles, 1992). When people monitor their progress, interest can play a role in judgments of "how things are going." For example, in the middle of reading a book, one student might find it to be particularly interesting, while another might find it to be boring. Interest can affect the degree to which a student persists in an activity, even when the student has high self-efficacy or positive ability beliefs for a skill. For example, a child who has high self-efficacy for reading might stop reading a particular book and switch to another if the first one is judged to be boring.

In addition to predicting choices and persistence in activities, interest has also been linked to deeper processing of information during learning and the use of certain kinds of strategies (Alexander & Murphy, 1998; Renninger et al., 1991). The precise associations between interest, strategy-use, and learning, however, varies according to the amount of knowledge a person has. Students who seem to benefit the most from interest are those who have a moderate amount of knowledge already (as opposed to a high or low amount). If readers know a moderate amount about a topic and are interested in learning more, they should make more gains and use reading strategies more than students who know less or know more about the topic before reading.

Appraisal of Outcomes

In addition to monitoring their progress and appraising their actions "midstream," people also estimate the likelihood that certain future events will occur and evaluate their performance after their goals have been met. The idea that people think about what will happen next has been implicit in many of the discussions so far. For example, when people monitor their progress, they not only think about how well things are going, they also think about how well things will go in the future. Moreover, people with high self-efficacy for a task (e.g., finishing *Moby Dick* or *War and Peace*) believe that although they might be still far from their goal, they can still reach it if they try something else or double their efforts.

In this section, we focus on how people evaluate outcomes both before they occur and after they occur. In particular, we focus on the factors that influence the judgments people make when they ask themselves forward-looking questions such as, "What will happen next?" "Why will it happen?" and "How will I feel about it if it does happen?" as well as backward-looking questions such as, "What happened?" "Why did it happen?" and "How do I feel about it?" As we will see, these questions pertain to four additional components of motivation: expectations, causal attributions, values, and emotions.

Expectations

An expectation is a belief about the likelihood of something happening in the future. In theories of motivation and decision making, the expectations that have received a lot of scrutiny are those pertaining to outcomes (Atkinson, 1964; Eccles et al., 1998; Slovic, 1990). Some examples of expectations for outcomes include statements such as, "It probably won't rain today," "It is pretty likely that I will get a 4.0 this semester," and "I think that I will enjoy this book."

When people form judgments about the likelihood that an outcome will happen, they consider both internal and external factors. By internal factors, it is meant such things as (1) how much skill it would take to attain the outcome and whether a person has the skill and (2) how much effort it would take to reach a goal and whether a person is likely to expend the necessary effort. By external factors, it is meant those things that are not under the control of the person (e.g., weather patterns; the number of A's given by some teachers; the writing skill of an author). So, when a person feels that there is only a 20% chance that he or she will get a 4.0 this semester, a portion of this estimate could derive from his or her perceptions of internal factors (e.g., "I have to work really hard to get an A"), and the remainder could derive from his or her perceptions of external factors (e.g., "I have to take Dr. Jones next semester, and she does not gives many A's").

Causal Attributions

In contrast to expectations that are forward-looking, causal attributions are initially backward-looking. In particular, causal attributions are made after an outcome has occurred. When someone makes a causal attribution, he or she assigns causality to some factor that seems to be responsible for the outcome (Weiner, 1986). For example, consider the situation in which two students get a C on the same test. One student might attribute this outcome to ineffective study strategies, and the other might attribute it to poor teaching on the part of his or her instructor.

When trying to explain achievement-related outcomes, research has shown that people tend to attribute their successes and failures to one of two main factors: ability or effort. For example, when students have trouble comprehending a passage, one might say, "I'm not a very good reader" (attributing the outcome to low ability), and another might say, "I didn't try very hard" (attributing the outcome to low effort). But students also have been found to cite bad luck, poor teaching, and a variety of other idiosyncratic factors in explaining outcomes (Weiner, 1986).

Weiner (1986) argues that causes such as ability and effort vary along three dimensions: stability, controllability, and locus. Whereas stable causes reflect a permanent aspect of a person or situation, unstable causes reflect a transient or variable aspect. Some people might consider their ability to be a stable attribute (if they have an entity view of their intelligence) and their effort to be an unstable attribute (if they often apply themselves in a variable way). Other people might view their ability to be an unstable attribute (if they have an incremental view) and their effort to be a stable trait (if they consider themselves to be "naturally lazy").

The perceived stability of a cause plays an important role in performance expectations. In particular, if people attribute their performance to a stable cause, it is normal for them to raise their expectations following success and lower their expectations following failure (Weiner, 1986). For example, consider the case of a student who thinks that there is a 60% chance that he or she will get a B on a test. If the student (1) ends up getting a C on the test, (2) attributes his or her failure to low ability, and (3) believes that ability is a stable trait, the student will probably think that he or she has less than a 60% chance of a B on the next test. However, if the student attributes his or her failure to a temporary lapse of effort, the student might continue to think that he or she has a 60% chance of a B on the next test.

In addition to viewing causes as being stable or unstable, students also consider some causes to be controllable (e.g., how hard they try) and other causes to be uncontrollable (e.g., how smart they are). Moreover, some causes of success and failure are believed to be internal (e.g., effort and ability) and others external (e.g., teacher bias, bad luck, hard tests).

Values

In theories of motivation and decision making, values have to do with the desirable and undesirable aspects of outcomes (Eccles et al., 1998; Feather,

1988; Slovic, 1990; Wigfield & Eccles, 1992). What makes something desirable or undesirable, of course, depends on the person. For example, whereas some people think that it is important to be rich, others think that it is important to be well-liked.

Wigfield and Eccles (1992) argued that there are four types of values that influence achievement behaviors: *attainment value*, *intrinsic value*, *utility value*, and *cost*. Attainment value has to do with whether it is important to do well on the task. To see the attainment value of something, ask yourself questions such as the following: "Do I care how well I do on this?" and "Is it important to me to do well?" The intrinsic value of a task concerns the enjoyment you would feel if you engaged in the task. I see the intrinsic value of something, ask yourself the following question: "Would I find it to be enjoyable or interesting?" Note that interest seems to play a role when people appraise actions (see above) and when they appraise outcomes. The utility value of a task concerns the relation between the task and future goals. To see the utility value of a task, ask yourself the question, "Will doing this help me meet my goals?" (e.g., taking a course help you get a job?). The cost of a choice concerns all of the negative aspects of performing a task, including negative emotions (e.g., embarrassment, anxiety) and the amount of effort needed. To see the cost of something, ask yourself, "What would I lose if I engaged in this task?"

Values affect behavior in the following way: People tend to seek out desirable outcomes and avoid undesirable outcomes, in which "desirable," means an outcome judged to be important, interesting, useful, or "low-cost" (Wigfield & Eccles, 1992), and "undesirable," means unimportant, uninteresting, useless, or costly outcomes.

Although values are an important reason why people make the choices they do, values alone do not determine achievement behavior. In particular, people only try to attain desirable outcomes if there is a reasonably good chance that they can attain them (Slovic, 1990; Wigfield & Eccles, 1992). For example, whereas most students will tell you that getting an A is more desirable than getting a B, only those students who think that is it possible to get an A will try to get it. Thus, *both* expectancies and values affect motivation.

Emotions

In addition to expectancies, attributions, and values, the final factor that affects how an outcome is appraised is the emotion associated with it. Whereas the attainment of some outcomes is likely to engender "positive" emotions in the person who attains them (e.g., joy, pride, self-esteem), other outcomes are likely to engender "negative" emotions (e.g., anxiety, guilt, shame). Clearly, most people want to experience the positive more often than the negative emotions. Thus, we would expect that people would try to attain outcomes that engender positive feelings and avoid those outcomes that engender negative feelings (Frijda, 1994).

Of all the emotions that may affect motivation, there are four that have received the most attention from motivation researchers: anxiety, shame, pride, and self-esteem. Let's examine the two negative emotions first and the two positive emotions second.

Anxiety is a complex emotion that is closely related to fear and worry. Researchers have identified both a self-evaluative component and a somatic component of anxiety (Wigfield & Eccles, 1989). The self-evaluative component consists of negative cognitions about being able to do well on something (e.g., "I'm afraid I'll probably flunk the exam"), and the somatic component involves the actual emotional and bodily reaction associated with thinking about the potential failure. Studies show that the self-evaluative component of anxiety relates more strongly to school performance than the somatic component.

Shame is an emotional response that is engendered when an individual feels responsible for poor behavior (Weiner, 1986). Students are most likely to feel shame when they attribute their failures to low ability. When students attribute their poor performance to low effort, they are more likely to feel guilty than embarrassed. Many adults who have reading problems are ashamed that they read poorly and do what they can to avoid reading in front of others.

In sum, then, the two negative emotions come into play when a student is thinking about possible failure in the future or when they are thinking about failures that occurred in the past. In contrast, the two positive emotions are the consequences of successes rather than failure. For example, when students feel that they are responsible for their successes through hard work or ability, they are likely to feel *pride*. In a sense, they say, "What I did was good and I am entirely responsible for it." *Self-esteem* is a generalized sense of pride and competence that is accrued across many episodes of success.

As mentioned above, emotions play a role in assessments of the desirability of outcomes. Students think that outcomes that engender happiness or pride are more desirable than outcomes that engender anxiety, guilt, or shame. Thus, emotions play a role in decisions regarding which outcomes to strive for. In addition, we have seen that some negative emotions play a debilitating role when people are in the middle of trying to attain outcomes. Anxiety can promote maladaptive coping behaviors (e.g., avoiding academic situations; thinking about failure rather than studying properly), and learned helplessness can foster low levels of effort and persistence.

The Importance of Social Relationships

Earlier it was noted that children have social goals in addition to academic goals. It was also shown that children who coordinate both kinds of goals do better in school than children who just focus on one kind of goal. Here, we elaborate on this notion by describing the importance of feeling connected to the classroom and feeling cared for by a teacher (Wentzel & Wigfield, 1998). Recent studies have shown that children who feel that they belong in school and that they are part of something are motivated to do well in school. In other words, to the extent that classrooms foster feelings of belongingness, children emulate the engaged student described earlier in this chapter. Relatedly, there is a high correlation between believing that your teacher cares about you and doing well in school.

Before school, of course, young children have special relationships with their parents. In particular, it is often the case that shared book reading promotes a great deal of positive affect between parent and child, as well as a sense of closeness. Children especially enjoy reading before bedtime and often feel comforted by the ritual and affection that occurs just before sleeping. Over time, one would expect books to symbolize this positive experience.

Once children leave school as young adults, they sometimes form book clubs and share their reading experiences with others. The desire to talk about powerful or intriguing aspects of a book with another person tends to enhance the reading experience and social relationships, as well (Wigfield & Guthrie, 1997).

One further way to consider the role of social relationships pertains to connections to an author. Very often, readers who have a favorite author develop the sense that they identify with, or relate to, the person in some way. To enhance this relationship from afar, they might learn everything they can about the person through biographies and so on.

Intrinsic versus Extrinsic Motivation

Before moving on to a consideration of developmental and individual differences in motivation, it is important to examine one final issue that, in many ways, captures a lot of what has been said so far: the distinction between intrinsic and extrinsic motivation. People who engage in behaviors in order to receive praise, gain tangible rewards, or avoid punishment are *extrinsically motivated* (e.g., a fourth grader who writes a poem to win the prize for the best one). In contrast, people who engage in behaviors to feel competent, gain mastery over some skill, or satisfy their curiosity are *intrinsically motivated* (e.g., a fourth grader who continues to write poems after the contest is over). In effect, when you are intrinsically motivated, you are the one making yourself do something, and you are engaging in an activity for that activity's sake (e.g., read for the sake of reading). When you are extrinsically motivated, in contrast, someone else is in control of how you behave. Overall, we can say that whereas intrinsic motivation concerns engaging in a task as an end in itself, extrinsic motivation concerns using a task as a means to an end (Deci & Ryan, 1985).

Researchers who have examined intrinsic motivation suggest that people are naturally inclined to seek feelings of competence, gain control over their environment, set challenges for themselves, and satisfy their curiosities (Berlyne, 1966; Deci & Ryan, 1985; Stipek, 1993). That is, no one has to make you want to feel competent and so forth, you just naturally want to. Researchers have found that feelings of competence naturally follow successes, particularly if a student believes he or she controlled the success. When given a choice of an easy, moderately difficult, or hard task, most people choose the moderately difficult one. Finally, the introduction of novelty, surprise, or events that lack an explanation seem to engender attention and sustained interest.

It is relatively easy to make someone who is intrinsically motivated into someone who is extrinsically motivated. The key factors in this shift are the frequent introduction of external rewards (e.g., prizes, personal recognition) or punishments, as well as the use of competition and social comparison in the classroom (Ames, 1986; Deci & Ryan, 1985;).

Given what has been said so far, we can see that learning goals, the incremental view of intelligence, self-efficacy, interest, and values all have to do with intrinsic motivation. In contrast, performance goals, the entity view of intelligence, and the behaviorist notions of reinforcement and punishment have to do with extrinsic motivation.

It should be noted that the distinction between intrinsic and extrinsic motivation, as well as the data that support this distinction, have been hotly debated (Cameron & Pierce, 1994). Behaviorists scoff at the idea that people engage in behaviors because these behaviors are intrinsically satisfying. Moreover, they question the meaning of results that suggest one can dampen intrinsic motivation by supplying an external reward. If a "reward" such as praise or money causes a behavior (e.g., reading) to decrease over time, it is by definition a punishment, not a reinforcer. Another problem for theorists who advocate the intrinsic/extrinsic motivation distinction is the fact that the effects of intended rewards vary according to their type. Across a number of studies, people rewarded with verbal praise or positive feedback show more intrinsic motivation than nonrewarded individuals (as indicated by doing the task even when they are told they can stop). In contrast, those who receive a tangible reward (e.g., money) demonstrate significantly less intrinsic motivation than nonrewarded individuals. These definitional and empirical problems may require revisions in contemporary accounts that emphasize intrinsic motivation, but the matter is highly controversial (see Ryan & Deci, 1996).

Summary

We have seen that motivation constructs can be grouped under three main headings: goals, knowledge, and metacognitive processes. A goal is a future-oriented specification of what someone wants. Knowledge has to do with knowing how to attain goals using procedures or strategies. The metacognitive processes include (1) monitoring of progress, (2) using your beliefs and preferences to appraise ongoing actions, (3) evaluating the likelihood and desirability of outcomes, and (4) explaining why outcomes occurred. In addition, we have found that people can either be intrinsically or extrinsically motivated for an activity. Given this description of the nature of motivation, we would expect to find that motivated individuals would have different goals and knowledge than less motivated individuals, and would also engage in metacognitive processes differently. In the next two sections, we examine whether this is the case.

THE DEVELOPMENT OF MOTIVATION

So far, we have examined the constituent parts of motivation. In this section, we examine the literature to see whether there is evidence that these constituent parts change over time. That is, we attempt to answer questions such as, "Do older students have different goals than younger students?" "Do older students have different means–end beliefs than younger students?" and "Do older students engage in the metacognitive aspects of motivation differently than younger students?"

Goals

Researchers who have examined motivational goals have made few developmental comparisons. As a result, little is known about developmental trends in the "natural" expression of learning, performance, proximal, distal, academic, or social goals (Eccles et al., 1998). There is, however, some reason to believe that whereas younger children might be more likely to engage in a task for its own sake—adopt learning goals, older students might be more likely to do so because they believe they should or because they want to get a good grade—adopt performance goals (Dweck & Elliot, 1988; Nicholls, 1983). Similarly, there is reason to suspect that whereas social goals might become more important with age, academic goals might become less important with age. If a number of studies were to confirm these expectations, it would mean that students would be less likely to challenge themselves or strive for high grades with age.

Although motivation researchers have not compiled extensive evidence in support of the claim that goals change with age, researchers who study other topics have. For example, as noted in Chapters 8 and 9, researchers who study reading comprehension have found that older and younger children have different goals when they read (Paris & Byrnes, 1989; Paris et al., 2001). Researchers who study writing have revealed similar findings (Page-Voth & Graham, 1999; Scardamalia & Bereiter, 1986).

Knowledge

Unlike the goals component that concerns the reasons *why* students engage in specific behaviors, the knowledge component has to do with *what* they do. As mentioned in the previous section, older students and younger students often engage in the same behaviors (e.g., read) but do so for different reasons (e.g., "to pronounce words properly" vs. "to learn something"). But it is also true that older students could have the same goals as younger students (e.g., get an A) but nevertheless try to attain these goals in different ways (e.g., using different studying techniques).

Metacognitive Processes

We have seen so far that there are two possible answers to questions of the form "Why are older children doing X and younger children doing Y?" The first is that older children have different goals than younger children. The second is that older children have different means–end beliefs than younger children. In this section, we discuss some additional answers that focus on the three subdivisions of metacognitive processes examined earlier: monitoring of progress, appraisal of actions, and appraisal of outcomes.

Monitoring of Progress

Research has shown that older children are more likely to monitor their performance than younger children (e.g., Baker & Brown, 1984; Markman, 1981). This developmental trend has both positive and negative consequences for younger children. Because they do not monitor how far they have progressed toward a goal, younger children cannot become discouraged by the realization that they have not progressed very far. As a result, it may not matter what their standards are or how highly they think of themselves. All young children would probably continue with the same course of action that they started with. But whereas young children gain something by not being discouraged as often as older children, they lose something in that they will not "fix" a strategy that is not working.

Appraisal of Actions

Very few studies have examined the possibility of developmental differences in personal standards or self-efficacy (Eccles et al., 1998). Bandura (1986) suggests that personal standards become progressively internalized as children interact with parents, peers, and teachers. Both direct instruction and modeling play a role in this internalization process. From this account, we can speculate that older students might be more likely to have standards than younger students. We cannot, however, say whether the former have higher standards than the latter.

With respect to self-efficacy, children develop a sense that they have control over successes by virtue of having many experiences in which their actions produced success and proportionately fewer experiences of failure (Bandura, 1986). Given the standard curriculum in which certain skills are reintroduced year after year, one would expect that older children would feel more self-efficacious than younger children when asked to think about the same type of tasks (because the latter have had more practice with these tasks). In support of this claim, Zimmerman and Martinez-Pons (1990) found that mean levels of self-efficacy for both verbal skills and math skills increased significantly from the 5th to 11th grades. However, one study showed that the mean levels of self-efficacy for reading dropped between the 4th and 5th grades (Wigfield & Guthrie, 1997). Perhaps not surprisingly, the average amount of daily reading also dropped from 22 min per day to 12 min a day, as well. This finding suggests that 5th graders may have had multiple bouts of failure experiences by way of especially challenging books.

If personal standards stay the same over time, and more and more children come to believe that they can be successful, it would be predicted that older children as a group would have more motivation than younger children. If standards increase over time, we would expect the levels of motivation of older children to be that much more enhanced. However, if children lower their standards at the same rate that they increase their sense of self-efficacy, we would expect roughly similar levels of motivation in younger and older students. Clearly, given the complex interactions among goals, standards, and self-efficacy, more developmental research is needed to sort out developmental trends in overall motivation levels.

As for ability beliefs, research has revealed three ways in which these beliefs change over time. First, children's self-concept becomes increasingly differentiated with age. That is, the gap between their academic and nonacademic beliefs becomes wider, as does the gap between their math and verbal self-concepts (Marsh, 1989). Concretely, this means that whereas younger students hold themselves in high regard for all subject areas, older students feel that they are better in some areas than others.

Second, there appears to be a curvilinear trend in which the self-concept declines during preadolescence and early adolescence, levels out in middle adolescence, and then increases in late adolescence and early adulthood (Marsh, 1989). These first two trends suggest that whereas elementary students show high levels of motivation and persistence for all subjects, middle school students show generally less motivation overall. In addition, middle school students apply themselves only in those subjects for which they have higher ability beliefs. During high school and beyond, motivation levels should return for most subject areas. But again, there is much more to motivation than ability beliefs, so research is needed to examine the patterns.

Third, whereas older students make a clear distinction between effort and ability, younger students seem to think that effort and ability are the same (Nicholls, 1983; Stipek, 1993). Thus, younger students tend to think that someone who is "really smart" is someone who "tries really hard." In contrast, once students acquire an "entity" view of intelligence, they come to believe that smart people do not have to try very hard (i.e., "things come easily to them").

Finally there are only a few studies that have examined the development of interests over time because researchers have often viewed interest as an individual-difference variable rather than a developmental-difference variable. In one study, Wigfield et al. (1989) asked first, second, and fourth graders to rate their enjoyment of various school subjects. They found that whereas there were no grade differences in children's liking of math or computers, there were differences in their liking of reading, music, and sports. In particular, both first and second graders liked reading more than fourth graders. The gap in ratings for reading between the first and fourth grades represented about a 15% drop. Also, whereas there was a 9% decline in children's liking of music over time, there was an 11% increase in their liking of sports over time. At all grade levels, children liked computers the best (average rating = 6.3 out of 7), followed by sports (average rating = 6.0), music (average rating = 5.25), reading (average rating = 5.25), and math (average rating = 5.0). Thus, the ratings for math were about 21% lower than those for computers.

Because elementary children are not given much choice over the subjects they learn, these age differences probably affect aspects of school performance such as attention, effort, and persistence, rather than selection. For example, during reading or music lessons, fourth-grade teachers would be more likely to find their students having problems with attention and persistence than first-grade teachers. Also, the overall average ratings suggest that math would not capture the attention of even the first graders.

In a study involving older students, Wigfield et al. (1991) asked children to rate their liking of social activities, sports, math, and English both before and after they made the transition to junior high school. Whereas students' liking of social activities and English stayed about the same over time, there was a 6% drop in interest in sports and a 10% drop in interest in math. In addition, there were large differences in what students found interesting. Students rated social activities and sports substantially higher (i.e., 25%) than math or English.

Appraisal of Outcomes

Research shows that young children are generally quite optimistic about things working out in their favor (Stipek, 1993). Part of their optimism stems from how they view their ability, another part derives from their attributions of success and failure, and still another part comes from their inability to differentiate between luck and skill (Nicholls, 1983). If young children hold an incremental view of their intelligence and feel that effort is they key to success, they will tend to be optimistic even after experiencing multiple failures. In particular, after performing poorly, they might say, "Oh well, I'll just have to try harder next time!" Moreover, if luck and skill are not sufficiently differentiated in their minds, they would feel that they have some influence over things that are out of their control (e.g., what will be on a test). Over time, social comparison, feedback from teachers, and other forms of experience inform children about the nature of ability, as well as what they can control and what they cannot. As a result, many children will come to feel that they can no longer control success and will lose their initial sense of optimism.

As mentioned earlier, a central component of children's values is the importance they attach to different topics (Wigfield & Eccles, 1992). In their study of first, second, and fourth graders, Wigfield et al. (1989) found that whereas there were no grade differences in the perceived importance of learning math, reading, social skills, or sports, grade differences emerged for learning computers and music. Both computers and music were judged to be less important with age.

In their study of children making the transition to junior high school, Eccles et al. (1989) found that there were significant drops ranging from 3% to 6% in the perceived importance of math, sports skills, and social skills between the sixth and seventh grades. The perceived importance of English was found to be lower at the start of the 7th grade but rebounded by the end of that year. Taken together, these two studies show that many subjects lose their value for students between the first and seventh grades.

Finally in the earlier section, "The Nature of Motivation," we learned that anxiety, learned helplessness, shame, and pride are emotions that play an important role in the motivation system. Here, we examine developmental trends in these emotions.

Most theorists assume that students develop test anxiety in response to repeated failure in evaluative situations (Stipek, 1993; Wigfield & Eccles, 1992). Research shows that young students who do poorly on tests do not become anxious right away. Rather, it is not until the end of elementary school that a consistent tendency to be anxious emerges in students.

The key to understanding student anxiety lies in how they define *failure*. Most students define a D or an F as a failure, so D and F students would be expected to be more anxious about tests than B or A students. And yet, students with high ability can also develop test anxiety, especially if they hold unreasonably high standards for themselves (Stipek, 1993). For example, a student who always gets 95% correct on tests might nevertheless treat such performances as failures if he or she feels that only 100% is good enough.

Personal standards seem to develop from three main sources: (1) parental expectations, (2) teacher behaviors and classroom structure, and (3) social comparisons (Mac Iver, 1987; Wigfield & Eccles, 1992). When parents and teachers are relatively "transparent" about what they want, when they hold very high standards for performance, and when classrooms are arranged such that it is easy for students to compare their performance to one another, students are more likely to develop anxiety than when the opposite is true.

Besides anxiety, two other emotions or emotion-related states that often emerge in response to repeated failure are shame and learned helplessness. Students who feel that they are responsible for performing poorly are likely to feel ashamed (Covington & Omelich, 1981; Weiner, 1986). Anyone who has experienced shame knows how uncomfortable it is to feel that way. Learned helplessness arises after students come to believe that they have no control over failure, and the feelings of shame that are associated with it (i.e., they cannot avoid it).

Pride, of course, is the opposite of shame and is felt when a student feels responsible for a successful performance. Both pride and shame emerge during the preschool period soon after children develop a clear sense of self (Stipek, Recchia, & McClintic, 1992). Thus, children enter elementary school with a pre-existing capacity to feel pride when they are successful. Given the age trends for monitoring of performance, conceptions of ability, and internalization of standards, it would be expected that only some students in the later elementary grades would consistently feel pride (i.e., those students who consistently do well on tests). In contrast, it would be expected that the majority of younger students would feel pride for a whole range of behaviors (e.g., being polite; trying hard).

Summary

The overall impression one gets from the developmental literature on motivation is that there are many reasons why older children should show less motivation to read than younger children (Eccles et al., 1998). First, older children are likely to have different goals than younger children (e.g., social goals vs. academic goals). Second, older children are more likely to monitor their performance and gauge it against standards than younger children. Third, students in the period ranging from late elementary school to early high school are more likely to have differentiated conceptions of their abilities, as well as an overall lower sense of competence than students in the early elementary years. Fourth, students are more likely to encounter failure with age. Those older students who attribute their poor performance to low ability and who think that failure is unavoidable are likely to have low expectations for future success, as well as negative emotional reactions such as anxiety, shame, and learned helplessness. At the very least, these students will not try very hard and will engage in a variety of avoidance behaviors (e.g., rarely reading). Finally, certain topics have been found to be not very interesting to students even in the first grade (e.g., math), and other topics start off interesting and become less interesting as students get older (e.g., reading). This is not to say, of course, that all students become less motivated with age. The most successful students will generally increase in their confidence level with age. The decrease in motivation will probably be limited to the least successful students in a grade. Nevertheless, there would be good reason to think that older children would be less likely than younger children to take advantage of opportunities to enhance their literacy skills, even when these opportunities are designed to be particularly engaging.

Considering these overall age trends in motivation, we can now ask the following question: What sorts of developmental mechanisms could explain these trends? The main culprits seem to be personal experiences, repetition, and lack of choice. As noted earlier, success and failure are important sources of information regarding one's competence. With age, children have many opportunities to fail as grading gets harsher, topics become more abstract, and skills become more complex. If only the top students maintain their high level of performance over time, the average levels of motivation within grade will inevitably fall. With respect to repetition, most subject areas become less interesting the longer one works in these areas. Most adults change their careers several times, so we should not be surprised at children getting a little tired of 12 years of reading. Finally, it is often the case that students have some or all of their reading choices selected for them. Studies suggest that students tend to be more engaged when they make their own choices of reading materials (Deci & Ryan, 1985). The lack of choice may be a particular problem for older students who, as noted earlier, find reading less interesting and important than younger students.

INDIVIDUAL DIFFERENCES IN MOTIVATION

In addition to understanding general normative trends in the development of the motivation to read and write, however, it is also useful to consider individual differences within grade in motivation. Although it is true that a fifth-grade teacher might have a harder time constructing literacy activities that will engage students than a second-grade teacher, it is also the case that some of the younger children may lack the motivation needed to benefit from instruction. Conversely, some of the older children may be particularly easy to reach. Thus, informed instructional decision-making requires knowledge of both normative trends and individual differences. Next we briefly examine two phenomena that are particularly salient examples of individual differences in motivation for literacy: precocious readers and leisure reading.

Precocious Readers

The population of preschoolers and kindergarteners can be subdivided into two kinds of children: (1) those who seem unusually interested in letters, word games, and books, and (2) those who show a more typical (less intense) interest in letters, words games, and books. Whereas children in the former group actively seek out or create literacy opportunities for themselves (e.g., by constantly asking their parents to either read to them or teach them letters), children in the latter group tend to have literacy experiences only when someone else (e.g., their mother) thinks of this option and presents it to them (Scarborough & Dobrich, 1994). Another difference between these children relates to how receptive they are to reading instruction when they are 3, 4, or 5 years old. Whereas children in the first group are agreeable to idea of learning the basics of reading (e.g., sounding out letters) at age 3 or 4 and may even ask their parents to teach them, those in the second group resist any attempts at instruction until they are at least 5 or 6.

It is nearly always the case that children who learn to read well before first grade (i.e., *precocious readers*) have the motivational profile of children in the first camp. Children who learn to read at the more typical ages of 5 or 6 tend to have the other motivational profile. Using the opportunity–propensity framework introduced at the beginning of this chapter, then, we would say that precocious children would be prone to take advantage of any literacy experiences that are presented to them (including those that provide direct instruction in decoding). Their less precocious peers, in contrast, would not be prone to take advantage of the same learning opportunities. Interestingly, many of the latter children would have the requisite abilities they need to take advantage of early reading instruction (e.g., phonological processing skills and knowledge of letters; see Chapters 4 and 7). The problem is not that they are unable to benefit from the instruction; rather, the problem is that they are not willing to do so.

Discussion Topic: Why do precocious readers and their less precocious peers differ in their motivational profiles? What components of motivation seem to be at the heart of this individual difference? Consider whether motivational constructs such as goals, means–end beliefs, interest, self-efficacy, and so on might be playing a role. After identifying the most likely differences (e.g., interest), consider the origins of this difference (e.g., Why are they more interested? Where did the interest come from?).

Leisure Reading

A second way to get a useful perspective on the role of motivation in literacy is to consider the amount of reading that children do on their own as a leisure activity. Because most children are unable to read books on their own until after the third or fourth grade, studies of independent leisure reading usually focus on children in the fourth grade or later. For example, large-scale surveys of fourth graders such as those conducted by the NAEP reveal the following about children's leisure reading habits. When presented with the item, "Reading is one of my favorite activities," 37% responded that the item was "a lot like me." However, another 39% and 25% responded that the item was only "a little like me" or "not like me," respectively (NCES, 2003). Hence, the majority (64%) did not consider reading to be one of their favorite activities. Similarly, when asked questions such as, "How much do you read for fun on your own time?" only 35–45% of children responded "almost every day." Even then, however, other studies report that children read an average of only 10–15 min a day—usually when required to do so for homework (Taylor et al., 1990; Wigfield & Guthrie, 1997). In contrast, NAEP and other studies (e.g., Greany & Hegarty, 1987) routinely report that more than 75% of children watch 2 hr or more of television per day. Hence, children who read every day, and do so for 30 min or more, are somewhat unusual.

Within the group of active readers is a small group that has been dubbed *ludic* readers (Nell, 1988). These children and adults (who comprise about 10% of any sample) place books near the top of their list for leisure activities and report that they get considerable pleasure out of reading. They frequently experience "getting lost" in a book and find that hours have slipped by while they are engrossed in the act of reading. Little is still known about the source of this extreme interest in books in ludic readers; demographically, we know that they (1) tend to be girls more often than boys, (2) tend to have higher standardized reading scores, and (3) have easy access to libraries and bookstores (Greany & Hegarty, 1987).

Discussion Topic: Imagine you were to conduct a study in which you were to measure constructs such as goals, means–end beliefs, self-efficacy, and so on in a sample of ludic fifth-grade readers and their more typical peers who read far less. Where would differences emerge (e.g., in their goals; in their interests)? After identifying the differences, propose an explanation as to how these differences came about. Why did ludic readers follow one developmental trajectory while their peers followed another?

INSTRUCTIONAL IMPLICATIONS

To consider the instructional implications of the literature on motivation, we propose some general guidelines using two approaches. First, we examine Ames's (1992) comprehensive proposal that attempts to link classroom structures and experiences to motivation. Second, we distill the literature on motivation into a series of heuristics or rules of thumb.

Ames (1992) summarized the literature on the links between classroom structures and motivation in the following way: Classrooms differ with respect to the tasks that children are asked to perform, the amount of authority relegated to students, and the kind of evaluative practices that are implemented. If these dimensions of a classroom are configured in particular ways, students will (1) focus on effort and learning, (2) have high intrinsic interest, (3) attribute their successes to effort and effort-based strategies, (4) employ effective learning and self-regulatory strategies, (5) demonstrate engagement, (6) demonstrate positive affect on high-effort tasks, (7) demonstrate feelings of belongingness, and (8) develop appropriate levels of failure tolerance. What kinds of task, authority, and evaluative structures produce these highly desirable motivation outcomes? In the case of tasks, activities should be meaningful, diverse, and occasionally novel, require short-term self-referenced goals, and require the effective use of learning strategies. With respect to authority, students should be given opportunities to participate in the decision making and make choices (as opposed to being told what to do and given a single option). Moreover, they should be given opportunities to develop responsibility and self-regulation of their behaviors (as opposed to being nagged and threatened). With respect to evaluations, grades should be given to acknowledge individual improvement, progress, effort, and mastery (as opposed to a one-shot attempt to get an absolute number of answers correct). Moreover, only the student, his or her parent or guardian, and the teacher should know of these grades. Finally, teachers should provide opportunities for improvement and encourage the view that mistakes are part of learning.

To this sound list of suggestions, the research described in this chapter suggests that teachers should also:

1. *Help students acquire and coordinate appropriate goals* (e.g., learning goals, proximal goals, social and academic goals).
2. *Empower students with appropriate means–end beliefs* (e.g., not only demonstrate skills but explain why they work).

3. *Provide devices to help students monitor their progress* (e.g., charts and other forms of feedback).

4. *Provide numerous experiences in which children of all skill levels feel successful and competent but also challenged* (e.g., individualized instruction to just beyond each student's skill level). Moreover, explicitly point out to students that they controlled successes that just occurred. Together, such experiences help students develop appropriately high standards, expectations, feelings of self-efficacy, and advantageous attributions.

5. *Adopt and communicate the incremental view of ability to students* (e.g., that intelligence is not fixed but increases as new skills are acquired; errors are normal in the early phases of learning).

6. *Point out to students the value and importance of learning certain skills using authentic and convincing argumentation* (e.g., why it is important to learn how to read, write, and communicate effectively).

7. *Frequently introduce novelty and information that cries out for explanation.*

11

Sociocultural Issues in Speaking, Reading, and Writing

Vignette: In the middle of conducting a study at a particular school in a low-income neighborhood, a famous researcher who studied motivation once encountered an African American boy who loved to read. After discussing books with him for a few minutes, the boy confided that he never read at home because he did not have very many books and those he had did not interest him. When the researcher and his teacher offered to let the boy bring books home, he adamantly refused because he said that kids in his neighborhood would make fun of him or threaten him if he walked by with books in his hands. The researcher eventually figured out a way to solve this problem: Once a week for a few months he surreptitiously dropped off a new book at the boy's home.

MAIN IDEAS OF THE CHAPTER

1. There are four factors that have been argued to affect the extent to which students have opportunities to learn literacy skills or take advantage of opportunities: their gender, their socioeconomic status (SES), their ethnicity, and their dialect.
2. The largest gender differences are found for sentence complexity during the preschool years (favoring girls), vocabulary and verbal fluency during the elementary school years (favoring boys), reading comprehension on challenging tests in older students (favoring girls), and writing quality and quantity in older students (favoring girls); these differences have typically been explained by arguing that girls have been given more opportunities to have conversations and read; girls may also be more intrinsically motivated for language and literacy.
3. SES appears to be a powerful determinant of the language and literacy skills that children acquire between birth and first grade; large differences are apparent by the time children reach fourth grade in vocabulary size and reading skills; again, opportunities seem to be the primary culprit.
4. Ethnic differences largely mirror those for SES; White and Asian students demon-

strate higher levels of achievement than Black or Hispanic students; differences in the level of opportunity prior to first grade are apparent.

5. Dialect is a regional or social variety of a language that is (a) distinguished by its pronunciation, grammar, or vocabulary, and (b) recognized as being different from the standard literary language or speech pattern of the culture in which it exists. A few studies suggest that dialect may pose problems for children when their own dialect does not match Standard English. In terms of the opportunity–propensity (O–P) framework, then, dialect could be an aspect of propensity that could explain differences in children's ability to take advantage of opportunities to acquire reading skills. However, methodological shortcomings of these studies preclude the possibility, for now, of knowing for certain the degree to which dialect is a key factor relative to other factors in the opportunity and propensity categories.

In Chapter 10, an O–P framework was introduced to explain individual differences in the rates at which students acquire language and literacy skills. As noted in that chapter, a basic premise of the O–P framework is that students are likely to attain high levels of achievement in a particular domain (e.g., reading) when two necessary conditions are met: (1) Students are regularly exposed to genuine opportunities to enhance their skills in that domain (the *exposure condition*), and (2) students have the propensity to take advantage of these opportunities (the *propensity condition*). The exposure and propensity conditions are considered to be necessary in the sense that students cannot attain a high level of skill if these conditions are not met. However, each of these conditions is also not sufficient by itself to promote achievement. For example, students sometimes show relatively slow growth in reading skills even when they are exposed to excellent opportunities to learn.

In Chapter 10, we focused on one factor that differentiates between students who benefit from opportunities to learn language and literacy skills, and students who do not seem to benefit: motivation. Motivation was said to be an aspect of the propensity to learn. In this chapter, we focus on several other factors that may influence the extent to which either of the exposure and propensity conditions are met: gender, SES, ethnicity, and dialect. Before discussing the literature on each of these factors, however, we need to first consider their possible roles in the overall O–P framework.

The role that any given factor plays derives from the general category to which it belongs. According to the O–P framework, predictors relate to each other and to achievement by virtue of being a member of one of the following three categories: opportunity factors, propensity factors, or distal factors (Byrnes & Miller, 2007). In particular, opportunities to learn are defined as culturally defined contexts in which an individual is presented with content to learn (e.g., by a teacher or parent, an author, a narrator of an educational television program) or given opportunities to practice skills. Thus, opportunities can occur both within school (e.g., in a classroom context) and outside of school (e.g., in the home context). One could ask the following three questions about such contexts: (1) has the content required on achievement tests been presented in these contexts? (2) has this content been presented accurately? and (3) has the content been presented effectively? Thus, any variables related to exposure (e.g., coursework, a teacher's emphasis, homework, amount of repetition) or teaching quality (e.g., use of proven techniques, communication skills, classroom management, equitable treatment of students) fall into the domain of an opportunity factor (Opdenakker, Van Damme, De Fraine, Van Langeghem, & Onghena, 2002; Pressley, Wharton-McDonald, & Raphael, 2002; Tate, 1995). We consider the role of such factors in Chapter 12.

Propensity factors, in contrast, are *any factors that relate to the ability or willingness to learn content once it has been exposed or presented in particular contexts.* Thus, cognitive factors such as intelligence, aptitude, cognitive level, and pre-existing skills would qualify, as would motivational factors such as interest, self-efficacy, values, and competence perceptions (Byrnes, 2003b; Corno et al., 2002; Eccles et al., 1998; Jones & Byrnes, 2006; Sternberg, Grigorenko, & Bundy, 2001). Self-regulation is a hybrid of cognitive (e.g., beliefs) and motivational (e.g., efficacy) orientations (Pintrich, 2000), so it would also qualify as a propensity factor. An additional assumption of the O–P framework is that when the opportunity and propensity conditions are fulfilled in an individual (i.e., he or she has been exposed to content in an effective manner and was willing and able to take advantage of this learning opportunity), higher achievement will follow directly. As a result, opportunity factors and propensity factors are considered to be *proximal causes* of achievement.

Although the two categories of opportunity factors and propensity factors capture the majority of predictive variables in the literature, there are other factors that also play a role but do not fit into either of these categories. The remaining factors become evident when one asks certain follow-up questions about achievement outcomes. For example, in response to the question, Why do some children show higher levels of reading skill than others at the end of first grade? O–P theorists would argue that the more skilled readers were not only given more opportunities to learn reading skills, they were also more willing and able to take advantage of these opportunities. If one accepts this answer, however, one can then ask follow-up questions such as the following: Why were the better readers given more opportunities? and Why were they more prone to take advantage of these opportunities? Factors that could explain the emergence or origin of opportunities and propensities include family SES, parental educational expectations for their children, children's own educational expectations, and prior educational experiences (Eccles et al., 1998; Oakes, 2005; Roscigno, 2000). For example, one might say that affluent children were given more opportunities to acquire reading skills because their parents read to them as preschoolers and could afford to buy a house in an excellent school district with excellent teachers. Because factors such as family income operate earlier in time and explain the emergence of opportunities and propensities, these factors are called *distal* factors in the O–P framework.

Having described the three categories of factors in the O–P framework, we are now in a position to consider the best ways to categorize factors such as gender, ethnicity, SES, and dialect. Should they be considered propensity factors, opportunity factors, or distal factors? As we just noted, SES is a distal factor because it could explain why some children had more opportunities to learn and were more prone to take advantage of these opportunities. As for gender and ethnicity, one recent proposal (Byrnes & Wasik, 2007) is that these factors are also appropriate for the distal category because implicit biases in parents or teachers could lead them to provide more literacy opportunities to children of one gender (e.g., females) or one ethnic group (e.g., White children). Dialect, in contrast, is more appropriately viewed as a propensity factor in that it has been said to adversely affect children's ability to acquire reading skills (see below). As we discuss each of the literatures on gender, SES, ethnicity, and dialect in turn, the significance of this categorization scheme will become evident.

THE ROLE OF GENDER IN LANGUAGE AND LITERACY SKILL ACQUISITION

A useful way to begin the discussion of gender is to briefly review what is known about gender differences in the development of language and literacy skills. After doing so, we can then consider how these differences might arise using the O–P framework as a guide.

Gender Differences That Require Explanation

Although the average person generally assumes that girls are much more skilled in the verbal domain than boys, reviews of the literature reveal a somewhat different story. For example, in an early and seminal review of the literature, Maccoby and Jacklin (1974) concluded that there are no gender differences in verbal skills before the age of 11, but there are gender differences after age 11 (e.g., on the SAT-verbal). However, more recent meta-analyses of both the older and newer literatures have found little support for this proposed developmental pattern (e.g., Hedges & Nowell, 1995; Hyde & Linn, 1988). Instead, the pattern seems to be a slight difference favoring girls at all age levels (average effect size of $d = 0.09$) when various kinds of verbal skills are all lumped together.

When verbal skills are segregated into different kinds, however, the story becomes a little more complicated. In the case of vocabulary, for example, meta-analyses suggest that the effect size is $d = -0.07$ for children below the age of 6 (suggesting that girls have slightly larger vocabularies), $d = 0.26$ for children between the ages of 6 and 10 (suggesting that boys have moderately larger vocabularies), and $d = -0.01$ for children between the ages of 11 and 18 (suggesting essentially no difference). The findings of the original developmental norms study for the Macarthur Communicative Development Inventories (CDI) largely supported these meta-analyses in showing that girls tend to be about 1 month ahead of boys in their acquisition of vocabulary during the preschool years (Fenson et al., 1994). However, gender only accounted for about 2% of the variance in vocabulary size in that study (meaning that 98% of the reason why children differed in their vocabulary involved something other than gender). In a different large-scale study of the effects of childcare on developmental outcomes (i.e., NICHD, 2000), researchers found once again that preschool girls seemed to have slight advantage over boys on the CDI vocabulary (correlation $r = .02$; $d = -0.04$), but the difference is so small that one would say that there was no difference. Thus, with the exception of the moderate difference favoring boys in the elementary school years, gender differences in vocabulary are essentially nonexistent at most age levels.

In contrast, differences do emerge when the focus shifts to other aspects of language such as sentence complexity and expressive language. For example, the aforementioned NICHD study of early childhood (NICHD, 2000) showed that the effect size for CDI sentence complexity was $d = -0.47$ for 2-year-olds (favoring girls). When the same children were 3 years old, the effect size for expressive language on the Reynell Language scales was $d = -0.39$ (favoring girls). Putting the findings for vocabulary and sentences together, then, it would appear that preschool boys and preschool girls know a similar number of words; girls, however, are more capable of combining these words together into more complex syntactic constructions than boys.

Conceivably, such a difference in language skill could translate into differences in reading scores when children enter first grade. However, meta-analyses of multiple small-scale studies of reading comprehension suggest that the average effect size is $d = -0.09$ for children between the ages of 6 and 10 (favoring girls), and $d = -0.02$ for children between the ages of 11 and 18 (Hyde & Linn, 1988). Thus, these findings suggest that possible syntactic advantages for girls do not seem to translate into reading comprehension superiority.

When large-scale studies of reading are examined, however, a different picture emerges. For example, the 2002 NAEP for reading study showed that the effect sizes were $d = -0.08$ for 4th graders, $d = -0.13$ for 8th graders, and $d = -0.23$ for 12th graders (Grigg, Daane, Jin, & Campbell, 2003). Together, NAEP studies and meta-analyses suggest that gender differences in reading comprehension are barely detectable in the early grades, but become moderately sized by the 12th grade, especially when children are given challenging tests such as NAEP. It is worth noting, though, that the SAT-verbal is also a challenging test that taps into reading comprehension skills. Here, boys have been found to have a slight advantage ($d = 0.07$; College Board, 2004). However, the SAT also taps into other skills, as well, such as analogical reasoning on which boys sometimes perform better than girls (Hyde & Linn, 1988).

Finally, we can examine the findings for writing skills. Studies have revealed gender differences for four aspects of writing: (1) fluency, (2) conformity to standard usage, (3) overall quality, and (4) the tendency to revise (Berninger & Fuller, 1992; Fitzgerald, 1987; Price & Graves, 1980). To illustrate, Berninger and Fuller (1992) investigated whether boys and girls in the early elementary grades differ in their verbal fluency (i.e., the speed with which they could name as many examples of something as they could), orthographic fluency (i.e., the speed with which they could write the letters of the alphabet in the correct order), and compositional fluency (i.e., the speed with which they could write stories and expository works). The results showed that whereas boys obtained higher scores for verbal fluency ($d = 0.21$; consistent with the findings for vocabulary in the elementary grades above), girls obtained higher scores for orthographic fluency ($d = -0.36$) and compositional fluency ($d = -0.34$ to -0.83). Furthermore, of the 28 children who were in the lowest 5% of the distribution for compositional fluency, 23 (82%) were boys.

Price and Graves (1980) obtained a similar gender split for the quantity of oral and written language. In particular, whereas boys produced more words in oral language than girls, boys were also twice as likely to make errors regarding double negatives, verbs, pronouns, and plural inflections in their writing and speech. Price and Graves labeled such errors "deviations from standard usage." Thus, there were both quantitative and qualitative differences in the writing of boys and girls.

Such quantitative and qualitative differences have also been found on large-scale national assessments such as the NAEP for writing. On NAEP, children are given a limited amount of time to write essays or stories that are scored for quality. Between 1984 and 1992, differences ranged between $d = -0.53$ and $d = -0.61$ for 12th graders (favoring girls; Hedges & Nowell, 1995). Ten years later on the 2002 NAEP, the differences were $d = -0.13$ for 4th graders, $d = -0.14$ for 8th graders, and $d = -0.29$ for 12th graders. This pattern shows that the gender gap seems to increase with age, but it is half as large as it used to be.

In sum, the largest gender differences are found for sentence complexity during the preschool years (favoring girls), vocabulary and verbal fluency during the elementary school years (favoring boys), reading comprehension on challenging tests in older students (favoring girls), and writing quality and quantity in older students (favoring girls). All other differences are fairly trivial.

Explaining These Gender Differences

A useful way to investigate the possible origin of these differences is to ask two central questions that derive from the O–P framework. In particular, given that children cannot acquire skills unless they are given opportunities to learn and have the propensity to take advantage of these opportunities, the framework implies that one should ask the following questions about gender differences: (1) Have children in one group (e.g., girls) been given more opportunities to learn than children in the other group (e.g., boys)? and (2) Are children in one group (e.g., girls) more willing or able to take advantage of these opportunities?

In the case of opportunities, for example, is it the case that parents and teachers converse more with girls in such a way that girls are asked to respond beyond one-word answers? A recent meta-analysis of parent–child communication (Leaper, Anderson, & Saunders, 1998) suggests that parents do, in fact, communicate more with their daughters than with their sons ($d = -0.29$). This increased level of communication could explain gender differences in complex sentence construction in preschoolers but could not explain the relative lack of gender difference in preschool vocabularies. Perhaps the lack of vocabulary differences is due to the fact that parents may talk more about certain topics (e.g., science) with boys than with girls (e.g., Crowley, Callanan, Tenenbaum, & Allen, 2001), but about other topics (e.g., emotions) more with girls than with boys (e.g., Fivush, Brotman, & Buckner, 2000). However, the overall amount of new vocabulary expressed to boys and girls might be similar.

Other questions that pertain to opportunities are the following: (1) Are girls provided with more opportunities to read or write? and (2) Is there a bias to place girls in the top reading groups over boys? We were unable to locate studies that documented the tendency of teachers or parents to provide more opportunities to girls either at home or through reading-group placement. There are, however, studies that suggest that girls themselves may seek out more opportunities to read and write than boys. For example, as noted in Chapter 10, studies of "ludic" readers have found that girls are more likely to engage in daily hours of leisure reading than boys (Greany & Hegarty, 1987; Neuman, 1986). Relatedly, studies using the Elementary Reading Attitude Survey have found that girls consistently hold more positive attitudes toward reading than boys, even though they score similarly on standardized tests of reading ability (Diamond & Onwuegbuzie, 2001; Kush & Watkins, 1996). In contrast to the explanation for syntactic complexity, then, it does not appear that girls acquire more reading and writing skills because they are given more opportunities to enhance their skills. Rather, it appears that they are more prone to seek out, or take advantage of, learning opportunities because they hold more favorable attitudes.

One further method for explaining gender differences is to appeal to other kinds of factors besides those that pertain to aspects of opportunities or propensities. In addition to showing possible differences between boys and girls in their opportunities and propensities, one can ask follow-up questions such as the following: Why were boys and girls given different opportunities to acquire language and literacy skills? and Why did they differ in their propensities to take advantage of these opportunities? Here, one can appeal to factors such as socialization (e.g., implicit cultural norms foster the belief that girls like to talk, read, and write more than boys, so parents are more inclined to create situations for girls in which speaking, reading, or writing can take place) or even biological differences. Consistent with the findings reported above for vocabulary and sentence complexity, one study of identical twins found that vocabulary seemed to have a higher heritability for boys than girls (20% vs. 8%), but sentence complexity seemed to have a higher heritability for girls than boys (28% vs. 10%). However, most of the variation (72–80%) was explained by shared environmental influences (Van Hulle, Goldsmith, & Lemery, 2004). A study of brain imaging in young adult males and females found that whereas brain activations for letter recognition and semantic category judgments did not differ between the sexes, females showed bilateral frontal activation for rhyme judgments, and males showed only left frontal activation (Shaywitz et al., 1995). Thus, genes and biology may play a small role in explaining gender differences, but factors such as environment and motivation seem to play a larger role. The fact that gender differences vary by age and aspect of language (vocabulary vs. sentence complexity) further mitigates against a strong physiological explanation of language differences.

THE ROLE OF SES IN LANGUAGE
AND LITERACY SKILL ACQUISITION

In keeping with the format used to understand gender differences, we first examine the differences that have emerged between higher-SES children and lower-SES children in the acquisition of language and literacy skills and then turn to possible explanations of these differences.

SES Differences That Require Explanation

Spoken Language

In a well-known observational study comparing interaction patterns of mothers and their children from three income levels (high SES, middle income, and on welfare), Hart and Risley (1995) found that differences in the size of children's vocabularies were relatively small during observations that were conducted when children were less than 20 months old. After that point, however, the high-SES children (whose parents were mostly college professors) gained an average of approximately 2 new words per day; the middle-income children gained about 1.5 words per day while the children of mothers on welfare gained less than 1 word per day, on average. By the time children in these groups were 4 years old, the gaps in vocabulary were too large to overcome via an experimental intervention that the authors had created. Thus, the authors realized that they needed to start some form of intervention much earlier.

Arriaga, Fenson, Cronan, and Pethick (1998) compared the vocabularies of 103 low-income children who were enrolled in a Head Start program and 309 middle-income children who were participants in the original norming study of the CDI. They found that 75% of their 16- to 30-month-olds fell below the median, and 35% fell below the 10th percentile for the CDI. In contrast, 50% of the middle-income norming sample fell below the median (by definition), and 10% fell below the 10th percentile (again by definition). In addition, the effect sizes for vocabulary and sentence complexity were $d = 0.52$ and 0.67, respectively (favoring middle-income children).

Chaney (1994) administered the Preschool Language Scale (PLS) and PPVT to 3-year-olds ($N = 43$) who attended daycare centers. She also obtained measures of their emergent literacy skills (e.g., phoneme deletion, print concepts), family SES, and home literacy environment. For the home literacy measure, points were awarded according to the answers provided by parents in an interview. Parents were asked about the amount and type of reading materials in their homes, use of local libraries, and use of literacy for a variety of purposes. Results showed that the best predictors of language skills were children's age and family literacy score (accounting for over 50% of the variance). Race added another 6% of the variance for the PLS but did not explain additional variance for the PPVT after family income and maternal education were controlled. Neither of the latter two SES components explained a significant amount of variance above and beyond that explained by age and family literacy.

In sum, then, SES appears to be a powerful determinant of the language skills that children acquire between birth and first grade. According to the theories and research presented in this book, these differences in language skills should lead to early differences in literacy skills, as well. In the next two sections, we consider whether this is the case.

Reading

The results of both small- and large-scale studies of reading are very consistent: Children from higher-SES families perform significantly better than children from lower-SES homes at all age levels. To illustrate, consider the findings of the Early Childhood Longitudinal Study—Kindergarten (ECLS-K). In the ECLS-K, a large national sample of kindergarteners ($N = 17,401$) was followed from the beginning of kindergarten until the end of third grade. We explored the public-access version of this database to determine the degree of association between SES and literacy scores at four assessment points: the beginning of kindergarten, end of kindergarten, end of first grade, and end of third grade. Children are grouped according to SES quintile in the ECLS-K database (e.g., falling in the bottom 20% for SES, falling in the next higher 20% between the 21st and 40th percentile). At the start of kindergarten, the gap in literacy skills between the top and bottom quintiles for SES corresponded to an effect size of $d = 1.12$. In addition, the average gap between each of the five quintiles was $d = 0.28$. For the remaining assessment points, the corresponding effect sizes for the top versus bottom SES comparison were $d = 1.25$ (end of kindergarten), 1.26 (end of first grade), and 1.30 (end of third grade). The average gap between successive quintiles (e.g., between the first and second or second and third) was $d = 0.32$ at each of these points. Thus, SES is clearly related to the amount of literacy skills evident in young children.

In older children, the results of the 2005 NAEP for reading reveal smaller but still large effects when parent education level serves as the index of SES. At the 8th-grade level, for example, the effect size corresponding to the gap between children whose parents graduated college and children whose parents dropped out of high school was $d = 0.79$. The contrast between children of college-educated parents and children of parents who earned only graduated high school was $d = 0.55$. The corresponding effect sizes for 12th graders were $d = 0.73$ and 0.57, respectively. Although the NAEP database does not have comprehensive indices of family income, it does code children according to their eligibility to receive free lunch at school (only low-income children whose parents earn below a certain amount are eligible). At the 8th-grade level, the effect size for the comparison between children eligible for free lunch and those not eligible was $d = 0.70$. At the 12th grade level, the effect size was $d = 0.54$.

Thus, the results for reading are very comparable to the results for spoken language skills. Each increase in the level of SES brings about a corresponding moderate increase in reading skills. However, these moderate gaps accumulate such that the gap between the most and least advantaged groups is rather large.

Writing

The results of the 2002 NAEP for writing reveal that the gap between children of college-educated parents and those of high school dropouts corresponded to effect sizes of $d = 0.79$ for 8th graders and $d = 0.53$ for 12th graders. The comparisons between those with high school diplomas and those with college diplomas yielded effect sizes of $d = 0.54$ and 0.50 for 8th graders and 12th graders, respectively. Using free lunch eligibility instead of parent education as the index of SES, the effect sizes were $d = 0.71$ and 0.53 for 8th and 12th graders, respectively.

Summary

Clearly, SES plays a powerful role in determining the level of language and literacy skill attained by children. The effect sizes range between 0.50 (moderate) and 1.30 (very large). In what follows, we consider why these differences might exist.

Explaining the Differences between SES Groups

As noted above for explanations of gender differences, a useful way to investigate the possible origin of these SES differences is to ask two central questions that derive from the O–P framework. In particular, given that children cannot acquire skills unless they are given opportunities to learn and have the propensity to take advantage of these opportunities, the framework implies that one should ask the following questions about SES differences:

1. Have children in some groups (e.g., high-SES, middle-income families) been given more opportunities to learn language and literacy skills than children in other groups (e.g., lower-income families, low-SES children)?
2. Are children in some groups more willing or more able to take advantage of these opportunities?

Let's consider answers to these questions in turn.

In the case of opportunities, for example, is it the case that higher-SES parents converse more with their children than lower-SES parents? Are higher-SES parents more likely to read books with their children (or read them in certain ways) than lower-SES parents? Are higher-SES students more likely to be assigned to higher reading groups than lower-SES students? Do teachers interact more (or more favorably) with higher-SES students during language arts lessons than with lower-SES students?

There are too few comparisons of the parent–child communication patterns to say with absolute certainty that there are SES differences in the amount and type of discourse between parents and children, but the aforementioned study of Hart and Risley (1995) provides some clues. In their monthly 1-hour observations of interactions, Hart and Risley found that when children were 11–18 months old, an average of 642 utterances were recorded in the hour-long observations of high-SES mothers and children, 482 (75%) of which were addressed to their children. For the middle-income mothers, the corresponding figures were 535 utterances total and 321 (60%) addressed to the child. For the low-SES mothers, the corresponding figures were 394 utterances per hour, 197 (50%) of which addressed to the child. Thus, there were large group differences in the amount of total discourse and the amount directed toward their children. In addition, there were qualitative differences in the style of communication used by parents. The communication style of the high-SES parents had the following characteristics:

- They talked beyond what was necessary to manage their children's behavior; their talk accompanied their actions (e.g., changing diapers) and described what their child was doing as a means to focus their attention.
- They actively listened and encouraged their children to say more or elaborate on what they were saying.
- They frequently gave children choices in the form of questions; this was a behavior-management technique as well (e.g., "Would you please flush the toilet?"; "Do you want to wash your hands?").
- They described aspects of an experience that was worth noticing, remembering, or naming.

Whereas families in all SES groups showed these qualities, they were more prominent and consistent in the recorded observations of the high-SES families. In general, there was a 3 to 1 proportional difference in the amount and type of communication experienced by the high- and low-SES children. Therefore, if the results of Hart and Risley can be generalized, the answer is clearly "yes" to the question above regarding whether high-income children are given more opportunities to acquire language than low-income children are.

Other studies have found comparable results. For example, Hoff-Ginsburg (1991) recorded conversations between lower-income (n = 30) or higher-income mothers (n = 33) and their children across four settings:

mealtime, reading, dressing, and playtime. The findings showed that the higher-income mothers directed a significantly larger number of utterances toward their children than lower-income mothers and were also more likely to reply contingently to their children's utterances in ways that continued a discussion about a particular topic. In contrast, lower-income mothers were significantly more likely to express directives at their children (i.e., utterances that told them to do certain things). Directives generally do not invite or require responding on the part of children.

In terms of book reading, we found (in a secondary analysis of ECLS-K data that was conducted for this chapter) that 60%, 76%, 82%, 87%, and 93% of parents in the first, second, third, fourth, and fifth quintiles for SES, respectively, reported that they read books to their children at least three times per week. The corresponding percentages for lower-SES parents reading books to their children everyday were 34%, 39%, 42%, 45%, 61%, respectively. Thus, higher-SES parents not only converse more with their children, they also read books to them more often.

After children enter first grade, opportunity differences appear again. Studies show that higher-SES children are more likely to be placed in the higher ability groups for reading than lower-SES children (Oakes, 2005) largely because the former come to school with a higher level of skill than the latter (Tach & Farkas, 2005). However, Tach and Farkas showed in their secondary analysis of ECLS-K data that SES still accounted for variance in ability group placement even after controlling for prior ability. There were also SES differences in teacher's perceptions of children's level of attention and behavioral regulation; such perceptions could have influenced group placement, as well. Longitudinal analyses showed that the gap widened between low- and high-SES students after they were placed in different ability groups.

THE ROLE OF ETHNICITY IN LANGUAGE AND LITERACY SKILL ACQUISITION

In keeping with the format used to make sense of gender and SES differences in language and literacy skills, we first discuss the kinds of ethnic differences that have been found for speaking, reading, and writing skills, and then, the possible explanations for these differences. By way of introduction, however, it is important to note that ethnic differences are not independent of SES differences because there are clear ethnic differences in family income and years of education. For example, the U.S. Census Bureau reports that the median incomes for Asian and White men in 2005 were $48,683 and $44,850, respectively (Webster & Bishaw, 2006). The corresponding medians for Black and Hispanic men were $34,433 and $27,380, respectively. In addition, the percentages of families living below the poverty line were 14%, 34%, 10%, and 28% for White, Black, Asian, and Hispanic families, respectively (DeNavas-Walt, Proctor, & Lee, 2006). In addition, the percentages of U.S. citizens older than 25 who have a bachelor's degree or higher are 26%, 14%, 44%, and 10% for White, Black, Asian, and Hispanic adults, respectively. Thus, whenever an ethnic or racial difference emerges, we must first consider the extent to which these differences are due to income and educational differences in the families.

Ethnic Differences That Require Explanation

Spoken Language Differences

With respect to spoken language, ethnic differences are more pronounced and consistent than those described above for gender differences. Consider, for example, several studies of low-income children in which the CDI was the outcome measure. Pan, Rowe, Spier, and Tamis-LeMonda (2004) found that White mothers reported that their 2-year-olds had larger productive vocabularies than Black ($p < .05$) or Hispanic mothers reported for their children ($p < .01$). Similarly, Roberts, Burchinal, and Durham (1999) found that, on average, Black children in their longitudinal study fell at the 53rd percentile when they were 18 months old, the 45th percentile when they were 24 months old, and the 27th percentile when they were 30 months old. Together, these studies of low-income children suggest that ethnic differences are not large at the earliest phases of language acquisition but are still detectable by age 2. This interpretation is corroborated by the findings of a large, national study ($N = 2,121$) of somewhat younger children at all income levels, in which it was observed that the effect sizes for productive vocabulary and sentence complexity for White and Black children were $d = 0.05$ at age 10 months and $d = 0.21$, at 16 months. In this age range, however, most children only have a few words in their vocabularies (see Chapter 4). Even so, Black children fall farther and farther behind as they progress through the preschool period.

Consistent with the idea that ethnic differences seem to increase after age 2, a variety of studies examining the performance of 3- to 5-year-old children on the PPVT-III have revealed fairly substantial differences. In contrast to the CDI that relies on maternal report, the PPVT-III asks children to choose the correct picture out of four possibilities that illustrates a word (e.g., *truck*) or phrase (e.g., *walking home*). Because children merely have to point to the correct picture rather than use the word themselves, the PPVT-III is said to be a measure of receptive vocabulary rather than productive vocabulary. Johnson et al. (1993) found that White 3-year-olds had significantly larger receptive vocabularies ($M = 105$) than Black 3-year-olds

($M = 88$; $d = 0.95$). The mean for the original standardization sample of 2,725 children (12% Black) for the PPVT-III was 100. In a study of 49 Black 3- to 5-year-olds in Head Start programs, Champion et al. (2003) reported a mean PPVT-III score of 87 ($d = 0.88$ between these children and the standardization mean). Nearly identical means were found by Pan et al. (2004) for 3-year-olds, Bracken, Howell, and Crain (1993) for 5-year-olds, and Howes, Sakai, Shinn, and Phillips (1995) for 2- to 5-year-olds. In Bracken et al., the effect size between White ($n = 38$) and Black children ($n = 22$) was $d = 1.52$. In a re-analysis of the Children of the National Longitudinal Survey of Youth of 1979 (CNLSY79) dataset that administered the PPVT to children every 4 months between the ages of 3 and 13, Farkas and Beron (2004) reported that there was a constant 20-word difference between White and Black children that was evident even at the first testing ($d > 1.0$). It grew no smaller or wider with age. In addition, an analysis of the scores at each testing suggested that Black children were approximately 1 year behind White children (i.e., White children knew certain words approximately 1 year earlier than Black children). However, further analyses showed that SES accounted for much of the difference between White and Black children.

Unfortunately, moderate to large ethnic differences are not limited to the CDI and PPVT-III. Rescorla and Achenbach (2002) found effect sizes of $d = 0.50$ for vocabulary and $d = 0.39$ for phrases when they gave the Language Development Survey (LDS) to a national probability sample of 278 White and Black children who were between the ages of 18 and 35 months. Scheffner-Hammer, Pennock-Roman, Rzasa, and Tomblin (2002) gave the second edition of the Test of Language Development—Primary (TOLD-2P) to 1,481 White 6-year-olds and 235 Black 6-year-olds. The effect sizes for the five component subtests were $d = 0.69$ (picture vocabulary), $d = 0.68$ (oral vocabulary), $d = 0.51$ (grammatic understanding), $d = 0.39$ (sentence imitation), and $d = 0.60$ (grammatic closure).

Thus, by the time children enter first grade, a variety of measures reveal ethnic differences in spoken language that are moderately large and consistent. Given arguments presented in previous chapters of this book, such differences should translate into ethnic differences in reading and writing skills when children enter elementary school. In what follows, we consider this possibility.

Reading

Although one could attempt to estimate effect sizes for reading using a handful of smaller-scale studies that exist in the literature (e.g., Stevenson, Chen, & Uttal, 1990), it is preferable to either (1) wait until enough additional studies are conducted to perform a meta-analysis that generates a meaningful average difference, or (2) construct effect sizes from several well-designed, large-scale studies in which representative samples of children were given carefully crafted, standardized assessments. The 2005 NAEP report is an example of the latter kind of study (Perie, Grigg, & Donahue, 2005). In 2005, several hundred thousand children in the 4th, 8th, and 12th grades were given an assessment based on a theoretical framework designed by experts in reading. On the basis of their performance on individual items, children were assigned scores ranging from 0 to 500. The scaled scores, in turn, corresponded to one of three levels of performance. For example, 4th grade children who scored in the range of 208 to 237 were assigned to the "basic" level of achievement. Children at this level were attributed the ability to (1) understand the overall meaning of what they read, (2) make obvious connections between the text and their own experiences, and (3) extend the ideas in the text by making simple inferences. Fourth graders who scored between 238 and 267, in contrast, were assigned to the "proficient level" because they showed the same skills as those in the "basic" level but also showed a more advanced level of comprehension and inference making. Children at the highest "advanced" level had scores greater than 267. The latter demonstrated the same skills as children at the basic and proficient levels but showed additional skills such as the ability to generalize about topics in the reading selections, show an awareness of how authors use literary devices, judge texts critically, and provide well-thought-out answers. At the 8th and 12th grades, comparable (but more advanced) frameworks were used to assign children to the basic, proficient, and advanced categories.

The last three NAEPs for reading (2002, 2003, and 2005) revealed that White ($M = 229$) and Asian 4th graders ($M = 229$) performed significantly better than Black ($M = 200$) and Hispanic 4th graders ($M = 203$) (Donahue, Daane, & Jin, 2005). The differences between the two top-scoring groups (White, Asian) and the two lower-scoring groups (Black, Hispanic) corresponded to large effect sizes that were comparable in size to those reported above for the PPVT-III ($d = 0.85$). It is also notable that whereas the means for White and Asian students correspond (unimpressively) to the high end of the basic level, the means for Black and Hispanic students fell just below the cutoff for the basic level. At the 8th grade, the story was pretty much the same. White and Asian students (M's of 271 and 271, respectively) performed significantly better than Black and Hispanic students (M's of 243 and 246, respectively). The effect sizes in this case were slightly smaller but still substantial ($d = 0.79$). Whereas the means for Black and Hispanic students were now just above the cutoff for the basic level, the means for White and Hispanic students were once again below the cutoff for the advanced level. Whereas the 2005 NAEP did not assess the reading skills of 12th graders, the 2002 NAEP did include this age group. As was found for younger ages, White and Asian students (M's = 292, 286, respectively) performed significantly better than Black and Hispanic students (M's = 267, 273, respectively). The largest effect size in this case was smaller than that found at younger ages (d = 0.69), but this finding could reflect the fact that a greater proportion of Black and Hispanic students drop out of high school than White and Asian students. In 2004, for example, the percentages of White, Black, and Hispanic students who dropped out were 6%, 12%, and 24%, respectively (Laird, DeBell, & Chapman, 2006).

Writing

As for ethnic differences in writing skills, too few small-scale studies have been conducted to compute reliable average effect sizes, so the best strategy once again is to turn to well-designed, large-scale studies such as NAEP. In 2002, the writing skills of 276,000 students at the 4th, 8th, and 12th grades were assessed. Children were given timed writing tasks to perform such as completing a story about a child discovering a castle in his or her backyard, or writing a persuasive argument to a friend. Scores could range between 0 and 300, and specific ranges of scores corresponded to basic, proficient, and advanced levels. For example, at the 4th grade, scores ranging between 115 and 175 were assigned to the basic level, scores ranging between 176 and 224 were assigned to the proficient level, and scores above 224 were assigned to the advanced level. Students performing at basic level demonstrated the ability to (1) respond appropriately to the assigned task in form, content, and language, (2) use some supporting details in their answer, (3) organize their response, and (4) demonstrate sufficient command of spelling, grammar, punctuation, and capitalization to communicate adequately to the reader.

The average scores for White, Asian, Black, and Hispanic 4th graders were 161, 167, 140, and 141, respectively. Whereas the effect size between White and Asian students was d = 0.18, the effect size between Asian and Black students was d = 0.79. Moreover, whereas the means for White and Asian students corresponded to the high end of the basic level, the means for Black and Hispanic students fell closer to the lower end of the basic level. At the 8th grade, the effect sizes between the two higher scoring groups (White, Asian) and two lower scoring groups (Black, Hispanic) were approximately d = 0.72; at the 12th grade, the effect sizes were approximately d = 0.63. Thus, the ethnic gap seemed to become smaller over time, but the finding for 12th graders could once again reflect the higher rate of dropping out in Black and Hispanic students.

Explaining These Ethnic Differences

In sum, then, ethnic differences are relatively small before age 2 but increase in size from that point on. By fourth grade, they are large for both reading and writing. As noted above for explanations of gender and SES differences, a useful way to investigate the possible origin of these ethnic differences is to ask two central questions that derive from the O–P framework. In particular, given that children cannot acquire skills unless they are given opportunities to learn and have the propensity to take advantage of these opportunities, the framework implies that one should ask the following questions about ethnic differences: (1) Have children in some groups (e.g., White or Asian children) been given more opportunities to learn language and literacy skills than children in other groups (e.g., Black or Hispanic children)? and (2) Are children in some groups more willing or able to take advantage of these opportunities? Let's consider answers to these questions in turn.

Opportunity Differences

In the case of opportunities, for example, is it the case that White and Asian parents converse more with their children than Black or Hispanic parents? Are White and Asian parents more likely to read books with their children (or read them in certain ways) than Black or Hispanic parents? Are White and Asian students more likely to be assigned to higher reading groups than Black or Hispanic students? Do teachers interact more (or more favorably) with White students during language arts lessons than with Black or Hispanic students?

Earlier, we noted the differences between high-SES, middle-SES, and low-SES mothers that were revealed in Hart and Risley's (1995) observational study. High-SES mothers not only communicated more with their children, they also communicated in ways that are likely to promote language growth. Here we can note that whereas all of the high-SES parents were White, all of the low-SES mothers on welfare were Black. Thus, any ethnic or racial differences that emerged in communication styles could largely be attributed to SES differences.

In addition to ethnic differences in conversation patterns, a further locus for ethnic differences in the domain of opportunity could be in the extent and nature of book reading in families of different ethnicities. There, again, are few studies that directly focus on this topic, but the existing studies are certainly suggestive. In one study conducted in the Netherlands (Leseman & de Jong, 1998), reading behaviors of native Dutch (*n* = 47), immigrant Turkish (*n* = 19), and immigrant Surinamese parents (*n* = 23) were recorded. The authors reported that there was a high degree of overlap in the behaviors expressed by the parents in each group, but there were also some noticeable differences. For example, whereas the Dutch mothers showed a higher level of "going beyond the text" in higher-level ways (e.g., explaining what was happening, making evaluative statements, and extending comments made by children), the Turkish and Surinamese mothers were more likely to repeat the text verbatim or complete narrative sentences started by their children. In another study conducted in the United States, Anderson-Yockel and Haynes (1994) likewise found considerable overlap in the reading behaviors of 10 White lower-income mothers and 10 African American lower-income mothers. The primary differences pertained to the fact that White mothers asked a greater number of "wh-" (e.g., what or where) questions and "yes–no" questions than Black mothers. No differences emerged for behaviors such as labeling referents in pictures, descriptions, or providing positive and negative feedback. However, the lack of difference in some cases could be due to the small sample size for each group. For labeling, the means were 24.55 (White) versus 15.28 (d = 0.54). In addition, the White mothers reported reading books to their children 4 times a week compared to 2.8 times a week reported by the Black mothers.

Despite the small sample sizes in the Anderson-Yokel and Haynes study, such findings for book reading are comparable for those that we discovered in an unpublished secondary analysis of the ECLS-K database. As noted above, in the ECLS-K, a large national sample of kindergarteners (N = 17,401) were followed until they reached the end of third grade. At the first assessment in the fall of their kindergarten year, parents were interviewed about a variety of matters including how often they read to their children. Whereas 87% of White mothers reported that they read books to their children at least 3 times a week, 50% said they read to their children every day. The corresponding figures for other ethnic groups were: Asian (77%, at least 3 times a week; 46% every day), Hispanic (71%, at least 3 times a week; 39%, everyday), and Black (68%, at least 3 times a week; 35% everyday). In addition, there were significant differences in the numbers of books their children were reported to have. White children were reported to have significantly more books (M = 95.31) than Asian children (M = 49.22), who had significantly more than Hispanic (M = 42.92) and Black children (M = 39.62). The means for Black and Hispanic children did not differ. Thus, it would seem that White and Asian children are read to more often and have access to a wider variety of books than Black and Hispanic children.

Besides conversational differences and book reading differences, a third aspect of opportunities to acquire literacy skills pertains to whether there are ethnic differences in ability group assignment once children enter first grade. The answer is once again clearly "yes" that there are ethnic differences in this form of opportunity (Oakes, 2005). White and Asian students are much more likely to be assigned to the higher reading groups than Black or Hispanic students beginning in first grade. To a large extent, this differential assignment reflects ethnic differences in the level of skill that children bring to first grade. That is, children found to have advanced skills at the start of first grade are assigned to the higher reading groups. Oakes (2005) argues, however, that there are also ethnic and racial biases in the assignment of children to ability groups that may supercede or enhance differences manifested in entry test scores. She also argues that standardized tests are not valid for low-income minority children. The nature and amount of reading experience clearly differs among reading groups (i.e., top reading groups read more often and more challenging works), so White and Asian students are provided with more opportunities to learn once in school, as well. Moreover, some have argued that the differences caused by ability grouping are further exacerbated by effects that occur within groups. Tate (1995), for example, argues that even when children of different ethnic and racial groups are in the same ability group with the same teacher, the interactions of teachers and students differ according to ethnicity. Hence, he argues that it is wrong to assume that being in the same classroom means that children were given the same opportunity to learn.

In sum, then, there is evidence that children in different ethnic groups are given differing amounts of exposure to experiences that could foster growth in their spoken language and literacy skills. These differences are present both before children start and during their formal schooling. According to the O–P framework, these differences in opportunities should produce differences in the level of literacy skill that children demonstrate on standardized reading and writing assessments.

Propensity Differences

Earlier it was noted that the O–P framework implies that one should ask the following questions about ethnic differences:

1. Have children in some groups (e.g., White or Asian children) been given more opportunities to learn language and literacy skills than children in other groups (e.g., Black or Hispanic children)?
2. Are children in some groups more willing or more able to take advantage of these opportunities?

We answered the first of these questions in the previous section on opportunity differences. Here, we turn to the second question.

Is it the case that White students are more prone to take advantage of opportunities to learn reading and writing skills in 1st through 12th grades because they are more willing and able to do so? Byrnes and Miller (2007) subdivided the propensity to learn into cognitive, motivational, and self-regulatory aspects. The cognitive aspects primarily include having the prerequisite skills needed to learn material that is presented at a certain level. Although there are large ethnic differences in the level of prerequisite skill children bring to first grade (Lee & Burkham, 2002), children are placed into reading groups using prerequisite skills as a guide and are taught at the level dictated by these skills. Hence, one would not expect ethnic differences in cognitive propensity to be the primary factor to explain increasing gaps with age as much as ability grouping itself. As for motivational propensity, there is no evidence of ethnic or racial differences in self-reported motivation in the early grades (Graham, 1994). If anything, Black students report having stronger motivation to read than White students (e.g., Baker & Wigfield, 1999). Thus, one would not appeal to motivational differences to argue that children in one group were more willing to take advantage of opportunities. There may be self-regulatory differences, however, in that teachers in the ECLS-K study rated White and Asian first graders as being higher than Black and Hispanic first graders on dimensions such as being attentive, persistent, eager to learn, independent, flexible, and organized (Byrnes & Wasik, 2008). On the composite scale that could range from 1 to 4, the ratings for Asian students ($M = 3.26$) were significantly higher than the ratings for White students ($M = 3.09$), which were significantly higher than the ratings for Hispanic ($M = 2.98$) and Black students ($M = 2.81$). The gap between the Asian and Black students amounts to an effect size of $d = 0.65$. According to the O–P framework, students who are more self-regulated are more likely to benefit from opportunities to learn than students who are less self-regulated. Thus, of the three aspects of the propensity to learn, the largest ethnic differences are for prerequisite skills and self-regulation. Given ability grouping, self-regulation differences could be the primary factor responsible for any further increases in ethnic differences in literacy skills that accrue after first grade.

Why Are There Differences in Opportunities and Propensities?

We have seen that there are ethnic differences in three aspects of the opportunity to acquire language and literacy skills (i.e., amount and style of parent communication with children, amount and style of book reading, and ability grouping), as well as ethnic differences in two aspects of the propensity to acquire these skills (i.e., the language and literacy skills that children bring to first grade and degree of self-regulation evident in first grade). Collectively, these differences in opportunities and propensities could explain the large ethnic gaps in reading and writing achievement that are evident by the fourth grade. However, the O–P framework suggests that it is useful to ask follow-up questions as to why these differences in opportunities and propensities emerged in the first place.

As noted above, we have a good sense as to why there are ethnic differences in ability grouping because children in various ethnic groups differ in the level of skill they bring to first grade, and the assignment process may not be as systematic or unbiased as it could be (Oakes, 2005). However, it is not clear why there are ethnic and SES-based differences in the amount and style of talk directed at children and the amount and style of book reading. Higher-SES parents presumably have a clearer sense of the need for their children to be ready for school (both academically and behaviorally) than lower-SES parents. They may also be more likely to view themselves as being responsible for imparting knowledge to their children and more likely to have the time and resources to impart this knowledge (or, alternatively, the resources to enroll their children in preschools or nursery schools); lower-SES parents may not view themselves being responsible for imparting school-related knowledge and may wait for teachers to impart knowledge when children enter first grade. In addition, even when they do view themselves as having a role in getting their children ready for school, they may lack the time to provide school-related skills and the financial resources to enroll their children in preschool. The ECLS-K database reveals that whereas 55% of White and Asian children attended a daycare center, preschool, or nursery school prior to kindergarten, only 32% of Black, Hispanic, and Native American children did.

As to the question, *why are White and Asian children more likely than Black or Hispanic children to come to first grade with the propensities they need to benefit from literacy instruction?* we have seen that differing preschool opportunities lead to their having differing levels of the prerequisite skills needed to be placed in more advanced reading groups. Children in these groups do not differ in their motivational profiles, so they all seem equally willing to engage in learning opportunities in first grade. There are, however, ethnic differences in their self-regulation or approach to learning. As noted above, kindergarten and first-grade teachers in the ECLS-K study rated White and Asian students as being more attentive, persistent, eager to learn, independent, flexible, and organized than Black or Hispanic children. Some have argued that this difference in aspects of behavioral readiness stem from differences in the parenting styles of White and Asian parents on the one hand and Black and Hispanic parents on the other (e.g., Brooks-Gunn & Markman, 2005). Brooks-Gunn and Markman (2005) report that when researchers measuring readiness gaps control for parenting differences, the ethnic gaps narrow by 25–50%. In addition, training programs have been successful in helping low-income parents engage in strategies that are likely to instill the behavioral, self-regulatory skills that children need to be successful in school. Low-income mothers can also be trained to read books to their children in ways that are effective for vocabulary growth and other aspects of emergent literacy (e.g., Hargrave & Sénéchal, 2000; Huebner & Meltzoff, 2005).

Summary

Ethnic differences in language skills start off fairly small and grow over time. By the time children enter first grade, there are already appreciable differences in their literacy skills, as well. These differences emerge because children of well-educated parents experience more frequent opportunities to acquire language and literacy skills. After first grade begins, differences are exacerbated because of (1) ethnic differences in the assignment to ability groups and (2) ethnic differences in children's self-regulation.

THE ROLE OF DIALECT IN LANGUAGE AND LITERACY SKILL ACQUISITION

The fourth sociocultural factor that has been implicated in studies of the language and literacy skills of students is dialect. In what follows, we explore the role of dialect by providing answers to three questions: (1) What is a dialect? (2) Is there evidence that dialect affects the acquisition of reading skills? and (3) What should teachers do when their students' dialects differ from Standard English?

What Is a Dialect?

Linguists define *dialect* as a regional or social variety of a language that is (1) distinguished by its pronunciation, grammar, or vocabulary, and (2) recognized as being different from the standard literary language or speech pattern of the culture in which it exists (e.g., Schilling-Estes, 2006). To illustrate, there are distinct dialects of Spanish evident in countries such as Spain, Mexico, and Venezuela. Similarly, there are distinct dialects of English evident in countries such as the United Kingdom, the United States, Australia, Canada, and India. In each case, words are pronounced somewhat differently, grammatical constructions are considered appropriate in some of these countries but not others, and different words are sometimes used for the same objects (e.g., *truck* and *elevator* in the United States vs. *lorry* and *lift* in the United Kingdom). Yet, the varieties are all considered the same language (e.g., English).

As the definition above implies, moreover, there are also various dialects within the same country. Consider, for example, the different dialects of English that can be found in cities such as Chicago (Illinois), Boston

(Massachusetts), Fargo (North Dakota), and New Orleans (Louisiana) in the United States. Although there is considerable overlap among these dialects in terms of pronunciation, word use, and grammar, there are also identifiable differences that often lead people to say that there are certain "accents" (e.g., a Boston accent or a southern accent) or styles of speaking.

One further dialectical difference that has generated considerable interest among linguists (and also considerable controversy within and outside the field of linguistics) is the difference between *Standard English (SE)* and *African American Vernacular English (AAVE)* (Charity et al., 2004). AAVE has also been called Black English, Black English Vernacular, and Ebonics. It differs from SE in several ways including the omission of final consonants (e.g., the final sound in the word *bad*), reduction of final consonant clusters (e.g., *mos* instead of *most; hep* instead of *help*), and substituting stops or labiodental fricatives for interdental fricatives (e.g., *dis* instead of *this, bof* instead of *both*). There are also grammatical differences in areas such as omitting or using the nonstandard forms of the verb "to be," nonstandard past tense constructions (e.g., *I don't know what happen*), missing auxiliaries (e.g., *What he do?*), and lack of agreement in number or subject-verb relations (e.g., *50 cent* instead of *50 cents; there go the rainbow* instead of *there goes the rainbow*) (Jackson & Roberts, 2001).

Given the close connections between language and literacy skills that have been emphasized repeatedly in this book, there is good reason to expect that dialectical differences could be part of the explanation for to why some children have a harder time learning to read than others (Snow et al., 1998). Among other things, sight vocabulary of written words maps onto spoken vocabulary, graphemes correspond to specific phonemes, and grammatical competence in spoken language predicts reading comprehension (NICHD Early Child Care Research Network, 2005). However, the fact that there are grounds for suspecting a role for dialect is not the same as providing data that dialect is important. Is there evidence that dialect does, in fact, predict the level of reading skill that a child attains? In other words, to what extent is dialect an aspect of propensity that could explain children's ability to take advantage of opportunities to acquire reading skills? If dialect does predict, what should teachers do about dialectical differences (if anything)?

Is There Evidence That Dialect Affects the Acquisition of Reading Skills?

Although researchers have argued since the 1960s (at least) that dialect probably does make a difference in the process of learning to read, there are surprisingly few studies in the literature that confirm this claim. Before describing the handful of studies that have been conducted, it is important to point out that dialect is normally confounded with other variables that predict growth in reading skills such as SES, race, phonological processing, and vocabulary size. In order to prove that dialect matters, these other variables have to be statistically controlled. For example, if certain struggling readers are both low-income and speakers of AAVE, how can one know for sure that it is AAVE and not income that is responsible?

With that in mind, we can consider four studies that have examined the association between dialect and reading. In the first, Thurmond (1977) created two versions of the same standardized reading test and gave one version to groups of White ($n = 20$) and Black students ($n = 26$) who were enrolled in low-track classes in an urban high school. One version of the reading test was the standard form that had passages written in SE. Thurmond created the other version by using her own knowledge of AAVE to convert the same passages written in SE to AAVE. She found that Black students performed significantly better on the AAVE version than they performed on the SE version. However, White students did not perform significantly worse on the AAVE version, which poses problems for her hypothesis. There was also no indication that the White and Black students were from the same SES stratum.

Taking a different approach, Hart, Guthrie, and Winfield (1980) hypothesized that phonological differences between SE and AAVE would interfere with first graders' ability to learn spelling–sound correspondences. They noted that the tendency in AAVE to sometimes drop the final consonant cluster in words that end in *t* or *d* would create homonyms in AAVE that are not present in SE. For example, dropping the final sound in *told* could create two homonyms that differ in meaning (i.e., *toll* as in payment to cross a bridge and *toll* for saying something in the past). To examine the consequences of this phenomenon, they created three sets of stimulus materials and presented them to low-SES Black children who spoke AAVE ($n = 15$), low-SES White children ($n = 15$), and middle-SES White children ($n = 15$). One set was called "dialect free" because the stimulus words in the set (e.g., *dog*) would not be pronounced differently by White and Black children in ways that create homonyms only for one group. A second set was called "dialect-conflict/homonym" because the words would be pronounced differently by the groups in ways that create homonyms only for the Black children (e.g., *told*). The third set was called "dialect-conflict/nonhomonym" because White and Black children would pronounce them differently, but homonyms would not be created (e.g., *land*). In the first part or phase of the test, the experimenter showed a card with a word on it and simultaneously said the word. For half of the cards, she would leave off the final consonant. For all cards, the child was asked to say, "yes" if the spoken word matched the printed word. Next came a decoding phase in which the same cards were presented, but the child had to pronounce them, not the experimenter. Errors in pronunciation were noted. Results for the first phase showed no differences among the three groups in recognizing when the spoken word matched the written word. However, for the second decoding phase, low-SES Black children made more pronunciation errors than low- and middle-SES White children. They further noted that the probability was 36% that a low-SES child would correctly decode a word when he or she had correctly identified matches or mismatches in phase I. The corresponding percentage for low-SES White children was 61%, which suggested they were more equipped to convert their receptive language skills to productive language skills.

In a third study, Steffensen, Reynolds, McClure, and Guthrie (1982) presented speakers of SE and AAVE with a cloze task in which they had to insert either content words or verbs in the sentences of a passage that had such words omitted. Then, in the second part of the study, children had to supply appropriate time adverbials (e.g., . . . *for 20 years* in *He had been living there for 20 years*) in 15 short paragraphs. Results showed that the AAVE speakers made more errors than SE speakers when inserting missing verbs in the cloze task in the first part of the study, but no differences were found for content words. AAVE speakers also had considerably more difficulty choosing the correct time adverbial based on tense.

In the fourth and most recent study, Charity et al. (2004) expected that some speakers of AAVE would know more about SE than might be evident in their normal conversations in natural settings. In addition, they expected that those who knew more would be more equipped to learn how to read than those who knew less. To measure familiarity with SE, children had to imitate sentences that had just been dictated by an experimenter in SE. The goal was to see whether familiarity predicted reading achievement in a sample of 217 low-income Black children who attended schools in Cleveland, New Orleans, and Washington, DC. From the imitation task, a phonological score and grammatical score was derived. Results showed that the partial correlations (controlling for memory, SES, and location) between SE familiarity and reading measures ranged between .30 and .58 in kindergarteners, first graders, and second graders. These findings suggest that children did seem to become better readers when they showed more familiarity with SE. However, there is reason to think that a child who can imitate a sentence that has been presented orally has some skill in the area of phonological processing. As noted in Chapter 4, phonological processing skill is one of the best predictors of becoming a good reader. Without a control for phonological processing, it cannot be said for certain that dialect per se contributed to the results, but the findings are certainly suggestive.

Summary

Although the evidence is not completely airtight, the four studies collectively suggest that dialect may indeed pose problems for children when their own dialect does not match SE. In terms of the O–P framework, then, dialect could be an aspect of propensity that could explain differences in children's ability to take advantage of opportunities to acquire reading skills. However, methodological shortcomings of these studies (e.g., small sample size, not all relevant factors have been controlled) preclude the possibility, for now, of knowing for certain the degree to which dialect is a key factor relative to other factors in the opportunity and propensity categories. Additional studies are clearly needed.

What Should Teachers Do When Their Students' Dialects Differ from Standard English?

It turns out that this question has sparked a number of heated debates in the United States since the 1960s. The most recent flare-up occurred in the 1990s when the Oakland, California, school district attempted to implement an Ebonics curriculum as a strategy to elevate the performance of their children (Perry & Delpit, 1998). The two positions on this issue can be summarized as such. Some look upon AAVE as a form of slang or an imperfect form of the higher-level dialect known as SE (Delpit, 1998). These individuals also argue that AAVE could interfere with a children's ability to read and that speaking in this manner would put an individual at a disadvantage in the job market. As such, AAVE should not be encouraged or modeled by teachers. If anything, teachers should do what they can to correct children when they hear aspects of AAVE used instead of SE in a particular situation.

Advocates on the other side of the debate, in contrast, argue that AAVE is not a degenerate form of SE or slang. Rather, they argue that it is a complex dialect in its own right that should be considered on par with SE (Delpit, 1998). In addition, language forms are central to issues of culture, community, and identity. Expressing oneself through the AAVE dialect is part of what it means to be an engaged and valued member of a community of individuals who also use this dialect in day-to-day interactions. Advocates argue that it is not right to ask someone to give up that aspect of their social identity; moreover, those being asked to change would find the request offensive and denigrating. Asking someone to do so is repressive and reflects perceptions of power and dominance in the culture. Sociocultural theories also argue that language is the primary means through which cultural values and understandings are transmitted from one generation to the next (Vygotsky, 1978). Asking someone to abandon his or her first language is asking the person to abandon his or her cultural beliefs and traditions. Further, just as advocates of bilingual education argue that non-English-speaking immigrants should be taught content (e.g., math) in their own native tongue for several years until they learn English, advocates of the second "encourage AAVE" perspective argue that classroom discourse and reading materials should be grounded in AAVE. They note that, eventually, children will acquire SE on their own and will flexibly use it in the contexts that call for it (e.g., work contexts, school contexts) but then switch back to AAVE in contexts that call for AAVE (e.g., chatting with a friend in the neighborhood). Finally, they argue that much of the firestorm over Ebonics was due to misrepresentations in the media. The Oakland board did not call for the elimination of SE and complete immersion in AAVE. Rather, they called for an infusion of AAVE dialogue and reading materials, combined with an emphasis on phonics instruction and activities that highlight similarities and differences between SE and AAVE in a nonthreatening way.

So, which of these positions is the right way to proceed? Deciding among these perspectives requires that we first analyze them to see which aspects are open to empirical refutation or confirmation and which aspects are not empirical in this sense because they reflect a set of values. The claims of the first "discourage AAVE" position that could be evaluated empirically include the claims that (1) AAVE could interfere with a children's ability to read and (2) speaking in this manner would put an individual at a disadvantage in the job market. Well-designed studies could be conducted to see whether each of these claims is true. We have already seen that the jury is still out in the case of dialect because additional studies are needed. As for the link between dialect and employability, quite a number of studies have been conducted but most of these have asked undergraduates (not actual employers) to rate the employability of taped speakers. In addition, whereas speakers of AAVE have been rated by undergraduates as being less suited only for executive positions (as predicted), studies of other dialects show that a speaker's ethnicity matters more to these judgments than his or her dialect (Cargile, 2000; Carlson & McHenry, 2006; Singer & Eder, 1989). Thus, the jury may still be out on the second claim, as well.

As for the values aspect of the first position, there are claims or assumptions that are not open to empirical refutation because they concern beliefs about what is important or how people should behave. Advocates of the first position seem to insinuate that everyone *should* express themselves in SE because it is the official, sanctioned, and more advanced language of the U.S. culture; moreover, there is something desirable or virtuous about having all students conform to the canons of SE.

As for the empirical and value-based claims of the second "encourage AAVE" position, the empirical claims include the suggestion that speakers of AAVE find it offensive and repressive to be corrected by teachers when they deviate from SE, that achievement will be higher if the curriculum is infused with AAVE, and that children will eventually acquire facility in SE on their own and show the ability to switch dialects depending on the circumstance. Systematic reviews of the evidence in support of these claims are currently lacking.

The values-based claims include the following: (1) It is not appropriate to impose the language and customs of the larger culture on communities that speak AAVE (doing so amounts to hegemony), and (2) all dialects should be valued and respected equally (i.e., one is not a better, more advanced, or more preferred way to speak).

In principle, then, evidence could accrue to help decide among these positions, but the values inherent in the two positions will make a resolution difficult to obtain. If nothing else, values and personal agendas can prompt people to disregard any evidence that accrues against one's position (Klaczynski, 2000). Thus, we predict that the Ebonics debate will linger on for many years. A lack of resolution means that school systems will remain in limbo as they grapple with what to do.

CONCLUSIONS

In this chapter, we have examined the evidence that gender, SES, ethnicity, and dialect are related to the rate at which children acquire language and literacy skills. We noted that gender, SES, and ethnicity are considered distal factors in the O–P framework because they can be used to explain why some children were given, or sought out, more opportunities to converse, read, or write than other children. Dialect, in contrast, was said to be a propensity factor that could explain why some children are more equipped to benefit from opportunities to learn than other children.

We saw that modest gender differences are found for sentence complexity during the preschool years (favoring girls), vocabulary and verbal fluency during the elementary school years (favoring boys), reading comprehension on challenging tests in older students (favoring girls), and writing quality and quantity in older students (favoring girls). All other differences are fairly trivial. In contrast, ethnic differences are relatively small before age 2 but increase from that point on. By fourth grade, they are large for both reading and writing and remain large through high school (favoring White and Asian students). The findings for SES mirror those for ethnicity, which should be the case given that SES and ethnicity are often confounded (e.g., the SES of White students is higher than the SES of Black students).

Discussion Topic: Use the O–P framework to design an intervention that would eliminate gender, SES, or ethnic differences. In other words, how would one target distal, opportunity, or propensity factors in the lives of these students? How would one increase or improve opportunities? How are motivational and cognitive propensities fostered? What could parents or teachers do differently? When would the intervention begin?

PART V

Instructional Techniques and Programs

12

General Principles
of Effective Instruction

In Chapter 1, it was noted that the selection of topics in Chapters 3 through 10 was guided by three main assumptions. The first was that *teaching is a goal-directed activity*. In other words, teachers are trying to accomplish certain things when they give a lecture on some topic or ask students to engage in various activities at school or at home. Successful teachers know how to accomplish their goals and do so on a regular basis. Unsuccessful teachers, in contrast, try to make things happen in their classrooms but have trouble getting the results that they (or the people they answer to) want.

The second assumption was that *teachers are more likely to attain their instructional goals on a regular basis if they have a detailed understanding of the inner workings of their students' minds than if they lack this understanding*. In Chapters 3 through 10, you were provided with this "inner workings" knowledge every time answers were given to the "nature of" question that was asked in most of these chapters (e.g., "the nature of spoken language competence"; "the nature of writing skill"). Teachers who have this "inner workings" knowledge have the *conceptual knowledge they need to understand and select appropriate instructional procedures*.

The third guiding assumption was that *education is a developmental mechanism* that fosters the acquisition of skills and transforms students from being in less optimal developmental states to being in more optimal states (see Chapter 1). Every time developmental mechanisms and the component processes of skills were revealed in Chapters 3 through 10, it became rather straightforward to figure out what should be done to enhance language and literacy skills of a particular kind. For example, when it was shown that (1) middle-SES parents converse more with their children and converse in different ways than lower-SES parents, and (2) middle-SES children come to first grade with a higher level of spoken language skill than lower-SES children, the implication is that one could enhance the spoken language skills of lower-SES children using an intervention that draws on the behaviors of the middle-SES parents. For example, lower-SES parents or day care providers could be trained to read to their children or converse with them in the manner of higher-SES parents. Such a derivative approach has been found to be successful (e.g., Hargrave & Sénéchal, 2000; Wasik, Bond, & Hindman, 2006).

However, in order for a derivative approach to be even more successful, it should be in line with both the domain-specific theories and research presented in Chapters 3 through 10, and with the principles that derive from domain-general theories and frameworks that apply to the learning of any content area. This chapter presents some of these domain-general principles. At the end of the chapter, you will be asked to use these principles to evaluate the instructional strategies and programs that are presented in Chapter 13. For example, one principle is that instructional activities should be meaningful for children. Each of the programs presented in Chapter 13 can be rated in terms of its meaningfulness.

As a prelude to understanding the importance of the general principles, however, it is useful to first acknowledge and explain the centrality of decision making in instructional competence. That is, in order to understand how principles help teachers make better decisions, we need to first understand what it means to make good decisions and how decision-making skills help teachers be more successful.

EFFECTIVE TEACHERS ARE SKILLED DECISION MAKERS IN THE CLASSROOM

To say that instruction is a goal-directed activity is to say that teachers engage in instruction-related behaviors to accomplish something in particular. For example, a teacher might think that by explaining a topic in a particular way, students will understand it better. Similarly, another teacher might expect that students would prefer to acquire certain ideas in science by engaging in a group project instead of listening to a lecture about the same ideas. In both cases, teachers expect that certain outcomes would occur (e.g., students would understand ideas better) if they engage in certain behaviors (e.g., explaining these ideas in a specific way). In addition, these examples illustrate the fact that in choosing to engage in certain behaviors (e.g., telling students to form groups to work on a project), teachers are also choosing to *not* engage in other behaviors (e.g., lecturing on a topic). Therefore, it should be apparent that all teachers make multiple decisions throughout a school day. However, we also know that only some of these teachers accomplish goals such as raising student achievement on a regular basis. It follows, then, that successful teachers must be highly skilled decision makers (Borko & Shavelson, 1983; Good & Brophy, 1990; Manley-Casimir & Wassermann, 1989).

To more fully understand the connection between decision making and classroom success, it is helpful to flesh out the construct of decision making a little further. Although contemporary theories suggest that competent decision making involves a number of component skills, two are particularly important: *accurate causal knowledge* and the *ability to coordinate multiple goals* (Byrnes, 2005). If teachers are choosing to engage in particular activities in order to accomplish certain goals, they are unlikely to accomplish these goals if they are mistaken about what consequences are likely to follow from their actions. For example, consider the case of a first-grade teacher who (wrongly) believes that children only need a single exposure of a printed word to learn its proper spelling and reliably recognize this word in the future. Such a belief may prompt this teacher to only present new words once rather than give children ample repeated exposures. As a result, we would expect that students assigned to this teacher would show poorer sight word reading at the end of first grade than students of another teacher who did use repetition. Thus, accurate causal knowledge helps teachers identify and implement actions that will be likely to lead to the outcomes they want. In other words, accurate causal knowledge helps teachers make better decisions.

In addition to having accurate causal knowledge, the second aspect of competent teaching relates to the fact that there usually are several different ways to accomplish the same goal. For example, the same material could either be presented in a way that students find entertaining and interesting, or presented in a way that students find dry and uninteresting. Competent decision-makers figure out ways to accomplish several goals at once (Byrnes, Miller, & Reynolds, 1999). To illustrate, consider the case of a preschool teacher who wants children to learn how to spell their own names. One way to accomplish this goal is to have each child go to the blackboard every day and write his or her name five times. A second way is to use children's names as the password that has to be entered when the children log on to the computer in their classroom to play a favorite game. A third way is to assign children tasks each day (e.g., snack helper) and put their names next to these tasks on cards on the classroom wall. As these examples illustrate, all three strategies are causally effective for accomplishing the same goal of having children learn their names, but the second and third approach are more interesting and motivating than the first. Thus, if teachers have multiple goals such as "helping students learn their names" (goal 1) and "maintaining student interest and motivation" (goal 2), teachers demonstrate a higher level of decision-making skill when they figure out how to accomplish both goals than when they accomplish only one of these goals.

Ideally, effective teachers recognize that they could create classroom environments and assign tasks that not only lead to substantial increases in knowledge over the course of an academic year (a cognitive goal), but also lead to other outcomes such as students (1) feeling good about what they have accomplished (a motivational, emotional goal), (2) feeling self-efficacious about their ability to accomplish learning tasks in a subject area (a motivational goal), (3) feeling like a valued member of the classroom community (a social goal), and (4) maintaining an interest in learning more about a particular topic area (a motivational goal). The principles to be discussed in the next section are geared toward providing insight into how to accomplish one or more of these goals.

However, it is important to note that these principles have to be tempered by the fact that in most classrooms in the United States, teachers face a number of constraints that may limit their ability to accomplish multiple goals even if they wanted to. For example, if teachers are required to cover content within a specific timeframe (e.g., 2 weeks), but they want to implement an instructional strategy that is very time-consuming, they will ultimately decide that they cannot implement that strategy. Thus, *effective teachers who have time constraints recognize the importance of implementing strategies that are efficient.* For example, *discovery learning*, which consists of teachers setting a goal of having students figure out solutions or answers completely on their own, can be very effective for promoting interest and understanding, but it is not very efficient. In contrast, *direct instruction*, which consists of teachers walking children through solutions in a step-by-step manner, is highly efficient and the fastest way to go, but children may not develop the same level of understanding and interest that they would develop with discovery learning. Once again, we see the need for teachers to figure out ways to accomplish multiple goals.

A second kind of constraint that could affect decisions pertains to the costs associated with a particular strategy. To illustrate, consider the case of teachers who attend a conference or workshop in which a new instructional strategy to promote literacy skills is presented. These teachers may use their highly developed conceptual knowledge of the inner workings of student minds to judge that this new instructional strategy is likely to be successful in terms of its ability to raise student test scores and student motivation levels. However, they may also use their knowledge of their school's funding to judge that they could not afford to purchase the materials required to implement this program. These teachers would have to reluctantly decide against using this strategy.

Other kinds of constrains include (1) school policies regarding the faithful implementation of a particular curriculum package (i.e., teachers are not free to improvise or implement it in a way that they think is more effective than the manner proposed by the developers of the package) and

(2) sociocultural pressures exerted by principals, other teachers in the school, or parents who have strongly held beliefs against using particular strategies, materials, or approaches.

Because effective teachers are skilled decision makers who try to accomplish several goals at once, they would be unlikely to adopt instructional strategies that (1) would not work within time limits imposed by their school systems, (2) would be more expensive than their school or they could afford, or (3) would meet considerable resistance from colleagues or parents. Rather, they would adopt ways to work within constraints to satisfy the primary cognitive and motivational goals that they have for their students.

As will become clear later in this chapter, any of the instructional strategies that are presented in the next chapter can be rated in terms of (1) its compatibility with domain-specific theories (e.g., on vocabulary learning), (2) its compatibility with domain-general principles (to be described next), (3) its efficiency, (4) its costs, and (5) the likelihood that it would be received in a negative manner by interested and influential parties.

DOMAIN-GENERAL PRINCIPLES OF EFFECTIVE INSTRUCTION

We have noted that competent decision makers have accurate causal knowledge of the likely consequences of their actions. In other words, they know the difference between teaching strategies that are likely to "work" and teaching strategies that are unlikely to "work." In this section, we provide some initial insight into ways to tell the difference between ineffective and effective approaches by considering the extent to which these approaches are compatible with four domain-general principles. These principles derive from the claims of domain-general theories of learning, cognitive development, or motivation that have considerable empirical support for many (but not all) of their claims: *Principle 1: Learning activities should be meaningful*; *Principle 2: Routines, repetition, and exposure are important*; *Principle 3: Learning activities should be appropriately challenging*; and *Principle 4: Instruction should involve a combination of scaffolding, modeling, and fading*. Let's examine each of these principles in turn.

Principle 1: Learning Activities Should Be Meaningful

Some of the most influential theoretical perspectives that have emerged in the past 100 years have emphasized the importance of having children engage in meaningful activities. For example, Jean Piaget, John Dewey, Lev Vygotsky, Gestalt psychologists, and Schema theorists all stress the centrality of meaning in the learning process (Nelson, 1996; Piaget & Inhelder, 1969; Vygotsky, 1978). However, each perspective characterizes meaning in a somewhat different way. For example, Schema theorists and Piagetians equate meaning with *children's ability to understand an activity and its products*. For example, some activities to promote phonological processing skills ask children to listen to a set of three words (e.g., *bear, hair,* and *tree*) and identify the word that does not sound like the others (i.e., *tree*). Although a 5-year-old would probably understand what he or she is being asked to do, a 2-year-old probably would not. The idea of identifying a member of a set that does *not* fit may be rather foreign to young children, and explanations of this concept would probably sail over their heads. Similarly, just as a fourth grader may have difficulty understanding why the answer to the problem $\frac{1}{2} + \frac{1}{4}$ is $\frac{3}{4}$, *a 3-year-old may not understand why the answer to the request "What would the word pink sound like if we dropped its last sound?" is the word pin*. The answers to the math and phonological-processing questions can be thought of as the products of mental activities. Correct answers will either make sense to children or they will not. So, when a strategy from the next chapter is evaluated, we can ask, are children in some target age range likely to understand this activity or the answers to questions about this activity?

A second way that activities can be judged to be meaningful is if *children can see the relevance of the activity to goals that they are trying to accomplish in a particular situation*. Piaget argued in his early books on infancy (Piaget, 1952) and later books with titles such as *Success and Understanding* (Piaget, 1978) that children try to invent procedures for accomplishing certain ends. At first, they might stumble upon, or be shown, a solution that leads to success. Eventually, after thinking about the problem a little further and solving related problems, they gain the conceptual knowledge they need to understand why the solution was successful. In other words, they are often successful before they understand why. Once this conceptual understanding is achieved, however, they can behave in a highly intelligent way when presented with a class of similar problems and become more successful in their problem-solving attempts than they would be without the understanding.

The Piagetian approach differs somewhat from the approach of Siegler and colleagues who have demonstrated that children readily adopt a more successful strategy when shown it (e.g., Siegler & Crowley, 1994). For example, when trying to win at tic-tac-toe, there is a strategy that quickly allows a player to create two possible routes to win that the opponent can do little about. After being shown this strategy, children adopt it immediately because they can see how they would always beat their opponent when they use it. The difference between the approaches of Piaget and Siegler may derive from the fact that whereas Piaget selected children who did not yet understand an activity, Siegler selected children who already understood it (e.g., how to play tic-tac-toe). The basic idea of both approaches, however, is that children will tend to be more successful when they not only are shown a strategy but understand why it works and how it helps them accomplish their goals (e.g., win a game).

The relevance of goal-relevant meaning for literacy learning is apparent when one contrasts various approaches to vocabulary instruction. When children are acquiring spoken language in natural contexts (e.g., conversations with their mothers), they have communicative goals (see Chapter 3), but they may also have other goals such as getting their mothers to give them a desired object (e.g., a favorite toy or food item). We learned in Chapter 5 that children learn an average of 5 to 6 new words per day simply by having communicative goals and learning words relevant to these goals as they converse or listen to stories. In other words, they may be highly interested in some object (e.g., a favorite television or book character) and want to learn the name of this object. Such words are learned must faster and more readily than other words that are also presented by parents. These findings suggest that classrooms could promote vocabulary development by instigating goals in children and creating contexts in which new words could help them accomplish their goals. For example, they may ask children to research some topic and present the information to the class. Here, they would have communicative goals regarding the need to explain certain concepts to the class, and the terms associated with these concepts help them meet these communicative goals. Such an approach would contrast with a more standard approach in which children are given the task of memorizing 20 new words every 2 weeks using vocabulary workbooks. In the latter, they are not learning words to satisfy communicative goals. Rather, they are learning words to satisfy goals such as getting a good grade on a vocabulary test. So, when evaluating strategies in the next chapter, we can ask, would children consider this activity a way of learning something that will help them accomplish communicative or literacy goals?

A third way to characterize meaning is related to the second but derives from various sociocultural theories of learning (Rogoff & Chavajay, 1995). These theories suggest that all learning takes place within culturally defined contexts such as "dinner time at home," "book reading before bedtime at home," "math class at school," and "religious services at church." In these contexts, participants engage in activities that have some association with the larger culture in which they are embedded. Meal times, for example, often involve eating foods that are common in, and representative of, their own culture but not other cultures (e.g., egg rolls in Japan vs. hamburgers in the United States). In schools, children are asked to acquire skills that are judged to be important by policymakers in their societies. In industrialized cultures, these skills may pertain to domains such as math or reading. In developing cultures, in contrast, the skills may relate to farming, tailoring, or weaving. Sociocultural theorists argue that the cognitive development of children is "inherently involved in their participation in sociocultural activities" (Rogoff & Chavajay, 1995, p. 871). As they participate in these contexts, they become more skilled, especially when given guidance from others who have more expertise than they have. As they gain expertise, moreover, the manner in which they participate changes. For example, they may be given more difficult tasks or leadership roles.

Sociocultural theorists also argue that activities in a domain only gain meaning when they are part of culturally defined contexts and are carried out for authentic, goal-directed reasons. In other words, the activity and the context are inextricably bound (Barab & Plucker, 2002). This perspective contrasts sharply with a more traditional view that suggests that students have abilities in their minds that may or may not be deployed in various situations. When abilities are viewed as traits possessed by individuals and housed in their minds, instruction becomes viewed as the process of transmitting content into minds. In addition, advocates of the traditional view see nothing problematic in divorcing a skill from its natural context, decomposing it into component operations, and asking students to practice the components until they achieve mastery. So, for example, instead of having students acquire math skills in real contexts that call for these skills (e.g., while cooking, shopping, or reconciling a checkbook), the skills are taught one by one using worksheets. Similarly, instead of having students acquire reading skills as they read authentic children's books, teachers might create word families using flash cards with rhyming words on them. Because the words are read out of their natural context, the activity is said to be meaningless by sociocultural theorists. So, yet another way to judge the activities presented in the next chapter is to ask, are children participating in actual, culturally defined contexts as they attempt to master the skill? How similar is the context to actual contexts in the world in which the skill would be applied?

Principle 2: Routines, Repetition, and Exposure Are Important

To readers familiar with the history of psychological theory and education in the United States, it may seem strange to discuss a principle about repetition right after discussing a principle on meaning. After all, many of the perspectives listed in the previous section (e.g., Vygotsky) gained prominence because they argued against perspectives that primarily emphasized repetition (e.g., Pavlov, Thorndike). However, close inspection of the points made by many of the scholars who emphasized meaning suggests that they did not argue that repetition does not matter or should be completely avoided; rather, they argued that learning is optimized when instruction involves *both* meaning and repetition. The perspectives of theorists such as Ivan Pavlov and E. L. Thorndike were judged to be problematic because they *only* emphasized repetition.

When Piaget discussed his concepts of *schemes, assimilation,* and *accommodation,* for example, he pointed out that children need to regularly implement newly acquired schemes in order for them to become consolidated (Byrnes, 2001a; Piaget, 1952). A scheme is a goal-directed behavior or sequence of behaviors. In infancy, schemes may be limited to simple behaviors that are directed at objects (e.g., the "grasping" scheme used to pick up objects) or combinations of actions to attain goals (e.g., using the pushing scheme first to remove an obstacle, followed by the grasping scheme to pick up the desired object). In older children, scheme may pertain to skills related to sports (e.g., bicycling, skiing) or strategies used in math or science (e.g., varying all factors except one in an experiment). Whatever the level, schemes are applied in a progressively wider manner to more situations. If schemes are not repeated, they do not become consolidated and may be lost from a child's repertoire. In addition, Piaget argued that children cannot eventually imagine themselves engaging in a behavior in a planning stage until they repeatedly perform an activity. That is, they must perform an activity a number of times before they can form a mental representation of this activity and see themselves acting out the behavior in their minds. Repetition promotes the internalization of the scheme.

In an analogous way, Vygotsky argued that children need to repeatedly grapple with a newly acquired skill and slowly appropriate it (i.e., make it their own) within meaningful, culturally defined contexts. An action does not become meaningful for children the first time it is presented. Rather, it slowly acquires a cultural meaning over time as children participate in contexts and engage in the action repeatedly (Vygotsky, 1978).

Schema theorists have likewise pointed out that *event representations* require a number of repetitions before they become organizing principles for children's and adults' behaviors (Anderson, 1990; Nelson, 1996). Event representations (also called *scripts*) are mental representations that capture the commonalities in events such as going to a restaurant, birthday party, funeral, and so on. Informally, event representations tell us what normally happens at certain kinds of events. To have a sense of an event representation, take a moment and write down the series of events that happen when one goes to a restaurant or attends a birthday party. In the case of a restaurant, the following events tend to occur in the following order: (1) you are met by a hostess who asks, "How many?" (2) you are escorted to your seat and handed a menu, (3) you are approached by a server who asks if you would like a drink, and so on. Young children acquire analogous event representations of recurring situations in their home lives such as lunch time, bath time, library visits, and trips to fast food restaurants. Somewhat older children in structured settings in preschool, kindergarten, and later grades also acquire event representations of recurrent events (e.g., snack time) and the order of these events during a school day. Nelson (1996) argues that a considerable amount of language acquisition occurs within these recurrent situations. Event representations provide structure to these situations and highlight categories of central objects and activities. Once highlighted, children learn the names of these objects and activities. Thus, event representations are thought to be powerful facilitators of language acquisition that are acquired as children repeatedly participate in the same activities. An event representation does not form during a single exposure.

Thus, three perspectives that are traditionally aligned with the construct of meaningful learning (i.e., Piaget, Vygotsky, and Schema theorists) also emphasized the importance of repetition in the service of goals. These accounts complement rather than contradict the accounts of other theorists who highlight the importance of repetition for promoting mental representations that are easily evoked from memory. A central tenet of cognitive psychology is that memory traces are more easily accessed when they are formed after a number of repeated exposures (Anderson, 2004). To illustrate, consider the trick used by successful business people to learn names. After being introduced to someone and being told the person's name, successful business people add the name to the end of many conversational turns (e.g., "Nice to meet you, Tom"; "How do you know the hostess, Tom?" "Well, you know, Tom, I have never really been a big fan of . . . "). In a large number of laboratory studies, cognitive psychologists have shown how recall is clearly a function of the number of practice trials and exposures. The only time when multiple exposures are not required is during "flashbulb" experiences in which something traumatic happens (e.g., the 911 events). All other experiences and facts are soon forgotten if repeated exposures do not occur.

In sum, theorists from a variety of perspectives agree that children rarely acquire knowledge in a single exposure. When evaluating programs and strategies in the next chapter, we can ask, does the program involve providing ample opportunities to repeat and practice a new language or literacy skill? Does it give time to consolidate a strategy or appropriate it?

Principle 3: Activities Should Be Appropriately Challenging

At least two cognitive theorists (i.e., Piaget, Vygotsky) and a variety of motivational theorists argue that teachers should occasionally cast instructional activities at a level that is just beyond their students' current cognitive level in order to maximize knowledge growth and motivation. From the cognitive standpoint, the argument is that students' knowledge may grow laterally (in terms of breadth) if material is presented at their current cognitive level, but their thinking will never advance beyond that level. Of course, a cognitive theorist would only agree with such a claim if he or she espoused the idea of qualitatively distinct levels of understanding or distinct levels of skill. For example, Piaget argued that children progress through four levels of thought between birth and adulthood (Piaget & Inhelder, 1969): the sensorimotor level (birth to about 18 months), the preoperations level (18 months to about 4 years old), the concrete operations level (5 to 10 years old), and the formal operations level (11 and beyond). At the preoperations level, children have mental representations that are very grounded in perceptual similarity. These representations may make them think (incorrectly) that whales and trout are both fish (or dogs and horses are both dogs) because the members of these two pairs bear some similarity in appearance. Concrete operational thought is more abstract and less grounded in physical appearance, so these children would be more equipped to understand that whales and dogs are similar because both are mammals (even though they do not look very much alike). Although a preschool teacher could promote lateral knowledge growth by presenting information about categories using only those cases that both fit the proper definition and share a resemblance to the prototypes for categories (e.g., dogs, horses, and cats in the case of *mammals* or *animals*), eventually children need to be challenged with cases that violate the perceptual similarity metric but fit the scientific definition (e.g., whales and humans in the case of *mammals*; humans and worms in the case of *animals*). In order to move from one level to the next higher level, Piaget argued that children need to be confronted with information that contradicts their current understanding.

Vygotsky (1978) agreed with the general premise of Piaget but took a somewhat different approach. He believed that intellectual skills are progressively mastered by children over time. When they first learn a skill (e.g., reading), they make many errors and rely heavily on teachers for corrective advice. After large amounts of practice and feedback from teachers, however, children ultimately reach a point at which they can perform the skill well on their own. In between the absolute-novice level and the complete-mastery level, there is a point at which a child could perform well if someone were to give him or her just a little help (e.g., a hint). For Vygotsky (1978, p. 86), the *zone of proximal development* is "the distance between the actual developmental level as determined by independent problem solving and the level of potential development as determined through problem solving under adult guidance or in collaboration with more capable peers." Teachers and peers foster intellectual growth by providing instruction at a level that is just beyond the level of independent mastery but still within a student's zone of proximal development.

To illustrate how the Piagetian and Vygotskian approaches would be applied to the case of literacy skills, consider the age trends reported in Chapter 4 for phonological processing. We learned that children progress from being able to hear whole words in the speech stream at about 10 to 12 months, to being able to hear portions of words that are larger than the phoneme level (e.g., syllables, onsets and rimes) by age 3, to being able to hear phonemes by age 5. Given these age trends, the Piagetian and Vygotskian approaches suggest that it would not be wise to attempt to move young children from hearing whole words to hearing phonemes in one step. However, it would be reasonable to move a child from the whole-word to syllable level or from the syllable to phoneme level. Both theorists would also agree that a child would never move from one level to the next with being challenged to do so.

However, it is important to re-emphasize a point made in Chapter 10 that care must be taken to maximize a child's level of success in order to foster an optimal level of motivation. All students prefer the experience of success over the experience of failure. If students are asked to perform tasks that they repeatedly perform poorly, they lose a sense of efficacy for these tasks and try very hard to avoid doing them. If we are forced to perform the tasks and cannot avoid them, we acquire a sense of learned helplessness (see Chapter 10). It is for this reason that we suggested that teachers need to occasionally challenge students. Classical motivation theorists assume that motivation is maximized when the likelihood of performing well on a task is 50%, but students themselves prefer to work on tasks in which the probability of success is closer to 90% (Clifford, 1991). The classical account is based on the assumption that tasks that are perceived as too easy or already mastered are boring to students. Conversely, tasks that are too difficult raise the specter of failure and embarrassment. Moderately challenging tasks maximize interest value and give the opportunity of feeling pride if success occurs.

For both cognitive and motivational reasons, then, literacy activities should be within a child's capacity but occasionally challenging, as well. When the programs and activities of the next chapter are evaluated, we can ask, how challenging would they be to students in the target age group? Would students find the task too easy or too hard? What is the likelihood that the activity would promote knowledge growth to the next level of performance?

Principle 4: Instruction Should Involve a Combination of Scaffolding, Guided Participation, Modeling, and Fading

In the sections on Principles 1 and 3 (on meaningfulness and challenge), we considered several constructs that happen to derive from core tenets of *the sociocultural perspective on learning*. In this section, we consider several other constructs from this perspective and provide further insight into their importance by making connections to other traditions in the fields of cognitive psychology and cognitive development. The constructs include scaffolding, guided participation, modeling, and fading.

The construct of *scaffolding* was alluded to in the previous section on Principle 3 when the zone of proximal development was discussed. It was noted that students can sometimes show a higher level of performance when given a little support from their teachers than when trying to solve a problem on their own. Examples of such support include (1) giving a hint, (2) demonstrating how to solve a few example problems first and then asking students to solve a similar one on their own, and (3) starting a problem and asking students to finish it (Vygotsky, 1978). Just as a real masonry scaffold allows a mason to build higher and higher courses of bricks, parents, teachers, and more capable peers can provide the supports that allow a student to reach a higher level of performance. To illustrate the concept of scaffolding with a literacy example, consider the following excerpt of a lesson in which a first-grade teacher in Wharton-McDonald, Pressley, and Hampston's (1998) study was teaching children about the word families that have the *-oa* (long *-a*) sound:

TEACHER: How about something that Mom puts in the oven—a kind of meat?

STUDENT 1: Meat loaf!

TEACHER: I was thinking of something else, but that's a good one too.

STUDENT 2: Roast beef!

TEACHER: Yes. *Roast.* Put that on your list.

STUDENT 3: *r-o-a-s-t.*

TEACHER: (*Writes* roast *on an easel pad.*) Does that look right?

STUDENTS: Yes.

TEACHER: OK. Now, I like that word that Kevin thought of. What was that?

STUDENT 1: *Loaf.*

TEACHER: OK. Put that on your lists. Kevin, how do you spell *loaf?*

STUDENT 1: *l-o-a-f.*

TEACHER: (*Writes* loaf *on the easel pad.*) OK. Now how about something that comes in a bar?

STUDENTS: Soap! (*A student spells* soap *and the teacher writes it on the pad.*)

TEACHER: What happens when you put wood in water?

STUDENTS: It floats!

TEACHER: What's something you wear when it is chilly outside?

STUDENT 4: A coat!

TEACHER: And what did Anthony wear in the story we read yesterday?

STUDENT 5: A cloak.

TEACHER: What's the difference between a coat and a cloak?

STUDENT 5: A cloak doesn't have any sleeves.

Several things are notable about this excerpt. The teacher could have presented the same material by herself on the easel pad by writing the words *roast*, *loaf*, *soap*, *coat*, and *cloak* and asking students to copy them down (a direct instruction approach). Conversely, she could have been more open-ended by asking students to spend 15 min coming up with their own examples of words in this family without any hints or help (a discovery learning approach). By taking a middle ground and using scaffolding, children themselves are coming up with the right answers but doing so in a more efficient manner. Although some would recommend the scaffolding approach over the direct instruction approach simply because it involves active learning on the part of students (and the premise that active learning is better is neither questioned nor analyzed further), another reason to recommend it derives from the work in the memory literature on the *generation effect* (e.g., McDaniel, Riegler, & Waddill, 1990). A number of studies have shown that when students are asked to actively process information in some way or come up with the memory strategy on their own, their performance is significantly higher than when they do not engage with the material in such ways. In addition, a skilled scaffolder is someone who knows what children already know and provides hints or other supports that help the children demonstrate this existing knowledge. It is possible for scaffolding attempts to fail because teachers either have misconceptions about what their students know or give prompts that are not especially effective. For example, imagine that the teacher said, "How about a kind of soil that has lots of organic material in it?" for the word *loam*. One would expect that few first graders would know this word. Or, for the word *oat*, imagine if the hint was, "A grain that has lots of soluble fiber."

Scaffolding is actually a more specific example of the more general approach known as *guided participation* (Rogoff & Chavajay, 1995). The modifier "guided" is included to distinguish the approach from discovery learning. Without guidance, students will often struggle to find good source materials or figure out how to constrain their search for answers. One could even argue that students may never arrive at the correct answer in some situations. Consider the (real) example in which math teachers have provided open-ended tasks to students with the goal that students would eventually discover the need for negative integers. It took several hundred years for mathematicians to do so, but, even then, only the brilliant mind of Descartes came up with this category of numbers. How likely is it that an average or even gifted high school student would invent negative integers without guidance? The term "participation" is included to denote the fact that development is taking place in culturally defined contexts in which there are roles and responsibilities that participants carry out. The suggestion is that all literacy learning activities should be culturally meaningful and authentic (as noted above) but also designed in ways that teachers provide enough guidance to help students come up with correct answers on their own, in an efficient manner.

As noted earlier, however, there is more than one way to provide support to students. The scaffolding example above illustrates a case in which students already know the solutions to problems but are having trouble retrieving it or knowing that the answer applies. In many other cases, students do not know how to proceed and need to be shown a solution. In the standard direct instruction approach, a teacher would walk students through a new solution in a step-by-step manner. Very often, the solution is presented in a detached manner (i.e., this is how it is done—by anyone). Here the focus is on the solution, not the teacher or any other problem-solver. Sociocultural theorists, in contrast, take a different approach. They advocate teachers *modeling* how they would solve the problem. In addition to showing the steps, teachers explain what they are doing and why. In this way, the discourse is more like a first-person narrative than a third-person description. After the solution is modeled a few times, teachers then ask students to imitate their actions and provide a similar verbal commentary.

As noted above, any solution that is more advanced than students can currently handle will be slowly appropriated by them as they make repeated attempts. Thus, teachers trained in the sociocultural framework expect that children's first attempts at imitation will be filled with false starts and other kinds of errors. As a result, teachers will need to observe students and provide feedback that helps students see which aspects of their attempts are on the right track and which are incorrect. With repeated attempts, the proportion of correct aspects will exceed the proportion of incorrect aspects. When this occurs, teachers need to provide less and less feedback. Sociocultural theorists call this progressive reduction in feedback *fading*. At the same time that teachers give away responsibility for success, students are taking on more and more responsibility. As they do, they slowly *internalize* successful strategies and become *self-regulated learners* rather than other-regulated learners. To get students to the point of being self-regulated, the three-step sequence has to be followed (i.e., modeling plus explanation, followed by student attempts at imitation, followed by feedback that progressively fades).

As the programs and strategies in the next chapter are presented, you can determine the extent to which the instructions imply that teachers should engage in the three-step sequence advocated by sociocultural theorists and whether scaffolding and other forms of guided participation are implicated. There is reason to think that strategies implemented according to the principles of sociocultural theory are more effective than strategies implemented according to principles of standard direct instruction or discovery learning approaches.

SUMMARY: IDENTIFYING EFFECTIVE APPROACHES

In this chapter, we have argued that successful teachers are skilled decision makers who know the difference between instructional approaches that are likely to be effective and instructional approaches that are unlikely to be effective. Throughout this book, we have argued that effective approaches are compatible with what we know about the inner workings of students' minds and developmental mechanisms. The chapters on spoken language competence, phonological processing, vocabulary, grammatical understanding, reading, writing, and motivation provide insight into these mental processes. Thus, the first step in evaluating any approach presented in the next chapter (or elsewhere) is to determine whether the approach is in line what we know about the nature and development of specific aspects of language or literacy skill (e.g., phonological processing). Just as a physician can judge whether a new medicine will be likely to work using his or her knowledge of the inner workings of biological systems of the human body, skilled teachers should be able to judge whether a new instructional technique is in line with how the mind works. In addition, however, we can also consider the extent to which approaches are in line with the four principles of effective instruction that derive from domain-general theories of learning and motivation.

To facilitate the evaluation process, we have created a six-step process for evaluating that focuses on issues of compatibility with domain-specific information in Chapters 3 through 10 and domain-general theories of learning. This guide can be revisited each time a particular approach is considered:

- *Step 1: Determine the focal skill that is being targeted.* For example, is the program designed to improve phonological awareness? Vocabulary? Reading comprehension?
- *Step 2: Identify the relevant chapters in this text that pertain to the*

focal skill. For example, if the program is designed to enhance phonological processing, refer to Chapter 4; if it targets writing skills, refer to Chapter 9; and so on. Note that the motivation chapter (Chapter 10) and brain chapter (Chapter 2) may apply to any of the targeted skills and should be consulted.

• *Step 3: Read the "nature of," "developmental trends," and "developmental mechanisms" sections of relevant chapters.* Find where the targeted age group falls in the developmental trends section and where they hope to be. The developmental mechanisms section describes the processes that cause increases in skills. Does the program include similar or related processes? For example, if the program is targeted at vocabulary and the developmental mechanisms section of Chapter 5 suggests that parent conversations and book reading improve vocabulary, does the program ask teachers to have conversations or read books with students? Programs that are consistent with the information in the relevant chapters should be rated higher than programs that are inconsistent. The consistent ones are more likely to work than the inconsistent ones.

• *Step 4: Determine the extent to which the program (1) would be meaningful to children (Principle 1 of this chapter), (2) involves sufficient repetition, exposure, or routines (Principle 2), (3) is appropriately challenging (Principle 3), and (4) involves scaffolding, guided participation, modeling, and fading (Principle 4).* Programs that are in line with these principles should be rated higher than programs that are not in line with or are silent on these principles.

• *Step 5: Evaluate the program in terms of its likely effect on the motivation of students.* Consult Chapter 10. Would students find it interesting? Would it promote their sense of self-efficacy? After being successful, would they feel pride?

• *Step 6: Finally, evaluate the program in terms of its efficiency, its costs, and the likelihood it would be received in a negative manner by interested and influential parties.* Remember that skilled decision makers try to accomplish multiple goals. Recommend an approach only if it is compatible with the inner processes of students' minds, likely to be motivating, and not problematic in terms of factors such as efficiency and costs. Is this approach practical? How expensive is it? Would it meet resistance? Are there other obstacles that stand in the way of it being implemented and successful?

13

Language and Literacy
Programs That Work

An essential part of educational research is translating theory into practice. In Chapters 3 through 9, the focus was on theory and research regarding: (1) the various component skills of language and literacy competencies, (2) age trends in the development of these skills and developmental mechanisms that explain these age trends, and (3) the specific problems that can occur when children do not develop the necessary precursors for reading. In Chapters 10 through 12, we discussed factors that help explain why some children respond to effective instruction more readily than others, and we also described some broad aspects of effective instruction. In this chapter, the focus becomes much more practical in that we describe specific examples of programs that were designed to improve children's language and literacy skills. Obviously, all of the strategies and techniques that are implied by theory and research are only useful if they can be applied to actual classrooms. We review interventions designed to teach struggling readers. The goal is to provide the reader with current reading interventions that have been successfully implemented in classrooms to help children learn to read.

The field of reading is flooded with numerous reading interventions that are available through publishers and other resources. The What Works Clearinghouse (*www.whatworks.ed.gov*) chronicles all of the new early literacy and beginning reading programs, including programs that show no discernable impact on children's literacy development. This chapter focuses on programs that have empirical data suggesting that the programs do promote children's literacy development. You will be asked to evaluate these programs in terms of their consistency with contemporary theories and research. In other words, you will be asked to figure out *why* these programs may work.

In order to narrow the focus of interventions presented in this chapter, the following selection criteria were used. First, all interventions selected were designed for children who are in preschool through third grade. In some instances, the programs can be used with older children, but here we focus on children in the early years as their reading skills are beginning to develop. Second, all of the programs focus on reading or precursor skills needed for the development of reading. For interventions that include other content areas, only the reading component will be presented. Third, only interventions that have research documenting their effectiveness were included. Using this selection criterion allows us to know with some certainty that the intervention has an empirically tested, positive impact on the children learning to read. Although this is not intended to be comprehensive review of all programs, the discussion provides a representative sample of effective language and literacy interventions.

As a way to systematically present the interventions, they are divided into three groups: (1) interventions that address emergent literacy skills that are precursors to reading, such as oral language development and vocabulary development, (2) interventions that address beginning reading skills, including word analysis and word recognition, and (3) interventions that focus specifically on comprehension strategies. Some programs focus both on the emergent language and literacy skills, which are important precursors for the development of reading skills.

INTERVENTIONS THAT DEVELOP EMERGENT LITERACY SKILLS

There are several commercially available emergent literacy programs that have been developed by experts in the field of reading. For example, Opening the World of Learning (OWLS), developed by Judith Schickedanz and David Dickinson (2005); Building Language for Literacy, by Susan Neuman, Catherine Snow, and Susan Canizares (2000); and Where Bright Futures Begin (2007), developed by a team of early literacy experts for Houghton Mifflin (Bredekamp, Morrow, & Pikulski, 2006), are widely used programs based on widely held beliefs about best practices in early childhood. Whereas all of these programs are based on contemporary theories and research in language and literacy (such as those presented in Chapters 3 through 9), they have not been compared to other programs in controlled experiments (at the time of this writing). As a result, they are not discussed in this chapter. Another program, Doors to Discovery, developed by Susan Landry and colleagues for the Wright Group, does have an evaluation that indicated that the program produced no discernable effects on children's early literacy skills (Assel, Landry, Swank, & Gunnewig, 2007). Therefore, this program was also not included in this review.

This section will review five programs: 1) Dialogic Reading, 2) the Johns Hopkins Language and Literacy project (JHLLP), 3) Sound Foundations, 4) Phonemic Awareness in Young Children: A Classroom Curriculum, and 5) Stepping Stones to Literacy (SSL). Two programs, Dialogic Reading and the JHLLP, focus on the development of language and vocabulary skills in young children. Sound Foundations and Phonemic Awareness in Young Children: A Classroom Curriculum are programs that develop phonemic awareness skills in young children. SSL focuses on phonemic awareness skills as well as awareness of print. All programs have been empirically evaluated with children at risk for reading failure and show positive effects for young children.

Dialogic Reading

Dialogic Reading is a method of reading picture books in which children are provided with multiple opportunities to talk and engage in conversation while the adult becomes an active listener, asking questions, adding information, and promoting the child's use of descriptive language. In Dialogic Reading, the adult helps the child become the teller of the story. The adult becomes the listener, the questioner, and the audience for the child. A method of questioning called PEER is used. In the PEER methods, the adult (1) Prompts the child to say something about the book, (2) Evaluates the child's response, (3) Expands the child's response by rephrasing and adding additional information to it, and (4) Repeats the prompt to make sure that the child has learned from the expansion. All of these strategies are done to increase the amount of conversation between the child and the adult. In addition, time is spent on developing children's vocabulary within the context of the storybook.

To date, 14 studies have been conducted on Dialogic Reading with preschoolers from various economic backgrounds and in one-to-one, small-group, and large-group situations. In the studies, children in the Dialogic Reading intervention consistently performed significantly better than children in comparison groups. For example, Whitehurst et al. (1988) investigated the impact of middle-income parents using Dialogic Reading techniques while reading one-on-one with their children. After a 1-month intervention, posttests on the Peabody Picture Vocabulary Test—Revised (PPVT—R) and Expressive One Word Picture Vocabulary Test (EOWPVT) indicated effect sizes of +0.69 and +1.10, respectively. Nine months after posttesting, children were tested on the same measures, yielding an effect size of +0.01 for the PPVT—R and +0.79 for the EOWPVT.

In a subsequent study, Whitehurst et al. (1994) examined the impact of using Dialogic Reading strategies at home, in day care, and in day care plus at home on low-income children's language and literacy development. During the 6-week intervention, day care teachers read daily for approximately 10 min and parents were given books to read at home; both parents and teachers were trained in Dialogic Reading techniques. The results indicated that for the PPVT—R, there was an effect size of +0.13 for day care only-condition and +0.24 for the day care plus home-reading condition. For the EOWPVT, the effect sizes were +0.18 for day care-only and +0.43 for day care-plus school. The double dose of reading at day care and at home had an impact on students' scores.

Read Together, Talk Together is the commercial program sold by Pearson Publishing, which is based on research in Dialogic Reading. The program includes teacher–parent notes, which will guide the adult reader, providing tips and sample questions for each of the 20 books. There are videotapes that show modeling of the Dialogic Reading approach.

Evaluation

In Chapter 12, a method for evaluating programs was described. It is reproduced here to guide the evaluation process. As you evaluate each program, you should progress through the following six steps:

- *Step 1: Determine the focal skill that is being targeted.* For example, is the program designed to improve phonological awareness? Vocabulary? Reading comprehension?
- *Step 2: Identify the relevant chapters in this text that pertain to the focal skill.* For example, if the program is designed to enhance phonological processing, refer to Chapter 4; if it targets writing skills, refer to Chapter 9; and so on. Note that the motivation chapter (Chapter 10) and brain chapter (Chapter 2) may apply to any of the targeted skills and should be consulted.
- *Step 3: Read the "nature of," "developmental trends," and "developmental mechanisms" sections of relevant chapters.* Find where the targeted age group falls in the developmental trends section and where they hope to be. The developmental mechanisms section describes the processes that cause increases in skills. Does the program include similar or related processes? For example, if the program is targeted at vocabulary and the developmental mechanisms section of Chapter 5 suggests that parent conversations and book reading improve vocabulary, does the program ask teachers to have conversations or read books? Programs that are consistent with the information in the relevant chapters should be rated higher than

programs that are inconsistent. The consistent ones are more likely to work than the inconsistent ones.

• *Step 4: Determine the extent to which the program (1) would be meaningful to children (Principle 1 of Chapter 12), (2) involves sufficient repetition, exposure, or routines (Principle 2), (3) is appropriately challenging (Principle 3), and (4) involves scaffolding, guided participation, modeling, and fading (Principle 4).* Programs that are in line with these principles should be rated higher than programs that are not in line with or are silent on these principles.

• *Step 5: Evaluate the program in terms of its likely effect on the motivation of children.* Consult Chapter 10. Would students find it interesting? Would it promote their sense of self-efficacy? After being successful, would they feel pride?

• *Step 6: Finally, evaluate the program in terms of its efficiency, its costs, and the likelihood it would be received in a negative manner by interested and influential parties.* Remember that skilled decision makers try to accomplish multiple goals. Recommend an approach only if it is compatible with the inner processes of students' minds, likely to be motivating, and not problematic in terms of factors such as efficiency and costs. Is this approach practical? How expensive is it? Would it meet resistance? Are there other obstacles that stand in the way of it being implemented and successful?

The Johns Hopkins Language and Literacy Project

The Johns Hopkins Language and Literacy Project (JHLLP) is a comprehensive professional development program designed to train teachers in specific strategies to enhance young children's language and literacy development. The JHLLP has two main components: (1) an intensive and ongoing staff development, and (2) lesson plans and materials that support the development of children's language and literacy.

Teachers are trained in five interactive modules: (1) interactive book reading, (2) guiding conversations across the curriculum, (3) phonemic awareness, (4) alphabet knowledge, and (5) writing. During training, teachers learn the importance of each training module, along with specific procedures for implementing activities that support children's language and literacy development. For example, in the interactive book reading module, Head Start teachers are guided through explanations of why book reading is important and how it contributes to language development. Teachers, then, receive explicit instructions on specific strategies for effectively reading a book. After the group training, JHLLP trainers model the procedures in each teacher's classroom. The teachers practice the strategies for 1 to 2 weeks; then they are observed and provided with feedback on how well they implemented the strategies in their classrooms.

In addition to training, JHLLP provides materials that support book reading and vocabulary development. Teachers receive prop boxes that correspond to the classroom themes such as *Welcome to School* or *What Grows in My Garden*. Prop boxes include books related to the theme, objects representing theme-related vocabulary in the books, and lesson plans detailing theme-related activities. The objects that represent the vocabulary words are presented to the children during the book-reading activities and are also available for children to play with during center time and free play. The books represent various genres including fiction, informational, and concept books. The comprehensive lesson plans outline theme-related book-reading and phonemic awareness activities, as well as art, center, and family involvement activities. The lesson plans are designed for teachers to follow as daily schedules and to adapt to the developmental age of their students.

Two studies show the effectiveness of JHLLP. Wasik and Bond (2001) implemented this program in a Title I preschool program. Half of the teachers were randomly assigned to participate in the language and literacy training, and the remaining half were not provided with training. Children in classrooms where the teachers were involved in the training, and the program materials were used, scored significantly better than children in no-treatment comparison classrooms on assessments of expressive and receptive vocabulary that was specific to the JHLLP curriculum. In addition, the children in the intervention classrooms scored significantly better than children in comparison classrooms on standardized receptive and expressive measures of vocabulary, the PPVT—R and the EOWPVT—3rd. Also, teachers who received the training created more opportunities in their classroom to talk with children and to use vocabulary words from the storybooks. Similar findings were found in Wasik, Bond, and Hindman's (2006) study in which JHLLP was implemented with Head Start teachers in a high-poverty, urban school district. Teachers were randomly assigned to either the intervention or comparison group. After a year of training that focused on teaching teachers to develop oral language and vocabulary skills with young children, the children were assessed on the PPVT—R and the EOWPVT—3rd. Children in the intervention classrooms performed significantly better on these measures of receptive and expressive vocabulary than children in classrooms where the teachers did not participate in the intervention.

Evaluation

Readers should use the six-step framework described above to evaluate this program (see Chapter 12). What focal skills are being targeted? What do we know about age trends for these skills and developmental mechanisms that promote them? Would the program be meaningful and challenging to children? Would it be motivating? What practical issues stand in the way of its being adopted or being implemented?

Sound Foundations

This program focuses on phoneme invariance by teaching children that different words can begin or end with the same sound (Byrne & Fielding-Barnsley, 1991a). The program uses a kit that includes large color posters depicting scenes with objects that are used to work on the phonemes and also games, worksheets, and an audiotape, all designed to teach the concept of sound-sharing among words.

A total of nine phonemes receive most attention. They are the continuant consonants /s/ (as in sit) and /l/, the stops /m/, /p/, /t/, and /g/, and the vowels /a/ (bat) and /e/ (bet). For each of the seven consonants there are two large pictorial posters, one containing many items beginning with the sound (e.g., sea, seal, sailor, sand) and one with items ending with the sound (e.g., bus, hippopotamus, horse, octopus). The posters for the vowels were beginning sounds only (e.g., ambulance, apple, acrobat). About 60% of the pictured items in each poster begin (or end) with the target sound.

For the nine key phonemes, as well as for the other phonemes represented by the remaining letters of the alphabet (b, c, d, f, and so on), there are worksheets that contain outline drawings of objects and characters. On each worksheet, about half of the items begin with the critical sound, and the child's task is to locate and color the target items. For the nine key phonemes (but not for the remainder), worksheets for end sounds were also created. In addition, there are outline drawings of each poster in which critical items can be colored.

Two card games were devised on the basis of four of the key sounds (/s/, /p/, /t/, and /l/). One is a form of dominoes with two pictured objects on each card. The children are required to join cards sharing beginning sounds (or ending sounds in a second version of the game). The other game consists of cards with just one picture on each, and it is played according to the rules of "snap." Children place the cards face up on a pile and say "snap" when the new card matches the top one on the pile for initial (or final) sound. The first child to identify the match collects the pile. Stories and jingles that repetitively emphasize the seven consonants in initial and final positions and the vowels in initial position are made up by the teacher to reinforce the sounds.

Sixty-four preschoolers were trained in the Sound Foundations program in groups of four to six for approximately half an hour per week for 12 weeks (Byrne & Fielding-Barnsley, 1991a). Training consisted of learning to classify items in the posters, worksheets, and games on the basis of shared sounds—searching the /s/ posters for the things beginning or ending with that phoneme, for instance. The use of small groups allowed for intensive teaching, with close monitoring of individual children.

The control group comprised 62 (originally 64) children from the same preschools who were exposed to the program materials for the same amount of time in similar-sized groups, with the same experimenter. The control children, however, did not receive instruction in phoneme identity—instead, they learned to classify items on formal or semantic grounds (e.g., color, shape, animacy, edibility). The main findings from the preschool phase of the study were that the experimental group showed greater gains in phonemic awareness than the control group, the improvement in phonemic awareness extended to sounds that were not part of the training program, and the experimental children performed better than the controls in a structured test of printed word decoding.

A year later, at the end of kindergarten, the experimental group children were significantly ahead of the controls on pseudoword decoding, though not on real word identification or spelling (Byrne & Fielding-Barnsley, 1993). The children were reclassified into two groups: those who passed the test of phoneme invariance at the end of preschool (which included 60 children from the experimental group and 16 from the control group) and those who did not pass (3 experimental group children and 40 controls). The ones who passed outperformed the ones who did not pass on all three measures of literacy development, namely decoding, word identification, and spelling. In general, therefore, the program could be judged a success in teaching the idea of sound-sharing among words and in supporting early decoding development. Additionally, children who had come to understand the concept of phoneme identity in preschool, from whatever source, showed advanced literacy development during their first year at school.

Studies conducted 2 and 3 years after the intervention (Byrne & Fielding-Barnsley, 1995) indicated that children who received the Sound Foundations instruction performed significantly better than children who did not receive the intervention. This suggests important evidence for the sustainability of the Sound Foundation intervention over time.

Evaluation

Use the six-step framework described above to evaluate this program along lines such as its consistency with contemporary theories and research, meaningfulness, effect on motivation, and practicality.

Phonemic Awareness in Young Children: A Classroom Curriculum

This program is based on an intervention developed by Lundberg, Frost, and Petersen (1988) and grounded in the premise that teaching phonemic awareness to preschool and kindergarten children will increase the chances of their developing later reading and writing skills (Ball & Blackman, 1991; Tangel & Blachman, 1992). As part of this program, children are engaged in series of games and activities that include nursery rhymes, rhymed stories, and rhyme production; segmentation of sentences into separate words and investigations of word lengths; clapping and dancing to rhythms; segmentation and blending of word-initial, word-final, and word-internal phonemes. The program is designed to be implemented 15 to 20 min per day. The activities in the program are sequenced from least difficult to most difficult.

The program also includes several assessment activities that allow teachers to determine skills children already have learned and skills that need to be developed. For example, activities are included that assess students' ability to count the number of syllables and phonemes in words and to recognize words that rhyme. These are all important indicators of children's phonological-processing skills.

Phonemic Awareness in Young Children: A Classroom Curriculum has been evaluated and the findings were positive. Lundberg, Frost, and Peterson (1998) compared kindergarteners who received training in this program to kindergarteners who were from a district that historically outscored them in academic measures. At the end of a year of training, the two groups were comparable in both letter knowledge and higher-order language comprehension. The experimental children were significantly superior to the controls in sensitivity to rhymes, syllables, word length, and most important, to phonemes. In a follow-up of the children in first grade, one year after the training program ended, the children were compared again on measures of word recognition and spelling tests. The children who had been in the Phonemic Awareness in Young Children curriculum outperformed children who were not in the program. Retesting at second grade showed that the experimental children's advantage remained and even increased slightly. These findings clearly show the positive impact that the phonological processing program has on preliteracy skills as well as reading.

Evaluation

Use the six-step framework to evaluate this program.

Stepping Stones to Literacy

Stepping Stones to Literacy (SSL) is an emergent literacy supplemental curriculum designed to promote listening, print conventions, phonological awareness, phonemic awareness, and serial processing–rapid naming (quickly naming familiar visual symbols and stimuli such as letters or colors). The program is for kindergarten and older preschool students who are considered to be underachieving readers, based on teacher's recommendations, assessments, and systematic screening. As part of the intervention, students participate in 10- to 20-min daily lessons in a small group or individually.

There are two components to the curriculum. The lesson book is designed to allow teachers to work one-on-one with students. It contains 25 complete lessons for a total of 15 hr of instructional time, plus a section on serial processing. For ease of use, these resources are spiral bound together in an easel-type book that stands up for viewing and instruction. The second component is the instructor's manual, which contains a short overview of the program, the research base that supports its use and effectiveness as a reading intervention tool, and classroom materials that can be reproduced. The curriculum consists of 25 lessons, for a total of 9–15 hr of instructional time.

Nelson, Benner, and Gonzalez (2005) conducted a randomized field trial of SSL in elementary schools serving low-income children in a medium-sized city. Thirty-six kindergartners with phonological processing difficulties and behavioral problems were randomly assigned to an experimental and comparison condition. All of the children were identified through a systematic behavior and prereading screening process. Children who exceeded the normative criteria on standardized behavior rating scales and correctly segmented less than 18 phonemes and identified less than 27 letter names participated. Children in the experimental condition ($n = 18$) received Stepping Stones in addition to the standard reading instruction provided in the classroom. Children in the comparison condition ($n = 18$) received the standard reading instruction provided in the classroom. The standard kindergarten reading curriculum included various teacher-designed reading, listening, and writing activities (e.g., shared reading, storytelling, phonological and phonemic awareness, theme presentation of the letter-of-the-week, letter sounds). The standard curriculum provided in the classroom was guided by the district outcomes (i.e., concepts of print, phonemic awareness, valuing reading, integrating reading with speaking and writing, and decoding). At the end of the year, all children were assessed on the Comprehensive Test of Phonological Processing (CTOPP) (Wagner, Torgesen, & Rashotte, 1999), phonological awareness (PA) and rapid automatized naming (RAN) clusters, and Dynamic Indicators of Basic Early Literacy Skills (DIBELS) (Good & Kaminski, 2002) probes, including letter naming fluency (LNF), initial sounds fluency (ISF), phoneme segmentation fluency (PSF), and nonsense word fluency (NWF).

The results indicated that children who received SSL made statistically significant gains on the CTOPP (ES = +1.18) and DIBELS (ES = +.89). The results indicate that SSL has a positive effect on children's phonological awareness, rapid naming skills, and alphabetic understanding (i.e., NWF). This intensive supplemental curriculum with a focus on phonological processing skills has been shown to have positive impact on a limited sample of children.

Evaluation

Use the six-step framework to evaluate this program.

INTERVENTIONS THAT DEVELOP READING SKILLS

In this section, programs that focus primarily on beginning reading and the ability to recognize and decode words will be presented. There are a total of seven interventions presented in this section. Five of the interventions, Success for All (SFA), Direct Instruction (DI), Exemplary Center for Reading Instruction (ECRI), Early Intervention in Reading (EIR), and Carbo Reading Styles Program are comprehensive in nature and are designed to be used in a group setting in classrooms. Two of the interventions, Reading Recovery and Early Steps, are designed to be implemented in one-to-one tutoring sessions. All of the interventions are representative of programs used with children who are at risk for reading failure and provide intensive instruction to prevent or remediate learning problems.

Success for All

The SFA program is one of the most extensively studied and comprehensive schoolwide reform model designed for both English- and Spanish-speaking populations. The most widely used component of SFA is the beginning reading program that focuses on kindergarten through third grade. The key components of the SFA model include a highly structured reading program, small teacher-student ratios for reading lessons, tutoring for identified students, assessments and regrouping assignments at 8 week intervals, and an onsite, reading curricula facilitator. The reading curriculum for kindergarten and first graders is phonics-based, and each lesson includes instruction on letter sounds along with reading of little books that are written using phonetically controlled text that correspond to the letter sounds presented in the lesson.

When children attain a second-grade reading level, they are placed in Reading Wings, an updated version of the Cooperative Integrated Reading and Composition program (CIRC) (Stevens, Madden, Slavin, & Farnish, 1987). CIRC includes a greater emphasis on comprehension strategy instruction, along with vocabulary building, decoding practices and story-related writing. Students who are struggling with lessons are provided with one-to-one tutoring in order to increase their opportunities to learn the material presented in class. The homogeneous grouping of students allows for instruction to be targeted to the needs of students with similar abilities and skills.

Numerous evaluations have supported the effectiveness of SFA. Longitudinal studies have taken place in 23 schools in 9 districts throughout the United States (Slavin & Fashola, 1998). In large scale, randomized field trail of SFA, 38 schools and nearly 4,000 students (grades K–2) were evaluated to determine the effects of the intervention. The results indicate that students in SFA classrooms were reading better than students in regular classrooms (Borman et al., 2005). After 1 year in SFA, kindergartners and 1st graders were scoring 2 months ahead of their peers in the comparison group on tests measuring their ability to decode words. These groups were equally matched on other measures of reading. At the end of 2 years, SFA students were decoding words an average of 4.7 months ahead of their peers in comparisons groups. SFA students also scored 1.3 months and 1.7 months ahead of the control students on measures of written passages and word identification. Results are currently being analyzed to determine the impact of students' reading after being in SFA for 3 years.

Although these finding clearly indicate that SFA has a positive impact on students' reading ability, the students are still not reading at grade level. Since the students who are involved in SFA are typically the most at risk for reading failure, trying to get students to achieve reading at grade level is a challenge.

Evaluation

Use the six-step framework to evaluate this program.

Direct Instruction/DISTAR

Direct Instruction for Teaching and Remediation (DISTAR) (also commonly known as Direct Instruction or DI) is one of the oldest, and perhaps, most controversial reading programs that is still widely used with students who are having difficulty learning to read. DI provides highly scripted lessons in which teachers are given the exact wording and precise directions for everything they do and say in class. Students progress through six series (levels) of reading materials and are given screening and placement tests before each level. Assessments occur at regular intervals. The instruction focuses on a phonetic approach to reading. Students begin with instruction on phonological processing, including rhyming, letter identification, and sounds, and they progress to blending and decoding. There is some emphasis on comprehension but not to the same degree as on phonics instruction.

DI has been widely studied; one of the most comprehensive evaluations was conducted at nine of the sites that were part of the original Follow Through (FT) sites. FT was a federally funded program in the 1960s designed to teach high-poverty children to successfully learn to read. In this study, there were 9,255 students in the intervention sites and 6,485 in the comparisons sites (Adams & Engelmann, 1996). DI was one of only two FT initiatives that showed positive effects.

Meyer (1984) conducted a study that examined the long-term positive effects of elementary students who had 3 and 4 years of DI and compared their achievements at the end of high school to those of matched control groups. More than 63% of DI students graduated from high school compared to 38% from the control group. In addition, DI students had lower dropout rates (28%) compared to the control group (46%).

In more recent work, Adams and Engelmann (1996) reviewed 350 research studies, 37 of which met a strict criterion for analysis, including having a control group. Examining the effect sizes for those DI programs that deal specifically with reading, language, or spelling, these researchers found that the mean effect size for reading (15 studies) was $d = .69$; for language (7 studies) was $d = +.49$; and for spelling (3 studies) it was $d = 1.33$. Although the effects have been consistently positive for DI, the program has met with much opposition because of its highly scripted lessons and lack of teacher input (Axelrod, Moyer, & Berry, 1990; Kim & Axlerod, 2005).

Evaluation

Use the six-step framework to evaluate this program.

Exemplary Center for Reading Instruction

The Exemplary Center for Reading Instruction (ECRI) is a professional development program for elementary and secondary teachers to learn to use effective strategies to prevent reading failure. Teachers are trained in specific strategies such as word recognition, writing skills related to decoding, vocabulary development, and comprehension monitoring. In addition, teachers are trained in classroom organizational and assessment strategies such as eliciting rapid and accurate responses, maintaining on-task behavior, administering formative and summative assessments, and using assessment data to impact instruction.

Students are homogeneously grouped according to their reading level. Within each of these groups, the teacher demonstrates skills and then prompts responses from students to ensure understanding. The students spend time practicing the demonstrated skills. During this practice time, the teacher works with individuals and small groups of students to help them achieve mastery of the content. Similar to SFA and DI, ECRI provides detailed instruction for teachers and encourages frequent assessment of student progress.

A large-scale evaluation of ECRI was conducted on second through seventh graders in Morgan County, Tennessee. The design compared ECRI students to other students who were being taught through a traditional commercial basal series. All students were assessed on the Stanford Achievement Test (SAT) of Reading Comprehension and Vocabulary. ECRI students outperformed those in the control group with effect sizes ranging from +.48 to +.90 in reading comprehension and from +.31 to +1.40 in vocabulary. In addition, evaluations without control groups in California and Texas indicated that children in ECRI made percentile gains from +6.4 to +25.7 (Reid, 1986, 1997).

Evaluation

Use the six-step framework to evaluate this program.

Carbo Reading Styles Program

This program is based on the research of Marie Carbo and a team of teachers that indicates that children have distinct reading styles predisposing them toward learning using specific reading techniques. The program is theme-based and uses a variety of activities and related literature to improve children's performance across all content areas. Teachers are trained to accommodate their students' strengths and weaknesses with a variety of effective reading strategies.

The Carbo Reading Styles program has six main components. Strategies of Instruction consists of recorded readings, manipulatives, and a variety of reading instruction methods to accommodate students' strengths. Strategy for Staffing and Scheduling includes the formation of teams and the use of coaching models, heterogeneous groups, and block scheduling to accommodate grade-level planning. Heterogeneous Grouping, in which students read for 1 to 2 hr per day, is implemented individually or in small groups. Parental Involvement strategies pertain to techniques to teach parents about their children's strengths and how to work with them at home in a variety of ways. Reading Style Inventory is used to identify students' key strengths and weaknesses in order to determine the most effective reading methods, materials, and strategies for each student. The Carbo Recorded-Book Method consists of brief segments of high-interest materials that are recorded on tape at below-normal speeds. Students listen to the materials repeatedly and then read the passages aloud to teachers.

Several studies have been conducted that document the effectiveness of this intervention. LaShell (1986) conducted a matched study of two groups of 90 students in grades 2 through 6 who were identified as LD. All of the students were pre-and post-tested on (1) the reading styles inventory (RSI) used to identify recommended reading methods, (2) the Oral Gray Reading

Test used to assess reading achievement, and (3) the Intellectual Achievement Responsibility Questionnaire used to measure locus of control. The intervention group was classified according the specific reading methodologies as recommended by the RSI and was taught using the Carbo method. The control group was taught using conventional methods. The results revealed that students in the intervention group achieved a 17-month gain in reading compared to those in the control group who achieved only a 4-month gain.

Barber, Carbo, and Thomasson (1998) conducted an evaluation in three school districts across grades 1 through 6 with a total of 269 children. Eight teachers used the Carbo method and eight used the district's traditional approach. Each site administered their district's standardized reading measures in the fall and spring of the year. Effect sizes for the treatment groups in grades 1 and 2 were positive, ranging from .47 to 2.37. However, for grade 3 through 6, the treatment groups did not perform as well, ranging from –.15 to .33. It appears that the instruction in the Carbo method may be more beneficial to younger readers.

Evaluation

Use the six-step framework to evaluate this program.

Early Interventions in Reading

Early Interventions in Reading (EIR) is a program developed by Barbara Taylor, a reading researcher and practitioner at the University of Minnesota. The program is designed to provide extra instruction to small groups of students in kindergarten through sixth grade who are identified as at risk for reading problems. The program focuses book reading and emergent literacy activities, along with professional development for teachers.

The kindergarten component of the program uses whole-class instruction with small-group follow-up for the children lowest in oral language and emergent literacy abilities. Book reading is a central activity, including listening to stories for enjoyment, discussion of these stories related to children's lives, creative dramatics, and emergent literacy development. Within book reading, concepts of print, rime, phonemic segmentation and blending, and letter and sound recognition are taught with emphasis on exposure—not mastery.

In first and second grade, teachers work with groups of 5 to 7 of the lowest-achieving children for about 20 to 30 min per day. The literacy instruction follows a routine and regular pace with regular monitoring of progress; instruction includes repeated reading of familiar stories, coached reading of a new story, phonemic awareness training and systematic phonics instruction, guided sentence writing, and vocabulary and comprehension instruction. The teacher focuses on coaching the children in strategies, in which they have been trained, that will make them become independent readers.

In grades 3 and 4, the teacher works with small groups for 20 min per day, 4 days a week, using narrative and informational picture books and focusing on attacking multisyllabic words and fluency, vocabulary, and comprehension strategies. In grade 4, children learn to use the reciprocal teaching model. Here, students take turns practicing the skills in front of the others while the teacher provides feedback. On the 4th day, the children read their picture book to a younger child who is in the grade 1 or 2 EIR program, and they coach these younger children as they read their EIR story.

There have been several evaluations conducted on the EIR program (for a complete review see Taylor, 2001). Taylor, Frye, Short, and Shearer (1992) randomly assigned 12 of 13 first-grade teachers in four schools in a large midwestern school district to either the EIR intervention or to a nontreatment control condition. There were 31 low-achieving readers who received the EIR intervention and 28 children in the control group. The EIR children received 20 min a day of the EIR instruction in addition to their regular classroom instruction. During a 3-day cycle, the children reread familiar books, read a new story with the teacher, and engaged in phonemic awareness and phonics activities called "sound boxes" or "making words." On days 2 and 3, the children reread familiar stories with their teacher, reread their new story, and wrote a sentence about the story. During the lessons, the teacher coached and provided feedback to the child on his or her performance. The children did as much reading and writing as possible. The children also spent 5 min per day reading a new story to an assistant trained in coaching word recognition (to help the children work on word identification skills). In the control group, the six teachers reported that they spent extra time with their lowest-achieving readers, reteaching reading skills and listening to the children read. In both the intervention and control classes, all teachers followed the district's whole language approach. Therefore, the EIR intervention provided the word-attack strategies that were missing from the district curriculum.

The results indicate that after controlling for fall scores on the Gates–MacGinitie Reading Test, the EIR students had significantly higher scores than the control students on the Gates–MacGinitie Reading Test reading comprehension subtest, $t(55) = 2.19$, $p = .03$, effect size = $+0.56$. The EIR children went from the mean percentile of 29 on the Gates in the fall to a mean of 37 in the spring. In contrast, the control students went from a mean percentile of 34 in the fall to a mean of 27 in the spring. In addition, 50% of the EIR children could read a trade book with 93% accuracy, compared to the children in the comparison group who could read the same book with only 23% accuracy. These results suggest that the EIR intervention had a significant impact on the reading and comprehension skills of first graders. Subsequent studies did not use a randomized treatment control design and also found positive effects for EIR (Taylor, 1995, 2001)

Evaluation

Use the six-step framework to explain why this program was effective. Is it consistent with theories and research? Is it motivating? Is it practical?

Reading Recovery

Reading Recovery (RR) is a widely known and much researched one-to-one tutoring intervention primarily for first graders who are at risk for reading failure. RR was developed by New Zealand educator and researcher Marie M. Clay. In RR, individual students receive a half-hour lesson each school day for 12 to 20 weeks with a specially trained RR teacher. As soon as students can read within the average range of their class and demonstrate that they can continue to achieve, their lessons are discontinued, and new students begin individual instruction.

The first few weeks of the RR session is called "roaming around the known," and involves the teacher determining where the students' strengths and weaknesses lie and what skills and concepts need to be addressed during tutoring. Each lesson consists of reading familiar stories, reading a story that was read for the first time the day before, working with letters and/or words using magnetic letters, writing a story, assembling a cut-up story, and reading a new book. Within these activities, the teacher demonstrates problem-solving strategies and provides just enough support to help the child develop effective strategies.

A significant amount of research has been conducted on RR, and the findings consistently indicate that the intervention is effective. In a comprehensive analysis of the data on RR, Shanahan and Barr (1995) published an independent evaluation of RR. The goal of the authors was to offer a thorough, systematic analysis of all available empirical work on RR. They reviewed all published evaluations and any available unpublished ones that included sufficient basic information to allow meaningful analysis. When it was possible to analyze data in a more precise and direct manner, data were combined across studies.

Their review concluded that many children who were in RR eventually improved to the level of their average-achieving peers. They asserted that RR was effective. It is clear that many children leave the program with well-developed reading strategies, including phonemic awareness and knowledge of spelling. Although some initially low-achieving students will succeed without RR, evidence indicates that many others would need such an intervention.

Quay, Steele, Johnson, and Hortman (2001) compared RR children in a Georgia school district with a control group who were equivalent in gender, ethnicity, and achievement. At the end of the school year, multivariate and univariate analyses of variance indicated that the RR children were significantly superior to the control group children on (1) The Iowa Test of Basic Skills (ITBS) language tests; (2) The Gates–MacGinitie Reading Test; (3) the six tests of an Observation Survey of Early Literacy Achievement; (4) classroom teachers' assessments of achievement in mathematics, oral communication, reading comprehension, and written expression; (5) classroom teachers' ratings of personal and social growth in work habits, following directions, self-confidence, social interaction with adults, and social interaction with peers; and (6) promotion rates. The data strongly suggest that the RR is an effective intervention for high-risk first-grade readers.

Evaluation

Use the six-step framework to evaluate this program, and explain why it may have generalizable effects.

Early Steps

This is a one-to-one tutoring program developed by Darrell Morris, who also created the Howard Street Tutoring Program (Morris, Perney, & Shaw, 1990). The Early Steps program is designed for first graders who are at risk for reading failure. Certified teachers in Title I schools are trained in the program strategies. The goal of Early Steps is to identify and remediate reading problems before children have an opportunity to face multiple failures. Like RR, the Early Steps program follows a daily lesson plan of: (1) reading a familiar book to develop fluency, (2) working with letters and words, (3) writing a story to practice word analysis, spelling, and reading, and (4) reading a new book to learn new words and practice comprehension.

Early Steps differs from RR in that it uses a word-study method, which is a systematic study of the orthographic patterns in words. This word study is purposefully isolated from meaningful context so that the child fully attends to the patterns being studied. In RR, the analysis of words is not presented systematically and is done in the context of reading. Also, teacher training in Early Steps differs from training in RR on three dimensions: (1) selection of tutors, (2) frequency of training sessions, and (3) structure of training. In Early Steps, tutors, as well as the first-grade reading teacher, participate in training. In RR, only the tutors participate. Unlike the 30 trainings provided by RR, there are 12 trainings throughout a school year. In addition, observations of tutoring sessions are not conducted by one tutor as others watch. Instead, each tutor has the opportunity to tutor one of his or her own students and receive feedback, observe two other tutor–child pairs, and participate in two observation-related discussions with the trainer.

Santa and Høien (1999) evaluated the impact of Early Steps on at-risk first-grade readers. Four neighborhood schools were selected to participate in the study—two experimental and two control schools. The study included 49 children from lower- to middle-income families. The design of the study included pre-, post-, and retention assessments of an experimental group and control group. Various tests were used to assess spelling performance, word recognition, nonword reading, and reading comprehension. The results at the end of grade 1 and at the beginning of grade 2 indicated that the experimental group performed significantly better than the control group on all variables assessed. In addition, data showed that the children with the lowest pretest levels, the very high-risk children, benefitted most from the intervention. They improved to the point that they nearly equaled the average performance level after an intervention period of 8 months. Santa and Høien (1999) attributed the positive effects to the fact that Early Steps is a balanced approach to beginning reading that targets the phonological and word-study skills of children most at risk in this domain.

Similar results were found from a study conducted by Morris, Tyner, and Perney (2000). Six intervention and five comparison schools were involved in this study in a mid-size urban school district in Tennessee. In each of the six intervention schools, one to three first-grade teachers and a Title I reading teacher participated in the study. Across all six schools, a total of 43 at-risk first graders were identified in September and provided with an average of 91 one-to-one tutoring sessions throughout the year. At the end of the year, students in the Early Steps program scored significantly better than children in the comparison groups on measures of word recognition, spelling, passage reading, Woodcock pseudoword task, and Woodcock passage comprehension. Morris, Tyner, and Perney (2000) attributed these improvements in student performance to the systematic study of words and to the critical role of the trainer of tutors.

Evaluation

Use the six-step framework to evaluate this program and explain why it seemed to be effective.

INTERVENTIONS THAT DEVELOP
COMPREHENSION SKILLS

Although it is difficult to separate reading from comprehension, the programs discussed in the previous section focus primarily on teaching children to "break the code" and the strategies needed for beginning reading. Two programs, concept-oriented reading instruction (CORI) and Accelerated Reader Best Classroom Practices (ARBCP), focus on skills needed to comprehend larger segments of text.

Concept-Oriented Reading Instruction

CORI integrates comprehension strategies and motivational practices to promote effective reading. The underlying premise of CORI is that students' reading comprehension is intrinsically related to their engagement and interest in reading. In CORI, students are explicitly taught the following comprehension strategies: (1) activating background knowledge, (2) questioning, (3) searching for information, (4) organizing graphically, and (5) identifying story structure. In addition, the following practices are implemented to promote engagement in reading: (1) using content goals in reading instruction, (2) providing hands-on activities, (3) affording student choice, (4) using interesting text, and (5) promoting collaboration in reading instruction.

CORI is based on the framework of science inquiry in which students explore ecological issues such as survival of birds or aquatic life. The program is themed-based and uses numerous trade books and a basal series within each of the four, 6-week themes. During a 12-week unit, students read at least 16 self-selected books, using the comprehension strategies to fully understand the content.

Teachers are trained in a 10-day summer workshop that includes viewing examples of instruction, performing the reading strategies, discussing motivational practices, constructing reading-science integrations, identifying books appropriate for instruction, and planning for the themes using a teacher's guide supplied by the project. Teachers also receive follow-up training and guidance as they implement the program throughout the year.

In systematic evaluations, CORI has demonstrated a positive impact on students' reading comprehension, reading motivation, and use of reading strategies. Guthrie, Anderson, Alao, and Rinehart (1999) assessed the effectiveness of CORI compared to traditional classrooms in low-income schools. Five CORI classrooms, three third grades and two fifth grades, were matched with traditional classrooms on similarities among students, teachers, and schools. All students were pretested on standardized reading measures and post-tested measures on reading engagement and conceptual learning. At the end of the school year, students in the CORI classrooms increased their strategy use, conceptual learning, and their comprehension of text more than students in traditional instruction classrooms.

Guthrie et al. (2004) randomly assigned four schools to either the CORI intervention or Strategy Instruction (SI), which is comprehension strategy instruction without the motivation component. The eight teachers in the CORI schools attended the summer training and implemented the intervention for 12 weeks during the fall of the year. All students in the CORI and SI classrooms were pre- and post-tested on measures of reading comprehension, strategy use, and reading motivation. Analysis of the data revealed that students in the CORI group outperformed students in the SI group on all measures.

Evaluation

Evaluate this program using the six-step framework. Is it consistent with contemporary theories and research on reading comprehension? Would students find the activities meaningful, challenging, and motivating? Is it practical or expensive?

Accelerated Reader Best Classroom Practices Program

Accelerated Reader Best Classroom Practices (ARBCP; also abbreviated AR) (formerly called Accelerated Reader/Reading Renaissance) is a guided reading intervention that focuses on the development of reading comprehension. The program is designed for children from kindergarten through sixth grade. The program has two components. The Reading Renaissance component uses the techniques of guided reading. There are a set of recommended principles that teachers use to help guide students' reading of the text. The second component, Accelerated Reading, is a computer-based program used to facilitate reading practices by providing students and teachers with feedback from quizzes based on children's comprehension of books that they have read. The program provides children the opportunity to practice reading books at their independent level and gives feedback on their comprehension.

A primary component of Reading Renaissance is a dedicated 30–60 min block of time for reading practice. Depending on the age and skill levels of the students, three activities might occur during the reading block: (1) reading texts to a child, (2) reading texts to a child using a paired-reading technique, or (3) independent reading by the child. In prekindergarten through third grade, reading practice is heavily weighted toward the first two segments. As children develop decoding skills, they transition increasingly to independent reading. Initially, students take an assessment to determine their independent reading level, and the students select books marked at this level. After completing each subsequent book, students take a comprehension quiz and earn points based on the number of correct responses and the reading level of the book. Teachers use the quizzes to assess appropriate reading texts for each student, monitor student progress, and identify students who may need remediation.

Ross, Nunnery, and Goldfeder (2004) conducted a randomized controlled trial evaluation of the AR program. The study included a subset of 45 teachers and 910 students in grades K–3 in 11 schools in a southern school district of the United States. Within each school, a minimum of two teachers within one grade volunteered to be randomly assigned to implement either the intervention or the comparison group. AR was implemented in the intervention group, and a commercially available basal reading program used across all schools was implemented in the control groups.

The findings suggest a positive and statistically significant effect of AR on third-grade student performance on the reading comprehension measure, which was the STAR reading test (effect size = +0.25). On measures of general reading, as measured by the Star Early Literacy test, AR had positive and statistically significant effects for kindergarten, first-, and second-grade students.

Nunnery, Ross, and McDonald (2006) conducted a similar study of AR with students in the third through sixth grade. This randomized field experiment was designed to evaluate the program's impacts on the reading achievement of 978 urban students. Forty-four teachers across schools volunteered to participate in the study. Teachers were randomly assigned to either implement the AR or served as controls. In general, the results were positive in favor of the intervention group across all three grades. However, the largest effects were found for third graders, in which an effect size of +.36 was generated. The result indict that the AR program increases reading achievement in general, and reading comprehension specifically, in low-achieving students.

FINAL THOUGHTS

In this chapter, we presented a number of programs for you to evaluate. As noted in Chapter 1, we wrote this book with the goal of providing you with the conceptual knowledge needed to understand why certain programs work and why others are not as effective. We have also noted that the conceptual knowledge presented in Chapters 3 through 9 is generative in the sense that it should help you understand how to create your own version of a successful reading program. Hopefully, our goals have been met, and you are now equipped to make informed and better decisions related to language and literacy instruction.

References

Abbott, R. D., & Berninger, V. W. (1993). Structural equation modeling of relationships among developmental skills and writing skills in primary- and intermediate-grade writers. *Journal of Educational Psychology, 85,* 478–508.

Ackerman, B. P. (1978). Children's understanding of speech acts in unconventional directive frames. *Child Development, 49,* 311–318.

Acredolo, C. (1992). Comment on "The age 4 transition." *Human Development, 35,* 178–181.

Adams, A. M., & Willis, C. (2001). Language processing and working memory: A developmental perspective. In J. Andrade (Ed.), *Working memory in perspective* (pp. 79–100). New York: Psychology Press.

Adams, G. L., & Engelmann, S. (1996). *Research on Direct Instruction: 25 years beyond DISTAR.* Seattle, WA: Educational Achievement Systems.

Adams, M. J. (1990). *Beginning to read: Thinking and learning about print.* Cambridge, MA: MIT Press.

Akhtar, N., & Tomasello, M. (1997). Young children's productivity with word order and verb morphology. *Developmental Psychology, 33,* 952–965.

Alba, J. W., & Hasher, L. (1983). Is memory schematic? *Psychological Bulletin, 93,* 203–231.

Alexander, P. A., & Murphy, P. K. (1998). Profiling the differences in students' knowledge, interest, and strategic processing. *Journal of Educational Psychology, 90,* 435–447.

Ames, C. (1986). Effective motivation: The contribution of the learning environment. In R. S. Feldman (Ed.), *The social psychology of education* (pp. 235–256). Cambridge, UK: Cambridge University Press.

Ames, C. (1992). Classrooms: Goals, structures, and student motivation. *Journal of Educational Psychology, 84,* 261–271.

Anderson, J. R. (1990). *Cognitive psychology and its implications* (3rd ed.). New York: Freeman.

Anderson, J. R. (1995). *Learning and memory: An integrated approach.* New York: Wiley.

Anderson, J. R. (2004). *Cognitive psychology and its implications* (6th ed.). New York: Worth Publishers.

Anderson, R. C., Wilson, P. T., & Fielding, L. G. (1988). Growth in reading and how children spend their time outside of school. *Reading Research Quarterly, 23,* 285–303.

Anderson-Yockel, J., & Haynes, W. O. (1994). Joint book-reading strategies in working-class African American and White mother–toddler dyads. *Journal of Speech and Hearing Research, 37,* 583–593.

Anglin, J. M. (1993). Vocabulary development: A morphological analysis. *Monographs of the Society for Research in Child Development, 58* [238], v–165.

Anthony, J. L., & Lonigan, C. J. (2004). The nature of phonological awareness: Converging evidence from four studies of preschool and early grade school children. *Journal of Educational Psychology, 96,* 43–55.

Applebee, A. N., Langer, J. A., Mullis, I. V. S., & Jenkins, L. B. (1990). *The writing report card, 1984–1988: Findings from the national assessment of educational progress.* Princeton, NJ: Educational Testing Service.

Arlin, P. (1981). Piagetian tasks as predictors of reading and math readiness. *Journal of Educational Psychology, 73,* 712–721.

Arriaga, R. I., Fenson, L., Cronan, T., & Pethick, S. J. (1998). Scores on the MacArthur Communicative Development Inventory of children from low- and middle-income families. *Applied Psycholinguistics, 19,* 209–223.

Aslin, R. N., & Smith, L. B. (1988). Perceptual development. *Annual Review of Psychology, 39,* 435–473.

Assel, M. A., Landry, S. H., Swank, P., & Gunnewig, S. (2007). An evaluation of curriculum, setting, and mentoring on the performance of children enrolled in pre-kindergarten. *Reading and Writing, 20,* 463–494.

Atkinson, J. W. (1964). *An introduction to motivation.* Princeton, NJ: Van Nostrand.

Atwell, N. (1987). *In the middle: Writing, reading, and learning with adolescents.* Portsmouth, NH: Heinemann.

Avons, S. E., Wragg, C. A., Cupples, L., & Lovegrove, W. J. (1998). Measures of phonological short-term memory and their relationship to vocabulary development. *Applied Psycholinguistics, 19,* 583–601.

Axelrod, S., Moyer, L., & Berry, B. (1990). Why teachers do not use behavior modification procedures. *Journal of Educational and Psychological Consultation, 1*(4), 309–320.

Baddeley, A. D. (1990). *Human memory: Theory and practice.* Boston: Allyn & Bacon.

Baker, L. (1984). Spontaneous versus instructed use of multiple standards for evaluating comprehension: Effects of age, reading proficiency, and type of standard. *Journal of Experimental Child Psychology, 38,* 289–311.

Baker, L., & Brown, A. L. (1984). Metacognitive skills and reading. In P. D. Pearson, M. Kamil, R. Barr, & P. Mosenthal (Eds.), *Handbook of reading research* (Vol. 1, pp. 353–394). White Plains, NY: Longman.

Baker, L., Fernandez-Fein, S., Scher, D., & Williams, H. (1998). Home experiences related to the development of word recognition. In J. L. Metsala & L. C. Ehri (Eds.), *Word recognition in beginning literacy* (pp. 263–287). Mahwah, NJ: Erlbaum.

Baker, L., & Wigfield, A. (1999). Dimensions of children's motivation for reading and their relations to reading activity and reading achievement. *Reading Research Quarterly, 34,* 452–477.

Ball, E. W., & Blackman, B. A. (1991). Does phoneme awareness training in kindergarten make a difference in early word recognition and developmental spelling? *Reading Research Quarterly, 26*(1), 49–66.

Bandura, A. (1986). *Social foundations of thought and action: A social cognitive theory.* Englewood Cliffs, NJ: Prentice-Hall.

Bandura, A. (1997). *Self-efficacy: The exercise of control.* New York: Freeman.

Bandura, A., & Schunk, D. (1981). Cultivating, competence, self-efficacy, and intrinsic interest through proximal self-motivation. *Journal of Personality and Social Psychology, 41,* 586–598.

Bandura, A., & Wood, R. (1989). Effect of perceived controllability and performance standards on self-regulation of complex decision making. *Journal of Personality and Social Psychology, 56,* 805–814.

Bangert-Downs, R. L. (1993). The word processor as an instructional tool: A meta-analysis of word processing in writing instruction. *Review of Educational Research, 63,* 69–93.

Barab, S. A., & Plucker, J. A. (2002). Smart people or smart contexts? Cognition, ability, and talent development in an age of situated approaches to knowing and learning. *Educational Psychologist, 37,* 165–182.

Barber, L., Carbo, M., & Thomasson, R. (1998). *A comparative study of the Reading Styles Program to extant programs of teaching reading.* Bloomington, IN: Phi Delta Kappa.

Barch, D. M., Braver, T. S., Nystrom, L. E., Forman, S. D., Noll, D. C., & Cohen, J. D. (1997). Dissociating working memory from task difficulty in human prefrontal cortex. *Neuropsychologia, 35,* 1373–1380.

Barr, H. M., & Streissguth, A. P. (1991). Caffeine use during pregnancy and child outcomes: A 7-year prospective study. *Neurotoxicology and Teratology, 13,* 441–448.

Barr, H. M., Streissguth, A. P., Darby, B. L., & Sampson, P. D. (1990). Prenatal exposure to alcohol, caffeine, tobacco, and aspirin: Effects on fine and gross motor performance in 4-year-old children. *Developmental Psychology, 26,* 339–348.

Barry, D. (1989). *Dave Barry slept here.* New York: Random House.

Bartlett, E. (1982). *Children's difficulties in establishing consistent voice and space/time dimensions in narrative text.* Paper presented at the meeting of the American Educational Research Association.

Bates, E. (1976). *Language and context: The acquisition of pragmatics.* New York: Academic Press.

Bates, E., Bretherton, I., & Snyder, L. (1988). *From first words to grammar: Individual differences and dissociable mechanisms.* New York: Cambridge University Press.

Bates, E., Marchman, V. A., Thal, D., Fenson, L., Dale, P., Reznick, J. S., et al. (1994). Developmental and stylistic variation in the composition of early vocabulary. *Journal of Child Language, 21,* 85–123.

Baumann, J. F. (1981). Effect of ideational prominence on children's reading comprehension of expository prose. *Journal of Reading Behavior, 13,* 49–56.

Baumann, J. F. (1984). The effectiveness of a direct instruction paradigm for teaching main idea comprehension. *Reading Research Quarterly, 20,* 93–115.

Baumann, J. F. (1986).Teaching third-grade students to comprehend anaphoric relationships: The application of a direct instruction model. *Reading Research Quarterly, 21,* 70–90.

Bayliss, D. M., Jarrold, C., Baddeley, A. D., & Leigh, E. (2005). Differential constraints on the working memory and reading abilities of individuals with learning difficulties and typically developing children. *Journal of Experimental Child Psychology, 92,* 76–99.

Beal, C. R. (1990). The development of text evaluation and revision skills. *Child Development, 61,* 247–258.

Beaton, A. (1997). The relation of planum temporale asymmetry and morphology of the corpus callosum to handedness, gender, and dyslexia: A review of the evidence. *Brain and Language, 60,* 255–322.

Bellinger, D., & Needleman, H. L. (1994). Developmental toxicity of methyl mercury. In H. L. Needleman & D. Bellinger (Eds.), *Prenatal exposure to toxicants: Developmental consequences.* Baltimore: Johns Hopkins University Press.

Benton, S. L., Glover, J. A., Kraft, R. G., & Plake, B. S. (1984). Cognitive capacity differences among writers. *Journal of Educational Psychology, 76,* 820–834.

Bereiter, C., & Scardamalia, M. (1982). From conversation to composition: The role of instruction in a developmental process. In R. Glaser (Ed.), *Advances in instructional psychology* (Vol. 2, 1–64). Hillsdale, NJ: Erlbaum.

Berko, J. (1958). The child's learning of English morphology. *Word, 14,* 150–177.

Berko Gleason, J. (2005). *The development of language* (6th ed.). Needham Heights, MA: Allyn & Bacon.

Berlyne, D. (1966). Curiosity and exploration. *Science, 153,* 25–33.

Berninger, V. W., & Fuller, F. (1992). Gender differences in orthographic, verbal, and compositional fluency: Implications for assessing writing disabilities in primary grade children. *Journal of School Psychology, 30,* 363–382.

Berninger, V. W., Mizokawa, D., & Bragg, R. (1991). Theory-based diagnosis and remediation of writing disabilities. *Journal of School Psychology, 29,* 57–79.

Bernstein Ratner, N. (2005). Atypical language development. In J. Berko Gleason (Ed.), *The development of language* (6th ed., pp. 324–395). Needham Heights, MA: Allyn & Bacon.

Berry, J. M., & West, R. L. (1993). Cognitive self-efficacy in relation to personal mastery and goal setting across the life span. *International Journal of Behavioral Development, 16,* 351–379.

Bialystok, E. (1988). Aspects of linguistic awareness in reading comprehension. *Applied Psycholinguistics, 9,* 123–139.

Bjorklund, D. F. (2004). *Children's thinking: Developmental function and individual differences* (4th ed.). Pacific Grove, CA: Brooks/Cole.

Bloom, L. (1998). Language acquisition in its developmental context. In W. Damon (Series Ed.), *Handbook of child psychology: Vol. 2. Cognition, perception, and language* (pp. 309–370). Hoboken, NJ: Wiley.

Bloom, L., & Tinker, E. (2001). The intentionality model and language acquisition: Engagement, effort, and the essential tension in development. *Monographs of the Society for Research in Child Development, 66,* 1–89.

Bloom, P. (2000). *How children learn the meanings of words.* Cambridge, MA: MIT Press.

Bolig, J. R., & Fletcher, G. O. (1973). The MRT vs. ratings of kindergarten teachers as predictors of success in first grade. *Educational Leadership, 30,* 637–640.

Bond, G. L., & Dykstra, R. (1967). The cooperative research program in first-grade reading instruction. *Reading Research Quarterly, 2,* 10–141.

Borko, H., & Shavelson, R. J. (1983). Speculators on teacher education: Recommendations from research on teachers' cognitions. *Journal of Education for Teaching, 9,* 210–214.

Borman, G. D., Slavin, R. E., Cheung, A., Chamberlain, A., Madden, N., & Chambers, B. (2005). The national randomized field trial of Success for All: Second-year outcomes. *American Educational Research Journal, 42,* 673–696.

Borman, G. D., Slavin, R. E., Cheung, A., Chamberlain, A. M., Madden, N. A., & Chambers, B. (2005). Success for All: First-year results from the national randomized field trial. *Educational Evaluation and Policy Analysis, 27,* 1–22.

Bornstein, M., & Tamis-LeMonda, C. S. (1989). Maternal responsiveness and cognitive development in children. *New Directions for Child Development* (no. 43), 49–61.

Bowerman, M. (1986). First steps in acquiring conditionals. In E. C. Traugott, A. ter Meulen, J. S. Reilly, & C. A. Ferguson (Eds.), *On conditionals* (pp. 285–307). New York: Cambridge University Press.

Bowey, J. A. (1995). Socioeconomic status differences in preschool phonological sensitivity and first-grade reading achievement. *Journal of Educational Psychology, 87,* 476–487.

Bowey, J. A., & Patel, R. K. (1988). Metalinguistic ability and early reading achievement. *Applied Psycholinguistics, 9,* 367–383.

Bracken, B. A., Howell, K. K., & Crain, R. (1993). Prediction of Caucasian and African-American preschool children's fluid and crystallized intelligence: Contributions of maternal characteristics and home environment. *Journal of Clinical Child Psychology, 22,* 455–463.

Braine, M. D. S. (1976). Children's first word combinations. *Monographs of the Society for Research in Child Development, 41,* v–104.

Bredekamp, S., Morrow, L. M., & Pikulski, J. J. (2006). *Houghton Mifflin Pre-K [kit]: Where Bright Futures Begin!* Boston: Houghton Mifflin.

Breedlove, S. M. (1994). Sexual differentiation of the human nervous system. *Annual Review of Psychology, 45,* 389–418.

Brenneman, K., Massey, C., Machado, S. F., & Gelman, R. (1996). Young children's plans differ for writing and drawing. *Cognitive Development, 11,* 397–420.

Brooks-Gunn, J., & Markman, L. B. (2005). The contribution of parenting to ethnic and racial gaps in school readiness. *The Future of Children, 15,* 139–168.

Broomfield, K. A., Robinson, E. J., & Robinson, W. P. (2002). Children's understanding of white lies. *British Journal of Developmental Psychology, 20,* 47–65.

Brown, A. L., & Day, J. D. (1983). Macrorules for summarizing texts: The development of expertise. *Journal of Verbal Learning and Verbal Behavior, 22,* 1–14.

Brown, A. L., Day, J. D., & Jones, R. (1983). The development of plans for summarizing texts. *Child Development, 54,* 968–979.

Brown, G. D. A. (1998). The endpoint of skilled word recognition: The ROAR model.

In J. L. Metsala & L. C. Ehri (Eds.), *Word recognition in beginning literacy* (pp. 121–138). Mahwah, NJ: Erlbaum.

Brown, R. (1958). How shall a thing be called? *Psychological Review, 65,* 14–21.

Brown, R., & Hanlon, C. (1970). Derivational complexity and order of acquisition in child speech. In J. R. Hayes (Ed.), *Cognition and the development of language* (pp. 11–54). New York: Wiley.

Brown, R. W. (1973). *A first language: the early stages.* Cambridge, MA: Harvard University Press.

Bruer, J. T. (1998). Brain science, brain fiction. *Educational Leadership, 56,* 14–18.

Bryant, P. E., MacLean, M., Bradley, L., & Crossland, J. (1990). Rhyme and alliteration, phoneme detection, and learning to read. *Developmental Psychology, 26,* 429–438.

Bryden, M. P., McManus, I. C., & Bulman-Fleming (1994). Evaluating the empirical support for the Geschwind–Behan–Galaburda model of cerebral lateralization. *Brain and Cognition, 26,* 103–167.

Bullock, M., Gelman, R., & Baillargeon, R. (1982). The development of causal reasoning. In W. J. Friedman (Ed.), *The developmental psychology of time* (pp. 209–253). New York: Academic Press.

Burton, M. W., Small, S. L., & Blumstein, S. E. (2000). The role of segmentation in phonological processing: An fMRI investigation. *Journal of Cognitive Neuroscience, 12,* 679–690.

Bus, A. G., & van IJzendoorn, M. H. (1999). Phonological awareness and early reading: A meta-analysis of experimental training studies. *Journal of Educational Psychology, 91,* 403–414.

Byrne, B., & Fielding-Barnsley, R. (1991). *Sound Foundations.* Artamon, Australia: Leyden Educational Publishers.

Byrne, B., & Fielding-Barnsley, R. (1993). Evaluation of a program to teach phonemic awareness to young children: A 1-year follow-up. *Journal of Educational Psychology, 85,* 104–111.

Byrne, B., & Fielding-Barnsley, R. (1995). Evaluation of a program to teach phonemic awareness to young children: A 2- and 3-year follow-up and a new preschool trial. *Journal of Educational Psychology, 87*(3), 488–503.

Byrnes, J. P. (1991). Acquisition and development of *if* and *because*: Conceptual and linguistic aspects. In S. A. Gelman & J. P. Byrnes (Eds.), *Perspectives on language and cognition: Interrelations in development* (pp. 354–393). New York: Cambridge University Press.

Byrnes, J. P. (1998). *The nature and development of decision-making: A self-regulation model.* Hillsdale, NJ: Erlbaum.

Byrnes, J. P. (2001a). *Cognitive development and learning in instructional contexts* (2nd ed.). Needham Heights, MA: Allyn & Bacon.

Byrnes, J. P. (2001b). *Minds, brains, and learning: Understanding the psychological and educational relevance of neuroscientific research.* New York: Guilford Press.

Byrnes, J. P. (2003a). Cognitive development during adolescence. In G. R. Adams & M. Berzonsky (Eds.), *Blackwell handbook on adolescence.* Oxford, England: Blackwell Publishers.

Byrnes, J. P. (2003b). Factors predictive of mathematics achievement in White, Black, and Hispanic 12th graders. *Journal of Educational Psychology, 95,* 316–326.

Byrnes, J. P. (2005). Self-regulated decision-making in children and adolescents. In J. E. Jacobs & P. A. Klaczynski (Eds.), *The development of judgment and decision-making in children and adolescents* (pp. 5–38). Mahwah, NJ: Erlbaum.

Byrnes, J. P., & Fox, N. A. (1998).The educational relevance of research in cognitive neuroscience. *Educational Psychology Review, 10,* 297–342.

Byrnes, J. P., & Miller, D. C. (2007). The relative importance of predictions of math and science achievement: An opportunity-propensity analysis. *Contemporary Educational Psychology, 32,* 599–629.

Byrnes, J. P., Miller, D. C., & Reynolds, M. (1999). Learning to make good decisions: A self-regulation perspective. *Child Development, 70,* 1121–1140.

Byrnes, J. P., & Wasik, D. C. (2008). Factors predictive of knowledge growth in mathematics during kindergarten and first grade: An opportunity propensity analysis. Manuscript under review.

Cain, K., Oakhill, J., & Bryant, P. (2004). Children's comprehension ability: Concurrent prediction by working memory, verbal ability, and component skills. *Journal of Educational Psychology, 96,* 31–42.

Cain, K., Oakhill, J., & Lemmon, K. (2004). Individual differences in the inference of word meanings from context: The influence of reading comprehension, vocabulary knowledge, and memory capacity. *Journal of Educational Psychology, 96,* 671–681.

Cain, K. M., & Dweck, C. S. (1995). The relation between motivational patterns and achievement cognitions through the elementary school years. *Merrill-Palmer Quarterly, 41,* 25–52.

Callanan, M. A. (1991). Parent–child collaboration in young children's understanding of category hierarchies. In S. A. Gelman & J. P. Byrnes (Eds.), *Perspectives on language and thought: Interrelations in development* (pp. 440–484). New York: Cambridge University Press.

Cameron, J., & Pierce, W. (1994). Reinforcement, reward, and intrinsic motivation: A meta-analysis. *Review of Educational Research, 64,* 363–423.

Caplan, D., & Waters, G. S. (1999). Verbal working memory and sentence comprehension. *Behavioral and Brain Sciences, 22,* 77–126.

Carey, S., & Bartlett, E. (1978). Acquiring a single new word. *Papers and Reports on Child Language Development, 15,* 17–29.

Carey, S. A. (1985). *Conceptual change in childhood.* Cambridge, MA: MIT Press.

Cargile, A. (2000). Evaluations of employment suitability: Does accent always matter? *Journal of Employment Counseling, 37,* 165–177.

Carlson, H. K., & McHenry, M. A. (2006). Effect of accent and dialect on employability. *Journal of Employment Counseling, 43,* 70–81.

Carpenter, M., Nagell, K., & Tomasello, M. (1998). Social cognition, joint attention, and communicative competence from 9 to 15 months of age. *Monographs of the Society for Research in Child Development, 63,* 1–143.

Carpenter, P., Just, M. A., Keller, T. A., Cherkassky, V., Roth, J. K., & Minshew, N. (2001). Dynamic cortical systems subserving cognition: fMRI studies with typical and atypical individuals. In J. L. McClelland & R. S. Siegler (Eds.), *Mechanisms of cognitive development: Behavioral and neural perspectives* (pp. 353–383). Mahwah, NJ: Erlbaum.

Carpenter, P. A., & Just, M. A. (1987). *The psychology of reading and language comprehension.* Boston: Allyn & Bacon.

Carpenter, P. A., Miyake, A., & Just, M. A. (1995). Language comprehension: Sentence and discourse processing. *Annual Review of Psychology, 46,* 91–120.

Carpenter, R. L., Mastergeorge, A. M., & Coggins, T. E. (1983). The acquisition of communicative intentions in infants eight to fifteen months of age. *Language and Speech, 26,* 101–116.

Carretti, B., Cornoldi, C., De Beni, R., & Romano, M. (2005). Updating in working memory: A comparison of good and poor comprehenders. *Journal of Experimental Child Psychology, 91,* 45–66.

Carroll, J. M., & Snowling, M. J. (2001). The effects of global similarity between stimuli on children's judgment of rime and alliteration. *Applied Psycholinguistics, 22,* 327–342.

Case, R. (1998). The development of conceptual structures. In W. Damon (Series Ed.), D. Kuhn, & R. S. Siegler (Vol. Eds.), *Handbook of child psychology: Vol. 2. Cognition, perception, and action* (pp. 745–800). New York: Wiley.

Caselli, C., Casadio, P., & Bates, E. (1999). A comparison of the transition from first words to grammar in English and Italian. *Journal of Child Language, 26,* 69–111.

Catania, A. C. (1998). *Learning* (4th ed.). Englewood Cliffs, NJ: Prentice-Hall.

Catts, H. W. (1993). The relationship between speech-language impairments and reading disability. *Journal of Speech and Hearing Research, 36,* 948–958.

Chall, J. S. (1967). *Learning to read: The great debate.* New York: McGraw-Hill.

Chall, J. S. (1983). *Stages of reading development.* New York: McGraw-Hill.

Champion, T. B., Hyter, Y. D., McCabe, A., & Bland-Stewart, L. M. (2003). A matter of vocabulary: Performances of low-income African American Head Start children on the Peabody Picture Vocabulary Test-III. *Communication Disorders Quarterly, 24,* 121–127.

Chaney, C. (1994). Language development, metalinguistic awareness, and emergent literacy skills of 3-year-old children in relation to social class. *Applied Psycholinguistics, 15,* 371–394.

Charity, A. H., Scarborough, H. S., & Griffin, D. M. (2004). Familiarity with school English in African American children and its relation to early reading achievement. *Child Development, 75,* 1340–1356.

Chenn, A., Braisted, J. E., McConnell, S. K., & O'Leary, D. D. M. (1997). Development of the cerebral cortex: Mechanisms controlling cell fate, laminar and areal patterning, and axonal connectivity. In W. M. Cowan, T. M. Jessell, & S. L. Zipursky (Eds.), *Molecular and cellular approaches to neural development* (pp. 440–473). New York: Oxford University Press.

Chomsky, N. (1957). *Syntactic structures.* The Hague, The Netherlands: Mouton.

Chomsky, N. (1959). A review of B. F. Skinner's *Verbal behavior. Language, 35,* 26–58.

Chomsky, N. (1965). *Aspects of the theory of syntax.* Cambridge, MA: MIT Press.

Chomsky, N. (1980) *Rules and representations.* New York: Columbia University Press.

Chomsky, N. (1981). On cognitive structures and their development: A reply to Piaget. In M. Piatelli-Palmerini (Ed.), *Language and Learning: The debate be-*

tween Jean Piaget and Noam Chomsky (pp. 23–55). Cambridge, MA: MIT Press.

Chow, B. W. Y., McBride-Chang, C., & Burgess, S. (2005). Phonological processing skills and early reading abilities in Hong Kong in Chinese kindergarteners learning to read English as a second language. *Journal of Educational Psychology, 97*, 81–87.

Cipielewski, J., & Stanovich, K. E. (1992). Predicting growth in reading ability from children's exposure to print. *Journal of Experimental Child Psychology, 54*, 74–89.

Clark, E. V. (1991). Acquisitional principles in lexical development. In S. A. Gelman & J. P. Byrnes (Eds.), *Perspectives on language and thought: Interrelations in development* (pp. 31–71). New York: Cambridge University Press.

Clay, M. (1985). *The early detection of reading difficulties.* Auckland, New Zealand: Heinemann.

Clifford, M. M. (1991). Risk-taking: theoretical, empirical, and educational considerations. *Educational Psychologist, 26*, 263–297.

Cohen, J. (1992). A power primer. *Psychological Bulletin, 112*, 155–159.

College Board. (2004). *Profile of seniors.* Princeton, NJ: Educational Testing Service.

Coltheart, M., Curtis, B., Atkins, P., & Haller, M. (1993). Models of reading aloud: Dual-route and parallel-distributed-processing approaches. *Psychological Review, 100*, 589–608.

Compton, D. L. (2003). Modeling the relationship between growth in rapid naming speed and growth in decoding skill in first grade children. *Journal of Educational Psychology, 95*, 225–239.

Corno, L., Cronbach, L. J., Kupermintz, H., Lohman, D. F., Mandinach, E. B., Porteus, A. W., et al. (2002). *Remaking the concept of aptitude: Extending the legacy of Richard E. Snow.* Mahwah, NJ: Erlbaum.

Covington, M., & Omelich, C. (1981). As failures mount: Affective and cognitive consequences of ability demotion in the classroom. *Journal of Educational Psychology, 73*, 796–808.

Coyle, J. T., Oster-Granite, M. L., Reeves, R. H., & Gearhart, J. D. (1988). Down syndrome, Alzheimer's disease, and the trisomy 16 mouse. *Trends in the Neurosciences, 11*, 390–394.

Crain-Thoreson, C., & Dale, P. S. (1992). Do early talkers become early readers? Linguistic precocity, preschool language, and emergent literacy. *Developmental Psychology, 28*, 421–429.

Creusere, M. A. (1999). Theories of adults' understanding and use of irony and sarcasm: Applications to and evidence from research with children. *Developmental Review, 19*, 213–262.

Crowley, K., Callanan, M. A., Tenenbaum, H. R., & Allen, E. (2001). Parents explain more often to boys than to girls during shared scientific thinking. *Psychological Science, 12*, 258–261.

Daiute, C. (2002). Social relational knowing in writing development. In E. Amsel & J. P. Byrnes (Eds.), *Language, literacy, and cognitive development.* Mahwah, NJ: Erlbaum.

Danner, F. (1976). Children's understanding of intersentence organization in the recall of short descriptive passages. *Journal of Educational Psychology, 68*, 174–183.

DeCasper, A. J., & Fifer, W. P. (1980). Of human bonding: Newborns prefer their mothers' voices. *Science, 208,* 1174–1176.

Deci, E., & Ryan, R. (1985). *Intrinsic motivation and self-determination in human behavior.* New York: Plenum Press.

DeFries, J. C., Gillis, J. J., & Wadsworth, S. J. (1993). Genes and genders: A twin study of reading disability. In A. M. Galaburda (Ed.), *Dyslexia and development: Neurobiological development of extraordinary brains* (pp. 187–204). Cambridge, MA: Harvard University Press.

de Jong, P. F., & van der Leij, A. (1999). Specific contributions of phonological abilities to early reading acquisition: Results from a Dutch latent variable longitudinal study. *Journal of Educational Psychology, 91,* 450–476.

DeLoache, J. S., Miller, K. F., & Pierroutsakos, S. L. (1998). Reasoning and problem solving. In W. Damon (Series Ed.), D. Kuhn, & R. S. Siegler (Vol. Eds.), *Handbook of child psychology: Vol. 2. Cognition, perception, and language* (pp. 801–850). Hoboken, NJ: Wiley.

Delpit, L. D. (1998). What should teachers do? Ebonics and culturally responsive instruction. In T. Perry & L. D. Delpit (Eds.), *The real ebonics debate: Power, language, and the education of African American Children* (pp. 17–28). Boston, MA: Beacon Press.

Dempster, F. N. (1992). The rise and fall of the inhibitory mechanism: Toward a unified theory of cognitive development and aging. *Developmental Review, 12,* 45–75.

DeNavas-Walt, C., Proctor, B. D., & Lee, C. H. (2006). *Income poverty and health insurance coverage in the United States: 2005* (U.S. Census Bureau, Current Population Reports, P60–231). Washington, DC: U.S. Government Printing Office.

de Villiers, J. (1991). Why questions? In T. Maxfield & B. Plunkett (Eds.), University of Massachusetts Occasional Papers in Linguistics Special Edition.

de Villiers, J., & de Villiers, P. (1973). A cross-sectional study of the acquisition of grammatical morphemes in child speech. *Journal of Psycholinguistic Research, 2,* 267–278.

Devlin, J. T., Matthews, P. M., & Rushworth, M. F. S. (2003). Semantic processing in the left inferior prefrontal cortex: A combined functional magnetic resonance imaging and transcranial magnetic stimulation study. *Journal of Cognitive Neuroscience, 15,* 71–84.

Dewitz, P., Carr, E., & Patberg, J. P. (1987). Effects of inference training on comprehension and comprehension monitoring. *Reading Research Quarterly, 22,* 99–121.

Diamond, A., Prevor, M. B., Callender, G., & Druin, D. P. (1997). Prefrontal cortex cognitive deficits in children treated early and continuously for PKU. *Monographs of the Society for Research in Child Development, 62,* 1–205.

Diamond, P. J., & Onwuegbuzie, A. J. (2001). Factors associated with reading achievement and attitudes among elementary school-aged students. *Research in the Schools, 8,* 1–11.

Dick, F., Bates, E., Wulfeck, B., Utman, J. A., Dronkers, N., & Gernsbacher, M. A. (2001). Language deficits, localization, and grammar: Evidence for a distributive model of language breakdown in aphasic patients and neurologically intact individuals. *Psychological Review, 108,* 759–788.

Dimino, J., Gersten, R., Carnine, D., & Blake, G. (1990). Story grammar: An approach for promoting at-risk secondary students' comprehension of literature. *The Elementary School Journal, 91,* 19–32.

Dimino, J., Taylor, R. M., & Gersten, R. M. (1995). Synthesis of the research on story grammar as a means to increase comprehension. *Reading and Writing Quarterly: Overcoming Learning Difficulties, 11,* 53–72.

Donahue, P. L., Daane, M. C., & Jin, Y. (2005). *The nation's report card: Reading 2003.* Washington, DC: U. S. Department of Education, National Center for Educational Statistics.

Donovan, C. A., & Smolkin, L. B. (2006). Children's understanding of genre and writing development. In C. A. MacArthur, S. Graham, & J. Fitzgerald (Eds.), *Handbook of writing research* (pp. 131–143). New York: Guilford Press.

Dore, J. (1975). Holophrases, speech acts, and language universals. *Journal of Child Language, 2,* 20–40.

Dorval, B., & Eckerman, C. O. (1984). Developmental trends in the quality of conversation achieved by small groups of acquainted peers. *Monographs of the Society for Research in Child Development, 49,* 1–72.

Driesen, N. R., & Raz, N. (1995). The influence of sex, age, and handedness on corpus callosum morphology: A meta-analysis. *Psychobiology, 23,* 240–247.

Duffy, G., & Roehler, L. (1987). Improving classroom reading instruction through the use of responsive elaboration. *Reading Teacher, 40,* 514–521.

Dweck, C. (1986). Motivational processes affecting learning. *American Psychologist, 41,* 1040–1048.

Dweck, C., & Elliot, E. (1983). Achievement motivation. In P. H. Mussen (Ed.), *Handbook of Child Psychology: Vol. IV. Socialization, Personality, and Social Development* (pp. 643–691). New York: Wiley.

Dweck, C., & Leggett, E. (1988). A social-cognitive approach to motivation and personality. *Psychological Review, 95,* 256–273.

Eccles, J. S., Wigfield, A., Flanagan, C., Miller, C., Reuman, D., & Yee, D. (1989). Self-perceptions, domain values, and self-esteem: Relations and changes at early adolescence. *Journal of Personality, 57,* 283–310.

Eccles, J. S., Wigfield, A., & Schiefele, U. (1998). Motivation to succeed. In W. Damon (Series Ed.) & N. Eisenberg (Vol. Ed.), *Handbook of child psychology: Vol. 3. Social, emotional, and personality development* (5th ed., pp. 1018–1095). New York: Wiley.

Eckler, J. A., & Weininger, O. (1989). Structural parallels between pretend play and narratives. *Developmental Psychology, 25,* 736–743.

Edelman, G. R. (1992). *Bright air, brilliant fire: On the matter of the mind.* New York: Basic Books.

Ehri, L. C. (1995). Phases of development in learning to read words by sight. *Journal of Research in Reading, 18,* 116–125.

Eimas, P. D. (1975). Auditory and phonetic coding of the cues for speech: Discrimination of the [r-l] distinction by young infants. *Perception and Psychophysics, 18,* 341–347.

Eimas, P. D., & Miller, J. L. (1980). Discrimination of the information for manner of articulation. *Infant Behavior and Development, 3,* 367–375.

Eimas, P. D., Siqueland, E. R., Jusczyk, P. W., & Vigorito, J. (1971). Speech perception in infants. *Science, 171,* 303–306.

Elliot, A. J., McGregor, H. A., & Gable, S. (1999). Achievement goals, study strategies, and exam performance: A mediational analysis. *Journal of Educational Psychology, 91,* 549–563.

Elman, J. L. (1989). Connectionist approaches to acoustic/phonetic processing. In W. D. Marslen-Wilson (Ed.), *Lexical representation and process* (pp. 227–260). Cambridge, MA: MIT Press.

Elrod, M. M. (1986). Children's understanding of indirect requests. *Journal of Genetic Psychology, 148,* 63–70.

Englert, C. S., Stewart, S. R., & Hiebert, E. H. (1988). Young writer's use of text structure in expository text generation. *Journal of Educational Psychology, 80,* 143–151.

Ericsson, K. A. (1996). *The road to excellence: The acquisition of expert performance in the arts, science, sports, and games.* Mahwah, NJ: Erlbaum.

Farkas, G., & Beron, K. (2004). The detailed age trajectory of oral vocabulary knowledge: Differences by class and race. *Social Science Research, 33,* 464–497.

Feather, N. T. (1988). Values, expectancies, and course enrollment: Testing the role of personal values within an expectancy-valence framework. *Journal of Educational Psychology, 80,* 381–391.

Feifel, H., & Lorge, I. (1950). Qualitative differences in the vocabulary responses of children. *Journal of Educational Psychology, 41,* 1–18.

Feitelson, D., Tehori, B. Z., & Levinberg-Green, D. (1982). How effective is early instruction in reading? Experimental Evidence. *Merrill-Palmer Quarterly, 28,* 485–494.

Fenson, L., Dale, P. S., Reznick, J. S., Bates, E., Thal, D. J., & Pethick, S. J. (1994). Variability in early communicative development. *Monographs of the Society for Research in Child Development, 59,* v–173.

Fielding, L. G., Anderson, R. C., & Pearson, P. D. (1990). *How discussion questions influence children's story understanding* (tech. rep. No 490). Urbana: University of Illinois, Center for the Study of Reading.

Finlay, B. L., & Darlington, R. B. (1995). Linked regularities in the development and evolution of mammalian brains. *Science, 268,* 1578–1584.

Fitzgerald, J. (1987). Research on revision in writing. *Review of Educational Research, 57,* 481–506.

Fivush, R., Brotman, M. A., & Buckner, J. P. (2000). Gender differences in parent–child emotion narratives. *Sex Roles, 42,* 233–253.

Fodor, J. A. (1975). *The language of thought.* New York: Crowell.

Fodor, J. A. (1983). *The modularity of mind.* Cambridge, MA: MIT Press.

Fowler, A. E., Gelman, R., & Gleitman, L. R. (1994). The course of language learning in children with Down syndrome. In H. Tager-Flusberg (Ed.), *Constraints on language acquisition: Studies of atypical children* (pp. 91–140). Hillsdale, NJ: Erlbaum.

Fowler, W. (1971). A developmental learning strategy for early reading in a laboratory nursery school. *Interchange, 2,* 106–124.

Foy, J. G., & Mann, V. (2003). Home literacy environment and phonological awareness in preschool children: Differential effects for rhyme and phoneme awareness. *Applied Psycholinguistics, 24,* 59–88.

Freedman, A. (1987). Development in story writing. *Applied Psycholinguistics, 8,* 153–170.

Frege, G. (1975). On sense and reference. In P. Geach & M. Black (Eds.), *Translations from the Philosophical Writings of Gottlob Frege* (pp. 56–78). Oxford, UK: Blackwell Scientific Publications. (Original work published 1892)

French, L., & Nelson, K. (1985). *Young children's knowledge of relational terms: Some ifs, ors, and buts.* New York: Springer-Verlag.

Frijda, N. (1994). Emotions are functional, most of the time. In P. Ekman & R. J. Davidson (Eds.), *The nature of emotion* (pp. 112–122). New York: Oxford University Press.

Galaburda, A. M. (1993). *Dyslexia and development: Neurobiological aspects of extra-ordinary brains.* Cambridge, MA: Harvard University Press.

Garner, R. (1981). Monitoring of passage inconsistency among poor comprehenders: A preliminary test of the 'piecemeal processing' explanation. *Journal of Educational Research, 74,* 159–162.

Garner, R. (1987). Strategies for reading and studying expository texts. *Educational Psychologist, 22,* 299–312.

Garner, R., Alexander, P., Slater, W., Hare, V. C., Smith, T., & Reis, R. (1986). Children's knowledge of structural properties of expository text. *Journal of Educational Psychology, 78,* 411–416.

Garner, R., Hare, V. C., Alexander, P., Haynes, J., & Winograd, P. (1984). Inducing the use of a text lookback strategy among unsuccessful readers. *American Educational Research Journal, 21,* 789–798.

Garrett, M. F. (1990). Sentence processing. In D. N. Osherson & H. Lasnik (Eds.), *An invitation to cognitive science, Vol. 1: Language* (pp. 133–175). Cambridge, MA: MIT Press.

Garton, A. F., & Pratt, C. (1990). Children's pragmatic judgments of direct and indirect requests. *First Language, 10,* 51–59.

Garvey, C. (1975). Requests and responses in children's speech. *Journal of Child Language, 2,* 41–63.

Gathercole, S. E., Alloway, T. P., Willis, C., & Adams, A. (2006). Working memory in children with reading disabilities. *Journal of Experimental Child Psychology, 93,* 265–281.

Gathercole, S. E., & Baddeley, A. D. (1989). Evaluation of the role of phonological STM in the development of vocabulary in children: A longitudinal study. *Journal of Memory and Language, 28,* 200–213.

Gayan, J., Smith, S. D., Cherny, S. S., Cardon, L. R., Fulker, D. W., Brower, A. M., et al. (1999). Quantitative-trait locus for specific language and reading deficits. *American Journal of Human Genetics, 64,* 157–164.

Gelman, S. A., & Taylor, M. (1984). How two-year-old children interpret proper and common names for unfamiliar objects. *Child Development, 55,* 1535–1540.

Gentner, D. (1988). Metaphor as structure mapping: The relational shift. *Child Development, 59,* 47–59.

Gernsbacher, M. A. (1996). The Structure-Building Framework: What it is, what it might also be, and why. In B. K. Britton & A. C. Graesser (Eds.), *Models of understanding text.* (pp. 289–311). Mahwah, NJ: Erlbaum.

Gervais, J., Tremblay, R. E., Desmarais-Gervais, L., & Vitaro, F. (2000). Children's persistent lying, gender differences, and disruptive behaviors: A longitudinal analysis. *International Journal of Behavioral Development, 24,* 213–221.

Geschwind, N., & Behan, P. (1982). Left-handedness: Association with immune disease, migraine, and developmental learning disorder. *Proceedings of the National Academy of Sciences, 79,* 5097–5100.

Geschwind, N., & Galaburda, A. M. (1985). Cerebral lateralization: Biological mechanisms, associations, and pathology I: A hypothesis and a program for research. *Archives of Neurology, 42,* 428–459.

Geschwind, N., & Galaburda, A. M. (1987). *Cerebral lateralization.* Cambridge, MA: MIT Press.

Geva, E. (1983). Facilitating reading comprehension through flowcharting. *Reading Research Quarterly, 18,* 383–405.

Giedd, J. N., Rumsey, J. M., Castellanos, F. X., Rajapakse, J. C., Kaysen, D., Vaituzis, A. C., et al. (1996). A quantitative MRI study of the corpus callosum in children and adolescents. *Developmental Brain Research, 91,* 274–280.

Gillon, G. T. (2000). The efficacy of phonological awareness intervention for children with spoken language impairment. *Language, Speech, and Hearing Services in Schools, 31,* 126–141.

Gleitman, L. R. (1990). The structural sources of verb meanings. *Language Acquisition, 1,* 3–55.

Glenberg, A. M., Gutierrez, T., Levin, J. R., Japuntich, S., & Kaschak, M. (2004). Activity and imagined activity can enhance young children's reading comprehension. *Journal of Educational Psychology, 96,* 424–436.

Glover, J. A., Ronning, R. R., & Bruning, R. H. (1990). *Cognitive psychology for teachers.* New York: Macmillan.

Goldinger, S. D., Pisoni, D. B., & Luce, R. D. (1995). Speech perception and spoken word recognition: Research and theory. In N. J. Lass (Ed.), *Principles of experimental phonetics* (pp. 277–327). Toronto: B. C. Decker.

Goldman-Rakic, P. S. (1994). Specification of higher cortical functions. In S. H. Broman & J. Grafman (Eds.), *Atypical cognitive deficits in developmental disorders: Implications for brain function* (pp. 3–18). Mahwah, NJ: Erlbaum.

Goldstein, D. M. (1976). Cognitive-linguistic functioning and learning to read in preschoolers. *Journal of Educational Psychology, 68,* 680–688.

Golinkoff, R. M., Mervis, C. B., & Hirsh-Pasek, K. (1994). Early object labels: The case for a developmental lexical principles framework. *Journal of Child Language, 21,* 125–155.

Gombert, J. E., & Fayol, M. (1992). Writing in preliterate children. *Learning and Instruction, 2,* 23–41.

Good, R. H., & Kaminski, R. A. (2002). *Dynamic Indicators of Basic Early Literacy Skills: Administration and scoring guide.* Eugene, OR: University of Oregon.

Good, T. L., & Brophy, J. E. (1990). *Educational psychology: A realistic approach* (4th ed.). New York: Longman/Addison Wesley Longman.

Goodman, C. S., & Tessier-Lavigne, M. (1997). Molecular mechanisms of axon guidance and target recognition. In W. M. Cowan, T. M. Jessell, & S. L. Zipursky

(Eds.), *Molecular and cellular approaches to neural development* (pp. 108–137). New York: Oxford University Press.

Goodman, K. S., & Goodman, Y. (1979). Learning to read is natural. In L. B. Resnick & R. A. Weaver (Eds.), *Theory and practice of early reading* (pp. 51–94). Hillsdale, NJ: Erlbaum.

Goodman, Y. M. (1991). Comments in "Beginning to read: A critique by literacy professionals and a response by Marilyn Jager Adams." *The Reading Teacher, 44,* 375.

Gopnik, A., & Choi, S. (1995). Names, relational words, and cognitive development in English and Korean speakers: Nouns are not always learned before verbs. In M. Tomasello & M. Merriman (Eds.), *Beyond names for things: Young children's acquisition of verbs* (pp. 63–80). Hillsdale, NJ: Erlbaum.

Gopnik, A., & Wellman, H. M. (1992). Why the child's theory of mind really is a theory. *Mind and Language, 7,* 145–171.

Gordon, R. R. (1988). Increasing efficiency and effectiveness in predicting second grade achievement using a kindergarten screening battery. *Journal of Educational Research, 81,* 238–244.

Goswami, U. (1998). The role of analogies in the development of word recognition. In J. L. Metsala & L. C. Ehri (Eds.), *Word recognition in beginning literacy* (pp. 41–64). Mahwah, NJ: Erlbaum.

Gough, P. B., Hoover, W. A., & Peterson, C. L. (1996). Some observations on a simple view of reading. In C. Cornoldi & J. Oakhill (Eds.), *Reading comprehension difficulties: Processes and intervention* (pp. 1–13). Mahwah, NJ: Erlbaum.

Graesser, A., Golding, J. M., & Long, D. L. (1991). Narrative representation and comprehension. In R. Barr, M. L. Kamil, P. Mosenthal, & P. D. Pearson (Eds.), *Handbook of reading research: Vol. II* (pp. 171–205). New York: Longman.

Graesser, A. C., Millis, K. K., & Zwaan, R. A. (1997). Discourse comprehension. *Annual Review of Psychology, 48,* 163–189.

Graham, S. (1994). Motivation in African-Americans. *Review of Educational Research, 64,* 55–117.

Graham, S. (1997). Executive control in the revising of students with learning and writing difficulties. *Journal of Educational Psychology, 89,* 223–234.

Graham, S. (2006). Writing. In P. A. Alexander & P. H. Winne (Eds.), *Handbook of educational psychology* (pp. 457–478). Mahwah, NJ: Erlbaum.

Graham, S., Berninger, V. W., Abbott, R. D., Abbott, S. P., & Whitaker, D. (1997). Role of mechanics in composing of elementary school students: A new methodological approach. *Journal of Educational Psychology, 89,* 170–182.

Graham, S., & Golan, S. (1991). Motivational influences on cognition: Task involvement, ego involvement, and depth of information processing. *Journal of Educational Psychology, 83,* 187–194.

Graham, S., & Harris, K. R. (1996). Self-regulation and strategy instruction for students who find writing and learning challenging. In C. M. Levy & S. Ransdell (Eds.), *The science of writing: Theories, methods, individual differences, and applications* (pp. 347–360). Mahwah, NJ; Erlbaum.

Graham, S., Harris, K. R., Fink-Chorzempa, B., & MacArthur, C. (2003). Primary grade teachers' instructional adaptations for struggling writers: A national survey. *Journal of Educational Psychology, 95,* 279–292.

Greany, V. (1980). Factors related to amount and time of leisure reading. *Reading Research Quarterly, 15,* 337–357.

Greany, V., & Hegarty, M. (1987). Correlates of leisure-time reading. *Journal of Research in Reading, 10,* 3–20.

Greenough, W. T., Black, J. E., & Wallace, C. S. (1987). Experience and brain development. *Child Development, 58,* 539–559.

Greenwald, E. A., Perksy, H. R., Campbell, J. R., & Mazzeo, J. (1999). *The NAEP 1998 writing report card for the nation and the states.* Washington, DC: U.S. Department of Education, Office of Educational Research and Improvement, National Center for Educational Statistics.

Grice, H. (1975). Logic and conversation. In P. Cole & J. Morgan (Eds.), *Syntax and semantics: Vol. 3. Speech acts* (pp. 41–58). New York: Academic Press.

Griffiths, Y. M., & Snowling, M. J. (2001). Auditory word identification and phonological skills in dyslexic and average readers. *Applied Psycholinguistics, 22,* 419–439.

Grigg, W. S., Daane, M. C., Jin, Y., & Campbell, J. R. (2003). *The nation's report card: Reading 2002.* Washington, DC: U. S. Department of Education, National Center for Educational Statistics.

Gurney, D., Gersten, R., Dimino, J., & Carnine, D. (1990). Story grammar: Effective literature instruction for high school students with learning disabilities. *Journal of Learning Disabilities, 23,* 335–348.

Guthrie, J. T., Anderson, E., Alao, S., & Rinehart, J. (1999). Influences of Concept-Oriented Reading Instruction on strategy use and conceptual learning from text. *Elementary School Journal, 99,* 343–366.

Guthrie, J. T., Cox, K. E., Knowles, K. T., Buehl, M., Mazzoni, S. A., & Fasulo, L. (2000). Building toward coherent instruction. In L. Baker, M. J. Dreher, & J. T. Guthrie (Eds.), *Engaging young readers: Promoting achievement and motivation* (pp. 209–236). New York: Guilford Press.

Guthrie, J. T., Wigfield, A., Barbosa, P., Perencevich, K., Taboada, A., Davis, M., et al. (2004). Increasing reading comprehension and engagement through Concept-Oriented Reading Instruction. *Journal of Educational Psychology, 96,* 403–423.

Halpern, D. F. (1992). *Sex differences in cognitive abilities* (2nd ed.). Hillsdale, NJ: Erlbaum.

Hammill, D. D., & McNutt, G. (1980). Language abilities and reading: A review of the literature on their relationship. *Elementary School Journal, 80,* 268–2770.

Hansen, J., & Pearson, P. D. (1983). An instructional study: Improving the inferential comprehension of good and poor fourth-grade readers. *Journal of Educational Psychology, 75,* 821–829.

Hargrave, A. C., & Sénéchal, M. (2000). A book reading intervention with preschool children who have limited vocabularies: The benefits of regular reading and dialogic reading. *Early Childhood Research Quarterly, 15,* 75–90.

Hart, B., & Risley, T. R. (1995). *Meaningful differences in the everyday experience of young children.* New York: Paul H. Brookes.

Hart, J. T., Guthrie, J. T., & Winfield, L. (1980). Black English phonology and learning to read. *Journal of Educational Psychology, 72,* 636–646.

Harter, S. (1985). Competence as a dimension of self-evaluation: Toward a comprehensive model of self-worth. In R. L. Leahy (Ed.), *The development of the self* (pp. 55–121). Orlando, FL: Academic Press.

Hassold, T., Sherman, S., & Hunt, P. A. (1995). The origin of trisomy in humans. In C. J. Epstein, T. Hassold, I. T. Lott, L. Nadel, & D. Patterson (Eds.), *Etiology and pathogenesis of Down Syndrome* (pp. 1–12). New York: Wiley-Liss.

Hayes, J. R. (1996). A new framework for understanding cognition and affect in writing. In C. M. Levy & S. Ransdell (Eds.), *The science of writing: Theories, methods, individual differences, and applications* (pp. 1–27). Mahwah, NJ: Erlbaum.

Hayes, J. R., & Flower, L. S. (1980). Identifying the organization of writing processes. In L. Gregg & E. Steinberg (Eds.), *Cognitive processes in writing: An interdisciplinary approach* (pp. 3–30). Mahwah, NJ: Erlbaum.

Hayes, J. R., & Flower, L. S. (1986). Writing research and the writer. *American Psychologist, 41,* 1106–1113.

Hayes, J. R., Flower, L. S., Schriver, K. S., Stratman, J., & Carey, L. (1987). Cognitive processes in revision. In S. Rosenberg (Ed.), *Advances in psycholinguistics: Vol. 2. Reading, writing, and language processing* (pp. 176–240). New York: Cambridge University Press.

Heath, S. B. (1983). *Ways with words: Language, life and work in communities and classrooms.* Cambridge: Cambridge University Press.

Hedges, L. V., & Nowell, A. (1995). Sex differences in mental test scores, variability, and numbers of high-scoring individuals. *Science, 269,* 41–45.

Heyns, B. (1978). *Summer learning and the effects of schooling.* New York: Academic Press.

Hidi, S., & Boscolo, P. (2006). Motivation and writing. In C. A. MacArthur, S. Graham, & J. Fitzgerald (Eds.), *Handbook of writing research* (pp. 144–157). New York: Guilford Press.

Hinds, T. S., West, W. L., Knight, E. M., & Harland, B. F. (1996). The effect of caffeine on pregnancy outcome variables. *Nutrition Review, 54,* 203–207.

Hintzman, D. L. (1986). "Schema abstraction" in a multiple-trace memory model. *Psychological Review, 93,* 411–428.

Hirsh-Pasek, K., & Golinkoff, R. M. (1991). Language comprehension: A new look at some old themes. In N. Krasnegor, D. M. Rumbaugh, R. L. Schiefelbusch, & M. Studdert-Kennedy (Eds.), *Biological and behavioral determinants of language development* (pp. 301–320). Hillsdale, NJ: Erlbaum.

Hoff, E. (2001). *Language development* (2nd ed.). Belmont, CA: Wadsworth/Thomson Learning.

Hoff-Ginsburg, E. (1991). Mother–child conversation in different social classes and communicative settings. *Child Development, 62,* 782–796.

Howes, C., Sakai, L. M., Shinn, M., & Phillips, D. (1995). Race, social class, and maternal working conditions as influences on children's development. *Journal of Applied Developmental Psychology, 16,* 107–124.

Huebner, C. E., & Meltzoff, A. N. (2005). Intervention to change parent–child reading style: A comparison of instructional methods. *Journal of Applied Developmental Psychology, 26,* 296–313.

Hunt, K. W. (1970). Syntactic maturity in school children and adults. *Monographs of the Society for Research in Child Development, 35* (No. 134), pp. 1–67.

Huttenlocher, J., Haight, W., Bryk, A., Seltzer, M., & Lyons, T. (1991). Early vocabulary growth: Relation to language input and gender. *Developmental Psychology*, *27*, 236–248.

Huttenlocher, P. R. (1993). Morphometric study of human cerebral cortex development. In M. H. Johnson (Ed.), *Brain development and cognition: A reader* (pp. 112–124). Cambridge, MA: Blackwell Publishers.

Hyams, N., & Wexler, K. (1993). On the grammatical basis of null subjects in child language. *Linguistic Inquiry*, *24*, 421–459.

Hyde, J. S., & Linn, M. C. (1988). Gender differences in verbal ability: A meta-analysis. *Psychological Bulletin*, *104*, 53–69.

Hynd, G. W., Marshall, R., & Gonzales, J. (1991). Learning disabilities and presumed central nervous system dysfunction. *Learning Disability Quarterly*, *14*, 283–296.

Hyönä, J., Lorch, R. F., & Kaakinen, J. K. (2002). Individual differences in reading to summarize expository text: Evidence from eye fixation patterns. *Journal of Educational Psychology*, *94*, 44–55.

Iverson, B. K., & Walberg, H. J. (1982). Home environment and school learning: A qualitative synthesis. *Journal of Experimental Education*, *50*, 144–151.

Jackson, N. E. (1992). Precocious reading of English: Origins, structure, and predictive significance. In P. S. Klein & A. J. Tannebaum (Eds.), *To be young and gifted* (pp. 171–203). Norwood, NJ: Ablex.

Jackson, S. C., & Roberts, J. E. (2001). Complex syntax production of African American preschoolers. *Journal of Speech, Language, and Hearing Research*, *44*, 1083–1096.

Johnson, D. L., Swank, P., Howie, V. M., Baldwin, C. D., Owen, M., & Luttman, D. (1993). Does HOME add to the prediction of child intelligence over and above SES? *Journal of Genetic Psychology*, *154*, 33–40.

Johnson, D. W., & Johnson, R. T. (1987). *Learning together and alone*. Englewood Cliffs, NJ: Prentice-Hall.

Johnson, M. H. (1997). *Developmental cognitive neuroscience: An introduction*. Cambridge, MA: Blackwell Publishers.

Johnston, P., & Afflerbach, P. (1985). The process of constructing main ideas from text. *Cognition and Instruction*, *2*, 207–232.

Jones, K. K., & Byrnes, J. P. (2006). Characteristics of students who benefit from high-quality mathematics instruction. *Contemporary Educational Psychology*, *31*, 328–343.

Jusczyk, P. W. (1997). *The discovery of spoken language*. Cambridge, MA: MIT Press.

Jusczyk, P. W., Luce, R. D., & Charles-Luce, J. (1994). Infants' sensitivity to phonotactic patterns in the native language. *Journal of Memory and Language*, *33*, 630–645.

Jusczyk, P. W., Pisoni, D. B., & Mullinex, J. (1992). Some consequences of stimulus variability on speech processing on 2-month-old infants. *Cognition*, *43*, 253–291.

Just, M. A., & Carpenter, P. A. (1987). *The psychology of reading and language comprehension*. Boston: Allyn & Bacon.

Kandel, E. R. (1991). Nerve cells and behavior. In E. R. Kandel, J. H. Schwartz, & T. M. Jessell (Eds.), *Principles of neural science* (3rd ed., pp. 18–32). Norwalk, CT: Appleton & Lange.

Karmiloff-Smith, A. (1995). *Beyond modularity: A developmental perspective on cognitive science*. Cambridge, MA: MIT Press.

Karmiloff-Smith, A., Grant, J., Berthoud, I., Davies, M., Howlin, P., & Udwin, O. (1997). Language and Williams syndrome: How intact is 'intact'? *Child Development, 68,* 246–262.

Katz, N., Baker, E., & McNamara, J. (1974). What's in a name? A study of how children learn common and proper names. *Child Development, 45,* 469–473.

Keil, F. C. (1989). *Concepts, kinds, and cognitive development.* Cambridge, MA: MIT Press.

Kelley, D. B. (1993). Androgens and brain development: Possible contributions to developmental dyslexia. In A. M. Galaburda (Ed.), *Dyslexia and development: Neurobiological aspects of extra-ordinary brains* (pp. 21–41). Cambridge, MA: Harvard University Press.

Kelley, S. D. (2001). Broadening the units of analysis in communication: Speech and nonverbal behaviours in pragmatic comprehension. *Journal of Child Language, 28,* 325–349.

Kellogg, R. T. (1996). A model of working memory in writing. In C. M. Levy & S. Ransdell (Eds.), *The science of writing: Theories, methods, individual differences, and applications* (pp. 57–72). Mahwah, NJ: Erlbaum.

Kemper, T. L. (1988). Neuropathology of Down Syndrome. In L. Nadel (Ed.), *The psychobiology of Down Syndrome* (pp. 269–289). Cambridge, MA: MIT Press.

Kessler, B., & Treiman, R. (1997). Syllable structure and the distribution of phonemes in English syllables. *Journal of Memory and Language, 37,* 295–311.

Kim, T., & Axelrod, S. (2005): Direct Instruction: An educators' guide and a plea for action. *The Behavior Analyst Today, 6,* 111.

Kintsch, W. (1982). Text representations. In W. Otto & S. White (Eds.), *Reading expository material* (pp. 87–102). New York: Academic Press.

Kipp, K., Pope, S., & Digby, S. E. (1998). The development of cognitive inhibition in a reading comprehension task. *European Review of Applied Psychology, 48,* 19–25.

Klaczynski, P. A. (2000). Motivated scientific reasoning biases, epistemological beliefs, and theory polarization: A two-process approach to adolescent cognition. *Child Development, 71,* 1347–1367.

Klima, E. S., & Bellugi, U. (1967). Syntactic regularities in the speech of children. In J. Lyons & R. J. Wales (Eds.), *Psycholinguistic papers: The proceedings of the 1966 Edinburgh Conference.* Edinburgh, UK: Edinburgh University Press.

Knopik, V. S., Alarcon, M., & DeFries, J. C. (1997). Common and specific gender influences on individual differences in reading performance: A twin study. *Personality and Individual Differences, 25,* 269–277.

Knudson, R. E. (1992). The development of written argumentation: An analysis and comparison of argumentative writing at four grade levels. *Child Study Journal, 22,* 167–181.

Kosslyn, S. M., & Koenig, O. (1994). *Wet mind: The new cognitive neuroscience.* New York: Free Press.

Kuczaj, S. A. (1990). Constraining constraint theories. *Cognitive Development, 5,* 341–344.

Kuhl, P. K., & Miller, J. D. (1982). Discrimination of auditory target dimensions in the presence or absence of variation in a second dimension by infants. *Perception and Psychophysics, 31,* 279–292.

Kuhn, D. (1992). Piaget's child as scientist. In H. Beilin & P. B. Pufall (Eds.), *Piaget's theory: Prospects and possibilities* (pp. 185–208). Hillsdale, NJ: Erlbaum.

Kush, J. C., & Watkins, M. W. (1996). Long-term stability of children's attitudes toward reading. *Journal of Educational Research, 89,* 315–319.

Laird, J., DeBell, M., & Chapman, C. (2006). *Dropout rates in the United States: 2004* (NCES 2007-024). U.S. Department of Education, Washington, DC: National Center for Educational Statistics. Retrieved May 4, 2007, from *nces.ed.gov/pubsearch*.

Lakoff, G. (1987). *Women, fire, and dangerous things: What categories reveal about the mind.* Chicago, IL: University of Chicago Press.

Langer, J. A. (1986). *Children's reading and writing: Structures and strategies.* Norwood, NJ: Ablex.

LaShell, L. (1986). An analysis of the effects of reading methods upon reading achievement and locus-of-control when individual reading style is matched for learning-disabled students. *Dissertation Abstracts International, 48,* 0362.

Lasnick, H. (1990). Syntax. In D. N. Osherson & H. Lasnik (Eds.), *An invitation to cognitive science: Vol. 1. Language* (pp. 5–22). Cambridge, MA: MIT Press.

Lau, I. C., Yeung, A. S., Jin, P., & Low, R. (1999). Toward a hierarchical, multidimensional English self-concept. *Journal of Educational Psychology, 91,* 747–755.

Lauren, L., & Allen, L. (1999). Factors that predict success in an early literacy intervention project. *Reading Research Quarterly, 34,* 404–424.

Leaper, C., Anderson, K. J., & Saunders, P. (1998). Moderators of gender effects on parents' talk to their children: A meta-analysis. *Developmental Psychology, 34,* 3–27.

Ledbetter, P. J., & Dent, C. H. (1988). Young children's sensitivity to direct and indirect request structure. *First Language, 8,* 227–246.

Lee, V. E., & Burkham, D. T. (2002). *Inequality at the starting gate: Social background differences in achievement as children begin school.* Washington, DC: Economic Policy Institute.

Leonard, L. B. (1998). *Children with specific language impairment.* Cambridge, MA: MIT Press.

Lesaux, N. K., & Siegel, L. S. (2003). The development of reading in children who speak English as a second language. *Developmental Psychology, 39,* 1005–1019.

Leseman, P. P. M., & de Jong, P. F. (1998). Home literacy: Opportunity, instruction, cooperation, and social-emotional quality predicting early reading achievement. *Reading Research Quarterly, 33,* 294–318.

Levin, I., & Bus, A. (2003). How is emergent writing based on drawing? Analyses of children's products and their sorting by children and mothers. *Developmental Psychology, 39,* 891–905.

Lewis, M., Stanger, C., & Sullivan, M. W. (1989). Deception in 3-year-olds. *Developmental Psychology, 25,* 439–443.

Linderholm, T., & van den Broek, P. (2002). The effects of reading purpose and working memory capacity on the processing of expository text. *Journal of Educational Psychology, 94,* 778–784.

Lindsey, K. A., Manis, F. R., & Bailey, C. E. (2003). Prediction of first-grade reading in Spanish-speaking English-language learners. *Journal of Educational Psychology*, *95*, 482–494.

Loban, D. W. (1976). *Language development: Kindergarten through grade twelve* (Research Report No. 18). Urbana, IL: National Council of Teachers of English.

Locke, J. L. (1993). *The child's path to spoken language*. Cambridge, MA: Harvard University Press.

Locke, J. L., & Pearson, D. M. (1992). Vocal learning and the emergence of phonological capacity: A neurobiological approach. In C. A. Ferguson, L. Menn, & S. Stoel-Gammon (Eds.), *Phonological development* (pp. 91–129). Timonium, MD: York Press.

Lundberg, I., Frost, J., & Petersen, O. (1988). Effects of an extensive program for stimulating phonological awareness in preschool children. *Reading Research Quarterly*, *23*(3), 263–284.

Maccoby, E., & Jacklin, C. N. (1974). *The psychology of sex differences*. Stanford, CA: Stanford University Press.

Mac Iver, D. (1987). Classroom factors and student characteristics predicting students' use of achievement standards during ability self-assessment. *Child Development*, *58*, 1258–1271.

MacKensie-Keating, S., McDonald, L., Tanchak, D., & Erickson, D. (1996). Natural rates of compliant behavior in preschool children in day care settings. *Early Child Development and Care*, *124*, 91–103.

MacWhinney, B. (1998). Models of the emergence of language. *Annual Review of Psychology*, *49*, 199–227.

MacWhinney, B. (2006). Emergentism—Use often and with care. *Applied Linguistics*, *27*, 729–740.

MacWhinney, B., Leinbach, J., Taraban, R., & McDonald, J. (1989). Language learning: Cues or rules? *Journal of Memory and Language*, *28*, 255–277.

Magliano, J. P., Trabasso, T., & Graesser, A. C. (1999). Strategic processing during comprehension. *Journal of Educational Psychology*, *91*, 615–629.

Malmgren, K., & Leone, P. E. (2000). Effects of a short term auxiliary readingprogram on the reading skills of incarcerated youth. *Education and Treatment of Children*, *23*, 239–247.

Mandler, J. M., & Johnson, N. S. (1977). Remembrance of things parsed: Story structure and recall. *Cognitive Psychology*, *9*, 111–151.

Manley-Casimir, M., & Wassermann, S. (1989). The teacher as decision maker: Connective self with the practice of teaching. *Childhood Education*, *65*, 288–293.

Maratsos, M. (1983). Some current issues in the study of the acquisition of grammar. In P. Mussen (Series Ed.), J. H. Flavell & E. M. Markman (Vol. Eds.), *Handbook of child psychology: Vol. 3. Cognition, perception, and language* (4th ed., pp. 707–786). New York: Wiley.

Maratsos, M. (1998). The acquisition of grammar. In W. Damon (Series Ed.), D. Kuhn & R. S. Siegler (Vol. Eds.), *Handbook of child psychology: Vol. 3. Cognition, perception and language* (5th ed.). New York: Wiley.

Markman, E. M. (1979). Realizing that you don't understand: Elementary school children's awareness of inconsistencies. *Child Development*, *50*, 643–655.

Markman, E. M. (1981). Comprehension monitoring. In W. P. Dickson (Ed.), *Children's oral communication skills*. New York: Academic Press.

Markman, E. M. (1991). The whole-object, taxonomic, and mutual exclusivity assumptions as initial constraints on word meanings. In S. A. Gelman & J. P. Byrnes (Eds.), *Perspectives on language and thought: Interrelations in development* (pp. 72–106). New York: Cambridge University Press.

Markson, L., & Bloom, P. (1997). Evidence against a dedicated system for word learning in children. *Nature, 385*(6619), 813–815.

Marschark, M., Lang, H. G., & Albertini, J. A. (2006). *Educating deaf students: From research to practice*. Oxford, UK: Oxford University Press.

Marsh, H. W. (1989). Age and sex effects in multiple dimensions of self-concept: Preadolescence to early adulthood. *Journal of Educational Psychology, 81*, 417–430.

Marslen-Wilson, W. (1989). *Lexical representation and process*. Cambridge, MA: MIT Press.

Martin, I., & McDonald, S. (2003). Weak coherence, no theory of mind, or executive dysfunction. Solving the puzzle of pragmatic language disorders. *Brain and Language, 85*, 451–466.

Masten, A. S. (1986). Humor and competence in school-aged children. *Child Development, 57*, 461–473.

McCann, T. M. (1989). Student argumentative writing knowledge and ability at three grade levels. *Research in the Teaching of English, 23*, 62–72.

McCarthy, D. (1954). Language development in children. In. P. Carmichael (Ed.), *Manual of child psychology* (2nd ed.). New York: Wiley.

McCarthy, R. A., & Warrington, E. K. (1990). *Cognitive neuropsychology: A clinical introduction*. San Diego: Academic Press.

McClelland, J. L., & Rumelhart, D. E. (1981). An interactive model of context effects in letter perception: I: An account of the basic findings. *Psychological Review, 88*, 375–407.

McCutchen, D. (1986). Domain knowledge and linguistic knowledge in the development of writing ability. *Journal of Memory and Language, 25*, 431–444.

McCutchen, D. (2006). Cognitive factors in the development of children's writing. In C. A. MacArthur, S. Graham, & J. Fitzgerald (Eds.), *Handbook of writing research* (pp. 115–130). New York: Guilford Press.

McCutchen, D., Covill, A., Hoyne, S. H., & Mildes, K. (1994). Individual differences in writing: Implications of translating fluency. *Journal of Educational Psychology, 86*, 256–266.

McCutchen, D., Francis, M., & Kerr, S. (1997). Revising for meaning: Effects of knowledge and strategy. *Journal of Educational Psychology, 89*, 667–676.

McCutchen, D., & Perfetti, C. A. (1982). Coherence and connectedness in the development of discourse production. *Text, 2*, 113–139.

McDaniel, M. A., Riegler, G. L., & Waddill, P. J. (1990). Generation effects in free recall: Further support for a three-factor theory. *Journal of Experimental Psychology: Learning, Memory, and Cognition, 16*, 789–798.

McGee, L. M. (1982). Awareness of text structure: Effects on children's recall of expository text. *Reading Research Quarterly, 17*, 581–591.

McGhee, P. E. (1971). Development of the humor response: A review of the literature. *Psychological Bulletin, 76*, 328–348.

McKeown, M. G., & Curtis, M. E. (1987). *The nature of vocabulary acquisition.* Hillsdale, NJ: Erlbaum.

McKoon, G., & Ratcliff, R. (1992). Inference during reading. *Psychological Review, 99,* 440–466.

McNamara, J. (1982). *Names for things.* Cambridge, MA: MIT Press.

Meltzoff, A. N. (1995). Understanding the intentions of others: Re-enactment of intended acts by 18-month-old children. *Developmental Psychology, 31,* 838–850.

Menn, L., & Stoel-Gammon, C. (2005). Phonological development: Learning sounds and sound patterns. In J. Berko Gleason (Ed.), *The development of language* (6th ed., pp. 62–111). Needham Heights, MA: Allyn & Bacon.

Mertens, D. M. (2005). *Research and evaluation in education and psychology: integrating diversity with quantitative, qualitative, and mixed methods* (2nd ed.). Thousand Oaks, CA: Sage.

Mervis, C. B. (1987) Child-basic object categories and early lexical development. In U. Neisser (Ed.), *Concepts and conceptual development: Ecological and intellectual factors in categorization* (pp. 201–233). New York: Cambridge University Press.

Mervis, C. B., & Bertrand, J. (1995). Early lexical acquisition and the vocabulary spurt: A response to Goldfield & Reznick. *Journal of Child Language, 22,* 461–468.

Mervis, C. B., & Crisafi, M. A. (1982). Order of acquisition of subordinate-, basic-, and superordinate-level categories. *Child Development, 53,* 258–266.

Metsala, J. L. (1999). Young children's phonological awareness and nonword repetition as a function of vocabulary development. *Journal of Educational Psychology, 91,* 3–19.

Metsala, J. L., & Walley, A. C. (1998). Spoken vocabulary growth and the segmental restructuring of lexical representations: Precursors to phonemic awareness and early reading ability. In J. L. Metsala & L. C. Ehri (Eds.), *Word recognition in beginning literacy* (pp. 89–120). Mahwah, NJ: Erlbaum.

Meyer, B. J. F. (1985). Prose analysis: Purposes, procedures, and problems. In B. K. Britton & J. B. Black (Eds.), *Understanding expository text* (pp. 11–66). Hillsdale, NJ: Erlbaum.

Meyer, B. J. F., Brandt, D. M., & Bluth, G. J. (1980). Use of top-level structure in text: Key for reading comprehension of ninth-grade students. *Reading Research Quarterly, 16,* 73–103.

Meyer, L. (1984). Long-term academic effects of the Direct Instruction Project Follow Through. *Elementary School Journal, 84,* 380–394.

Miller, G. E., Giovenco, A., & Rentiers, K. A. (1987). Fostering comprehension monitoring in below average readers through self-instruction training. *Journal of Reading Behavior, 19,* 303–317.

Miller, L. M. S., Stine-Morrow, E. A. L., Kirkorian, H. L., & Conroy, M. L. (2004). Adult age differences in knowledge-driven reading. *Journal of Educational Psychology, 96,* 811–821.

Montague, M., Maddux, C. D., & Dereshiwsky, M. I. (1990). Story grammar and comprehension and production of narrative prose by students with learning disabilities. *Journal of Learning Disabilities, 23,* 190–197.

Moore, C., & Corkum, V. (1994). Social understanding at the end of the first year of life. *Developmental Review, 14,* 349–372.

Morphett, M., & Washburn, C. (1931). When should children begin to read? *Elementary School Journal, 31,* 496–503.

Morris, D., Perney, J., & Shaw, B. (1990). Helping low readers in grades 2 and 3: An after-school volunteer tutoring program. *The Elementary School Journal, 91*(2), 132–150.

Morris, D., Tyner, B., & Perney, J. (2000). Early Steps: Replicating the effects of a first-grade reading intervention program. *Journal of Educational Psychology, 92,* 681–693.

Morse, P. A. (1972). The discrimination of speech and nonspeech stimuli in early infancy. *Journal of Experimental Child Psychology, 14,* 477–492.

Moyer, K. E. (1980). *Neuroanatomy.* New York: Harper & Row.

Murphy, G. L. (2002). *The big book of concepts.* Cambridge, MA: MIT Press.

Muter, V., Hulme, C., Snowling, M., & Stevenson, J. (2004). Phonemes, rimes, vocabulary, and grammatical skills as foundations of early reading development: Evidence from a longitudinal study. *Developmental Psychology, 40,* 665–681.

Nagle, R. J. (1979). The predictive validity of the metropolitan readiness tests, 1976 edition. *Educational and Psychological Measurement, 39,* 1043–1045.

National Assessment of Educational Progress. (1990). *The writing trend cross sectional report, 1988.* Washington, DC: National Center for Educational Statistics.

National Center for Educational Statistics. (2003). *The 2003 reading report card.* Washington, DC: U.S. Department of Education.

Nell, V. (1988). The psychology of reading for pleasure: Needs and gratification. *Reading Research Quarterly, 23,* 6–50.

Nelson, J. R., Benner, G. J., & Gonzalez, J. (2005). An investigation of the effects of a prereading intervention on the early literacy skills of children at risk of emotional disturbance and reading problems. *Journal of Emotional and Behavioral Disorders, 13,* 3–12.

Nelson, K. (1973). Structure and strategy in learning to talk. *Monographs of the Society for Research in Child Development, 38*(1–2, Serial No 149), v–136.

Nelson, K. (1988). Constraints on word learning? *Cognitive Development, 3,* 221–246.

Nelson, K. (1996). *Language in cognitive development: Emergence of the mediated mind.* New York: Cambridge University Press.

Nelson, K., & Kessler, L. (2002). Developing a socially shared symbolic system. In E. Amsel & J. P. Byrnes (Eds.), *Language, literacy, and cognitive development: The development and consequences of symbolic communication* (pp. 27–57). Mahwah, NJ: Erlbaum.

Neuman, S. B. (1986). The home environment and fifth-grade students' leisure reading. *The Elementary School Journal, 86,* 335–343.

Neuman, S. B., Snow, C. E., Canizares, S. E. (2000). *Building language for literacy.* New York: Scholastic.

Newell, A., & Simon, H. A. (1972). *Human problem solving.* Englewood Cliffs, NJ: Prentice-Hall.

National Institute of Child Health and Human Development Early Child Care Research Network. (2000).The relation of child care to cognitive and language development. *Child Development, 71,* 960–980.

National Institute of Child Health and Human Development Early Child Care Research Network (2005). Pathways to reading: The role of oral language in the transition to reading. *Developmental Psychology, 41,* 428–442.

Nicholls, J. (1983). Conceptions of ability and achievement motivation: A theory and its implications for education. In S. Paris, G. Olson, & H. Stevenson (Eds.), *Learning and motivation in the classroom* (pp. 211–237). Hillsdale, NJ: Erlbaum.

Ninio, A., & Snow, C. E. (1999). The development of pragmatics: Learning to use language appropriately. In N. C. Ritchie & T. K. Bhatia (Eds.), *Handbook of child language acquisition* (pp. 347–383). Orlando, FL: Academic Press.

Noble, K., Glosser, G., & Grossman, M. (2000). Oral reading in dementia. *Brain and Language, 74,* 48–69.

Norris, J. A., & Bruning, R. H. (1988). Cohesion in the narratives of good and poor readers. *Journal of Speech and Hearing Disorders, 53,* 416–424.

Nunnery, J., Ross, S. M., & McDonald, A. (2006). A randomized experimental evaluation of the impact of Accelerated Reader/Reading Renaissance implementation on reading achievement in grades 3 to 6. *Journal of Students Placed At-Risk, 11,* 1–18.

Nussbaum, E. M., & Kardash, C. M. (2005). The effects of goal instructions and text on the generation of counterarguments during writing. *Journal of Educational Psychology, 97,* 157–169.

Nygaard, L. C., & Pisoni, D. B. (1995). Speech perception: New directions in research and theory. In J. L. Miller & P. D. Eimas (Eds.), *Speech, language, and communication* (pp. 63–96). Orlando, FL: Academic Press.

Oakes, J. (2005). *Keeping track: How schools structure inequality* (2nd ed.). New Haven, CT: Yale University Press.

Okagaki, L., & Sternberg, R. J. (1991). *Directors of development: Influences on the development of children's thinking.* Mahwah, NJ: Erlbaum.

Oller, D. K., & Eilers, R. E. (1988*).* The role of audition in infant babbling. *Child Development, 59,* 441–449.

Ollers, D. K., Eilers, R. E., Basinger, D., Steffens, M. L., & Urbano, R. (1995). Extreme poverty and the development of precursors to the speech capacity. *First Language, 15,* 167–189.

Opdenakker, M., Van Damme, J., De Fraine, B., Van Landeghem, G., & Onghena, P. (2002). The effects of schools and classes on mathematics achievement. *School Effectiveness and School Improvement, 13,* 399–427.

Page-Voth, V., & Graham, S. (1999). Effects of goal setting and strategy use on the writing performance and self-efficacy of students with writing and learning problems. *Journal of Educational Psychology, 91,* 230–240.

Palincsar, A. M., & Brown, A. L. (1984). Reciprocal teaching of comprehension-fostering and comprehension-monitoring activities. *Cognition and Instruction, 1,* 117–175.

Pan, B. A. (2005). Semantic development: learning the meaning of words. In J. Berko Gleason (Ed.), *The development of language* (6th ed., pp. 112–147). Needham Heights, MA: Allyn & Bacon.

Pan, B. A., Rowe, M. L., Spier, E., & Tamis-LeMonda, C. (2004). Measuring productive vocabulary of toddlers in low-income families: Concurrent and predictive validity of three sources of data. *Journal of Child Language, 31,* 587–608.

Paris, S. G. (1978). Coordination of means and goals in the development of mnemonic skills. In P. A. Ornstein (Ed.), *Memory development in children.* Hillsdale, NJ: Erlbaum.

Paris, S. G., & Byrnes, J. P. (1989). The constructivist approach to self-regulation and learning in the classroom. In B. J. Zimmerman & D. H. Schunk (Eds.), *Self-regulated learning and academic achievement: Theory, research, and practice.* New York: Springer-Verlag.

Paris, S. G., Byrnes, J. P., & Paris, A. H. (2001). Constructing theories, identities, and actions of self-regulated learners. In B. Zimmerman & D. Schunk (Eds.), *Self-regulated learning: Theories, research, practice* (2nd ed., pp. 253–287). New York: Guilford Press.

Paris, S. G., Wasik, B. A., & Turner, J. C. (1991). The development of strategic readers. In R. Barr, M. L. Kamil, P. B. Mosenthal, & P. D. Pearson (Eds.), *Handbook of reading research, Vol. II* (pp. 609–640). New York: Longman.

Pearson, P. D., & Fielding, L. (1991). Comprehension instruction. In M. Barr, M. L. Kamil, P. B. Mosenthal, & P. D. Pearson (Eds.), *Handbook of reading research, Vol. II* (pp. 815–861). New York: Longman.

Perfetti, C. A. (1985). *Reading ability.* New York: Oxford University Press.

Perfetti, C. A., & McCutchen, D. (1987). Schooled language competence: Linguistic abilities in reading and writing. In S. Rosenberg (Ed.), *Advances in applied psycholinguistics* (pp. 105–141). Cambridge: Cambridge University Press.

Perie, M., Grigg, W., & Donahue, P. (2005). *The nation's report card: Reading 2005.* Washington, DC: U.S. Department of Education, National Center for Educational Statistics.

Perry, T., & Delpit, L. D. (1998). *The real ebonics debate: Power, language, and the education of African American children.* Boston, MA: Beacon Press.

Petersen, S. E., Fox, P. T., Snyder, A. Z., & Raichle, M. E. (1990). Activation of extrastriate and frontal cortical areas by visual words and word-like stimuli. *Science, 240,* 1041–1044.

Piaget, J. (1926). *The language and thought of the child.* London: Kegan & Paul.

Piaget, J. (1952). *The origins of intelligence in children.* New York: International Universities Press.

Piaget, J. (1978). *Success and understanding.* Cambridge, MA: Harvard University Press.

Piaget, J. (1983). Piaget's theory. In P. H. Mussen (Ed.), *Handbook of child psychology: Vol. 1. History, theory, methods* (pp. 103–128). New York: Wiley.

Piaget, J., & Inhelder, B. (1969). *The psychology of the child.* New York: Basic Books.

Pinker, S. (1989). Language acquisition. In M. I. Posner (Ed.), *Foundations of cognitive science* (pp. 359–400). Cambridge, MA: MIT Press.

Pinker, S. (1994). *The language instinct.* New York: William Morrow.

Pinker, S. (1997). *How the mind works.* New York: W. W. Norton.

Pintrich, P. R. (2000). The role of goal orientation in self-regulated learning. In M. Boekaerts, P. R. Pintrich, & M. Zeidner (Eds.), *Handbook of self-regulation* (pp. 451–502). San Diego, CA: Academic Press.

Polak, A., & Harris, P. L. (1999). Deception by young children following noncompliance. *Developmental Psychology, 35*, 561–568.

Pollitt, E., Gorman, K. S., Engle, P. L., Martorell, R., & Rivera, J. (1993). Early supplemental feeding and cognition: Effects over two decades. *Monographs of the Society for Research in Child Development, 58* (No. 235), v–99.

Posner, M. I., Peterson, S. E., Fox, P. T., & Raichle, M. E. (1988). Localization of cognitive operations in the human brain. *Science, 240*, 1627–1631.

Pressley, M. (1997). The cognitive science of reading: Comments. *Contemporary Educational Psychology, 22*, 247–259.

Pressley, M., Almasi, J., Schuder, T., Bergman, J., Hite, S., El-Dinary, P. B., et al. (1994). Transactional instruction of comprehension strategies: The Montgomery County Maryland SAIL program. *Reading and Writing Quarterly, 10*, 5–19.

Pressley, M., & Hilden, K. (2006). Cognitive strategies. In W. Damon & R. M. Lerner (Series Eds.), D. Kuhn & R. S. Siegler (Vol. Eds.), *Handbook of child psychology: Vol. 2. Cognition, perception, and language* (6th ed., pp. 511–556). New York: Wiley.

Pressley, M., Johnson, C. J., Symons, S., McGoldrick, J. A., & Kurita, J. A. (1989). Strategies that improve children's memory and comprehension of text. *Elementary School Journal, 90*, 3–32.

Pressley, M., Wharton-McDonald, R., & Raphael, L. M. (2002). Exemplary first-grade teaching. In B. Taylor & P. D. Pearson (Eds.), *Teaching reading: Effective schools, accomplished teachers* (pp. 73–88). Mahwah, NJ: Erlbaum.

Price, G. B., & Graves, R. L. (1980). Sex differences in syntax and usage in oral and written language. *Research in the Teaching of English, 14*, 147–153.

Proctor, C. P., Carlo, M., August, D., & Snow, C. (2005). Native Spanish-speaking children reading in English: Toward a model of comprehension. *Journal of Educational Psychology, 97*, 246–256.

Purves, D., & Lichtman, J. W. (1985). *Principles of neural development.* Sunderland, MA: Sinauer Associates.

Qualls, C. D., & Harris, J. L. (1999). Effects of familiarity on idiom comprehension in African American and European American fifth graders. *Language, Speech, and Hearing Services in the Schools, 30*, 141–151.

Quartz, S. R., & Sejnowski, T. J. (1997). The neural basis of cognitive development: A constructivist manifesto. *Behavioral and Brain Sciences, 20*, 537–596.

Quay, L. C., Steele, D. C., Johnson, C. I., & Hortman, W. (2001). Children's achievement and personal and social development in a first-year Reading Recovery program with teachers in training. *Literacy Teaching and Learning: An International Journal of Early Reading and Writing, 5*(2), 7–25.

Quigley, S. P., & Paul, P. V. (1987). Deafness and language development. In S. Rosenberg (Ed.), *Advances in applied psycholinguistics: Vol. 1. Disorders of first-language development* (pp. 180–219). New York: Cambridge University Press.

Quine, W. O. (1960). *Word and object.* Cambridge, MA: MIT Press.

Quinn, P. C. (2006). On the emergence of perceptual organization and categorization in young infants: Roles for perceptual process and knowledge access. In L. Balter & C. S. Tamis-LeMonda (Eds.), *Child psychology: A handbook of contemporary issues* (2nd ed., pp. 109–131). New York: Psychology Press.

Rakic, P. (1993). Intrinsic and extrinsic determinants of neocortical parcellation: A radial unit model. In M. H. Johnson (Ed.), *Brain maturation and cognition: A reader* (pp. 93–111). Oxford, UK: Blackwell.

Randel, M. A., Fry, M. A., & Ralls, E. M. (1977). Two readiness measures as predictors of first and third grade reading achievement. *Psychology in the Schools, 14,* 37–40.

Ransdell, S., & Levy, C. M. (1996). Working memory constraints on writing quality and fluency. In C. M. Levy & S. Ransdell (Eds.), *The science of writing: Theories, methods, individual differences, and applications* (pp. 93–106). Mahwah, NJ: Erlbaum.

Rapcsak, S. Z. (1997). Disorders of writing. In L. J. Gonzalez Rothi & K. M. Heilman (Eds.), *Apraxia: The neuropsychology of action.* Hove, UK: Psychology Press.

Raynor, K., & Pollatsek, A. (1989). *The psychology of reading.* Englewood Cliffs, NJ: Prentice-Hall.

Recanzone, G. H., Schreiner, C. E., & Merzenich, M. M. (1993). Plasticity in the frequency representation of primary auditory cortex following discrimination training in adult owl monkeys. *Journal of Neuroscience, 13,* 87–103.

Recht, D. R., & Leslie, L. (1988). Effect of prior knowledge on good and poor readers' memory of text. *Journal of Educational Psychology, 80,* 16–20.

Reichardt, L. F., & Farinas, I. (1997). Neurotrophic factors and their receptors. In W. M. Cowan, T. M. Jessell, & S. L. Zipursky (Eds.), *Molecular and cellular approaches to neural development* (pp. 220–258). New York: Oxford University Press.

Reid, E. R. (1986). Practicing effective instruction: The Exemplary Center for Reading Instruction approach. *Exceptional Children, 52,* 510–519.

Reid, E. R. (1997). Exemplary Center for Reading Instruction (ECRI). *Behavior and Social Issues, 7,* 19–24.

Renninger, K. A., Hidi, S., & Krapp, A. (1991). *The role of interest in learning and development.* Hillsdale, NJ: Erlbaum.

Reschly, D. J., & Gresham, F. M. (1989). Current neuropsychological diagnosis of learning problems: A leap of faith. In C. R. Reynolds & E. Fletcher-Janzen (Eds.), *Handbook of clinical child neuropsychology* (pp. 503–519). New York: Plenum Press.

Rescorla, L., & Achenbach, T. M. (2002). Use of the Language Development Survey (LDS) in a national probability sample of children 18 to 35 months old. *Journal of Speech, Language, and Hearing Research, 45,* 733–743.

Reznick, J. S., & Goldfield, B. A. (1992). Rapid change in lexical development in comprehension and production. *Developmental Psychology, 28,* 406–413.

Rheingold, H. L., Gewirtz, J. L., & Ross, H. W. (1959). Social conditioning of vocalizations in the infant. *Journal of Comparative and Physiological Psychology, 52,* 68–73.

Rinehart, S. D., Stahl, S. A., & Erickson, L. G. (1986). Some effects of summarization training on reading and studying. *Reading Research Quarterly, 21,* 422–438.

Roberts, J. E., Burchinal, M., & Durham, M. (1999). Parents' reports of vocabulary and grammatical development of African American preschoolers: Child and environmental associations. *Child Development, 70,* 92–106.

Rogoff, B., & Chavajay, P. (1995). What's become of research on the cultural basis of cognitive development? *American Psychologist, 50,* 859–877.

Roller, C. M. (1990). The interaction between knowledge and structure variables in the processing of expository prose. *Reading Research Quarterly, 25,* 80–89.

Rosch, E. (1975). Cognitive representations of semantic categories. *Journal of Experimental Psychology: General, 104,* 192–233.

Roscigno, V. J. (2000). Family/school inequality and African-American/Hispanic achievement. *Social Problems, 47,* 266–290.

Rosenshine, B., & Meister, C. (1994). Reciprocal teaching: A review of the research. *Review of Educational Research, 64,* 479–530.

Rosenthal, R. (1994). Parametric measures of effect size. In H. Cooper, & L. V. Hedges (Eds.), *The handbook of research synthesis* (pp. 231–244). New York: Russell Sage Foundation.

Ross, S. M., Nunnery, J., & Goldfeder, E. (2004). *A randomized experiment on the effects of Accelerated Reader/Reading Renaissance in an urban school district: Preliminary evaluation report.* Memphis, TN: University of Memphis, Center for Research in Educational Policy.

Rubin, K. H., Bukowski, W., & Parker, J. (1998). Peer interactions, relationships, and groups. In W. Damon (Series Ed.) & N. Eisenberg (Vol. Ed.), *Handbook of child psychology: Vol. 3. Social, emotional, and personality development* (pp. 619–700). New York: Wiley.

Rumelhart, D. E., & McClelland, J. L. (1986). *Parallel distributed processing: Explorations in the microstructure of cognition.* Cambridge, MA: MIT Press.

Ryan, R. M., & Deci, E. L. (1996). When paradigms clash: Comments on Cameron and Pierce's claim that rewards do not undermine intrinsic motivation. *Review of Educational Research, 66,* 33–38.

Saffran, E. M. (2003). Evidence from language breakdown: Implications for the neural and functional organization of language. In M. T. Banich & M. Mack (Eds.), *Mind, brain, and language: Multidisciplinary perspectives* (pp. 251–281). Mahwah, NJ: Erlbaum.

Sandberg, A. D. (2002). Phonological recoding problems in children with severe congenital speech impairments: The importance of production speech. In E. Witruk, A. D., Friederici, & T. Lachmann (Eds.), *Basic functions of language reading, and reading disability* (pp. 315–327). Dordrecht, The Netherlands: Kluwer Academic Publishers.

Santa, C., & Høien, T. (1999). An assessment of Early Steps: A program for early intervention of reading problems. *Reading Research Quarterly, 34,* 54–79.

Savage, R., Cornish, K., Manley, T., & Hollis, C. (2006). Cognitive processes in children's reading and attention: The role of working memory, divided attention, and response inhibition. *British Journal of Psychology, 97,* 365–385.

Scarborough, H. S. (1998). Early identification of children at risk for reading disabilities: Phonological awareness and some other promising predictors. In B. K. Shapiro, A. J. Capute, & B. Shapiro (Eds.), *Specific reading disability: A view of the spectrum* (pp. 77–121). Mahwah, NJ: Erlbaum.

Scarborough, H. S., & Dobrich, W. (1994). On the efficacy of reading to preschoolers. *Developmental Review, 14,* 245–302.

Scardamalia, M., & Bereiter, C. (1986). Research on written composition. In M. C.

Wittrock (Ed.), *Handbook of research on teaching* (3rd ed., pp. 778–803). New York: Macmillan.

Scardamalia, M., Bereiter, C., & Goelman, H. (1982). The role of production factors in writing ability. In M. Nystrand (Ed.), *What writers know: The language, process, and structure of written discourse.* New York: Academic Press.

Scarr, S., & Weinberg, R. A. (1978). The influence of family background on intellectual attainment. *American Sociological Review, 43,* 674–692.

Schatschneider, C., Fletcher, J. M., Francis, D. J., Carlson, C. D., & Foorman, B. R. (2004). Kindergarten prediction of reading skills: A longitudinal comparative analysis. *Journal of Educational Psychology, 96,* 265–282.

Scheffner-Hammer, C., Pennock-Roman, M., Rzasa, S., & Tomblin, J. B. (2002). An analysis of the Test of Language Development—Primary for item bias. *American Journal of Speech Pathology, 11,* 274–284.

Schickedanz, J. A., & Dickinson, D. K. (2005).*Opening the World of Learning: A comprehensive early literacy program.* Parsippany, NJ: Pearson Early Learning.

Schilling-Estes, N. (2006). Dialect variation. In R. Fasold & J. Connor-Linton (Eds.), *An introduction to language and linguistics* (pp. 311–342). New York: Cambridge University Press.

Schunk, D. (1991). Goal-setting and self-evaluation: A social-cognitive perspective on self-regulation. In M. Maehr & P. Pintrich (Eds.), *Advances in motivation and achievement* (Vol. 7, pp. 85–113). Greenwich, CT: JAI Press.

Schunk, D., & Rice, J. (1989). Learning goals and children's reading comprehension. *Journal of Reading Behavior, 21,* 279–293.

Schunk, D. H., & Ertmer, P. A. (1999). Self-regulatory processes during computer skill acquisition: Goal and self-evaluative influences. *Journal of Educational Psychology, 91,* 251–260.

Searle, J. R. (1969). *Speech acts: An essay in the philosophy of language.* Cambridge, UK: Cambridge University Press.

Searle, J. R. (1983). *Intentionality: An essay in the philosophy of mind.* New York: Cambridge University Press.

Segal, N. L. (1989). Origins and implications of handedness and relative birth weight for IQ in monozygotic twin pairs. *Neuropsychologia, 27,* 549–561.

Seidenberg, M. S., & McClelland, J. L. (1989). A distributed, developmental model of word recognition and naming. *Psychological Review, 96,* 523–568.

Sell, M. A., Kreuz, R. J., & Coppermath, L. (1997). Parents' use of nonliteral language with preschool children. *Discourse Processes, 23,* 99–118.

Sénéchal, M., & LeFevre, J. (2002). Parental involvement in the development of children's reading skill: A five-year longitudinal study. *Child Development, 73,* 445–460.

Shanahan, T., & Barr, R. (1995). A synthesis of research on Reading Recovery. *Reading Research Quarterly, 30,* 958–996.

Shapiro, L. R., & Hudson, J. A. (1991). Tell me a make-believe story: Coherence and cohesion in young children's picture-elicited narratives. *Developmental Psychology, 27,* 960–974.

Share, D., & Levin, I. (1999). Learning to read and write in Hebrew. In M. Harris & G. Hatano (Eds.), *Learning to read and write: A cross-linguistic perspective* (pp. 89–111). New York: Cambridge University Press.

Shatz, M., & Gelman, R. (1973). The development of communication skills: Modification in the speech of young children as a function of listener. *Monographs of the Society for Research in Child Development, 38* (no. 152), 1–37.

Shaywitz, B. A., Shaywitz, S. E., Pugh, K. R., Constable, R. T., Skudlarski, P., Fulbright, R. K., et al. (1995). Sex differences in the functional organization of the brain for language. *Nature, 373,* 607–609.

Shaywitz, S. E. (1996). Dyslexia. *Scientific American, 94,* 98–104.

Shaywitz, S. E., Escobar, M. D., Shaywitz, B. A., Fletcher, J. M., & Makuch, R. (1992). Evidence that dyslexia may represent the lower tail of a normal distribution of reading ability. *The New England Journal of Medicine, 326,* 144–150.

Shaywitz, S. E., Shaywitz, B., Fletcher, J. M., & Escobar, M. D. (1990). Prevalence of reading disability in boys and girls. *Journal of the American Medical Association, 264,* 998–1005.

Shaywitz, S. E., Shaywitz, B., Pugh, K. R., Fulbright, R. K., Constable, R. T., Mencl, W. E., et al. (1998). Functional disruption in the organization of the brain for reading in dyslexia. *Proceedings of the National Academy of Science, 95,* 2636–2641.

Siegler, R. S. (1983). Information processing approaches to cognitive development. In P. H. Mussen (Ed.), *Handbook of child psychology: Vol. 1. History, theory, and methods.* New York: Wiley.

Siegler, R. S., & Crowley, K. (1994). Constraints on learning in nonprivileged domains. *Cognitive Psychology, 27,* 194–226.

Singer, M. S., & Eder, G. S. (1989). Effects of ethnicity, accent, and job status on selection decisions. *International Journal of Psychology, 24,* 13–34.

Singley, M., & Anderson, J. R. (1989). *The transfer of cognitive skill.* Cambridge, MA: Harvard University Press.

Skinner, B. F. (1957). *Verbal behavior.* New York: Appleton-Century-Crofts.

Skinner, E., Chapman, M., & Baltes, P. (1988). Control, means-ends, and agency beliefs: A new conceptualization and its measurement during childhood. *Journal of Personality and Social Psychology, 54,* 117–133.

Slater, W. H., Graves, M. F., & Piche, G. L. (1985). Effects of structural organizers on ninth grade students' comprehension and recall of four patterns of expository texts. *Reading Research Quarterly, 20,* 189–202.

Slavin, R. E., & Fashola, O. S. (1998). *Show me the evidence! Proven and promising programs for America's schools.* Thousand Oaks, CA: Corwin Press.

Slovic, P. (1990). Choice. In D. N. Osherson & E. E. Smith (Eds.), *Thinking.* Cambridge, MA: MIT Press.

Smith, E. E. (1989). Concepts and induction. In M. I. Posner (Ed.), *Foundations of cognitive science* (pp. 501–526). Cambridge, MA: MIT Press.

Smith, E. E., & Medin, D. L. (1981). *Categories and concepts.* Cambridge, MA: Harvard University Press.

Smith, M., Apperly, I., & White, V. (2003). False belief reasoning and the acquisition of relative clause sentences. *Child Development, 74,* 1709–1719.

Snow, C. E., Burns, S., & Griffin, P. (1998). *Preventing reading difficulties in young children.* Washington, DC: National Academies Press.

Spector, C. C. (1996). Children's comprehension of idioms in the context of humor. *Language, Speech and Hearing Services in Schools, 27,* 307–313.

Spelke, E., & Newport, E. L. (1998). Nativism, empiricism, and the development of knowledge. In W. Damon & R. L. Lerner (Eds.), *Handbook of child psychology: Vol. 1. Theoretical models of human development* (5th ed., pp. 275–340). Hoboken, NJ: Wiley.

Spires, H. A., Gallini, J., & Riggsbee, J. (1992). Effects of schema-based and text structure-based cues on expository prose comprehension in fourth graders. *Journal of Experimental Education, 60,* 307–320.

Stahl, S. A., & Murray, B. (1998). Issues involved in defining phonological awareness and its relation to early reading. In J. L. Metsala & L. C. Ehri (Eds.), *Word recognition in beginning literacy* (pp. 65–88). Mahwah, NJ: Erlbaum.

Stanovich, K. E. (1980). Toward an interactive-compensatory model of individual differences in the development of reading fluency. *Reading Research Quarterly, 16,* 32–65.

Stanovich, K. E. (1986). Matthew effects in reading: Some consequences of individual differences in the acquisition of literacy. *Reading Research Quarterly, 21,* 360–407.

Stanovich, K. E. (1988a). Explaining the differences between the dyslexic and the garden-variety poor reader: The phonological-core variable-difference model. *Journal of Learning Disabilities, 21,* 590–604, 612.

Stanovich, K. E. (1988b). The right and wrong places to look for the cognitive locus of reading disability. *Annals of Dyslexia, 38,* 154–177.

Stanovich, K. E., & Cunningham, A. E. (1992). Studying the consequences of literacy within a literate society: The cognitive correlates of print exposure. *Memory and Cognition, 20,* 51–68.

Stanovich, K. E., Cunningham, A. E., & Feeman, D. J. (1984). Intelligence, cognitive skills, and early reading progress. *Reading Research Quarterly, 29,* 278–303.

Stanovich, K. E., & Siegel, L. S. (1994). Phenotypic performance profile of children with reading disabilities: A regression-based test of the phonological-core variable-difference model. *Journal of Educational Psychology, 86,* 24–53.

Stanovich, K. E., West, R. F., & Harrison, M. R. (1995). Knowledge growth and maintenance across the lifespan: The role of print exposure. *Developmental Psychology, 31,* 811–826.

Stark, R. E. (1986). Prespeech segmental feature development. In P. Fletcher & M. Garman (Eds.), *Language acquisition* (2nd ed., pp. 149–173). Cambridge, UK: Cambridge University Press.

Steffensen, M. S., Reynolds, R. E., McClure, E., & Guthrie, L. F. (1982). Black English Vernacular and reading comprehension: A cloze study of third, sixth, and ninth graders. *Journal of Reading Behavior, 14,* 285–298.

Stein, N. L. (1982). What's in a story: Interpreting the interpretations of story grammars. *Discourse Processes, 5,* 319–335.

Stein, N. L., & Glenn, C. G. (1979). An analysis of story comprehension in elementary school children. In R. O. Freedle (Ed.), *New directions in discourse processing.* Norwood, NJ: Ablex.

Stein, N. L., & Policastro, T. (1984). The story: A comparison between children's and teacher's viewpoints. In H. Mandel, N. L. Stein, & T. Trabasso (Eds.), *Learning and comprehension of text.* Hillsdale, NJ: Erlbaum.

Steinmetz, H., Herzog, A., Schlaug, G., Huang, Y., & Lanke, R. (1995). Brain (a)symmetry in monozygotic twins. *Cerebral Cortex, 5*, 296–300.

Sternberg, R. J. (1985). *Beyond IQ: A triarchic theory of human intelligence.* New York: Cambridge University Press.

Sternberg, R. J., Grigorenko, E. L., & Bundy, D. A. (2001). The predictive value of IQ. *Merrill-Palmer Quarterly, 47*, 1–41.

Sternberg, R. S. (1987). The psychology of verbal comprehension. In R. Glaser (Ed.), *Advances in instructional Psychology, Vol. 3* (pp. 97–151). Hillsdale, NJ: Erlbaum.

Stevens, R. J., Madden, N. A., Slavin, R. E., & Farnish, A. M. (1987) Cooperative integrated reading and composition: Two field experiments. *Reading Research Quarterly, 22*, 433–454.

Stevenson, H. W., Chen, C., & Uttal, D. H. (1990). Beliefs and achievement: A study of black, white, and hispanic children. *Child Development, 61*, 508–523.

Stipek, D., Recchia, S., & McClintic, S. (1992). Self-evaluation in young children. *Monographs of the Society for Research in Child Development, 57* (No. 226).

Stipek, D. J. (1993). *Motivation to learn: From theory to practice* (2nd ed.). Boston: Allyn & Bacon.

Streissguth, A. P., Barr, H. M., Sampson, P. D., Darby, B. L., & Martin, D. C. (1989). IQ at age 4 in relation to maternal alcohol use and smoking during pregnancy. *Developmental Psychology, 25*, 3–11.

Streissguth, A. P., Sampson, P. D., Barr, H. M., Bookstein, F. L., & Olson, H. C. (1994). The effects of prenatal exposure to alcohol and tobacco: Contributions from the Seattle Longitudinal Prospective Study and implications for public policy. In H. L. Needleman, D. Bellinger, et al. (Eds.), *Prenatal exposure to toxicants: Developmental consequences* (pp. 148–183). Baltimore, MD: Johns Hopkins University Press.

Sulzby, E. (1991). Assessment of emergent literacy: Storybook reading. *The Reading Teacher, 44*, 498–500.

Swanson, H. L. (1999). What develops in working memory? A life span perspective. *Developmental Psychology, 35*, 986–1000.

Swanson, H. L. (2003). Age-related differences in learning disabled and skilled readers' working memory. *Journal of Experimental Child Psychology, 85*, 1–31.

Swanson, H. L., Sáez, L., Gerber, M., & Leafstedt, J. (2004). Literacy and cognitive functioning in bilingual and nonbilingual children at risk and not at risk for reading disabilities. *Journal of Educational Psychology, 96*, 3–18.

Swingley, D., & Aslin, R. N. (2002). Lexical neighborhoods and the word-form representations of 14-month-olds. *Psychological Science, 13*, 480–484.

Swoboda, P., Moore, P. A., & Leavitt, L. A. (1976). Continuous vowel discrimination in normal and at-risk infants. *Child Development, 47*, 459–465.

Tach, L. M., & Farkas, G. (2005). Learning-related behaviors, cognitive skills, and ability grouping when schooling begins. *Social Science Research, 35*, 1048–1079.

Tager-Flusberg, H. (2005). Putting words together: Morphology and syntax in the preschool years. In J. Berko Gleason (Ed.), *The development of language* (6th ed., pp. 148–179). Needham Heights, MA: Allyn & Bacon.

Talairach, J., & Tournoux, P. (1988). *Co-planar stereotaxic atlas of the human brain.* New York: Thieme Medical Publishers.

Tallal, P., Merzenich, M., Miller, S., & Jenkins, W. (1998). Language learning impairment: Integrating research and remediation. *Scandinavian Journal of Psychology, 39,* 197–199.

Talwar, V., & Lee, K. (2002). Emergence of white-lie telling in children between 3 and 7 years of age. *Merrill-Palmer Quarterly, 48,* 160–181.

Talwar, V., Lee, K., Bala, N., & Lindsay, R. C. L. (2002). Children's conceptual knowledge of lying and its relation to their actual behaviors: Implications for court competence examinations. *Law and Human Behavior, 26,* 395–415.

Tangel, D. M., & Blachman, B. A. (1992). Effect of phoneme awareness instruction on kindergarten children's invented spelling. *Journal of Reading Behavior, 24*(2), 233–261.

Tardif, T. Z. (1996). Nouns are not always learned before verbs: Evidence from Mandarin speakers' early vocabularies. *Developmental Psychology, 32,* 492–504.

Tate, W. F. (1995). Returning to the root: A culturally relevant approach to mathematics pedagogy. *Theory into Practice, 34,* 166–173.

Taylor, B. M. (1980). Children's memory for expository text after reading. *Reading Research Quarterly, 25,* 399–411.

Taylor, B. M. (1986). Summary writing by young children. *Reading Research Quarterly, 21,* 193–208.

Taylor, B. M. (1995). *The Early Intervention in Reading Program: Results and issues spanning six years.* Paper presented at the annual meeting of the American Educational Reading Association, San Francisco.

Taylor, B. M. (2001). *The Early Intervention in Reading Program (EIR(r)). Research and development spanning twelve years.* Edina, MN: Web Education Company.

Taylor, B. M., Frye, B. J., & Maruyama, G. M. (1990). Time spent reading and reading growth. *American Educational Research Journal, 27,* 351–362.

Taylor, B. M., Frye, B. J., Short, R. A., & Shearer, B. (1992). Classroom teachers prevent reading failure among low-achieving first-grade students. *The Reading Teacher, 45,* 592–597.

Teale, W. H. (1986). Home background and young children's literacy development. In W. H. Teale & E. Sulzby (Eds.), *Emergent literacy* (pp. 173–206). Norwood, NJ: Ablex.

Teale, W. H., & Sulzby, E. (1986). *Emergent literacy.* Norwood, NJ: Ablex.

Thal, D. J., Bates, E., Zappia, M. J., & Oroz, M. (1996). Ties between lexical and grammatical development: Evidence from early-talkers. *Journal of Child Language, 23,* 349–368.

Thiede, K. W., Anderson, M. C. M., & Therriault, D. (2003). Accuracy of metacognitive monitoring affects learning of texts. *Journal of Educational Psychology, 95,* 66–73.

Thurmond, V. B. (1977). The effect of Black English on the reading test performance of high school students. *Journal of Educational Research, 70,* 160–163.

Tomasello, M. (1992). *First verbs: A case study of early grammatical development.* New York: Cambridge University Press.

Tomasello, M. (2003). *Constructing a language: A usage-based theory of language acquisition.* Cambridge, MA: Harvard University Press.

Tomasello, M., & Brooks, P. J. (1999). Early syntactic development: A construction grammar approach. In M. Barrett (Ed.), *The development of language* (pp. 161–190). New York: Psychology Press.

Tomasello, M., Mannle, S., & Kruger, A. C. (1986). Linguistic environment of 1- to 2-year-old twins. *Developmental Psychology, 22,* 169–176.

Tomasello, M., & Merriman, W. E. (1995). *Beyond names for things: Young children's acquisition of verbs.* Hillsdale, NJ: Erlbaum.

Tomasello, M., & Mervis, C. B. (1994). The instrument is great, but measuring comprehension is still a problem. *Monographs of the Society for Research in Child Development, 59,* 174–179.

Torgesen, J. K., & Burgess, S. R. (1998). Consistency of reading-related phonological processes throughout early childhood: Evidence from longitudinal-correlational and instructional studies. In J. L. Metsala & L. C. Ehri (Eds.), *Word recognition in beginning literacy* (pp. 161–188). Mahwah, NJ: Erlbaum.

Trehub, S. E. (1973). Infants' sensitivity to vowel and tonal contrasts. *Developmental Psychology, 9,* 91–96.

Treiman, R., Mullennix, J., Bijeljac-Babic, R., & Richmond-Welty, E. D. (1995). The special role of rimes in the description, use, and acquisition of English orthography. *Journal of Experimental Psychology: General, 124,* 107–136.

Treiman, R., & Tincoff, R. (1997). The fragility of the alphabetic principle: Children's knowledge of letter names can cause them to spell syllabically rather than alphabetically. *Journal of Experimental Child Psychology, 64,* 425–451.

Treiman, R., Tincoff, R., & Richmond-Welty, E. D. (1996). Letter names help children to connect print to speech. *Developmental Psychology, 32,* 505–514.

Treiman, R., Weatherston, S., & Berch, D. (1994). The role of letter names in children's learning of phoneme-grapheme relations. *Applied Psycholinguistics, 15,* 97–122.

Treiman, R., & Zukowski, A. (1996). Children's sensitivity to syllables, onsets, rimes, and phonemes. *Journal of Experimental Child Psychology, 61,* 193–215.

Troia, G. A. (2006). Writing instruction for students with learning disabilities. In C. A. MacArthur, S. Graham, & J. Fitzgerald (Eds.), *Handbook of writing research* (pp. 324–336). New York: Guilford Press.

Tunmer, W. E., Herriman, M. L., & Nesdale, A. R. (1988). Metalinguistic abilities and beginning reading. *Reading Research Quarterly, 23,* 134–158.

van den Broek, P. (1989). Causal reasoning and inference making in judging the importance of story statements. *Child Development, 60,* 286–297.

van den Broek, P., Lorch, E. P., & Thurlow, R. (1996). Children's and adults' memory for television stories: The role of causal factors, story-grammar categories, and hierarchical level. *Child Development, 67,* 3010–3028.

van Dijk, T. A., & Kintsch, W. (1983). *Strategies of discourse comprehension.* New York: Academic Press.

Van Gelderen, A., Schoonen, R., de Gloppen, K., Hulstijn, J., Simis, A., Snellings, P., et al. (2004). Linguistic knowledge, processing speed, and metacognitive knowledge in first and second language reading comprehension: A componential analysis. *Journal of Educational Psychology, 96,* 19–30.

Van Hulle, C. A., Goldsmith, H. H., & Lemery, K. S. (2004). Genetic, environmental, and gender effects on individual differences in toddler expressive language. *Journal of Speech, Language, and Hearing Research, 47,* 904–912.

Vellutino, F. R., & Scanlon, D. M. (1987). Phonological coding, phonological awareness, and reading ability: Evidence from a longitudinal and experimental study. *Merrill-Palmer Quarterly, 33,* 321–363.

Vellutino, F. R., & Scanlon, D. M. (1991). The preeminence of phonologically based skills in learning to read. In S. A. Brady & D. P. Shankweiler (Eds.), *Phonological processes in literacy.* Hillsdale, NJ: Erlbaum.

Vellutino, F. R., Scanlon, D. M., Sipay, E. R., Small, S. G., Pratt, A., Chen, R. et al. (1996). Cognitive profiles of difficult-to-remediate and readily remediated poor readers: Early intervention as a vehicle for distinguishing between cognitive and experiential deficits as basic causes of specific reading disability. *Journal of Educational Psychology, 88,* 601–638.

Vihman, M. M. (1988). Later phonological development. In J. Bernthal & N. Bambson (Eds.), *Articulation and phonological disorders* (2nd ed., pp. 110–144). New York: Prentice-Hall.

Vihman, M. M. (1993). Variable paths to early word production. *Journal of Phonetics, 21,* 61–82.

Vygotsky, L. S. (1978). *Mind and language.* Cambridge, MA: Harvard University Press.

Waggoner, J. E., Messe, R., & Palermo, D. (1985). Grasping the meaning of metaphor: Story recall and comprehension. *Child Development, 56,* 1156–1166.

Wagner, R., Torgesen, J., & Rashotte, C. A. (1999). *Comprehensive Test of Phonological Processing (CTOPP).* Austin, TX: PRO-ED.

Walberg, H. J., & Tsai, S. (1984). Reading achievement and diminishing returns to time. *Journal of Educational Psychology, 76,* 442–451.

Walker, C. H. (1987). Relative importance of domain knowledge and overall aptitude on acquisition of domain-related information. *Cognition and Instruction, 4,* 25–42.

Wallach, L., Wallach, M. A., Dozier, M. G., & Kaplan, N. E. (1977). Poor children learning to read do not have trouble with auditory discrimination but do have trouble with phoneme recognition. *Journal of Educational Psychology, 69,* 36–39.

Walley, A. C. (1993). The role of vocabulary development in children's spoken word recognition and segmentation ability. *Developmental Review, 13,* 286–350.

Wasik, B. A. (1986). *Familiarity of content and inference making in young children.* Unpublished doctoral dissertation, Temple University.

Wasik, B. A., & Bond, M. A. (2001). Beyond the pages of a book: Interactive book reading in preschool classrooms. *Journal of Educational Psychology, 93,* 43–250.

Wasik, B. A., Bond, M. A., & Hindman, M. A. (2006). The effects of a language and literacy intervention on Head Start children and teachers. *Journal of Educational Psychology, 98,* 63–74.

Weaver, C. A., & Kintsch, W. (1991). Expository text. In R. Barr, M. L. Kamil, P. Mosenthal, & P. D. Pearson (Eds.), *Handbook of reading research* (Vol. II, pp. 230–245). New York: Longman.

Webster, B. H., & Bishaw, A. (2006). *Income, earnings, and poverty data from the 2005 American Community Survey* (U.S. Census Bureau, American Survey Reports, ACS-02). Washington, DC: U.S. Government Printing Office.

Weiner, B. (1986). *An attribution theory of motivation and emotion.* New York: Springer-Verlag.

Wentzel, K. R. (1989). Adolescent classroom goals, standards for performance, and academic achievement: An interactionist perspective. *Journal of Educational Psychology, 81,* 131–142.

Wentzel, K. R. (1991). Social and academic goals at school: Motivation and achievement in context. In M. Maehr & P. Pintrich (Eds.), *Advances in motivation and achievement, Vol. 7* (pp. 185–212). Greenwich, CT: JAI Press.

Wentzel, K. R., & Wigfield, A. (1998). Academic and social motivational influences on students' academic performance. *Educational Psychology Review, 10,* 155–175.

Wharton-McDonald, R., Pressley, M., & Hampston, J. M. (1998). Literacy instruction in nine first-grade classrooms: Teacher characteristics and student achievement. *The Elementary School Journal, 99,* 101–128.

Whitehurst, G., Arnold, D., Epstein, J., Angell, A., Smith, M., & Fischel, J. (1994). A picture book reading intervention in day care and home for children from low-income families. *Developmental Psychology, 30,* 679–689.

Whitehurst, G. J., Falco, F. L., Lonigan, C., Fischel, J. E., DeBarsyshe, B. D., Valdez-Menchaca, M. C., et al. (1988). Accelerating language development through picture book reading. *Developmental Psychology, 24,* 552–559.

Whitehurst, G. J., & Lonigan, C. J. (1998). Child development and emergent literacy. *Child Development, 69,* 848–872.

Whittlesea, B. W. A., & Cantwell, A. L. (1987). Enduring influence of the purpose of experiences: Encoding-retrieval interactions in word and pseudoword perception. *Memory and Cognition, 15,* 465–472.

Wigfield, A., Eccles, J., Harold-Goldsmith, R., Blumenfeld, P., Yoon, K. S., & Friedman-Doan, C. (1989). *Gender and age differences in children's achievement self-perceptions during elementary school.* Paper presented at the Biennial Meeting of the Society for Research in Child Development, Kansas City, April.

Wigfield, A., & Guthrie, J. T. (1997). Relations of children's motivation for reading to the amount and breadth or their reading. *Journal of Educational Psychology, 89,* 420–432.

Wigfield, A. W., & Eccles, J. S. (1989). Test anxiety in elementary and secondary school students. *Educational Psychologist, 24,* 159–183.

Wigfield, A. W., & Eccles, J. S. (1992). The development of achievement task values: A theoretical analysis. *Developmental Review, 12,* 265–310.

Wigfield, A. W., & Eccles, J. S. (2000). Expectancy-value theory of achievement motivation. *Contemporary Educational Psychology, 25,* 68–81.

Wigfield, A. W., Eccles, J., Mac Iver, D., Reuman, D., & Midgley, C. (1991). Transitions at early adolescence: Changes in children's domain-specific self-perceptions and general self-esteem across the transition to junior high school. *Developmental Psychology, 27,* 552–565.

Wilson, A. E., Smith, M. D., & Ross, H. S. (2003). The nature and effects of young children's lies. *Social Development, 12,* 21–45.

Wimmer, H., & Perner, J. (1983). Beliefs about beliefs: Representation and constraining function of wrong beliefs in young children's understanding of deception. *Cognition, 13,* 103–128.

Winick, M. (1984). Nutrition and brain development. In M. Winick (Ed.), *Nutrition in the 20th century* (pp. /1–86). New York: Wiley.

Wittgenstein, L. (1953). *Philosophical investigations*. New York: Macmillan.

Wright, R. E., & Rosenberg, S. (1993). Knowledge of text coherence and expository writing: A developmental study. *Journal of Educational Psychology, 85,* 152–158.

Younger, B. A., & Cohen, L. B. (1986). Developmental change in infants' perception of correlations among attributes. *Child Development, 57,* 803–815.

Zatorre, R. J. (2003). Sound analysis in auditory cortex. *Trends in Neurosciences, 26,* 229–230.

Zimmerman, B. J., & Kitsantas, A. (1999). Acquiring writing revision skill: Shifting from process to outcome self-regulatory goals. *Journal of Educational Psychology, 91,* 241–250.

Zimmerman, B. J., & Martinez-Pons, M. (1990). Student differences in self-regulated learning: Relating grade, sex, and giftedness to self-efficacy and strategy use. *Journal of Educational Psychology, 82,* 51–59.

Zinar, S. (1990). Fifth graders' recall of propositional content and causal relationships from expository prose. *Journal of Reading Behavior, 22,* 181–199.

Index

Page numbers followed by *f* indicate figures.